MENNONITES
IN
RUSSIA

MENNONITES
—IN—
RUSSIA

1788-1988

Essays in Honour of
Gerhard Lohrenz

Edited by
John Friesen

CMBC Publications
Winnipeg, Manitoba
1989

CMBC Publications
600 Shaftesbury Blvd.
Winnipeg, Manitoba
R3P OM4

Cover: Gerald Loewen
Cartography: Dianne Harms

Canadian Cataloguing in Publication Data

Main entry under title:

Mennonites in Russia, 1788-1988 : essays in honor of
　Gerhard Lohrenz

　Includes bibliographical references.
　ISBN: 0-920718-29-9

1. Mennonites — Soviet Union — History. 2. Lohrenz,
Gerhard, 1899-1986. I. Friesen, John. II. Lohrenz,
Gerhard, 1899-1986.
BX8119.R8M45 1989　　305.6'87'047　　C89-098166-3

Printed in Canada
by
Friesen Printers
Altona, Manitoba
ROG OBO

Contents

List of Maps and Tables

List of Photos

Acknowledgements

In many respects this book was a community project. The proposal to publish a volume of essays on Russian Mennonite history was made in the History-Archives Committee of the Conference of Mennonites in Canada. The Committee appointed an inter-Mennonite editorial committee consisting of Abe Dueck, Mennonite Brethren Bible College; George K. Epp, Menno Simons College, University of Winnipeg; Victor G. Doerksen, University of Manitoba; Doreen Klassen, Steinbach Bible College; Lawrence Klippenstein, Mennonite Heritage Centre; Adolf Ens and John Friesen, Canadian Mennonite Bible College. John Friesen was appointed editor.

Recognition must be given to the writers who took the time and effort to draw the Russian Mennonite story together around various themes. The bibliography and notes on archival resources were prepared by Lawrence Klippenstein. Special thanks goes to Adolf Ens who was involved in the whole project from beginning to end, providing counsel, advice and guidance at many points. Margaret Franz of CMBC Publications went well beyond her duties as copy editor in seeing the manuscript through to its final form.

A note of gratitude is also extended to Canadian Mennonite Bible College for allowing considerable secretarial time for keying the articles into the computer.

Maps were provided by James Urry, Walter Sawatsky, Dianne Harms and taken from the *Mennonite Encyclopedia*. They were prepared in their final form by Dianne Harms.

Spellings of Russian words and place names for both articles and maps were standardized, using the Library of Congress transliteration scheme. The exception to this usage was the retention of the traditional Russian Mennonite spellings of their own settlements, Chortitza and Molotschna.

The generous publication subsidies provided by the P.W. Enns Family Foundation, Winkler, Manitoba, and the History-Archives Committee are gratefully acknowledged.

Editor's Preface

This volume of articles about Mennonite life in Russia is designed to honour the memory and contributions of Gerhard Lohrenz. For many years he was archivist of the Conference of Mennonites in Canada. While teaching at Canadian Mennonite Bible College he gathered the core of CMBC's Mennonite Historical Library and its significant holdings in Russian Mennonitism. During his teaching career, and later, his retirement, Gerhard Lohrenz was a tireless promoter of Russian Mennonite history. He was concerned that the Russian experience not be forgotten. This volume is designed to recognize Lohrenz's inspirational roles, and to continue to stimulate the scholarly analysis of this important segment of the Mennonite story.

The publication of these essays arises out of the conviction that much research still remains to be done in the area of the Russian/ Soviet/Ukrainian Mennonite experience. While this volume presents the state of research up to the present, its intention is not to express the conclusion of an era, but rather to open up and inspire new research and to help raise new questions and suggest areas that require further study.

The volume covers the first two centuries of Mennonite life in Russia. Even though the book was not originally intended as a bicentennial publication, it happily is appearing in the two-hundredth year of the founding of the first Mennonite settlement on the banks of the Khortitza River in Russia.

It was difficult to decide how to conclude the book. Conditions in the Soviet Union are changing so rapidly that whatever one might say in a final chapter seemed to be out of date as soon as it was written. The story is taken up to the events of 1988. Later developments will need to be analyzed in subsequent publications.

This book has been a long time in formation. The earliest planning discussions were held with Gerhard Lohrenz shortly before his death. It is hoped that this volume will be a fitting tribute both to him and to the people he loved.

John Friesen
September 1989

Contributors

(listed in order of appearance)

Gerhard Ens, Editor, *Der Bote,* Winnipeg, Manitoba

Lawrence Klippenstein, Historian-Archivist, Mennonite Heritage Centre, Winnipeg, Manitoba

John Friesen, Associate Professor of History and Theology, Canadian Mennonite Bible College, Winnipeg, Manitoba

Adolf Ens, Associate Professor of History and Theology, Canadian Mennonite Bible College, Winnipeg, Manitoba

James Urry, Senior Lecturer in the Department of Anthropology, Victoria University of Wellington, Wellington, New Zealand

Harry Loewen, Professor and Chair in Mennonite Studies, University of Winnipeg, Winnipeg, Manitoba

Harvey Dyck, Professor of Russian and East European History, University of Toronto, Toronto, Ontario

Abe J. Dueck, Academic Dean and Associate Professor of Historical Theology, Mennonite Brethren Bible College, Winnipeg, Manitoba

Wesley Berg, Associate Professor of Music, University of Alberta, Edmonton, Alberta

Al Reimer, Professor of English, University of Winnipeg, Winnipeg, Manitoba

George K. Epp, Professor at Menno Simons College, University of Winnipeg, Winnipeg, Manitoba

John B. Toews, Professor of Church History, Regent College, Vancouver, British Columbia

Victor G.Doerksen, Professor and Head of the German Department, University of Manitoba, Winnipeg, Manitoba

Walter Sawatsky, Director of East-West Concerns, Mennonite Central Committee Canada, Winnipeg, Manitoba

Peter J. Klassen, Dean of the School of Social Sciences and Professor of History, California State University, Fresno, Californa

Dedication

To the memory of Gerhard Lohrenz (1899-1986)

Gerhard Lohrenz: His Life and Contributions

Gerhard Ens

I first heard of Gerhard Lohrenz when I was a young teacher-trainee in the darkest days of World War II. A farmer from the Springstein area whose name I have forgotten spoke in glowing terms of the quality of education which their young people in Springstein were receiving. In a newly expanded three-room school, which included all the classes from Grades I to XI, Gerhard Lohrenz was the teaching principal. "Teaching" meant taking the entire teaching load of the third room, Grades IX to XI; being "principal" meant acting at least minimally as supervisor of the two junior rooms. At that time Springstein was under an "official trustee." Hence, the role of the principal frequently included being a buffer between the Department of Education and the district ratepayers and parents who, especially during the war years, did not always see things the same way. The people soon learned to respect their outspoken teacher, especially when his Grade XI students, at that time ranked as junior matriculates, regularly surpassed the average provincial achievements and were as ready for university or senior matriculation studies as were the graduates of much larger and more prestigious schools.

By this time Gerhard Lohrenz, already past the age of 40, had had a long and sometimes rocky (or as he put it, "stormtossed") pilgrimage behind him. Born just days before the turn of the century — December 27, 1899 according to the Gregorian calendar — he was destined to witness and experience as a teenager and young adult the destruction of the Mennonite world in Russia as he had learned to know it, to appreciate it and love it in spite of its shortcomings and faults of which he was keenly aware and which he forthrightly and fearlessly criticized.

Gerhard Lohrenz was born in the village of Friedensfeld (No. 3) in the Zagradovka settlement located about 120 miles north of the city of Kherson on the environs of the Inguletz River. Zagradovka was the oldest of the numerous daughter colonies of the Molotschna settle-

1

ment. Daughter colonies were settled largely by landless families of the mother colony and were therefore, especially in their early stages, less affluent. By the time Gerhard Lohrenz came on the scene, however, Zagradovka was a prosperous colony, and the Lohrenz family was considered to be quite well-to-do by the standards of the late 19th century. Two years later, 1902, the family moved to the village of Neu Schoensee, where the elder Lohrenz had purchased his father-in-law's (and stepfather's) farm and buildings. In the course of the years he increased and expanded this property.

Here in the village of Neu Schoensee Gerhard Lohrenz grew up, the oldest (an older sister had died in infancy) in a family of five boys and two girls. Life in a pre-war Mennonite colony was secure, predictable and, no doubt, somewhat monotonous. Mechanization of farm operations was just beginning, so that farming sometimes was a backbreaking chore, an endless round of heavy physical labour from which even children were not exempt. Gerhard Lohrenz often reminisced about his parental home — of a strict but just and fair father and, very fondly, of a loving and wise mother, the daughter of Elder Gerhard Warkentin. The death at age 18 of his oldest brother Hans, with whom he was particularly intimate, affected him deeply, even as the death of his oldest daughter at the age of 15 was to affect him much later.

The Lohrenz family home in Zagradovka. This is a typical village homestead of the early part of the twentieth century.

Gerhard Lohrenz was a gifted child. He was able to enter the local *Zentralschule* (continuation school approximately on the junior high level) at age 12. Four years later he enrolled in the *Handelsschule* (literally a "school of commerce," but in fact more like a senior high school) at Alexanderkrone in the Molotschna Colony from which he graduated in 1918. In spite of his thirst for knowledge and his desire for a higher education, circumstances were such that any further formal schooling in Russia became impossible for Gerhard Lohrenz.

The ensuing days and years of German occupation of Ukraine, the Makhno terror, the struggle between the Red and White armies, the ultimate victory of the Red Army and the introduction of communist administration to the Mennonite settlements and villages were turbulent years for the Zagradovka settlement and the Lohrenz family. During the nightmare days of November 1919 when six of the 16 Zagradovka villages were attacked by Makhno's anarchists leaving 200 dead and many more wounded behind, Gerhard Lohrenz was away, serving as a Red Cross orderly with the White Army. A relatively mild bout with typhus in December 1919 ended this service. After his recovery he returned home and spent half a year in his home village which had not been attacked by the anarchists.

Both his illness and the terrible tragedy so close to his home affected his life profoundly. He did not look for easy solutions, however, and he was not inclined to use religion as a placebo. Therefore, when he experienced conversion in August 1920 it was a thorough commitment of his life to Jesus Christ, made in full knowledge of the cost of discipleship and the possible consequences in a land under an atheist government. Conversion was followed in 1921 by baptism by Elder Jacob A. Rempel of Gruenfeld in the neighbouring colony of Baratov-Shlakhtin.

In the meantime Gerhard Lohrenz had been drafted into the Red Army in which he again served in a noncombatant capacity as a "lumberjack" in the very forest which his father had helped to plant during his four years in the forestry service under the imperial tsarist regime. He was quickly advanced to an administrative position, which relieved him of physical labour, and later to administrative office work in the cities of Nikolaiev and Elisavetgrad. His service in the Red Army was also terminated by illness — this time by a very severe attack of typhus which left him unconscious for two weeks, hovering on the edge of death.

After his recovery he married his longtime friend, Anni Harder, on September 15, 1922. The young couple took up its first residence in

3

the Lohrenz parental home, and Gerhard Lohrenz worked on his father's *Wirtschaft* (Mennonite term for a farm operation). In 1923 and 1924 he took up civic duties. He was persuaded to accept, first, the position of secretary of the local village soviet (council) and, a little later, that of district chairman over an area comprising five villages. His service in an administrative capacity in the Red Army had given him both the necessary experience as well as a working knowledge of the new system.

Gerhard Lohrenz was an efficient but scrupulously fair administrator. He knew that orders had to be obeyed but he tried to soften them as much as possible for the local villagers. Once decided upon, however, he insisted on such orders being carried out. When he terminated his civic career it was not for sentimental reasons of not being able to turn the clock back to pre-revolutionary times, but because of a growing realization that on the long run his religious convictions were irreconcilable with the atheistic philosophy of the new regime.

Gerhard Lohrenz' growing conviction that emigration was the only solution for him and his people was, no doubt, strengthened by his attendance at the all-Mennonite Congress on January 13-18, 1925 in the city of Moscow. His church at Zagradovka saw fit to delegate the 25-year-old Lohrenz to this historic meeting. He was the youngest delegate as well as the last survivor of this "martyrs' synod" as it has come to be called. Except for the few who managed to emigrate every one of the participants was later arrested and exiled. Gerhard Lohrenz always considered himself fortunate to have had the opportunity to learn to know so many Mennonite leaders firsthand at this historic conclave.

Barely a month after the Moscow Conference the young Lohrenz family — they had one child, a daughter, and were expecting a second — were on their way to Canada. Gerhard and Anni were the only ones of their respective families to emigrate at this time. Some of Anni's family followed later, but the first time Gerhard should see some of his family members again would be a full half century later on some of his numerous visits to the Soviet Union. His brother Peter was able to visit him twice in Canada, decades after the Second World War.

In Canada the Lohrenz family tried farming. In spite of his farm background in the old country, Gerhard Lohrenz was not happy as a farmer in Gilroy, Saskatchewan. Hence, in fall 1928 the Lohrenz family — by now increased to three daughters and one son — moved to the village of Gretna, Manitoba, where the father was

4

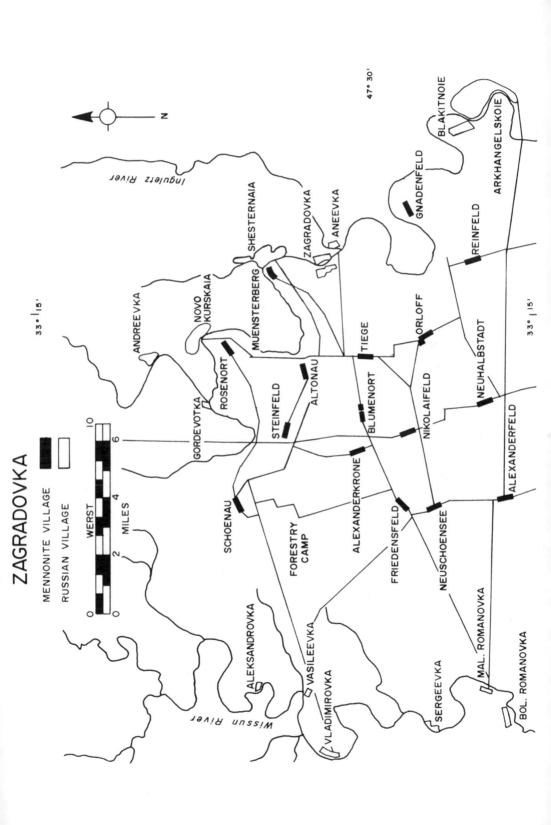

ZAGRADOVKA

enrolled as a Grade X student at the Mennonite Collegiate Institute. The greatest hurdle, of course, was the new language which seldom comes easily to an adult. However, in two years' time Gerhard Lohrenz satisfied all requirements for junior matriculation plus achieving some Grade XII credits. A year later, 1931, he graduated from the Manitou Normal School with a second-class teaching certificate, which could be raised to first-class status simply by fulfilling the requirements for senior matriculation. Dearly he would have liked to continue his studies, but financial considerations prevented this.

Instead he accepted a teaching position in a non-Mennonite school near Beausejour, Manitoba. Lydiatt school district was populated largely by German Lutheran families. Here the Lohrenz family spent seven happy years, appreciated by their neighbours, the parents of their pupils, who respected their teacher and, by and large, did their best to please him. Gradually Gerhard Lohrenz upgraded his academic and professional standing; by 1940 he was the holder of a First Class A teaching certificate.

In the meantime he had accepted a teaching position in the school of the newly founded Mennonite settlement at Springstein, Manitoba, which in the early 1940s became the three-room school mentioned earlier. Before Lohrenz applied for and accepted this position he carefully weighed the pros and cons. On the plus side was the opportunity to raise a growing family in a Mennonite environment, the proximity to the city of Winnipeg with its opportunities for studies, and the chance to do high school work with well motivated students. On the down side were the prospects of an increased work load and the possibility of being drawn into church and family controversies to which Mennonites seem to be so prone. In Lydiatt, as an outsider, he had been able to stay aloof from such things.

But the Springstein years, 1938 to 1947, apart from the tragedy of the death of the oldest daughter, Mary, as a result of polio contracted in early childhood, were basically happy years. Once the community understood Lohrenz' firm stand in matters of faith and baptism both denominations in Springstein, the Mennonite Brethren and the General Conference congregations, accepted and supported their teacher. This support from the Mennonite Brethren side continued also when Lohrenz took an ever more active part in the General Conference group, permitting the congregation to elect (but not ordain) him as a lay minister. During these nine years at Springstein, Gerhard Lohrenz worked steadily at improving his academic standing towards a degree and a Collegiate certificate by means of extramural and Summer School courses at the University of Manitoba.

In 1947 Gerhard Lohrenz was approached by the board of the newly founded private high school of the Mennonite Brethren, Mennonite Brethren Collegiate Institute (MBCI) in Winnipeg, to become its principal and teacher. In spite of misgivings how he, a General Conference lay minister and a country school teacher, would fit into a Mennonite Brethren urban setting, he accepted the offer. He remained principal of MBCI for five years during which time he acquired his Bachelor of Arts (B.A.) degree at the University of Manitoba. During these years the school's reputation and enrollment rose steadily, so that he could hand back to the board a school greatly improved from the one he had taken over.

But now there was a new call waiting for him. Canadian Mennonite Bible College (CMBC) needed someone to build up its history department. With some hesitation Lohrenz accepted this new challenge. For 13 years he was a college professor, lecturing in the History of Western Civilization, Church History and Mennonite History. Since the faculty was small he also had to accept some other assignments, but his first love remained the history area. In some measure both the Mennonite Historical Library as well as the Mennonite Archives owe their very existence to Gerhard Lohrenz' efforts.

It was also after 1952 that Gerhard Lohrenz began to identify more and more closely with the General Conference. He not only joined the newly formed Sargent Avenue Mennonite Church in Winnipeg but he accepted ordination as minister in 1954 and as elder in 1959. At age 65 he resigned his position at the College and devoted himself entirely to pastoral work. At age 70 he also withdrew from the active pastorate and embarked on his third (or fourth) career, that of travelling tour guide, lecturer and writer. While he was by no means wealthy, his financial situation was secure and he could afford many things which had been beyond his reach for so many years. His 30 plus tours to the Soviet Union gave him and his tour guests more than just a glimpse behind the Iron Curtain. His intimate knowledge of the Soviet bureaucratic mind as well as his still surprising mastery of the Russian language made him an invaluable guide, eagerly sought out not only by travel agents but also, in at least one case, by an official trade mission of the provincial government to the Soviet Union. There must have been some satisfaction in receiving the red carpet treatment from a government from which he and his family had fled almost a half century earlier.

As a writer Gerhard Lohrenz published a very popular illustrated volume of Mennonite life in Russia, published in German as *Damit es nicht vergessen werde* and in English as *Heritage Remembered*,

7

along with 13 miscellaneous books on life in Russia and the violent disruption of this life beginning with World War I. In addition to being a member on numerous Conference boards and committees his membership and counsel were sought by the Manitoba Mennonite Historical Society, the Mennonite Village Museum Society, the Mennonite Centennial Committee, the Mennonite Memorial Committee, the University of Winnipeg's Chair of Mennonite Studies and Menno Simons College. He was honoured by the University of Winnipeg when it conferred on him the degree of Doctor of Divinity, *honoris causa* on October 26, 1974.

At the close of his life one dark shadow enveloped Gerhard Lohrenz. His beloved Njuta's (Anni's) health began to fail. During her last years she had to be institutionalized. Her responses weakened and she apparently no longer recognized him during his daily visits. This saddened him greatly. His wish that he would be able to be with her to the end was not to be fulfilled. He died quite suddenly on February 6, 1986, of a massive heart attack. Anni outlived him by over two years.

As a pioneer in Mennonite higher education as well as in Mennonite history research and scholarship the place of Gerhard Lohrenz in the history of his conference and his people is secure.

Books by Gerhard Lohrenz

(listed chronologically)

Sagradowka: Die Geschichte einer mennonitischen Ansiedlung im Süden Rußlands. Rosthern, Saskatchewan: Echo-Verlag, 1947.

The Mennonites of Western Canada: Their Origin and Background and the Brief Story of Their Settling and Progress Here in Canada. Winnipeg, Manitoba: By the author, 1974.

Lose Blätter. Vol. I, II, III. Winnipeg, Manitoba: By the author, 1974-1976.

Damit es nicht vergessen werde: Ein Bildband zur Geschichte der Mennoniten Preußens und Rußlands. Winnipeg, Manitoba: CMBC Publications, 1974; revised and enlarged edition, 1977.

Heritage Remembered: A Pictorial Survey of Mennonites in Prussia and Russia. Winnipeg, Manitoba: CMBC Publications, 1974; revised and enlarged edition, 1977.

Storm Tossed: The Personal Story of a Canadian Mennonite from Russia. Winnipeg, Manitoba: By the author, 1976.

The Fateful Years 1913-1923: The Story of a Young Mennonite of Southern Russia. . . Winnipeg, Manitoba: Christian Press, 1977.

The Odyssey of the Bergen Family. Winnipeg, Manitoba: By the author, 1978.

Stories from Mennonite Life. Winnipeg, Manitoba: By the author, 1980.

Mia, oder über den Amur in die Freiheit: Die Lebensgeschichte einer mennonitischen Frau, Maria DeFehr. Winnipeg, Manitoba: DeFehr Foundation, 1981.

The Lost Generation and Other Stories. Winnipeg, Manitoba: By the author, 1982.

Fire over Zagradovka. Winnipeg, Manitoba: By the author, 1983.

1788-1880

Mennonites moved to Russia for a variety of reasons. For centuries Mennonites from Thorn to Danzig along the Vistula River had lived under Polish rule. During the seventeenth century Polish royal power crumbled, and in 1772 Poland was partitioned by its three neighbours, Russia, Prussia and Austria. A large portion of the Mennonite community came under Prussian rule as the result of this partition. Mennonite religious and social life as it had developed under Polish rule was now threatened. This change in the political situation together with the Russian government's offer of free land, provided a powerful incentive for emigration. The move to Russia began in 1788.

The first section of this collection of essays focuses on the early years in Russia. The immigrant group's motivations were diverse, but its unifying aim was to create communities. However, despite good intentions, practical necessity and theological motivation, community was elusive and difficult to achieve. The immigrants came with few material resources. Leadership was weak and fragmented. Organized religious life was slow in being established. Competing factions made cooperation difficult. Separation of Mennonite community authority into civil and religious institutions created endless internal conflict. There were different visions of community, visions which were hard to reconcile into a harmonious whole.

Despite these difficulties, or maybe because of them, Mennonites in Russia sought courageously to form the needed institutions which would shape their life together. One of the most important of these was the village. The village was not only the social setting within which practically every Mennonite in these early years grew up; it also was the local administrative unit. The landowners elected village mayors (Schulzen) who were responsible for the administration of the Russian government's local law and order. The village became the unit which administered schools, the orphan's bureau (Waisenamt) and the fire insurance (Brandordnung). It facilitated the myriad of cooperative endeavors in everyday social and agricultural life.

However, it was also in the village that the diversity of the vision of community became apparent. Only landowners fully experienced the life of the village. The landless sat on the sidelines as observers without vote or voice. Eventually it became important to ask whether the village would be the setting where all families could have access to some land, or whether it would be the arena for competition in which some would own most of the land and the majority would be

11

landless. As economic developments expanded beyond agriculture to include milling, manufacturing and retailing, the clash between the egalitarian and competitive perspectives became ever more serious. Such differing visions of community had to exist side by side without resolution.

The church should have been the strongest resource for creating community. In it the beliefs, ideals and values of living together were formed and articulated. From the beginning, however, the church was one of the weak links in the shaping of community. The immigrants were divided into two groups, the Frisian and the Flemish. Both had difficulty establishing capable religious leadership in the Chortitza settlement. In the Molotschna settlement such leadership was less fragmented and stronger right from the outset.

Mennonite civil leadership, which had the force of law behind it, immediately clashed with religious leadership and limited it. This set the stage for some Mennonites to embrace enthusiastically the new political context with a more limited religious role for the church, while others viewed the new situation as a threat to the very existence of faith and faithfulness to God.

Despite its slow start, education became another important institution creating community. Schools were at first established in most of the villages. Their purpose was to prepare young people for responsibilities in village and church. The reforms of the 1820s and the 1840s introduced a new and much broader vision of education. This more open-ended view, which introduced students to the intellectual heritage of Europe, clashed with the smaller, more limited view of education of the earlier era. It became evident rather quickly that these two views of education expressed quite different visions of the Mennonite community.

It was within this context of these diverse views that the Russian government in the early 1870s created significant new anxieties when it threatened to abolish exemption from military service and insisted on taking a more direct role in the Mennonite school system. Not all Mennonites viewed these proposed changes with equal alarm and apprehension. Some felt that emigration was the only answer. When the Russian government showed itself flexible and open to negotiation in both areas, military service and education, about two-thirds of the Mennonites decided to remain. For the other one-third, however, the setting in Russia had become too threatening and the possibility for a new start in North America too alluring. This latter group emigrated to Canada and to the United States hoping in those new settings to create the community which had eluded them in Russia.

The Mennonite Migration to Russia 1786-1806

Lawrence Klippenstein

Mennonites of Royal (West) Prussia and Danzig had lived under Polish rulers for nearly 250 years. This extended experience included periods of productive and relatively peaceful community growth, as well as times of tension, distress and explicit harassments. During the eighteenth century when Poland was faltering politically, Mennonites enjoyed their greatest freedom.

In 1772 Prussia annexed Royal (West) Prussia. The Mennonites of that region now came under the rule of Prussian kings, first Frederick II, the Great (1740-1786) and then Frederick William II (1786-1797).[1] The Prussian government exercised much stronger centralized control and was less tolerant of minority religious groups. For that reason life for the Mennonites became an ever tighter web of pressures and restrictions. Eventually emigration seemed to be the only solution. To understand this situation one needs to consider some of the social and political developments which preceded the decision to emigrate.

The first Dutch settlers who reached the Vistula Delta in the sixteenth century had no trouble pleasing the aristocratic landowners of this region because they had the skills needed to improve conditions in the swampy flats of the northern lowlands.[2] Those Polish noblemen who had invited settlers to live on their land received the open support of their relatively tolerant kings whose official policies made such development possible. When many Mennonites were placed under the sometimes onerous obligations of emerging Lutheran parishes during the Reformation, they were frequently helped by Catholic bishops who saw advantages in offering guarantees of protection to the oppressed.[3]

Within this context, that is, a Poland which for that period has been called "the most democratic and least autocratic country in central and Eastern Europe," the new immigrant Mennonites from 1632 onward obtained a series of royal *Privilegia* which further stabilized their status as a minority without citizenship in the country.[4] How-

ever, since conferring citizenship remained an aspect of local jurisdiction and administration, Mennonites from time to time still had to
confront threats and harassments on these levels.[5]

During the seventeenth and early eighteenth centuries added
conflicts developed with the established churches, Lutheran and
Catholic alike. For a time, for instance, Mennonites had to defend
themselves against charges of Arianism. Often their views were also
erroneously identified with Socinianism, a form of the Polish reform
movement which stressed pacifism and adult baptism but rejected
the divinity of Christ.[6]

In East Prussia during the sixteenth century, Mennonites were
generally excluded as colonists or driven out of the area. However,
some businessmen were allowed to settle near Koenigsberg. Frederick I (1701-1713) and Frederick William I (1713-1740) invited Mennonite immigrants to settle in the Memel region. They were offered
freedom of conscience; yet when the issue of military service arose,
Mennonites were all expelled from the region.[7]

In 1722 the small Mennonite congregation at Koenigsberg
received the right to worship, but only if it met in private homes and
if the members paid the sum of 200 taler to the Prussian recruitment
treasury. In the following year when plundering Prussian soldiers in
the Tilsit community carried off a number of Mennonite men for the
grenadier regiment of Frederick William, the King was incensed.
However, he immediately ordered the Mennonites banished from
the realm. Some returned to the Polish areas where they had lived
originally.[8]

Such wanton acts of persecution were much less likely to occur
under the reign of Frederick William's successor, Frederick the Great
(1740-1786). The latter enunciated a forthright policy of religious
toleration and extended the policy to both Prussias when Prussia
forcibly took Royal Prussia from Poland in 1772. But Frederick's
recruitment regulations linked military obligations with the ownership of land. Mennonites therefore sent delegations to the king to
request exemption from military service. They pointed out the pro-
tective terms of previous Polish charters and asked for military
exemption in keeping with the tenets of their faith.[9]

The June 14, 1773, edict of Frederick the Great was, on the whole,
a positive response to the nine-point petition which Mennonites had
submitted the week before. There was, however, one ominous
qualification of the confirmation of privileges which it included.
Point eight of the petition had asked for the privilege of selling land
to and buying land from persons of other faiths, as had been the

practice till then. The new law permitted the purchase of additional lands by Mennonites only with the consent of the Ministries of War and State Domain which would decide if such sales were indeed in the interest of the nation as a whole. Since the interest of the state included primarily the maintenance of military strength in the Prussian army, it was evident that the consent of the Ministries might be hard to obtain.[10]

In the city of Danzig, Mennonites had always found the situation very complex. Their civic virtues, industry and skill in trades and business often earned them the protection of government authorities. However, frequently the local guilds and the clergy contested such toleration. During the entire Polish period, one source maintains, "they suffered almost continually from hostility and arbitrary oppression, in many cases unabashed extortion from high-ranking persons."[11]

Heavy fines were regularly imposed on the Mennonites. From 1749 to 1762 a regulation was enforced by the guilds of the city prohibiting Mennonite merchants in the suburbs from selling anything but brandy. In addition, on January 14, 1750, an arbitrary "protection fee" of 5,000 florins had been imposed on Mennonites living in or near the city. This measure impoverished quite a few of the Mennonite families in the Danzig congregation. Moreover, the renewal and re-issue of the *Privilegia* provided by the Polish kings came to an end at this point.[12]

Within the newly acquired Prussian areas, the relationship of Mennonites to the state had to be reviewed during the 1770s and 1780s. Initiatives at the Heubuden Conference of August 22, 1774, the visits of two Mennonite delegations to Berlin on July 8, 1774 and August 26, 1777, along with the submission of another petition on February 21, 1780, finally resulted in the fulfilment of the Mennonites' request for exemption from military service.

In early April, 1780, Frederick the Great gave his reply to the request in the highly prized *Gnadenprivilegium*, assuring the Mennonites full religious freedom and perpetual *(auf ewig)* exemption from recruitment and military service. To retain such rights they must remain loyal and industrious citizens of Prussia, must promise to carry out the general duties of such citizenship, and must conscientiously pay 5,000 taler to the military academy at Culm in exchange for the promised privileges.[13] However, they were forbidden to buy additional land unless they received permission from the government.

The Prusso-Polish Mennonites prospered despite all adversities.

Under Frederick the Great, according to one author, they almost created a heaven on earth. Nonetheless, Prussia was a military state. For purposes of his own, the king had enumerated the Mennonites of the two Prussias and Lithuania soon after the new accessions of 1772. There were 12,000 persons, who lived on 2,177 *Hufen,* or about 90,000 acres of choice land. Expansion was slowing down but it did not stop altogether. Between 1781 and 1784 Mennonites made 296 new purchases of land.[14] Yet they were constantly looking for additional land to provide for growing families. Increasingly local officials complained about the shortage of recruits in their cantons, well aware that Mennonites were not required to perform military service. It was an uneasy "truce." The future of the Mennonites in that area was unclear.

When Frederick the Great died in 1786, many wondered if the forces which had created the socioeconomic and other tensions of the distant and more recent past would not come to the fore once more. In the court of the new ruler, Frederick William II, there were some who wished to curtail the privileges of the Mennonites. The king, it seemed, was disposed to give them credence early in his reign. The edict of July 30, 1789, sought to codify the privileges assured by his predecessor; however it simultaneously restricted the purchase of more land.[15]

In the city of Danzig, which was still under Polish rule in the 1780s, Mennonites were facing several special problems. Frustrated in his hope to include Danzig in the annexation area, Frederick William II took a series of measures designed to weaken the city's economy and thus make its existence as a Polish city politically unviable. The ensuing high tariffs on Polish imports and exports through Danzig diverted much trade to Elbing and Koenigsberg, causing serious economic deprivation particularly for the poorer residents of the city. Many Mennonite families felt these pressures too and wondered, with their neighbours, when and how these precarious conditions might come to an end.[16]

What a later Mennonite historian would view as a providential happening came via a Russian German "caller of colonists," Georg Trappe. As one of numerous agents sent out by his government to find foreign settlers for Russia, Trappe had obtained his commission from the Vice Regent of New Russia, Prince Grigorii Alexandrovich Potemkin. The latter hoped that the recent new Transcaucasian colonization ukase, which had been issued by Catherine II (the Great) on July 14, 1785, would help him find settlers for his lands.[17]

In May, 1786, Trappe had made his way to the Vice Regent's palace.

He managed to convince Potemkin that colonists from Danzig could be successfully recruited to settle in New Russia. Trappe felt himself especially well qualified to contact the Mennonites because, he pointed out, he could speak their Low German language. By early June the intrepid "caller" reached Danzig where his aggressive personal influence was felt by many almost from the moment he arrived.[18]

Peter Hildebrand, one of the early emigrants who responded to the promises of Trappe, later wrote the following about his initial contacts with the recruiting enterprise:

> It happened in late August 1786 that I visited my friend in Neuendorf, a mile outside the city of Danzig. He told me that the Russian tsarina had sent us a gentleman to invite people to settle in Russia. He seemed especially interested in the Mennonites. It was a ray of hope for my soul. I saw it as a sign from God.
>
> It was also a challenge to me personally. Since I owned neither a house nor land, but merely rented my property, I saw it as God's will that my earlier plans to emigrate had been foiled. . . . Greatly comforted, I returned to my landlord in Bohnsack who said, "If ten families move, I will be the eleventh."[19]

Trappe discovered very quickly that he could expect only cold indifference, indeed outright hostility, from the city authorities who forthrightly opposed his designs in the Danzig community. However, Ältester Peter Epp, leader of the local Mennonite congregation, proved to be an attentive listener, and he soon became an enthusiastic supporter for emigration from Prussia to New Russia.[20]

On August 7 of that summer, Trappe publicly presented his proposals to both Mennonite congregations in Danzig. When the authorities became aware of these initiatives, they forbade Ältester Epp and another of the church leaders, Isaac Stobbe, to have any more contacts with Trappe. Till December 1787, these men refused any open comment on the question of emigration.[21]

Many Danzig area residents responded warmly to the Russian offer. By the end of August Trappe had signed up just under 250 families, 35 of them Mennonite, the rest mainly Lutheran. The majority were quite satisfied with the information they had received. The Mennonites, however, felt they needed a clearer understanding of what was being promised. They considered the terms of the 1763 and 1785 manifestos more carefully, decided that someone ought to investigate the settlement opportunities firsthand and agreed to attempt negotiating more detailed terms of colonization with authorities on location in New Russia.[22]

A three-man land scouting party was selected to go. It included Jakob Hoeppner, a small landholder and businessman from Bohnsack, the somewhat younger Johann Bartsch, a shoemaker from the village of Neugarten, and a lesser known individual, Jakob von Kampen, who withdrew before the group actually left for New Russia. Sixty persons signed the authorization of their investigation. They also obtained the firm endorsement of the Russian consulate in Danzig and were told that their plans would be communicated to St. Petersburg. An affirmative reply of welcome came back without undue delay.[23]

The office of immigration in Riga was informed that von Kampen could not come because of illness but that the other two, Hoeppner and Bartsch, would be arriving forthwith. After receiving a letter of commendation from Trappe, the two left Danzig on October 19/31, 1786 in the company of 141 German colonists, the first of Trappe's recruits actually to leave the country.[24] None of the Mennonite families who had signed up joined this emigrant party.

After an eight-day journey by ship, the delegates made their first stop in Riga, then travelled by sleigh overland to Dubrovno in an area which belonged to Vice Regent Potemkin. Here they were hosted by General Lieutenant Baron von Stahl who was an acquaintance of Trappe. From there they proceeded to Kremenchug. After a short stop to post letters home, the men travelled to Kherson, where they spent most of the winter.[25]

Inspection of a wide area in the Kherson region took up most of the winter of 1786-87. In their survey trips the scouts included large tracts of land along the left bank of the Dniepr, the region of the Molochnaia waters and the Crimean peninsula. After carefully evaluating their observations, they finally chose a sector of land on the lower Dniepr River, not far from the recently founded city of Kherson, at a place called Berislav.[26]

Here they found the good soil, the pasture and access to water which were needed for farming operations. The site also lay adjacent to a major transportation route, the road built by the Russians to facilitate military communications from the north across the Perekop neck into the Crimea. With Kherson in the immediate vicinity, markets were also assured. The setting as a whole was not dissimilar to the lowlands of the Vistula Delta and its hinterland which the Mennonites had learned to appreciate in West Prussia earlier.

On April 22, 1787, the delegates submitted to Potemkin in Kremenchug their decision on site selection and a statement of the conditions of settlement which they felt would attract a large number of Mennonite families to colonize their region. What they asked for in their "Twenty Point Petition" was essentially the fulfillment of promises made in the 1763 and 1785 Russian imperial manifestos of colonization, very similar to what other colonists could also have expected. However, there were items relating to the Berislav locality which were unique to this statement, as were, more importantly, the particular practical terms of settlement which the delegates felt were essential to create a viable permanent settlement.[27]

The requests for religious freedom and worship headed the list as Article 1. However, no mention was made of one factor vital to the Russian stipulations, that is, relationships to other religious groups. It was illegal, for example, to proselytize among Russian Orthodox nationals. Non-Christians could, however, be evangelized. Trappe had indeed held out to Mennonites the prospects of a mission field among the Crimean Tartars, quite in keeping with the 1763 manifesto. However, there is little evidence to suggest that the concern for missionary work played any significant role in the Mennonite discussions about emigration to New Russia.[28]

Hoeppner and Bartsch did explicitly include the points about exemption "for all time" *(v vechn'ia vremiana)* from military service, and the rendering of acts of allegiance according to Mennonite practice, specifically not swearing the oath.[29] The manifesto of 1763 had granted exemption from state service as long as an immigrant lived in Russia. Those wishing to enlist voluntarily would not be hindered, but rather given a wage at the time of enrollment.

According to Potemkin, Mennonites were free from extra obligations for a number of years. After that period they were required to fulfill the obligations of "ordinary public service" *(obiknovenoi zemskoi):* billeting soldiers during times when military detachments might be marching through, or transporting provisions for military purposes (*podwod* services). Article 4 of the Petition had asked for exemption "for all time" from these duties as well. In fact a community of Hutterites which had moved to Vishenka at the invitation of Count Rumiantsev in 1770 had been able to negotiate these very same exemptions.[30]

The central request of the entire Petition was for a huge tract of land along the Dniepr near the tributary called Konskaia Vody, enough to provide for each family a grant of 65 dessiatins (about 175 acres) of arable land. They also asked specifically for the island of

Tavan and several smaller ones, including Kairo Island, lying oppo-site Berislav, from which they might harvest hay and obtain wood. Furthermore, they asked for the right to engage in trade and industry, for a ten-year exemption from taxes and for other practical requests such as the loan outlined in the 1763 manifesto, advances of money for food and transport, which they hoped they would not have to repay, and another loan to support them until their first harvest.

They wanted to have the land properly surveyed and divided among families. They also asked for government protection for their settlements and property and for the use of nearby quarantine sheds to provide shelter for new colonists. Besides that they requested materials to construct houses "in the German manner" and mill-stones to establish mills.

In addition to these forms of help, they petitioned for a ten-year exemption from taxes and a fixed land tax of ten kopecks per dessiatina. They expected further that Trappe would be put in charge of the entire migration enterprise and that he would be the Director and Curator of the new colony. With a view towards later develop-ment they asked as well that land be set aside in the Crimea to accommodate Mennonites who might want to settle in that area.[31]

The Petition had not been thrown together overnight. It was, as David G. Rempel has put it, "a carefully weighted and prepared statement of intent to emigrate to New Russia."[32] Potemkin's reply, affirmative in most aspects of the requests, did not come until July 5, 1787.[33] He had preoccupied himself with the preparations which preceded the visit of Catherine to the Crimea, planned for that summer. At Kremenchug, then the Vice Regent's capital, Hoeppner and Bartsch were presented to the tsarina in the presence of the entire diplomatic corps of her entourage. She insisted that the dele-gates accompany her on the rest of the trip. It was an invitation that they felt they dared not refuse, even though it worried them greatly because such a detour might delay the emigration for perhaps a whole year.

During the course of these travels, the delegates spent a day or two of royal entertainment at the Potemkin estate on the Khortitza River just below the famous Dniepr Rapids.[34] Little did they realize that in two years this would be the precise spot on which their people would have to settle. The men asked for permission to go to St. Petersburg to have their agreement ratified at the court. At first Potemkin objected but then changed his mind, and even provided them with all necessary facilities to get to the capital as quickly as possible.

Other delays in St. Petersburg gave the delegates further anxieties about getting back. However, Trappe was able to introduce them to influential personages in the government and the court. These were important contacts which would be useful later on. Thus in Gachina, for example, they were able to meet the heir to the throne, Prince Paul, as well as his wife, Maria. The delegates took this chance to pass on to them a copy of the Mennonite Confession of Faith. They were encouraged by the warm and friendly reception they were given on this occasion.

At the conclusion of this stay they received a document which summarized the agreement they had drawn up with Potemkin earlier that year. Count Bezborodko, the chancellor who had prepared and countersigned the document, pointed out to them that it had been approved by the tsarina. It was dated August 12, 1787, although it was not officially published until later in September.[35]

By late fall 1787, Hoeppner and Bartsch were back in Danzig again. Accompanied by Trappe, they had returned via Warsaw in Poland, to

The Hoeppner monument on Khortitza Island. A century after founding the Chortitza settlement, Mennonites erected monuments to honour the two deputies, Jacob Hoeppner and Johann Bartsch.

Photo: Mennonite Heritage Centre Archives

21

gain the support of the Polish king in their endeavors. In Danzig they found that discouraging and disparaging remarks about the emigration had undermined the hopes of some potential emigrants.

However, a number of families had become firmer in their resolve to leave. Six Mennonite heads of families had arrived in Danzig some months before the delegates' return. They claimed that they had sold all their possessions in their Prussian home villages in order to join those who were leaving Danzig for southern Russia. The men were Hans Hamm, Kornelius Willems, Peter Regier, Jacob Harder and Dietrich Isaak, who brought his unmarried brother-in-law, Abraham Krahn.[36] They managed to get the needed documents from the Russian consul in Danzig and decided not to await the return of the delegates but to proceed to Riga at once.[37] This was the first group which actually moved. These persons, as well as later emigrants, needed to depart from Danzig which was under Polish jurisdiction, because Prussia was refusing to issue emigration visas directly to Russia.

The others needed more preparation time before they were ready to leave. With renewed energy, Trappe sought to direct the enthusiasm stirred up by the return of the delegation and the information which they brought from Kremenchug and St. Petersburg. Among other things, he distributed a brochure in which he reiterated once more the proffered benefits of the emigration, while squelching, as well as he could, the negative rumours which might discourage the move.

At the Neugarten New Year's Day service of 1788, Trappe also handed out invitations to all who came to hear personal details from the delegates themselves. Specifically, the invitation asked everyone to gather on January 19 at the offices of the Russian consul in Langgarten to hear the reading of the original *Privilegium* which had been brought back from the Russian capital and to ask any questions that might remain about the Russian offer.

A large crowd gathered on the appointed day. Everyone was cordially received and taken on a tour of the premises. The group then heard speeches from the consul and Trappe. When the meeting ended, seven families declared themselves ready to go with Hoeppner as vanguard of the total body that might come later on.[38]

After the delegates had once more stated the terms of settlement offered by the tsarina, the crowd's enthusiasm reached its peak. Thereupon Trappe produced a document for each of the delegates, detailing the special privileges and awards which Potemkin had designated for the negotiators themselves.

Hoeppner and Bartsch were to receive the two flour mills promised in the Petition with the condition that the Russian government would be reimbursed for its construction expenses after the 15-year exemption had expired. The mills would then become the personal property of the two men. In addition to the 65 dessiatins given to every family, each of the two men would also get 29 dessiatins of meadow on Tavan Island. They would have the right to keep a store and a bakery and to sell their products anywhere they wished. Each owner of the mill would be given a grant of 800 rubles, repayable in 15 years.

They would each have the right to brew beer and vinegar and to sell their products without restrictions in town and country. Neither Hoeppner nor Bartsch would be required to repay government outlays for their travel and for the subsistence and travel of their families. These were generous gifts, but would later lead to no end of trouble for both men.[39]

As emigration fever rose to a high pitch, local authorities set out in earnest to hold back the swelling tide. Danzig authorities, encouraged by the Prussian Resident in Danzig, von Lindenovsky, did what they could to dissuade prospective emigrants from leaving. Efforts were made to discredit the entire Russian colonization policy. Danzig citizens were also warned that promises to settle them on state-owned lands would be broken and that they would find themselves on Potemkin's private estates instead. Harsh charges brought against the potential emigrants led the congregation of Danzig to dissociate itself from Trappe and the Russian consulate.

Trappe called the charges "outright lies." He pressured Sokolovski to inform the Russian capital that Danzig was refusing to allow its people to leave freely. One of the Prussian newspapers passed on a rumour that Trappe had been heard to boast to an English banker about the way he had bribed the entire Danzig council so that it would allow residents to leave.[40]

When the dust of this acrimony had settled, only 26 families, that is, 138 Mennonites out of more than 1,000 who had applied, found themselves with permission to leave. However, there were others in the Prussian hinterland of the city who were planning to join. Stobbendorf at Tiegenhof had 18 families who had obtained permission. Seventy more had registered their intent in Elbing and surrounding areas. Authorities now resorted to endless chicanery and bureaucratic foot-dragging as they delayed the issuance of exit visas and prohibited outright any but the poorest of applicants to actually make the move.[41]

Thus it was that the emigrants of 1788-1789 came to include almost no people of means. They were mainly low income families, tradesmen and craftsmen including blacksmiths, cartwrights, carpenters, cabinetmakers, tanners, harness- and saddle-makers, tailors, weavers, millers and brewers. It is not surprising that they had some difficulty adjusting to the agricultural demands which their settlement in Chortitza would make on them.

The advance party of emigrants, led by Hoeppner himself, had left by wagon train on March 10/22, 1788.[42] A farewell service took place at the Bohnsack church before the departure. The group of seven families, about fifty persons, spent its first night at Stutthof *am Frischen Haff.* Then came a stretch of travelling by sleigh over dangerously thin ice. Five weeks later they arrived in Riga, where they rested for a time. In four weeks they started up again; by June 12/24 they arrived in Dubrovno where Baron von Stahl once again hosted the company of travellers. They would have to wait here until the following spring, lodged in the facilities opened for them by the Russian government.[43] The group was told that the Russo-Turkish War made the southern Russian region insecure for settlement until later the following year.[44]

Meanwhile, another much larger group gathered on July 28 at Rosenort to take leave. They had hoped to elect ministers at a brotherhood meeting but this did not happen. No one among the emigrants was considered suitable for such an assignment because of rivalry between the Frisians and Flemish. The indecision made the authorities even more reluctant to hand out passes. Some families now decided to leave secretly. Bartsch did head up a group which left Danzig in late fall.

Failure to obtain adequate ministerial leadership became a major problem as the groups struggled to overcome the dislocations caused by the Flemish-Frisian differences that prevailed. Trappe, now in England, persuaded the Mennonite leaders of Amsterdam to send to the Danzig Mennonites an exhortation to unity. Its effect, of course, was difficult to determine.[45] The next group received an especially strong admonition from the Ältester Cornelius Regier, a plea that they might exercise much love and seek to leave divisions behind.

By winter 1789, a total of 228 families had gathered in Dubrovno, waiting for the beginning of the final leg of the journey which would take them to the region designated for them in the Petition.[46] A certain peace now settled over the group as the families waited for further developments in spring.

Yet the matter of pastoral care literally clamoured for attention. Several men, Jakob Wiens, Gerhard Neufeld and Jakob Schoet (one Frisian, two Flemish), were asked to lead church services by reading sermons such as those by I. Kroeker. However, they had no authority to perform marriages, lead communion services or baptize new believers. By now twelve couples were in fact waiting to be married.

A plea sent to the home congregations brought together a Danzig brotherhood meeting where four persons among the emigrants were appointed to serve as ministers: Jacob Wiens, Gerhard Neufeld, Behrend Penner and David Giesbrecht. None of them was an *Ältester*, however. Peter Dyck and Cornelius Friesen were chosen as deacons. Then a dispute arose because some of the Frisians felt under-represented among the four new ministers. Ältester Peter Epp of Danzig was finally persuaded to join the emigrants. Before he could leave, however, Epp became sick and died. The situation was not a happy one and worse was still to come.[47]

Before leaving Danzig, the first group had decided that when they reached Dubrovno, six men should go ahead to receive the lumber which was to be waiting for them downstream at Kremenchug. It was a difficult journey. The roads were very bad and the weather alternated between rain and cold, unpleasant and depressing. At Mogilev they replenished their supplies; at Velikoverst, not far from Chernigov, they decided to wait for better weather. Travelling improved as they drew closer to Kremenchug. But when they arrived they were told that the lumber was not yet there.

Almost immediately Hoeppner was invited to an audience with Potemkin, who informed him that Berislav still lay in the war theatre, so that the area they had chosen for settlement would remain closed to all colonists. He proposed that they take their party to the region of Khortitza Island on the Dniepr, about 70 versts from the city of Ekaterinoslav. Without waiting for a response, Potemkin advised the deputies to look over the site and report back as soon as possible. The deputies were almost certain that no alternative site would meet their wishes and desires as well as the Berislav region which they had been promised earlier. This development was a further bitter disappointment.[48]

Meanwhile, the whole group had begun to move, some families on wagons, others on barges along the Dniepr. Only a few of the more well-to-do families had their belongings with them; the others had shipped theirs via the Russian consulate in Danzig. The supplies were to go by ship to Riga, then to the Dniepr on wagons, and finally down the river to Kremenchug and Ekaterinoslav where they could be claimed by the owners. Four weeks after the earlier group of seven arrived in Kremenchug, it was joined by the remaining members of the contingent. A number continued on down the river while the rest waited for Hoeppner to return from his visit to the Chortitza region. When Hoeppner did return, he spent three weeks trying to catch up with Potemkin who had moved from the capital to Olgopol.

When they met, Hoeppner learned that the views of Potemkin had not changed. The Mennonite families must move to Khortitza on the Dniepr. The Berislav area, it was pointed out, remained in a danger area of Turkish and Russian fighting. A group of Lutheran German families, who had emigrated in the same wave, now settled in the Novomoskov region in a community which they named Josephtal. The Mennonites, meanwhile, were trying hard to sustain their own hopes.

In Hoeppner's absence, and with Trappe also away, Potemkin had appointed Major Jean von Essen to serve as "director" of the new Mennonite settlement. The latter, it seemed, had secretly planned to improve his financial fortunes through this assignment. In this he was disappointed, as he also was in reaching another of his goals, that is, settling the Lutherans and Mennonites in one community at Chortitza.

The first Mennonite families reached Chortitza and landed just below the rapids on the Dniepr around July 20, 1789.[49] By now their spirits had slumped decidedly. As Hildebrand put it, "Till Kremenchug I enjoyed the journey, and felt quite good about the area we were in. But the closer we came to the Chortitza region, the worse things looked."[50] Hoeppner and Bartsch joined the rest a little later that same month.

Making their way down the narrow valley of the Khortitza River where it flows into the Dniepr, the new arrivals saw before them the depressed sight of a ruined village and, on the crest of the slope to the south, a "palace" in the process of being dismantled. To the right of this structure were the green trees of a small orchard. Those who had come by barges down the Dniepr had landed at "Tsar's Landing," about a verst above the mouth of the Khortitza River. After looking around for a few days, they pitched their tents under a magnificent oak tree. This tree is still standing and is thought to be one of the oldest trees in the Soviet Union.[51]

By now Bartsch too had arrived. A new cry arose immediately when the crates of luggage were unloaded and in many instances found to be filled not with their belongings, but with stones. Some crates were partially smashed. Only a small sum of the money promised was in their possession so far.[52]

The new settlers spent their first weeks and months living in tents or camping under their wagons. Heavy rains fell in the late summer so that a number of individuals became sick. Some died almost immediately. Much of the wood which they had been promised did not arrive, so there was no hope of building wooden homes. For four years they would live in huts made of earth, sunk partly into the ground. However, some sites for villages were chosen already in the summer of 1789, and a little hay was harvested on the low hills that same year.[53]

From the beginning a group of 36 Frisian families chose to settle separately. They elected Johann Klassen and Franz Pauls as ministers of their group and formed a congregation of their own. A number of families were taken across the river to Alexandrovsk for the winter. Sheltered in the Sloboda Volovskaia, they received flour, salt and other supplies from government stores so that they could survive until the spring. Many of them had no intention of moving back to Khortitza-Dniepr junction, a location in which they felt it was not possible to survive. They demanded land in another location.[54]

Those who were most disappointed and discouraged vented their anger and frustration on Hoeppner and Bartsch. These men, they

For a century and a half Mennonite children played on the branches of the great oak which stood on the banks of the Khortitza River.

Photo: Mennonite Heritage Centre Archives

27

vowed, must be made to pay for their folly and treachery. Others, who were more resolute and realistic, explored the outer areas of their settlement, looking at the steppes farther away from the valleys. Here they found the soil more suitable for farming and concluded that some good crops could be raised on this terrain. Low-lying wooded areas and the bottoms of the valleys were quite suited to livestock. Gradually, more and more came to agree with Anton Klassen, who had declared almost immediately: "I can wish for no better land; it is equal to any we had back home. . . . I think we can make a living here as well." Hildebrand, too, felt that things could have been worse.[55]

The more enterprising families returned from Alexandrovsk in spring 1790 to build earthen huts and to settle in. The entire group had, in fact, been firmly informed that no other options remained and that they must begin at once to build their homes or be punished for their obstinacy. Sometimes several families cooperated to cut hay for their horses and cows, which a few of the more well-to-do had managed to buy. Hoeppner built his home on the island of Khortitza already during the first fall.[56]

In this way, eight villages of the settlement were founded by 1790. Chortitza, which became the centre, lay in the Upper Khortitza Valley. Originally , it had 34 families. Rosenthal (Valley of Roses), where Bartsch built his home, was a neighbouring village with 20 families. The two villages merged into one community as the years went by. The Island of Khortitza, seven versts long and three wide, was settled by 12 families including the Hoeppners. Its forests were a special asset, although these were to be utilized by the entire Colony.[57] The island settlement was also referred to as the *Kamp*.

Einlage, situated at a bend in the Dniepr, was named after a community on the Nogat in Prussia. It lay near a crossing of the Dniepr River where the Chumak Road reached Kitchkas as it advanced eastward to the region of the Don.[58] At the outset Einlage had 41 families. Kronsweide, founded by 35 familes, was built somewhat north of the other villages and on the west bank of the Dniepr. In 1833 it was transferred to another location, leaving only six of the original owners at the old site which was renamed Alt (Old) Kronsweide. It was a settlement of the Frisian families of the colony. Neuenburg had one of the flattest sections of the region. It originally consisted of 16 families, and lay on the road leading to the Dniepr crossing at Kitchkas.

Neuendorf, like Neuenburg, owed its name to a former home village in Prussia. Its first settlers numbered 38 families. It and

Schoenhorst were located in the Tomokovka Valley. Both villages had similar landscape and soil quality. Schoenhorst included 32 original families.[59] The Mennonites would discover later that the total land allotment of these eight villages amounted to 21,469 dessiatins of good arable land, with 987 dessiatins for haying, 249 dessiatins of wooded land and 1,293 dessiatins apparently of little use at all.[60]

Under the general supervision of the inept Major von Essen, Hoeppner and Bartsch sought to inspire and direct the enterprise as well as they could. The bitter accusations and charges which they faced upon their arrival smouldered beneath the surface of community relations throughout these early years. In 1793 the two men handed over all their official documents to the church leaders of the Colony. This actually signified their resignation from leadership in the Colony.

When this still did not quiet the opponents of Bartsch and Hoeppner, the church leaders decided to ask for help from the Prussian brethren. On April 18, 1794, Ältester Cornelius Regier and a colleague, the minister, Cornelius Warkentin, came to the Colony to help resolve the dispute. Confessions came from those who felt they had been part of the problem. Eighteen signed a document which it was hoped could terminate the quarrelling and disunity and unite everyone into one Flemish community.[61]

By this time, additional families were beginning to arrive from Prussia. The Prussian government's edict of July 30, 1789, had added new restrictions to land purchases by Mennonite farmers. In 1793 the Danzig and Thorn Mennonites also came under Prussian rule during the second partition of Poland. They were now brought under the edict of 1789 and had to pay an extra 600 taler to support the Culm Academy. These developments quickly revived troublesome issues which had touched off the first phase of the emigration five years before.

One hundred and eighteen families, totalling 623 persons, joined the New Russia settlement in 1793-1796. All of these families were Frisians. This raised the number of families resident on the Dniepr to 350 for a total of more than 2,000 persons. These later arrivals were somewhat more well-to-do than the earlier families. They brought along 400 horses and a good many head of cattle. Since they also had some governmental support funds, they could provide a significant stimulus to the development of the whole settlement.[62]

It was felt that Chortitza did not have sufficient good quality land to accommodate the second wave of immigrants with the regular allotment of 65 dessiatins per family. However, across the Dniepr, south of the fort of Alexandrovsk, they could obtain some vacant lands which, with the purchase of a small area from a private land-owner, were sufficient for seventeen families. In 1796-97 this group, entirely of Frisian background, founded the ninth village of the settlement and called it Schoenwiese (beautiful meadow).[63] The church leader for these families was Ältester Heinrich Janzen, who also had the Frisian community of Kronsweide placed under his pastoral jurisdiction.

Another fifteen families moved about 80 versts north to the vicinity of the Lutheran communities of Rybalsk and Josephtal, not far from the recently founded town of Ekaterinoslav. Though somewhat removed from Chortitza it, like Schoenwiese, was always treated as part of the original colony.[64] This tenth village, located on the river Kilshin, was called Kronsgarten (garden of the crown).

The others of the additional 118 families were temporarily settled in five of the original villages, with the expectation that ultimately additional land would be available in a good location. Hoeppner hoped very much that they could be given lands near Berislav at the site of their original agreement, thus perhaps to reclaim what had been lost in 1788-89. This did not happen. However, in the end he was able to persuade authorities to provide the areas which the families of Schoenwiese and Kronsgarten had procured.[65]

By 1797 the first two waves of immigration to the Chortitza Colony had come to an end. Ten villages had been established. However, it was not yet certain that the venture as such would succeed. The first decade had been difficult, at times extremely so. Some progress had been made, to be sure, but permanent stability was not yet assured.

Mennonite immigration ceased almost entirely during the reign of Paul (1796-1801). By all appearances the new tsar actually had intended to continue the colonization policies of his mother, Catherine II. However, certain diplomatic considerations and the concerns of dealing, first of all, with making improvements in the colonies brought a temporary end to the move.[66]

Nevertheless, some very important steps were taken to shore up the foundations of the new colony at Chortitza and to reassess the approach to colonization generally. One such move was the establishment on March 4, 1797, of a special section of the Senate called "Department of State Economy, Guardianship of Foreigners and Rural Husbandry." It was this section which, in the case of the Mennonites, sought to determine what was causing economic difficulties in their new colony and suggested measures that might

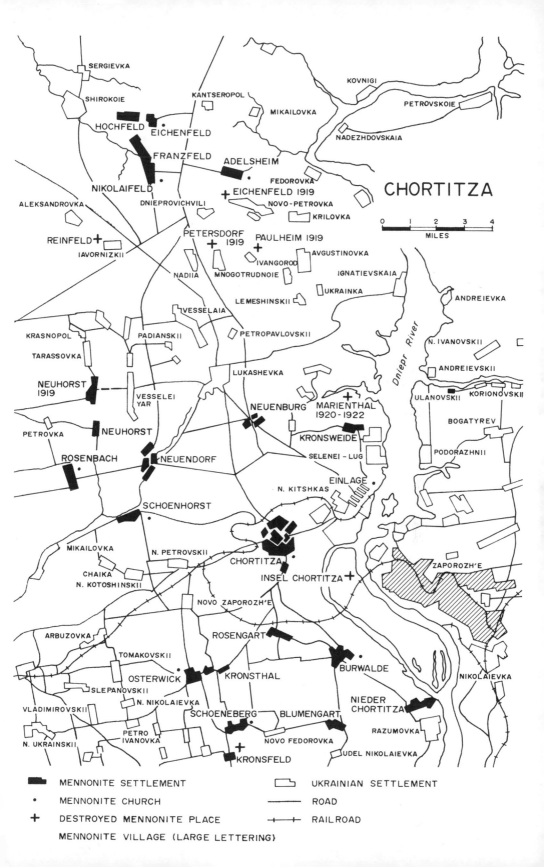

CHORTITZA

SERGIEVKA

SHIROKOIE

KANTSEROPOL

KOVNIGI

PETROVSKOIE

MIKAILOVKA

HOCHFELD EICHENFELD

NADEZHDOVSKAIA

FRANZFELD

ADELSHEIM

NIKOLAIFELD

FEDOROVKA

EICHENFELD 1919

DNIEPROVICHVILI

NOVO-PETROVKA

ALEKSANDROVKA

KRILOVKA

REINFELD

PETERSDORF
1919

PAULHEIM 1919

IAVORNIZKII

AVGUSTINOVKA

IVANGOROD

NADIIA

MNOGOTRUDNOIE

IGNATIEVSKAIA

ANDREIEVKA

LEMESHINSKII

UKRAINKA

VESSELAIA

N. IVANOVSKII

KRASNOPOL

PADIANSKII

PETROPAVLOVSKII

ANDREIEVSKII

TARASSOVKA

LUKASHEVKA

NEUHORST
1919

VESSELEI
YAR

NEUENBURG

MARIENTHAL
1920-1922

ULANOVSKII

KORIONOVSKII

BOGATYREV

PETROVKA

NEUHORST

KRONSWEIDE

PODORAZHNII

ROSENBACH

NEUENDORF

SELENEI – LUG

EINLAGE

N. KITSHKAS

SCHOENHORST

MIKAILOVKA

N. PETROVSKII

CHORTITZA

ZAPOROZH'E

CHAIKA
N. KOTOSHINSKII

INSEL CHORTITZA

NOVO ZAPOROZH'E

ARBUZOVKA

ROSENGART

TOMAKOVSKII

BURWALDE

NIKOLAIEVKA

OSTERWICK

KRONSTHAL

SLEPANOVSKII

N. NIKOLAIEVKA

NIEDER
CHORTITZA

VLADIMIROVSKII

SCHOENEBERG

BLUMENGART

RAZUMOVKA

PETRO
IVANOVKA

NOVO FEDOROVKA

N. UKRAINSKII

KRONSFELD

UDEL NIKOLAIEVKA

Dniepr River

0 1 2 3 4
MILES

◼ MENNONITE SETTLEMENT   ▢ UKRAINIAN SETTLEMENT

• MENNONITE CHURCH   —— ROAD

+ DESTROYED MENNONITE PLACE   +—+ RAILROAD

MENNONITE VILLAGE (LARGE LETTERING)

improve the situation.

This department forthwith assigned State Councillor Samuel Contenius to the task of investigating matters in Chortitza and asked him to submit detailed reports on his findings. His studies, and those of others like him, led to the issuance of the "Special Instructions" of July 26, 1800, and May 16, 1801, which brought a new system of self-government to the villages and to the settlement as a whole. With this move came the opening of an office at Ekaterinoslav known as the *kontora opekunstva* or *Tutel Kanzlei* (Guardians Bureau) to oversee the proposed changes.[67]

Contenius also recommended that more land be acquired for landless Chortitza families. The result was the purchase of more than 12,000 dessiatins at Nizhnaia Khortitza where two more villages were set up in 1803. It was hoped that 150 families could be moved. However, the new communities of Burwalde (Baburka) and Nieder Chortitza (Nizhnaia Khortitza) were able to accommodate only 65 of these families. The others remained in the older villages.

The real Mennonite "coup" of this period, as many viewed it, was the acquisition of a *Privilegium* signed by Tsar Paul himself. Dated September 6, 1800, this document confirmed the legal basis on which Mennonites would rest their residence and other state rights for the next 117 years.

In fact the *Privilegium* was more than a confirmation of what had existed before. The new agreement extended the earlier terms considerably. To the conditions worked out by Hoeppner and Bartsch were now added other rights: the freedom to dispose of property according to Mennonite custom (except in cases of land received from the crown); freedom to build factories not only in the cities of New Russia but throughout the entire realm; the right to brew beer and vinegar; and the privilege of controlling all places for building houses and taverns in the colonies.[68]

In Chortitza the new *Privilegium* made a very favourable impression. Immediately reports on it were sent to Prussian Mennonites. After Paul died, his son, Alexander I, once more restored the vigorous immigration policies of Catherine II. A new law passed in 1804 formalized this renewed support for colonization, including help for Mennonites from Prussia. As a result a second major Mennonite immigration movement began almost immediately.[69] The Prussian government's continuing refusal to allow Mennonites to purchase land gave the impetus for more families to pull up stakes and leave.

On December 17, 1801, Frederick William III issued a supplement to the 1789 edict, adding further restrictions to acquisition of new land by his Mennonite subjects. As before, they were again deeply disturbed and sent numerous delegations to Berlin to find a solution to the dilemma caused by the new decree. The Prussian government made some concessions but did not offer enough. Once more Mennonites began to make preparations to leave for New Russia.

When it became known that more than 150 families had left by the autumn of 1803, Frederick William ordered that the supplementary law of December 17, 1801, should be tempered somewhat. This plus the difficulty of obtaining passports did reduce the number of people leaving, but neither measure could halt the emigration altogether.[70]

The new group of Mennonite emigrants from Prussia which had disturbed the king was in fact a contingent of 162 families from the Marienburg and Elbing regions. They received passports in 1803 and left during the same year. Apparently most of them were not well-to-do. They were, however, given a positive reception at the border of the Russian Empire. They also received considerable government assistance: ten rubles per person; payment for travelling expenses; money for buying feed, implements, stock and lumber; and money for food from the time of their arrival at their destination until the first harvest. After a ten-year period of exemption from taxes, the settlers were to repay this advance.

Another group of 166 families followed in the summer of 1804. A number of these brought with them considerable amounts of money, household goods and implements, as well as herds of cattle and sheep. Twenty-one additional families were added to these groups in 1805, again assisted financially by the government as the first newcomers had been. In 1806 another 15 families arrived in New Russia, bringing the total of this move to about 360 families. The war of 1806-1807 with Napoleon temporarily halted the exodus.[71]

The ultimate destination of all these groups was a settlement tract of about 120,000 dessiatins which lay east of the Molochnaia River and south of one of its tributaries, the Tokmak River, in the Taurida area. It was not one of the areas which the government had originally hoped to procure for the Mennonite immigrants and it did not meet the criteria for a final choice. The area was not near the Dniepr River, did not have any trees and was not located near a market town or port. Moreover, Nogai tribesmen roamed part of the area. However, the soil here was rich, black and ready for cultivation. The area was also relatively flat. One of the newer towns of the region, Orekhov, lay only 40 versts to the north. Another town, Bolshoi Tokmak, was situated on the northern boundary of the settlement tract.[72]

The hardships of pioneering in the "old" colony, Chortitza, were reduced considerably for the later arrivals in the new settlement at Molotschna. Those who left Prussia in fall 1803 actually spent the winter with Chortitza families, making it easier to get settled during the next spring. For the earlier settlers this hospitality brought some much-needed money. Also the exchange of information and other materials benefitted hosts and visitors alike.[73]

Foundations for eighteen villages were laid by the newcomers of 1803-1806 in the "new" colony along the Molochnaia River.[74] The farmsteads of the first two years formed a string of villages along the river beginning with Halbstadt not far from Bolshoi Tokmak in the north, to Altonau near the mouth of the Iushanlee tributary in the south. In between, beginning in the north, came the villages of Muntau, Schoenau, Fischau, Lindenau, Lichtenau, Blumstein and Muensterberg. Tiegenhagen was established just south of Muntau in 1805.

Each of the villages had an average of 20 full farms. These villages also had a total of 38 half farms as part of their holdings.

Two additional series of villages were added in 1805, the height of this settlement period. One of the groups, consisting of Petershagen, Ladekopp and Schoensee, stretched eastward along the Tokmak tributary. Further south, following roughly the Kurushan tributary and east of Blumstein and Muensterberg, appeared the villages of Ohrloff, Tiege, Blumenort and Rosenort. Each of these had 19 or 20 full farms; together they included 16 half farms as well. Fuerstenau, just west of Blumenort, was begun in 1806. This brought the land area of settlement to about 33,500 dessiatins (just over 90,000 acres), owned at this stage by about 360 families.

The Molotschna Colony operated under the new regulations of self-government. From the beginning it experienced the firm leadership of its director *(Oberschulz)*, Klaas Wiens. Among other things he also helped select many of the village names. The somewhat chaotic conditions of the settlement years experienced by the Chortitza Colony did not reoccur in the Molotschna settlement. Money and property brought from Prussia and a steady policy of government aid considerably increased the speed of development over what the older colony had gone through fifteen years before.

As it turned out the Molotschna settlement received a final, indeed its major boost from another wave of immigration which began in 1809. Thirty-eight new villages were brought into being by 1863, bringing the total to 56. Four "experimental farm"-type estates were established in the region as well. That raised the total number of

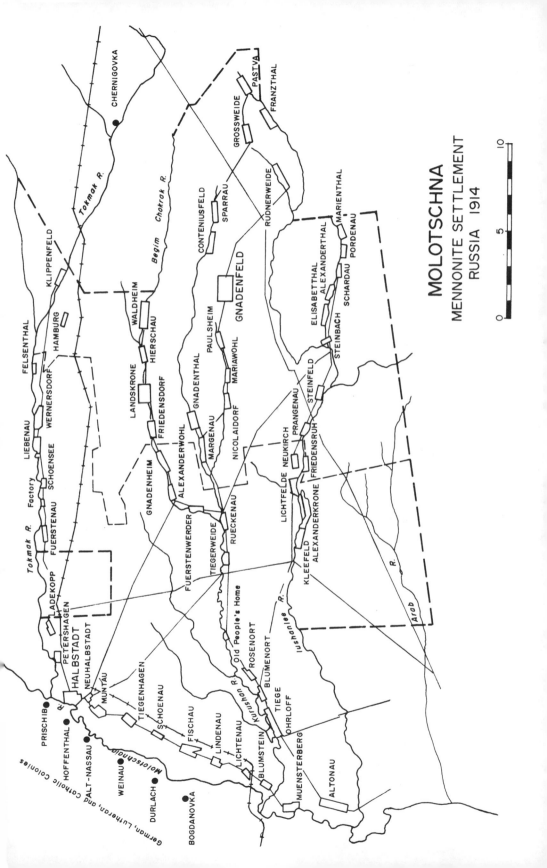

MOLOTSCHNA
MENNONITE SETTLEMENT
RUSSIA 1914

0 5 10

CHERNIGOVKA

PASTVA
FRANZTHAL
GROSSWEIDE
RUDNERWEIDE
SPARRAU
CONTENIUSFELD
MARIENTHAL
ALEXANDERTHAL
PORDENAU
SCHARDAU
STEINBACH
ELISABETHAL
GNADENFELD
PAULSHEIM
MARIAWOHL
GNADENTHAL
STEINFELD
FRIEDENSRUH
PRANGENAU
NEUKIRCH
LICHTFELDE
ALEXANDERKRONE
KLEEFELD
KLIPPENFELD

Tokmak R.

Begim Chatrak R.

WALDHEIM
HAMBURG
HIERSCHAU
LANDSKRONE
FRIEDENSDORF
ALEXANDERWOHL
MARGENAU
NICOLAIDORF
GNADENHEIM
RUECKENAU
TIEGERWEIDE
FUERSTENWERDER

FELSENTHAL
LIEBENAU
WERNERSDORF
SCHOENSEE
Factory
FUERSTENAU
Tokmak R.
LADEKOPP
PETERSHAGEN
HALBSTADT
NEUHALBSTADT
MUNTAU

PRISCHIB
HOFFENTHAL
ALT-NASSAU
WEINAU
DURLACH
BOGDANOVKA

German, Lutheran, and Catholic Colonies

Molotschnaia

TIEGENHAGEN
SCHOENAU
FISCHAU
LINDENAU
LICHTENAU
Kurushan R.
Old People's Home
ROSENORT
BLUMENORT
BLUMSTEIN
TIEGE
OHRLOFF
MUENSTERBERG
ALTONAU

Iushanlee R.

Arab R.

residents in this settlement to about 4250 families.[75]

Within a period of two decades the two "mother" colonies of Mennonite settlement in New Russia had been firmly put in place. Numerous other settlements followed in the ensuing years. The Mennonite colonies of New Russia, founded from 1789-1806, required two more decades to overcome their pioneering pains completely. After that, progress seemed assured, slower at first, but gaining pace as time went by. The Mennonites had come to New Russia to stay.

Notes

1. H.G. Mannhardt, "Die Mennoniten unter den preußischen Königen," *Mennonitische Volkswarte* 1 (November 1935): 431-443.

2. Basic treatment of the emigration of the first Dutch Mennonites to the Danzig area is found in Benjamin Unruh, *Die niederländisch-niederdeutschen Hintergründe der mennonitischen Ostwanderung im 16. 18. und 19. Jahrhundert* (Karlsruhe: Heinrich Schneider, 1955), 88-182; Herbert Wiebe, *Das Siedlungswerk niederländischer Mennoniten im Weichseltal zwischen Forden und Weisenberg bis zum Ausgang des 18. Jahrhunderts* (Marburg a.d. Lahn: Johann Gottfried Herder Institut, 1952); and in Horst Penner, *Die ost- und westpreußischen Mennoniten in ihrem religiösen und sozialen Leben in ihren kulturellen und wirtschaftlichen Leistungen*, vol. 1 (Weierhof: Mennonitischer Geschichtsverein, 1978), 39ff.

3. Hermann Nottarp, *Die Mennoniten in den Marienburger Werdern; Eine kirchenrechtliche Untersuchung* (Halle: Max Niemeyer Verlag, 1929), 19ff.

4. The Polish context of this movement has recently been reassessed and accentuated by John Friesen in "Mennonites in Poland: An Expanded Historical View," *Journal of Mennonite Studies* 4 (1986): 94-108. The most prominent *Privilegia* were those of King Wladislaus IV (1642), Johann Kasimir (1650 and 1660), Johann Sobieski (1694), August II (1732) and Stanislaus August Poniatowski (1764). Their texts are given in Wilhelm Mannhardt, *Die Wehrfreiheit der alt-preußischen Mennoniten* (Marienburg: Im Selbstverlag der altpreußischen Mennonitengemeinden, 1863), lx-lxviii.

5. Nottarp, *Die Mennoniten*, 26ff.

6. *Mennonite Encyclopedia*, s.v. "Socinianism." See also Lech Szdzucki, et al., *Socinianism and its Role in the Culture of the XVIIth and XVIIIth Centuries* (Warsaw-Lodz: Polish Academy of Sciences, 1983). The precarious position of Mennonites in the city of Danzig during these years is discussed in H.G. Mannhardt, *Die Danziger Mennonitengemeinde: Ihre Entstehung und ihre Geschichte von 1569-1919* (Danzig: Selbstverlag der Danziger Mennonitengemeinde, 1919), 48-79.

7. On East Prussian Mennonites see *Mennonite Encyclopedia*, s.v. "East Prus-

sia;" and Erich Randt, *Die Mennoniten in Ostpreußen und Litauen bis zum Jahre 1772* (Koenigsberg: Otto Kümmel, 1912). See also Penner, *Die ost- und westpreußischen Mennoniten,* 216ff., and Mannhardt, *Die Mennoniten,* 431.

8. William Schreiber, *The Fate of the Prussian Mennonites* (Goettingen: Goettingen Research Committee, 1955), 24ff., and Mannhardt, *Die Mennoniten,* 433.

9. The basic feature of the recruitment/land ownership linkage was the canton regulation of September 15, 1773, which made the apportionment of recruits for each canton directly proportional to the amount of land owned in such a district. See Hajo Holborn, *A History of Modern Germany, 1648-1840* (New York: Alfred A. Knopf, 1968), 19ff., for the earlier development of this system.

10. Mannhardt, *Wehrfreiheit,* 131-132, and Peter Brock, *Pacifism in Europe to 1914* (Princeton, New Jersey: Princeton University Press, 1972), 232-233.

11. *Mennonite Encyclopedia,* s.v. "Danzig Mennonite Church."

12. Ibid.

13. The payment of 5,000 taler at the Academy began retroactively on June 1, 1773. Mannhardt, *Wehrfreiheit,* 128-129, and Mannhardt, *Die Mennoniten,* 436.

14. Mannhardt, *Wehrfreiheit,* 128, 138-139. The names of the heads of households are listed in Penner, *Die ost- und westpreußischen Mennoniten,* 414ff. He noted a total of 12,603 persons, including East Prussian settlements.

15. Frederick William II felt the pressures especially of Lutheran churchmen who often discriminated against other religious groups. James Urry, "The Closed and the Open: Social and Religious Change among Mennonites in Russia (1789-1889)" (D.Phil. dissertation, Oxford University, 1978), 59. See also Mannhardt, *Die Mennoniten,* 437-438; Schreiber, *The Fate of Prussian Mennonites,* 29; Nottarp, *Die Mennoniten,* 42; Mannhardt, *Wehrfreiheit, 141;* Holborn, *A History,* 373-374.

16. David G. Rempel, "The Mennonite Migration to New Russia, 1787-1870," *Mennonite Quarterly Review* 9 (April, 1935): 87.

17. Trappe had been in the service of the Russian government since 1776 when he had received some tracts of land near St. Petersburg. R.P. Bartlett, *Human Capital: The Settlement of Foreigners in Russia, 1762-1804* (Cambridge: Cambridge University Press, 1979), 84. The manifesto for Transcaucasian settlement is discussed in 121ff. The patterns for immigration under Catherine II had been set down in two earlier manifestos of 1762 and 1763 which apparently did not affect the Danzig area at the time.

18. David G. Rempel, "From Danzig to Russia: The First Mennonite Migration," *Mennonite Life* 24 (January 1969): 9-10. On the lead-up to Trappe's appointment see also Grigorii Pisarevskii, *Iz istorii inostrannoi kolonizatzii v rossii v XVIII v.* (Moskva: Suegerev, 1909), 262ff., and David G. Rempel, "The Mennonite Commonwealth in Russia: A Sketch of its Founding and Endurance, 1789-1919," *Mennonite Quarterly Review* 47 (October 1973): 276ff.

19. Translated by author from Peter Hildebrand, *Erste Auswanderung der Mennoniten aus dem Danziger Gebiet nach Südrußland* (Halbstadt: Typographie von P. Neufeld, 1888), 5-6.

20. David Rempel, "The Mennonite Migration," 87. On the role of Epp in the migration see D.H. Epp, *Die Chortitzer Mennoniten: Versuch einer Darstellung des Entwickelungsganges desselben* (Rosenthal bei Chortitz, 1888), 2, and *Men-*

nonite Encyclopedia, s.v. "Epp, Peter." Epp's earlier difficulties with the Danzig authorities are described in H.G. Mannhardt, *Die Danziger Mennoniten,* 122.

21. Rempel, "From Danzig to Russia," 10-11; Mannhardt, *Die Danziger Mennoniten,* 128.

22. Rempel, "From Danzig to Russia," 10.

23. Epp, *Die Chortitzer Mennoniten,* 8; see also Alexander Rempel Collection, Mennonite Heritage Centre Archives, Winnipeg, Manitoba.

24. The letter of commendation took the form of a sort of contract between Trappe and the delegates. Dated September 22, 1786, the agreement set out the terms of support for the trip and charged any to whom it might be shown to give a warm welcome to the holders of the letter. Epp, *Die Chortitzer Mennoniten,* 10-11 has the text of the agreement.

25. Ibid., 12ff.

26. Potemkin had founded Kherson in 1778. A few years later he coerced a colony of Swedes to move to the Island of Dagoe where they founded the colony of Gammal Svenskby (or Staro Shvedskaia, which means Old Sweden). David G. Rempel, "The Mennonite Commonwealth," 274.

27. The original German text was entitled "Die von Ihre Russisch Kayserlichen Majestät allerunterthäniges von uns zu erbittende Punkte" and was referred to in official Russian documents as "Prositel'nyia stat'i mennonitov" (Petitioning Articles of the Mennonites). A reprint of the text as later presented to the Danzig community is in Epp, *Die Chortitzer Mennoniten,* 16-23. The Russian text was reprinted in Pisareveskii, *Iz istorii,* 299-300, and S.D. Bondar, *Sekta Mennonitov v Rossii v sviazi s istorii nemetzkoi Kolonazatzii na iuge rossii* (Petrograd: Tipo V.D. Smirnova, 1916), 191-197.

28. David G. Rempel, "The Mennonite Colonies in New Russia: A Study of their Settlement and Economic Development from 1789-1914" (Ph.D. dissertation, Stanford University, 1933), 67.

29. Military exemption had been an explicit promise of Catherine's colonization manifestos, although they did not refer to the question of swearing oaths. Pisarevskii, *Iz istorii,* 53, and Epp, *Die Chortitzer Mennoniten,* 18-19 (Articles IV and VIII).

30. The Count's offer in twelve points, headed by the promise of religious freedom and military exemptions, was reprinted in A.J.F. Zieglschmid, *Das Klein Geschichtsbuch der Hutterischen Brueder* (Philadelphia, Pennsylvania: The Carl Schurz Memorial Foundation, 1947), 324-325. See also John A. Hostetler, *Hutterite Society* (Baltimore and London: Johns Hopkins University Press, 1974), 94-95.

31. I am indebted for this succinct summary to Urry, "The Closed and the Open," 73-75. See also Rempel, "The Mennonite Commonwealth," 283ff., for a more detailed point by point discussion of the Petition.

32. Ibid.

33. The reservations of certain points of the Petition are given in the reprint of Epp, *Die Chortitzer Mennoniten,* 16-23.

34. When Potemkin had become vice-regent, he had appropriated for himself huge estates in New Russia, including some of the choicest areas around the lower Dniepr Rapids. Along the Upper and Middle Khortitza streams, he had established an estate called Khortitskoe Urochische. Close to the river, Nizhnaia

Khortitza, lay another smaller estate which belonged to him as well.

35. Rempel, "The Mennonite Commonwealth," 287-288.

36. Hildebrand, *Erste Einwanderung*, 29, and Unruh, *Hintergründe*, 204. The latter actually speaks of seven families and also refers to a Behrend Jantzen family, and to a certain Abraham Epp all moving to Russia already in 1787. See also Jacob Quiring, *Die Mundart von Chortitza in Süd-Rußland* (Muenchen: Druckerei Studentenhaus Muenchen Universitaet, 1928), 9, who adds Franz Barkman to the family heads.

37. Hildebrand, *Erste Auswanderung*, 29-30.

38. Rempel, "The Mennonite Commonwealth," 288-289. See also Hildebrand, *Erste Auswanderung*, 35ff., and Mannhardt, *Die Danziger Mennoniten*, 128-129.

39. The terms are set out in detail by Rempel in "The Mennonite Commonwealth," 289.

40. Rempel, "From Danzig to Russia," 15-16. See also Paul Karge, "Die Auswanderung west- und ostpreußischer Mennoniten nach Südrußland 1787-1820," *Elbinger Jahrbuch* 3 (1923): 83-84.

41. Karge, "Die Auswanderung," 86.

42. Unruh, *Hintergründe*, 205. Mannhardt noted that a group of four families from Danzig preceded them earlier on February 10. They were the families of Hans Sawatzky, Heinrich Klassen, Gerhard Rempel and Peter Reimer. Mannhardt, *Die Danziger Mennoniten*, 129. The royal order of April 24, 1787, may have heightened the emigration fever. It created further restrictions for the Mennonites and led to a flood of requests to leave. Karge, "Die Auswanderung," 67-68, 86ff.

43. Hildebrand, *Erste Auswanderung*, cited the time of departure as Easter Sunday at 9 p.m. Then he detailed the trip to Berislav, 46ff; see also Rempel, "The Mennonite Commonwealth," 292.

44. The first Russo-Turkish War of this period took place from 1768-1774; the second Russo-Turkish War was fought between 1787-1791. Nicholas Riasanovsky, *A History of Russia* (New York: Oxford University Press, 1963), 292-295.

45. Epp felt that the differing practices of the Danzig Mennonites lay at the heart of their church problems. Essentially the families were divided into two "factions," the Frisians and the Flemish, a division with deep roots going back to life in the Netherlands several centuries earlier, i.e., to a split which occurred there in 1566. Trappe was aware of these problems and saw their potential danger to the settlement ahead. Epp, *Die Chortitzer Mennoniten*, 39-40.

46. Official Russian sources for the most part cited the total of families as 228. This made up a group of just over 1,000 persons. Rempel, "The Mennonite Commonwealth," 293-294. Several western sources, however, allude to 288 families. See Quiring, *Die Mundart*, 10, and Adolf Ehrt, *Das Mennonitentum in Rußland von seiner Einwanderung bis zur Gegenwart* (Langensalza-Berlin-Leipzig: Verlag von Julius Beltz, 1932), 22.

The villages from which these families came cannot be accurately determined for all those involved. One source accounts for 152 of the families as follows: Tiegenhagen 41; Rosenort 41; Fuerstenwerder 5; Ohrloff 1; Ladekopp 6; Heubuden 17; Elbing 20; and Danzig 22. Only two of this list came from East Prussia. Quiring, *Die Mundart*, 14.

47. Hildebrand, *Erste Auswanderung*, 48-50. See also Epp, *Die Chortitzer*

Mennoniten, for a fuller discussion of Danzig Mennonite efforts to provide pastoral leadership for the departing families. A letter communicating decisions in Danzig is found in a chronicle record from the pen of Ältester Gerhard Wiebe of Elbing/Ellerwald in Prussia. "Verzeichnis der gehaltenen Predigten samt anderen vorgefallenen Merkwürdigkeiten in der Gemeinde Gottes in Elbing/Ellerwald von anno 1778 den 1sten Januar," 160-161 under an entry for March 1789, Gerhard Wiebe manuscript, Mennonite Heritage Centre Archives, Winnipeg, Manitoba. See also Epp, *Die Chortitzer Mennoniten,* 48-50, for a fuller discussion of Danzig Mennonite efforts to provide pastoral leadership for the departing families.

48. Hildebrand, *Erste Auswanderung,* 56-62.

49. This date is cited in *Kurze älteste Geschichte der Taufgesinnten (Mennoniten genannt)* (Odessa: Franzow und Nitzsche, 1852), 12. Other sources say simply "late July." A 1789 letter to the church in Danzig noted the arrival at Chortitza as being on July 22, 1789. "Ein Brief aus Chortitz vom Jahre 1789," *Mennonitische Warte* 4 (January 1938): 19-20.

50. Hildebrand, *Erste Auswanderung,* 64.

51. D.G. Rempel, "The Mennonite Migration to New Russia (1787-1870)," *Mennonite Quarterly Review* 9 (July 1935): 111-112. The Khortitza Valley and the island by that name belonged to Potemkin at this time. A commemorative service to recall two hundred years of Mennonite settlement in Russia was held at this tree in August 1989.

52. On promises of financial support and other help to come, see Rempel, "From Danzig to Russia," 20ff. He noted that the period 1788-1797 had cost the Russian government a total of 347,950 rubles. Cf., Rempel, "The Mennonite Commonwealth," 295ff.

53. "Ein Brief," 20-21.

54. A few of the families were also taken to the village of Volokhoskii near Ekaterinoslav for the winter. Epp, *Die Chortitzer Mennoniten,* 51.

55. Hildebrand, *Erste Auswanderung,* 76.

56. A letter from Bartsch and Hoeppner, dated February 11, 1790, provided a fairly detailed report on the situation of the first months of settlement in the summer and fall of 1789. Among other things, they mentioned a visit by two men from the Hutterite community of Vishenka. Gerhard Wiebe manuscript, 198-199. See also Epp, *Die Chortitzer Mennoniten,* 50-51, who says that Hoeppner and Bartsch together took a number of families to the island in the fall of 1789.

57. Khortitza (Chortitza in Mennonite usage) was the original Russian name of the river and the island near its mouth. The island had once been the site of the Zaporozhian Sech, earlier a fort and then a kind of "capital city" for the Zaporozhian Cossacks, who inhabited the area.

58. The Chumak road (Tschumakenweg) used for transporting salt from the Volga originally reached Kitchkas on the east bank of the Dniepr, then went on to the Kachovka and finally down to the Crimea via Perekop.

59. Marguerite Woltner, *Die Gemeindeberichte von 1848 der deutschen Siedlungen am Schwarzen Meer* (Leipzig: Verlag S. Hirzel, 1941), 10-12.

60. Rempel, "The Mennonite Commonwealth," 297. A dessiatina was the equivalent of about 2.7 acres.

61. Hildebrand, *Erste Auswanderung,* 82ff., and Epp, *Die Chortitzer Mennoni-*

ten, 58-62.

62. Mannhardt, *Die Mennoniten,* 437-438.

63. Woltner, *Gemeindeberichte,* 13-14. The village name was also "imported" from Prussia. See also Rempel, "The Mennonite Migration," 114 and "The Mennonite Commonwealth," 298-299; and Epp, *Die Chortitzer Mennoniten,* 54.

64. This group brought mainly its wagons, but received substantial help from the government: 500 rubles per family, plus 75 rubles a person for payment of travelling expenses and 800 rubles to construct a mill. The original land allotment of 780 dessiatins was sufficient only for 12 families. Hence an additional 195 dessiatins were provided adjoining the lands of the Lutheran colony of Rybalsk. Woltner, *Gemeindeberichte,* 14, 27-28.

A list of families in Kronsgarten was included in Karl Stumpp, *The Emigration from Germany to Russia in the Year 1763 to 1862* (Lincoln, Nebraska: AHSGR, 1978), 873-874. Stumpp erroneously referred to the village as "ev" (meaning Lutheran in the index), and yet also referred to it as "Mennonite," founded in 1780 [sic]. He does not directly refer to any families as coming in 1796-97 when the village was actually first settled. Benjamin Unruh did not include the Kronsgarten list among his findings, though he had listings for nine of the first ten villages founded in the "Old Colony," Chortitza.

65. Rempel, "The Mennonite Commonwealth," 298-299. They would later be the main groups to form the villages of Nieder Chortitza and Burwalde (both in 1803), those of Schoenberg, Rosengart, Blumengart (all 1816) and finally Neuhorst (in 1824). This would complete all the villages established as part of the Old Colony, eighteen in all. See also N.J. Kroeker, *First Mennonite Villages in Russia, 1789-1943, Khortitsa-Rosental* (Vancouver: By the author, 1981), 9-20.

66. It has been suggested that the emigration stalled during the time of Paul I because he was anxious not to give Prussia any cause for offense, potentially possible because of an error on the part of the Russian consul of Koenigsberg, J. Isakov. The latter had reported to Prince Kurakin in February, 1797, that several Mennonite families wanted to settle in Russia. The prince then asked Isakov to follow this up with assistance, but to do so secretly. His letter of instruction was sent by courier to prevent it from falling into Prussian hands. Isakov then got in touch with M. Mierau, a representative of the Mennonites, telling him to inform the 27 families "by first mail" that they should get ready to move. He gave Mierau written assurance that Russia would treat them well. Since both Mierau and Isakov used the mails, it was felt that the intended secrecy of the plan had been violated. Hence the government, fearing complications diplomatically, decided to let things rest for a time. G. Pisarevskii, *Pereselenie prusskikh mennonitov v Rossiu pri Alexandre I* (Rostov-on-Don: S.S. Sivozhelezov, 1917), 4-5, cited in Rempel, "The Mennonite Migration," 117-118.

67. On the work of Samuel Contenius, see A. M...r [sic], "Staatsrat Kontenius," *Heimatbuch der Deutschen aus Rußland* (1958): 147-152, and D.H. Epp, "Samuel Contenius," *Der Bote,* December 30, 1953, 11.

68. Rempel, "The Mennonite Commonwealth," 301-302. The original text is found in *Polnoe Sobranie Zakonov Rossiskoi* (PSZ) 26 (No. 19): 546.

69. The main work on this migration to date is Pisarevskii, *Pereselenie prusskikh mennonitiv v rossiu pri Alexandre I.* See also Rempel, "The Mennonite Commonwealth," 304ff. The new law of February 20, 1804, published in PSZ

(No. 21): 163 was called "Concerning Regulations for bringing in Foreigners as Settlers." It stressed not simply the settlement of vacant Russian lands, but the need for more skilled people who could be a model for nationals in New Russia. Ehrt, *Das Mennonitentum in Russland,* 26.

70. Karge, "Die Auswanderung," 70ff., and Rempel, "The Mennonite Commonwealth," 304ff.

71. Quiring, *Die Mundart,* 15ff, but with more detail in Woltner, *Gemeindeberichte,* 88ff. On the beginnings see also H. Goerz, *Die Molotschnaer Ansiedlung: Entstehung, Entwicklung und Untergang* (Steinbach, Manitoba: Echo Verlag, 1950/51).

72. Rempel, "The Mennonite Migration," 120ff.

73. Goerz, *Die Molotschnaer Ansiedlung,* 7ff.

74. The best description of the beginning of the first eighteen villages as well as later ones is in Woltner, *Gemeindeberichte,* 88ff.

75. Rempel, "The Mennonite Commonwealth," 306-307. See also *Mennonite Encyclopedia,* s.v. "Molotschna Mennonite Settlements."

Mennonite Churches and Religious Developments in Russia 1789-1850

John Friesen

When Mennonites left the Polish city of Danzig (now Gdansk) for New Russia in the spring of 1788, they were divided into two religious groups, the Frisians and the Flemish. This division proved to be a continuing liability for them as they attempted to establish church organizations in New Russia.

In the sixteenth century Frisian and Flemish Mennonites were distinguished by geographical origin in the Netherlands. Before long, however, it was not geographical distinctions but diverse church practices and views on church discipline which differentiated these two groups. Church practices which characterized the Flemish included the following: ministers read their sermons while seated before the congregation; baptismal candidates provided two character witnesses whose names were read from the pulpit; baptism was by pouring from a pitcher; in the communion ceremony the bread was distributed to the members who remained seated; and usually only the *Ältesten* were ordained by laying on of hands.[1] Frisian church patterns, on the other hand, included the following: ministers did not read sermons but preached more freely; baptismal candidates were not required to have two character witnesses; baptism was by sprinkling; in the communion ceremony the members filed past the *Ältester* who put the bread on their handkerchiefs. In the matter of church discipline, the Flemish were generally stricter, the Frisian churches somewhat more lenient.

While they lived under Polish rule, that is, from the mid-16th century until 1772, these groups usually would not accept members from each other without rebaptism. Marriage between people of the two groups was problematic because they were usually excommunicated. The Flemish were somewhat stricter in this regard than were the Frisians. Conflict between the two groups was beginning to mellow a little at the time of the emigration to New Russia. The first acceptance of a member into the other group without rebaptism occurred in 1768. However, by 1788 the walls of suspicion and tension between the two were far from coming down. Division within the Mennonite group which moved to New Russia represented not only a difference in minor external practices, but also a two-century-old mistrust of each other.

Leadership patterns in the two groups were very similar. At the head of each congregation was an *Ältester* who had responsibility for the general oversight, direction and leadership of the congregation. He also presided at communion services, baptized all new members, kept the church books which included membership lists of baptisms, births, remarriages and deaths, and enforced church discipline where necessary. In addition to the *Ältester* each congregation had a number of ministers, called *Lehrer* (teachers), whose function was to do much of the teaching and preaching in the congregation and in general to assist the *Ältester* in directing the congregation. Each congregation also had a number of deacons who looked after the material welfare of needy church members.[2]

These persons — *Ältester, Lehrer* and deacons of whom there could be six or more altogether in one congregation — constituted the leadership in the Mennonite community and collectively were called the *Lehrdienst.* This group would discuss issues, make recommendations to the members and represent the congregation before the government or other outside bodies. Whether this system operated democratically or autocratically frequently depended on the predisposition of the *Ältester.* However, since all members of the *Lehrdienst* were elected, the congregation could exercise some control on autocratic tendencies, especially when a new *Ältester* was selected. The people had very high regard for their leaders. Leaders were looked on as God's appointed, although they served in their positions without pay. The process of selection involved both the will of the people and the hand of God. In the selection process each adult male of the congregation voted for the person he thought best suited for the position. Then from a short list of about four, the lot was cast to make the final choice. Men thus chosen served for life; if the health of an *Ältester* failed, a co-*Ältester* was frequently selected.

The *Ältester* and *Lehrer* received no special training. Knowledge of the Bible, of theological issues and of their own heritage was acquired through self-study. Therefore quality of leaders varied widely due to differing aptitudes for study, degrees of individual initiative and personal financial means. Also a pattern developed whereby candidates were frequently selected from among those whose fathers or relatives had been leaders. This resulted in oral transmission of theological and biblical knowledge and passing on of ways to deal with various issues. Thus, a leadership class of families tended to develop.

Until the 1760s the language of worship in the Danzig Flemish church and in the rural churches had been Dutch. However, this language was in transition during the time of the first emigration in 1788. Increasingly churches were switching to German.[3] Since the late seventeenth century the German dialect they had been using in everyday conversation was the local Werder-Platt, a Low German spoken by the people in this area. By the 1760s this Low German dialect was being used more and more as the language of worship. However, the language situation was affected by another development, namely Prussia's acquisition in 1772 of the Polish province of Royal Prussia.

After 1772 most of the Mennonites along the Nogat and Vistula rivers found themselves under Prussian rule. Their children were being taught in schools which used Prussian High German as the language of instruction. Thus from 1772 to 1788, High German was entering the predominantly Low German Mennonite communities and was beginning to transform the language at the time of emigration in 1788.

Up to the middle of the seventeenth century the piety of Mennonites had been shaped largely through periodic contact with Mennonites in the Netherlands. However, as the language shifted from Dutch to Low German or High German, contact with the Netherlands decreased, and Mennonites were increasingly thrown on their own intellectual and theological resources. They had no institutions of higher education; hence lay leadership became their resource base. The body of literature they used was fairly limited, consisting primarily of the German Lutheran Bible, the writings of Dirk Philips and Menno Simons, the *Martyrs' Mirror* by van Braght, and *Die Wandelnde Seele* by Jan Philipsz Schabaelje, a Dutch Mennonite of the seventeenth century.[4] The influence of Pietism on Polish Mennonites was not very strong until after the first emigration to Russia.[5]

Chortitza

When Poland was forced to cede the province of Royal Prussia to Prussia in 1772, Mennonite churches outside of Danzig came under Prussian control.[6] In 1786, Frederick William I was crowned king of Prussia. It then became virtually impossible for Mennonites who refused to do military service to acquire additional land. For Mennonite communities this new situation threatened to increase greatly the number of landless people. At this point of discontent, Georg

Trappe came as a representative of the Russian crown to invite Mennonites to consider settling in New Russia. He knew Mennonites and their situation quite well and recognized that two issues were central to Mennonite self-understanding: exemption from military service and need for large tracts of land. He also articulated other religious dimensions which he felt would be inducements to emigration: that this move was clearly the leading of God and that no monarch guaranteed greater freedom of religion than Catharine.[7] Such freedom was certainly not guaranteed in America which, after its revolt, was so intolerant of Quakers that many had to flee, and also not in France to which these same Quakers had fled.[8]

In 1786 Trappe led a Mennonite delegation of two, Jacob Hoeppner and Johann Bartsch, to Russia to inspect the land and to negotiate terms of settlement. In 1787 the delegation returned and recommended emigration. When the first group prepared to leave, Trappe counseled Mennonites to appoint a good *Lehrer* for the emigrants, one "who will be concerned for the salvation of your soul and for the maintenance of a pious life among the people, in order that you may let your light shine in Russia, so that they may see your good works and praise your Father who is in heaven."[9]

The emigration to New Russia resulted in some efforts to bring about unity between Frisians and Flemish. The emigration began on March 22, 1788 and continued throughout the summer.[10] The Russian government had requested that the Mennonite groups unite so that it could relate to one set of leaders. In fact, however, no religious leaders had been elected or appointed prior to their departure. For some reason, Trappe did not accompany the emigrants, despite the fact that in the agreement with the Russian consul in Danzig on March 3, 1788, the government had explicitly agreed that Trappe would be the "director and ruler" of the Mennonites when they settled near Berislav.[11] Rather, Trappe made his way to Amsterdam and met with Dutch Mennonite leaders. With his encouragement, these leaders wrote a letter to the churches in the Danzig area on May 15, 1788, encouraging the Frisian and Flemish to unite and admonishing them not to ban members who married outside their group.[12] Even though this admonition may have had some effect on the relationship between the two groups, it did not resolve the basic conflict. On July 28, 1788, prior to the departure of another group of emigrants, a meeting was held in the Rosenort church to elect church leaders for the emigrating group.[13] However, this meeting was fruitless since those who were selected for leadership did not yet have their passports.

By the fall of 1788, 228 families had arrived in Dubrovno on the estate of Potemkin in the Mogilev region *(gubernia)*.[14] The majority of persons in this group were Flemish. No church or civic leaders existed among them except to the extent that Hoeppner and Bartsch exercised limited leadership by virtue of having been the delegates.[15] An attempt was made to now appoint church leaders. Three men, two Flemish and one Frisian, were elected to read sermons.[16] But they did not have the authority of ordained *Lehrer* to counsel and to perform marriages. Since there were twelve couples at Dubrovno who were waiting to be married, the latter concern was important.[17]

During the winter of 1788-89 the Dubrovno group repeatedly wrote to the Prussian churches requesting them to provide church leaders.[18] In response to their first letter, the Prussian church leaders merely told them to select a number of men to read sermons at their Sunday services. The reply to their second request advised them to elect ministerial candidates from their midst and send the candidates' names to Prussia where a selection would be made. The group submitted a list of candidates from which the Prussian Flemish church chose as *Lehrer* the three with the strongest support among the 228 families, Jacob Wiens, Gerhard Neufeld and David Giesbrecht. Lots were cast to select additional leaders from the remaining candidates. Chosen were Bernhard Penner as *Lehrer* and Cornelius von Riesen and Peter Dyck as deacons. All six were then ordained under authorization received by letter from the Prussian Flemish *Lehrdienst.*[19] The Dubrovno group now had four ministers. It seemed that the Frisians and Flemish would be united into one congregation. However, the choice of leaders brought in a potential problem: none of the four ministers selected by the Prussian leaders was Frisian. In his recollection of these events Peter Hildebrand regarded it as the leading of God that no Frisian was selected. To the Frisians it seemed a slight.

For a third time the group at Dubrovno wrote to Prussia and specifically urged Peter Epp, *Ältester* of the Danzig Flemish Church, to come to Dubrovno to help select an *Ältester.*[20] Epp was an old man, but because of the great need he decided to go. However, he died before he could undertake the journey. Without an *Ältester* the group lacked the traditional leader, the central authority figure so these church members could not celebrate communion. Discontent within the church grew.

A fateful event for the development of Mennonite church life took place in the summer of 1788 when the group from Dubrovno arrived in New Russia. Instead of allowing them to settle at Berislav, the region which had been promised to them by Potemkin and the Russian government, the vice-regent now ordered them to settle on the Dniepr near the mouth of the Khortitza Creek.[21] The switch was probably made because Potemkin owned the land in the Khortitza region and wanted settlers on his own land.[22] He had been appointed ruler over all of New Russia, and since he was a very close confidante of Catherine and, as a modern writer says, "manager of her male harem," protests against his decision were useless.[23]

The result of the change in location brought heightened dissatisfaction among the settlers. They vented their anger against Hoeppner who, they felt, had betrayed them. As already noted, the community also lacked a religious leader, an *Ältester,* who might have been able to speak on behalf of the people and possibly even rally their spirits to meet the new challenges.

Throughout 1789 and during the winter of 1790, the settlers' unhappiness grew as supplies which were promised did not arrive; baggage which they had sent down the Dniepr by boat and lumber were stolen.[24] Many still hoped to acquire a different place to settle. In spring 1790, the order to lay out villages came from Potemkin. Eight villages were established that summer: Chortitz, Rosenthal, Khortitza Island, Einlage, Kronsweide, Neuenburg, Neuendorf and Schoenhorst.[25]

The division between the Frisian and Flemish, which had surfaced in Dubrovno when the Frisian nominees for *Lehrer* had been passed over, expressed itself in the settlement of the villages. Kronsweide became a Frisian village and the centre of a Frisian church. Its members confirmed as *Lehrer* their two candidates, Cornelius Froese and David Schoet, who had been passed over by the Prussian Flemish *Lehrdienst.*[26] The records of the Frisian congregation are incomplete prior to 1800. According to some records it appears that a certain Johann Klassen may have been recognized as *Ältester* by them. Other sources indicate that Cornelius Froese was elected *Ältester* in 1792, but it is not clear whether he functioned in that office prior to his death in 1794.[27] Frisians who had settled in other villages before the Frisian church was organized joined the Flemish church.[28]

It was also in summer 1790 that the much larger Flemish church was organized. At a meeting in Chortitz, Bernhard Penner was elected *Ältester.* What the settlement needed was strong, energetic leadership; what they received was weak leadership. At the elections for ministers in Dubrovno, Penner had received one of the lowest number of votes, so his support in the community was not strong. He was also physically ill and was even poorer than most settlers. He was ordained as *Ältester* by his co-*Lehrer* Jacob Wiens, authorized to do so by letter from the Prussian Flemish Church, but his contribution to the church was very minimal.[29] On his request a co-Ältester, Johann Wiebe, a 25-year-old nephew of the Elbing Ältester Gerhard Wiebe, was elected. Because of his age and his strong sense of inadequacy, he declined to accept the office. Penner died shortly afterward, on July 29, 1791. Before his death he had written a letter requesting that the congregation elect a new *Ältester* and have him ordained by the home congregation in Prussia.[30] Wiebe was inclined to accept ordination if he could have a co-*Ältester*. The congregation elected David Epp, nephew of the recently deceased Ältester Peter Epp of Danzig, and requested that the two candidates go to Prussia to be ordained. Because of conflict in the congregation and Wiebe's indecision about whether he would accept ordination, the trip to Prussia was cancelled. Epp was then persuaded to accept the office and was ordained as *Ältester* by Jacob Wiens.[31] But, because part of the church and two members of the *Lehrdienst* disagreed with this act, leadership continued to be weak.

Several other troublesome issues aggravated the basic problems. The Flemish, as well as the Frisians, assumed that authority was bestowed on leaders through the combination of a call (election) by the congregation and confirmation of the call through ordination by another leader. Because both elements had to be present, the New Russia Flemish and Frisian congregations could not, by themselves, legitimate their leaders. Consequently Chortitza leadership could develop only slowly, leaving the churches weakened and de facto almost leaderless in the crucial early years.

Another emerging problem lay in the tension which persisted between religious and civil Mennonite authorities. The Russian government continued to relate to Hoeppner and Bartsch as representatives of the settlers. In Poland, the religious leaders — *Ältesten*, *Lehrer* and deacons — gave direction to the Mennonite communities. During the first few years in New Russia, leadership in the settlement had been largely consolidated in the hands of the deputies. By late 1791 when the two *Ältesten*, Epp and Wiebe, tried to assert authority, tension began to develop between them and the deputies.[32] Strong civil Mennonite leadership was a new factor in Chortitza which had not existed in the Mennonite community in Poland. In Russia this civil leadership was to play an increasingly important role, especially since the Russian government had decided to relate to it rather than to the religious leaders.[33]

From the summer of 1791 to the fall of 1793 conflicts and problems increased. In the Flemish church disagreement over Epp's ordination as *Ältester* led to the development of two parties.[34] The conflict increased when one group sent a letter to the governor of New Russia; another group sent a similar letter to Prussia, accusing the ministers of misappropriating 1129 rubles.[35]

The conflict became so severe that in the fall of 1793 the church sent *Ältester*-elect Johann Wiebe and Jacob von Bargen to Prussia to solicit help.[36] In response to this urgent appeal Ältester Cornelius Regier from Heubuden and Lehrer Cornelius Warkentin from Rosenort were sent to Russia by the Prussian Flemish leaders. The two men arrived in Chortitza on Good Friday, April 18, 1794.

Regier and Warkentin managed to reconcile the factions regarding the alleged misappropriation of money and drew up a document of reconciliation.[37] They involved both sides in the process so that unity seemed to have been restored. Regier, as *Ältester*, baptized thirty-one people in the Flemish church. The Frisian church also requested Regier's help since its *Ältester*, Cornelius Froese, had just died. Regier baptized thirteen candidates and helped to resolve a conflict which again erupted after Ältester Froese's death.[38]

Not long after Pentecost, probably due to the strenuous efforts of the preceding months, Regier died on June 16, 1794. Shortly before his death he ordained Warkentin as *Ältester*. Warkentin then held elections of ministers in both the Flemish and Frisian churches and ordained them. Now that the strife in the church had been settled, Johann Wiebe accepted the office of *Ältester*. Finally, after five years in Russia, the Chortitza Flemish church had leaders who were properly ordained.[39]

Regier and Warkentin also appointed a number of persons to civil administrative posts. They supervised the appointment of village mayors *(Dorfschulzen)* and settlement mayors *(Oberschulzen)* as well as a secretary in the Chortitza settlement office. The latter could speak both German and Russian.[40] These appointments were very important for the future development of Chortitza because they expressed the belief that Mennonite civil authorities were subordinate to Mennonite religious authorities. This system followed the pattern which existed in Poland and Prussia. Whether this pattern could be maintained in Russia was not at all clear.

Between 1793 and 1796 another 118 families arrived from Prussia. Many of these people were Frisian.[41] Some came from the Thiensdorf congregation near Elbing, a group that was quite strict about not marrying Flemish. They injected a strictness of discipline into the existing Frisian congregation in the Chortitza settlement. It was also at this time that the village of Schoenwiese near Ekaterinoslav was established. Sometime after 1794 but before 1800 the Frisian congregations, with centres at Kronsweide and Schoenwiese, elected Heinrich Janz as *Ältester*. [42]

After 1794 church life in the Chortitza settlement began to stabilize. Regular weekly worship services, baptism held at Pentecost and twice yearly communion services characterized the church year. The expression of religious commitment, of course, involved much more than attending religious services. All of life was to be organized around the people's religious commitment. For this reason it was crucial that the schools be under the control of the church and not under civil administration. The school curriculum was designed to provide people with the necessary reading and writing tools to become good church members. It was also important that village and colony civil administration express the faith of the church and not be separate from it. The authority of the religious leaders ought to be greater than that of the civil administrators. The equal land plots reflected their belief in the essential equality of all members; the communally-organized villages in which many responsibilities were shared symbolized their view that Christians should be interdependent within their community, mutually supporting each other in everyday activity.

After 1794, that is, after the authority of the church leaders was more firmly established, conflict broke out between the deputies Hoeppner and Bartsch on one hand and the church leaders on the other. The struggle was between established civil authority and a newly organized religious authority. [43] The Russian government had obviously favoured the delegates, even providing them with a separate *Privilegium*. [44] Both delegates, however, seem to have tried hard not to accept special favours. Both were successful farmers, and people soon began to be jealous of them. It also seemed that some people needed a scapegoat for the difficulties they had suffered. Both delegates were accused of wrongdoing and excommunicated from the church. Bartsch admitted his guilt and was reaccepted into the church. [45] Hoeppner was not ready to confess. He waited, was accused by the Flemish church before the Russian authorities and found guilty. The Frisian church did not enter this conflict.

Hoeppner's property was sold, and he was imprisoned. Shortly thereafter, in 1801, Tsar Paul died. The new tsar, Alexander, released many people in a general amnesty, including Jacob Hoeppner and his brother Peter. [46] The Frisian church immediately drew up a statement inviting Jacob Hoeppner as a member in their congregation. However, he never did join. The Flemish church worked hard to keep him out of the Chortitza Colony. Hoeppner thus became a casualty of the developing conflict between civil and religious authority within the Mennonite community.

The Russian government had not formally ratified the *Privilegium* which the two deputies had brought from Russia in 1787. This matter caused increasing concern for the settlers; without it their situation in Russia was precarious. In June 1798, the Mennonites sent two men to St. Petersburg to formalize the *Privilegium*. It is noteworthy that the two were church leaders, Ältester David Epp and Lehrer Gerhard Willms, and not civil leaders.[47]

After two years in St. Petersburg the two delegates returned with a *Privilegium* duly authorized by the Russian government, finally giving the Mennonite settlement a firm legal base. The *Privilegium* included commercial rights, like permission to brew and sell beer and vinegar, and control over inheritance patterns.[48]

After the turbulent early years, the situation in the two churches in the Chortitza settlement became more peaceful. Both had stable leadership. Schools were under the control of church leadership and were thus expected to complement the church in training the young people. Church leaders continued to carry considerable weight in relationship to the civil administration.

The smaller Frisian church was concentrated largely in the two villages of Kronsweide and Schoenwiese and seems to have exercised fairly strict discipline in its early days.[49] The long terms as *Ältesten* of Heinrich Janz (1800-1824) and Jakob Hildebrand (1826-1867) provided stable leadership. After the Molotschna Frisian church was established in Rudnerweide in 1820, the two Frisian churches supported each other and ordained each other's *Ältesten*.[50]

Much of the credit for developing a stable, united, strong Flemish church in Chortitza must go to Johann Wiebe who served as *Ältester* until 1823. He seemed to feel secure in his leadership, not easily threatened and willing to delegate authority. During the first fifteen years he had co-*Ältesten* David Epp (1794-1802), Peter Bargen (1802-1809) and Jakob Dyck, Sr. (1812-1823). After Wiebe's death Dyck continued to serve as *Ältester* until 1854.[51] Thus the two *Ältesten*, Wiebe and Dyck, served for a total of sixty years.

Two major events took place during the leadership of Jakob Dyck Sr. The first was the establishment of the Bergthal settlement and church. By 1836 approximately 40 percent (304 out of 749 members) of the Chortitza population was landless. This was not only an economic but also a religious problem. The Chortitza villages were established on the basis that every landowner *(Wirt)* had a vote in village affairs. Landless people were thus disenfranchised in civic matters although each baptized male had a vote in the church. This situation created inequality in the church, since the landed people felt that in church matters they should have a greater say than the landless. For a church which believed and tried to practice mutual confession and forgiveness among members, economic inequality was a problem because rich and poor rarely could relate as equals.

The Chortitza settlement arranged to purchase land north of the Sea of Azov in the Mariupol region and established the Bergthal settlement in 1836.[52] To avoid the problems of the early years of Chortitza, not only landless but also land-owning families moved to Bergthal so that experienced farmers could aid the inexperienced. In order to avoid some of the earlier religious tensions, only Flemish settled in Bergthal and organized one church. The first *Ältester* ordained by Jakob Dyck, Sr. was Jakob Braun who served from 1840 to 1866.[53] The Bergthal settlement established the same village pattern as Chortitza had. However, the equality of the early years gave way to inequality fairly rapidly. By 1867 over one-quarter of the families were again landless.

The church building in the village of Bergthal in the first daughter settlement (Bergthal) in Russia.   Photo: Mennonite Heritage Centre Archives

The second major crisis to confront Ältester Dyck in Chortitza was the issue of control of the schools. From the very early days, schools had been controlled by the church through its *Lehrdienst*. The school and church worked together to train children in the religious values of the community. The school curriculum was non-competitive, designed merely to help each student obtain the minimal literacy tools needed to play his or her role as an adult in the community.[54]

Until 1842 the Chortitza settlement had only village primary schools. In 1842 a secondary school *(Zentralschule)* was established with Heinrich Heese as teacher. The school was under the control of the Chortitza *Lehrdienst,* and was organized on orders from the Russian government's Ministry of State Domains.[55] Heese, of Lutheran background in Prussia, had come to Russia to escape service in the Napoleonic War, had taught himself Russian, and was appointed to run the Ohrloff *Vereinsschule* where he served from 1829 until 1840 when Johann Cornies abruptly dismissed him. From 1842 to 1846 he headed the Chortitza Zentralschule.

In 1846 the crisis hit. Cornies' Agricultural Union was given control over Chortitza, including its schools. Cornies promptly dismissed Heese and appointed his own choice, Heinrich Franz, who taught there from 1846 to 1858.[56] The Chortitza Flemish *Lehrdienst* was ignored and bypassed in this appointment. The church had lost control of the schools and with it the ability to control standards. A new school system was implemented which was designed to serve Johann Cornies' and the Russian government's vision of education, not the Mennonite church's view. For some this was progress, for others it represented the loss of something essential to the church's continued existence.

Church life in the Chortitza settlement from 1789 to the 1840s went through a number of phases. During the crucial early years — a lengthy period when leadership was essentially quite weak — the church was prevented from playing a decisive role. It is evident, however, that a strong religious commitment existed among the Chortitza settlers. When religious leadership was established under Johann Wiebe, the people rallied around him in a remarkable manner. Wiebe was able to establish that the church was paramount in the life of the settlement. The centrality of the church in the life of Chortitza was continued by Jakob Dyck. He provided stable leadership and maintained control over the life of the settlement until the Russian government, through its agent Johann Cornies, broke the church's control over Chortitza schools. Even though the church's scope of influence consequently was more limited, it continued to play an important role in the life of the settlement.

TABLE I
Chortitza Settlement: Churches and Leaders

Aeltester	Ordained by	Term
Flemish (Chortitzer) Church		
Behrent Penner	Jacob Wiens by authority of Prussian Flemish *Aeltesten*	1790-1791
David Epp co-*Aeltester*, 1794-1802	Jacob Wiens Chortitza, Flemish	1792-1802
Johann Wiebe co-*Aeltester*, except 1809-1812	Cornelius Warkentin Prussia, Flemish	1794-1823
Peter Bargen co-*Aeltester*	Johann Wiebe	1802-1809
Jakob Dyck, Sr. co-*Aeltester* 1812-23	Johann Wiebe	1812-1854
Franz Wiens co-*Aeltester*	Jakob Dyck, Sr.	1851-1853
Frisian (Kronsweider) Church		
Cornelius Froese	?	1792-1794
Heinrich Janz[en]	?	1800?-1824
Jacob Hildebrand	Franz Goertz, Sr. Rudnerweide, Frisian	1826-1867

Molotschna

In 1803 a new group of Mennonites left from various Prussian churches and headed for New Russia. A year later they established a new settlement east of the Molochnaia River and named it "Molotschna."

These new arrivals were more well-to-do, bringing with them more cash and hence able to purchase more supplies and equipment right from the start. The majority had been landowners in Prussia and thus brought along more management skills. Since church leaders — *Ältesten, Lehrer* and deacons — were elected from the membership, the higher level of personal experience and more abundant financial resources were bound to have an influence on the life of the church.

Linguistically, this group had experienced a generation of German education under the Prussian school system established after 1772 and 1793. The Molotschna settlers thus had facility in the use of High or classical German, whereas the Chortitza Mennonites felt more comfortable with Low German. Religiously, the Molotschna settlers had come under the influence of Pietist renewal emphases not experienced by the Chortitza settlers. This is not to say that all Molotschna people had accepted Pietism. It is rather to note that Pietism had entered the community and was making its impact both on those who accepted it and those who rejected it.

In 1804 and 1805 thirteen villages were established along the Molochnaia River and a cluster of four along its tributary, the Kurushan. Initially the inhabitants of these villages met for worship services in homes, served by *Lehrer* who had been ordained in the Danzig and West Prussian churches. In 1805 they elected their own *Ältester,* Jakob Enns, who was ordained by the Flemish *Ältester,* Johann Wiebe of the Chortitza settlement. In the Molotschna settlement, church life was thus organized right from the start and was spared the difficult early years which had plagued Chortitza.

During his fifteen years as *Ältester,* Enns encountered numerous challenges as he tried to mould a new church. Since his members came from various congregatons in Prussia, he faced the task of pulling this diverse group into a united harmonious spiritual community. During the first number of years most of the settlers' energy went into establishing their farms; very little was left for creative church development.

Although Jakob Enns brought to the task of *Ältester* some native skills of a moderately successful farmer, he also had some liabilities. He is described as being of "an exceedingly violent character,"[57] as energetic, of small spirit, having sudden fits of anger and being power hungry.[58] Even if one allows for some exaggeration by unsympathetic later writers, Enns seems to have had some serious weaknesses in dealing with religious issues that confronted him.

The Molotschna church was immediately faced with the issue of relating to the government. Under Polish rule up to 1772 and thereafter under Prussian rule, governments had not been overly sympathetic to Mennonite religious life. For example, Poland allowed Mennonites to build meeting houses only after the 1720s. However, in Russia things were different. Shortly after the Molotschna church was organized, Tsar Alexander I donated six thousand rubles to the

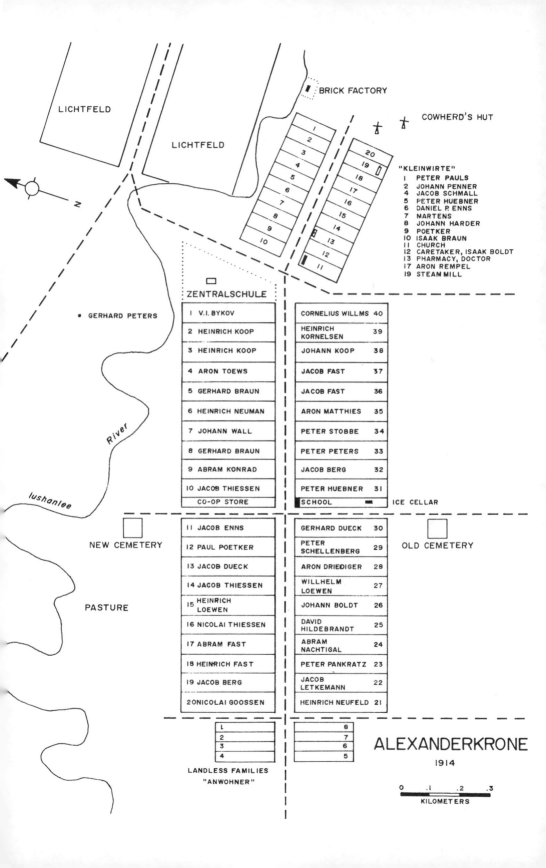

LICHTFELD

LICHTFELD

BRICK FACTORY

COWHERD'S HUT

N

"KLEINWIRTE"
1 PETER PAULS
2 JOHANN PENNER
4 JACOB SCHMALL
5 PETER HUEBNER
6 DANIEL P. ENNS
7 MARTENS
8 JOHANN HARDER
9 POETKER
10 ISAAK BRAUN
11 CHURCH
12 CARETAKER, ISAAK BOLDT
13 PHARMACY, DOCTOR
17 ARON REMPEL
19 STEAM MILL

• GERHARD PETERS

River

lushanlee

ZENTRALSCHULE

1 V.I. BYKOV	CORNELIUS WILLMS 40
2 HEINRICH KOOP	HEINRICH KORNELSEN 39
3 HEINRICH KOOP	JOHANN KOOP 38
4 ARON TOEWS	JACOB FAST 37
5 GERHARD BRAUN	JACOB FAST 36
6 HEINRICH NEUMAN	ARON MATTHIES 35
7 JOHANN WALL	PETER STOBBE 34
8 GERHARD BRAUN	PETER PETERS 33
9 ABRAM KONRAD	JACOB BERG 32
10 JACOB THIESSEN	PETER HUEBNER 31
CO-OP STORE	SCHOOL ICE CELLAR

NEW CEMETERY

OLD CEMETERY

PASTURE

11 JACOB ENNS	GERHARD DUECK 30
12 PAUL POETKER	PETER SCHELLENBERG 29
13 JACOB DUECK	ARON DRIEDIGER 28
14 JACOB THIESSEN	WILLHELM LOEWEN 27
15 HEINRICH LOEWEN	JOHANN BOLDT 26
16 NICOLAI THIESSEN	DAVID HILDEBRANDT 25
17 ABRAM FAST	ABRAM NACHTIGAL 24
18 HEINRICH FAST	PETER PANKRATZ 23
19 JACOB BERG	JACOB LETKEMANN 22
20 NICOLAI GOOSSEN	HEINRICH NEUFELD 21

1	8
2	7
3	6
4	5

LANDLESS FAMILIES
"ANWOHNER"

ALEXANDERKRONE

1914

0   .1   .2   .3
KILOMETERS

Molotschna church for building meeting houses.[59] This money was used to build a church in Ohrloff in 1809, and a second one in Petershagen in 1810. Evidently no serious questions were raised within the Mennonite community about accepting this generous gift from the friendly monarch.

The relationship to the Russian government was further complicated when it required that Mennonites organize their own local civil government with an *Oberschulze* at its head. The *Oberschulze,* who presided over local police and local juridical affairs, was elected by all male landowners in the settlement. Under Polish and Prussian rule the *Ältesten,* that is, the religious leaders, had been the acknowledged heads of the Mennonite community and spokespersons before the government. In Russia, there were two heads, the *Ältester* as the religious head, the *Oberschulze* as the civil head. The Russian government through the *Fürsorgekomitee,* which was responsible to the Department of the Interior, worked through the civil administrators.[60] This situation set the stage for power struggles and conflicts. The *Ältester* felt that the authority to which he was traditionally entitled was being challenged and diminished. In turn, the *Oberschulze* sensed that the authority which was bestowed on him according to Russian law was being challenged by a power-seeking *Ältester*. The conflict between *Ältester* and *Oberschulze* became so sharp that before long Enns placed the first *Oberschulze,* Klaas Wiens, under the ban. Sources indicate that there were numerous issues about which they disagreed. Most seemed to involve some form of conflict over authority.

P.M. Friesen believed the reason for conflict between *Ältester* and *Oberschulze* to be that "Mennonites had not yet learned to distinguish between spiritual and temporal authority and jurisdictions."[61] This may well be true. However, it is also true that Mennonites in Poland and Prussia had developed a theology which considered that all of life — religious, civil, secular, agricultural and educational — should be lived according to the Christian faith, and thus properly come under the authority of the church. The distinction between secular and spiritual which was being imposed on the Mennonite communities in New Russia was foreign to them, and in direct conflict with the historical view that the two realms ought to be united. In the conflict with Wiens, Enns lost, largely because he used unscrupulous methods.[62] He thus weakened the church and its leaders.

Enns was also challenged from another quarter. This occurred partly because of the peculiar situation in which the Mennonite church in Russia found itself, partly because of Ältester Enns' contentious character. In 1804 another West Prussian group, Klaas Reimer, Cornelius Jansen and thirty adults, arrived in Chortitza. In the following year they all moved to the Molotschna settlement. Reimer had been an ordained minister in the rural wing of the Danzig Mennonite Church. He considered the Danzig *Ältester* too liberal and hoped to find a less liberal, purer church in Russia.[63] What he saw in the Molotschna church alarmed him.[64] He was dismayed by the constant strife. He also believed that within a community of believers, such as the Molotschna settlement presumed itself to be, there should be no need to use corporal or worldly forms of punishment and force.[65] Surely, believers would respond to appeals to live Christian lives. However, it was evident that not all people in the Molotschna settlement were exemplary Christians. The problem was compounded because, according to Russian law, all Mennonites were required to live in the settlements assigned to them. Thus Mennonite identity was based not only on personal persuasion, as had been the case in Poland/Prussia, where joining the Lutheran church had always been an option for people who did not wish to live according to Mennonite principles. Mennonite identity was now being based on birth, and all Mennonites of varying personal convictions were now forced to be part of the church.

Reimer thought that church discipline should be used more vigorously to purify the church. When Mennonites did transgress the law and were punished or fined by the local Mennonite civil administration, Reimer believed that the Mennonite principle of nonresistance, of not using force and restricting discipline to the ban only, had been violated. Mennonites were resorting to worldly force to deal with matters of faith. In this situation Reimer expected Ältester Enns to exercise vigorous leadership but found him lacking. He felt that Enns' sermons were too formal and did not address the burning issues facing the church.[66]

Reimer and Jansen had numerous discussions with the Molotschna church leaderhip, but to no avail. Enns was defensive and felt threatened. Reimer was insistent and refused to compromise. In 1812 a group of eighteen people began to meet separately for worship and formed the church derisively called the little church, *Die Kleine Gemeinde.* Eventually the group adopted this name. It fought a long battle with Enns and his church over the issue of recognition. Enns did not want the group to separate and forbade the other *Ältesten* from ordaining Klaas Reimer as *Ältester.* Finally the *Kleine Gemeinde Lehrer,* Cornelius Jansen, ordained Klaas Reimer as *Ältester*. For years, though, *Kleine Gemeinde* ministers were not exempt from extra work for the colony administration from which all other ministers were excused. Finally in 1843 Johann Cornies interceded on their behalf. As a result the Minister of the Interior through the *Fürsorgekomitee* ordered the colony administration to extend to the *Kleine Gemeinde* ministers the same rights and privileges as all other ministers had.[67]

P.M. Friesen described the theological orientation of the *Kleine Gemeinde* as "narrow-minded, frightened, isolationist, opposed to education as well as extremely severe in matters of dress, residence and furniture."[68] Delbert Plett, in a study based on correspondence of the early years of the *Kleine Gemeinde,* presents quite a different picture. He argues that the *Kleine Gemeinde* made an attempt to warn the Molotschna Mennonites against the twin dangers of a deadening cultural Mennonitism and a corrupting Pietist Mennonitism, and to call them back to the historical Anabaptist Mennonite values and beliefs of adult baptism, refusal to swear the oath and nonresistance.[69]

By 1817 Jakob Enns was in poor health. He supervised the election of another *Ältester*, Jakob Fast, whom he ordained in the same year. Fast was *Ältester* for only three years before he died in 1820. But these three years were very eventful and had profound influences on subsequent church life in Molotschna.

During these three years two church groups emigrated from Prussia and settled in Molotschna. In 1819 a Frisian Mennonite group under the leadership of Aeltester Franz Goertz, Sr. arrived and, in the following year, established the Frisian Rudnerweide Mennonite Church at the extreme eastern end of the Molotschna settlement along the Iushanlee River valley and its tributaries.[70] Goertz, *Ältester* from 1820 to 1835, was followed by Benjamin Ratzlaff from 1835 to 1861.

This church was quite different from the large Flemish church. It came as a united body with an *Ältester* already ordained in Prussia and thus managed to avoid the internal conflicts which characterized the Flemish church. Goertz provided more freedom in the worship services. The *Lehrer* preached sermons they themselves had prepared instead of reading sermons written by their predecessors. The church had come under the influence of Pietism in Prussia and thus had incorporated special evening sessions like prayer meetings into church life. Periodically they also organized mission festivals.

Goertz had a concern for higher education and had a hand in inviting Tobias Voth to emigrate to the Molotschna to help in establishing the Ohrloff *Vereinsschule.* By bringing Voth into the settlement Goertz influenced the Molotschna settlement profoundly. In addition to his interest in promoting good education for young people and remedial education for adults, Voth emphasized singing, evening meetings, mission gatherings and organized a literary society to promote Christian and educational literature.[71]

Shortly after the organization of the Rudnerweide church, Franz Goertz and Ältester Jakob Fast of the large Flemish church decided to bring their two churches into full fellowship and recognition of each other.[72] Both leaders felt that the differences between them were merely external and not significant enough to prevent full fellowship.

In the same year, 1820, the Alexanderwohl congregation under the leadership of Ältester Peter Wedel also settled in the Molotschna.[73] It established villages in the centre of the Molotschna settlement along the Kurushan River. The group originated on the Przechovka estate near Schwetz in Prussia and was an "Old" Flemish congregation. The "Old" Flemish were more conservative and stricter on issues of church discipline than the other Flemish churches. On the way to Molotschna they were met by Tsar Alexander I who welcomed them to Russia. When they settled in Molotschna they named their village Alexanderwohl in honour of the Tsar. By the time this group settled in Russia, it seems to have come under Pietist influences. Klaas Reimer says in his autobiography that Ältester Peter Wedel became president of the Molotschna chapter of the Russian Bible Society, organized in December 1821.[74] By 1850, the Alexanderwohl *Lehrer* were preaching their own sermons rather than reading sermons written by others.[75]

Ältester Jakob Fast died in November 1820. In January 1821 the church elected Bernhard Fast to succeed him. He decided to emphasize the newly established cooperation between the Frisian and Flemish congregations by inviting the Frisian Rudnerweide *Ältester,* Franz Goertz, to ordain him. Shortly after his ordination the Ohrloff School Society opened the *Vereinsschule* in Ohrloff with Tobias Voth as the first teacher.

Almost immediately after Bernhard Fast was ordained, a major conflict broke out in his church between two groups which could be called the "conservers" and the "progressives." The "conservers" included about three-quarters of the membership and four *Lehrer,* led by Jakob Warkentin. The leader of the "progressives" was Bernhard Fast.[76] The "conservers" felt that the innovations Fast was introducing were undermining or at least threatening the traditional

Mennonite emphases of nonresistance, rejection of military service, discipleship and separation from the state. They objected to the union with the Frisian Rudnerweide Church because the Frisians had always seemed too liberal for most of the Flemish. They feared the new school in Ohrloff because it could bring about harmful changes.

The "conservers" were also vigorously opposed to the church joining a chapter of the Russian Bible Society. Fast had joined the Bible Society without informing his church or helping them to understand his reasons for this action. The opponents feared that this association with the Bible Society would subject them to military service since it involved them with an organization of the Russian state.[77] In his written response Fast emphasized the noble work that Bible societies were doing. Surely, he argued, no one would object to distributing Bibles. His opponents were not convinced, however, and pointed out that the Bible Society used military-type titles like President for its offices. Since the head of the Russian Bible Society at this time was Prince Alexander Golitsyn, a mystical pietist aristocrat who attempted to impose his view of Bible-centred education on Russian universities, the fear that relating to the Bible Society could involve some interference from St. Petersburg was probably not altogether without justification.[78]

The "conservers" were also indignant that Fast had granted a non-Mennonite, a certain Mr. Moritz, the right to partake of communion in the church.[79] To people who had always practised "closed" communion, that is, celebrating communion only among its members, and for whom communion signified fellowship, forgiveness and commitment to each other, the presence of a stranger in their midst violated their understanding of communion.[80] Resolving this issue was not helped when Fast lamely tried to excuse himself by claiming that Moritz had begged so vigorously that he had been unable to refuse him. Fast promised he would never invite an outsider to communion again.

The "conservers" were also apprehensive about Bernhard Fast's close association with Daniel Schlatter, a Swiss missionary who had developed his religious ideas from the Basel Mission Society, an organization founded under the influence of English mission societies.[81] Schlatter had been sent to Russia by the Basel Mission initially to teach at the newly organized Mennonite school at Ohrloff. However, by the time he arrived in Molotschna, Tobias Voth had been hired. Schlatter then took up mission work among the Nogai Tartars near the Molotschna settlement. He continued to maintain close contact with the leaders in the Molotschna churches who were interested in mission work.

The feelings between "conservers" and "progressives" were further poisoned when the Russian government requested that Mennonite religious feast days, like Christmas, Easter and Pentecost, be observed according to the Russian (Julian) calendar instead of the Gregorian calendar which had been used in Prussia.[82] To the "conservers" this signified unwarranted government interference in the religious life of their community.

The conflict between the two sides became ever more intense. In 1822 Fast resigned his position as *Ältester*. A general meeting was called, a reconciliation reached, and Fast was asked to take up his role as *Ältester* again.[83] However, the conflict continued and in 1824 the congregation split. Jacob Warkentin became *Ältester* of the "conserver" group which was named the Lichtenau Church or *Die Große Gemeinde.* Fast remained *Ältester* of one-quarter of the congregation which became known as the Ohrloff Church.

Even after the split the issue was not resolved. The question now was, who had the right to use the church building in Petershagen? The Warkentin group insisted that they had exclusive rights and, in 1827, appealed to the *Fürsorgekomitee* in Ekaterinoslav to confirm this right. It ruled that since the tsar had given money to build this church for the benefit of all Mennonites, no one group could claim exclusive use of it. [84]The Lichtenau Church then built a meeting place with its own funds.

Religious life in the Molotschna settlement was now divided into two, possibly three factions. One group of churches, the Ohrloff, Rudnerweide and Alexanderwohl congregations, developed its contact with Pietist groups. Regular correspondence was carried on with the Moravian Brethren at Herrnhut who kept the Molotschna Mennonites informed about mission activities in Greenland, Labrador, the West Indies and about missionary work among the Jews.[85] Correspondence was also carried on with a "Basel" group. Furthermore, these churches related to Pietist groups from Wuerttemberg which had settled west of the Molotschna Colony in German Lutheran villages. Thus the "progressive" Mennonite churches increasingly came under pietist influence.

However, most of the literature which was used by the Molotschna churches consisted of historical Mennonite writings. One of the most popular books was *Die Wandelnde Seele.* According to a *Kleine Gemeinde* booklet of 1845, other books used were Menno Simons' writings, T.J. van Braght's *Märtyrerbrüder: Der Spiegel der Gerech-*

tigkeit von einem Ältesten Dürk Philips von 1578, Peter Peters' *Der Weg nach Friedenstadt,* the confessions of Georg Hansen and Hans von Steen, and the writings of P. Jansz Twisck, a Dutch Flemish minister of the early seventeenth century.[86] The *Kleine Gemeinde* made the greatest effort to keep historical Mennonite writings in print.

The second group in the Molotschna settlement consisted largely of the Lichtenau Church. The situation in that church, which represented approximately three-quarters of Molotschna members, is more difficult to comprehend. All available sources from Molotschna seem to be unsympathetic to their group. It spawned no great writers and initiated few innovations. These congregations attempted to defend the faith which they had inherited from their forebears. The missionary, D. Schlatter, who visited Molotschna in 1825 reported among other observations that the "widows, orphans and the poor are well taken care of."[87] Although this was especially true of the Lichtenau church, it could be said that exercising support and mutual care within the church community was a matter of Christian obligation for all Mennonites. The test of the quality of faith and Christian life was whether this was happening, especially whether the weakest members were receiving care. For groups influenced by Pietism the tests of faith increasingly became those of attitudes relating to higher education, a more active church program and support of missions and Bible societies.

Delbert Plett argues that the *Kleine Gemeinde* represented a third orientation in Molotschna church life.[88] It attempted to transform the received heritage into new forms which they considered to be more consistent with the content of traditional Mennonite beliefs than the forms adopted from Pietism. Plett feels that the *Kleine Gemeinde,* by searching for new forms, avoided some of the "deadening" effects which resulted from the Lichtenau church's attempts to maintain the tradition unchanged. His conviction is that the orientation of the *Kleine Gemeinde* most faithfully reflected the original vision of the Anabaptist Mennonite movement.

For all Mennonite churches in Molotschna a major problem developed in the area of church discipline. According to practices followed in Poland/Prussia, church discipline was placed under the direction of the *Ältester* and carried out for the purpose of maintaining harmonious church life and commitment to common goals. However, as noted above, the civil authorities of the Mennonite community, the *Schulzen* and *Oberschulzen,* were empowered by the Russian government to maintain local civil order and to punish transgressors. They thus frequently encroached on the authority which the *Ältesten* thought belonged to them and used methods of punishment, fines and whippings which the *Ältesten* thought were inappropriate and not consistent with the faith of the churches. Since the force of Russian law supported the civil arm, the *Ältesten* felt increasingly powerless to influence the mores and life-style of the community. Drunkenness and other behaviour which they did not approve of was not illegal and thus not punished by the civil authorities; they thought they should intervene but felt powerless to do so.

A new factor entered Molotschna church life with the founding of the Agricultural Union in 1830. The Russian government wanted to improve agriculture in the Molotschna settlement and surrounding areas and gave the Union authority to implement change. Consistent with Russian bureaucracy its authority came from above and not from the people it served. It was directly responsible to the *Fürsorgekomitee* in Odessa which appointed Johann Cornies to head the Agricultural Union for life.[89]

The Union was problematic for the churches in a number of ways. Cornies was a member of the Ohrloff congregation, so the progressivism he promoted and implemented further aggravated the Lichtenau congregation. Since Cornies acted by decree and not by discussion, the "conservers" felt threatened by him and his methods. The authority structure in Molotschna was further complicated by the addition of a second civil authority which, at least in the area of agriculture, had authority superior to the existing civil and church structures. The Lichtenau *Schulzen* felt that Cornies infringed on their authority when, for example, he gave them orders to plant wood lots, hedges and rows of trees from one village to the next, implement the four-field system of land cultivation with summerfallow every fourth year, drain the water ponds and irrigate the valleys.[90] The "conserver's" resentment of the "progressives" was simply exacerbated by these orders. Most annoying was the fact that the "progressives" always seemed to have the force of Russian law behind them.

During the 1830s two more churches entered the Molotschna settlement. In 1835 a Flemish group, which had originated in the Schwetz region of Prussia, became established in the village of Gnadenfeld and named itself the Gnadenfeld Mennonite Church. In 1764 it had moved to Brenkenhofswalde-Franztal in Brandenburg where it came under the protection of the Moravian Brethren since the Brandenburg authorities did not know or recognize Mennonite churches.[91] Here it had organized a school which had become a strong promoter of Pietism through its teachers. Of all the churches in Molotschna, the Gnadenfeld group had been influenced most by Pietism. Its *Ältester,* Wilhelm Lange, was of Lutheran background. In Molotschna the Gnadenfeld congregation continued the Pietist practices it had begun in Brandenburg. The church organized annual mission festivals.[92] Women met to work and earn money for mission. Child dedication services were held. Baptismal candidates met weekly for instruction for two years. Children were baptized at age twelve. Regular singing sessions were organized which greatly improved singing in the congregation. In 1841 Wilhelm Lange was succeeded as *Ältester* by his younger relative, Friedrich Wilhelm Lange.

The Gnadenfeld congregation, consisting of forty families at the time of arrival, grew rapidly. Neighbours were attracted by its active program as well as by the powerful preaching. Some joined the congregation. The leaders frequently invited Lutheran Pietist pastors from neighbouring villages and thus established an open ecumenical mood in the congregation.

In 1836 the last of the immigrant church bodies settled in Molotschna. Also a Flemish group from the Schwetz region, it settled at Waldheim and formed the Waldheim Mennonite Church under Ältester Christian Schmidt. Eight years later he was removed from office by von Hahn, President of the *Fürsorgekomitee.* Circumstances surrounding the dismissal are not clear, but it may have been because Schmidt opposed Cornies. In terms of its religious orientation, the Waldheim group was "Old" Flemish. It combined some of the conservative elements of the Alexanderwohl congregation with some of the new pietistic practices and ideas of the Gnadenfeld *Gemeinde.*[93]

The tension which festered between the Lichtenau congregations and the Agricultural Union came to a head in the early 1840s. To a large extent the conflict became a test of strength between Ältester Jakob Warkentin and Johann Cornies. Warkentin frequently took action in areas which Cornies felt were under his jurisdiction. In the spring of 1842 Warkentin, together with Oberschulze Klassen, went to Odessa to see von Hahn, President of the *Fürsorgekomitee.* They brought accusations against Cornies and requested that he be exiled to Siberia.[94] After their discussion with von Hahn they were sure Cornies would be defeated. However, von Hahn had said he would personally have to investigate the accusation.[95] During the course of his own investigation in which he personally spoke to all the principals in the conflict, he changed his mind and came to the conclusion that Warkentin was the problem. He sent a circular letter through Molotschna stating that Warkentin was unworthy to be church leader. In May, three Molotschna *Ältesten,* Fast, Wedel and Ratzlaff, deposed Warkentin.

The Lichtenau church was now forcibly divided into three groups in order to weaken it: Lichtenau-Petershagen with Duerk Warkentin as *Ältester;* Margenau-Schoensee with Heinrich Wiens as *Ältester;* and Pordenau with Heinrich Toews as *Ältester.*

The bad feelings existing between these churches and Johann Cornies intensified in 1843 when the Agricultural Union was given control over all the schools. Cornies implemented standards for teachers, developed new curriculum, introduced new teaching methodologies, and ordered the construction of new school buildings according to a set model. The old school system, which was under the control of the churches, had functioned for the purpose of providing young people with tools necessary for life in the village. The new school system provided a world-expanding education which raised the intellectual horizons of the young people far beyond the village. The result of Cornies' changes was a new clash over the issues of authority and over the purpose of education.

Heinrich Wiens continued his opposition to Cornies' reforms. In 1847 the *Fürsorgekomitee* ordered him deposed and exiled.[96] After a farewell sermon in his church to which throngs of people came, he left for Prussia.[97] Later in life he returned to Russia and lived a quiet life. Many people in the three "conserver" congregations continued to see him as a martyr. His farewell sermon reflected a deep piety and a carefully formulated religious outlook. However, his attempt to "conserve" the ways of the past was crushed by the "progressives." Wiens' congregation was not allowed to elect a new *Ältester* for fourteen years.

A number of other developments occurred before the 1840s drew to a close. One was the deposing of Ältester Friedrich Wilhelm Lange of the Gnadenfeld church in 1849. Lange had been accused of some misdeeds in his household. Upon investigation the charges were proved substantially true. Lange was deposed by Bernhard Fast of Ohrloff. As a result Lange left the Mennonites and returned to the Lutheran church. The four Gnadenfeld ministers were also deposed, and from 1840 until 1854 the church was administered by Bernhard Fast. This was a serious blot on the development of church life in Molotschna, but its devastating effect upon Gnadenfeld is hard to fathom. The most progressive, the most pietistic of all the churches, was robbed of its leadership and left to drift.

The second problem was the rapid rise of a landless class. In churches which had historically emphasized fellowship, sharing, discipleship, and the giving and receiving of counsel within the church, the development of a relatively wealthy landowning class alongside a larger landless class posed serious theological problems. The division of Molotschna into competing civil and religious structures did not leave it in a strong position to solve this crucial issue.

The event which could be seen as closing this early period of Molotschna Mennonite church development was the organization of the "Molotschnaer Mennonite Church Covenant" in 1850.[98] The *Kirchenkonvent* included all *Ältesten* and *Lehrer* of the various Molotschna churches. These religious leaders had been meeting informally to discuss various issues from the earliest days of the settlement. All along they had dealt with issues concerning the relationship of churches to one another and with matters of discipline. One of their principle areas of responsibility prior to 1843 was the control over the school system. During the period of Johann Cornies' school reforms they had lost control over the schools.

With the formal organization of the *Kirchenkonvent* in 1850, the leaders' power in religious affairs became almost absolute and was clearly hierarchical. The *Fürsorgekomitee* dealt with this group regarding all religious matters. Within churches the decisions of the *Kirchenkonvent* were usually accepted without opposition or discussion. The authority of the local congregation and the rights of church members to speak to issues were seriously undermined. It is important to note that during this first period of development, the church's area of authority was gradually restricted to religious issues only. In this way a division between religious and secular issues had been created. Within the religious realm, authority and decision-making gradually shifted from the community to the leaders.

Conclusion

Developments in church life within the Chortitza and Molotschna settlements were fairly different. The Chortitza settlement experienced the ongoing divisions of the Frisian and Flemish churches, both having great difficulty in their early years. However, once leadership issues had been resolved, Chortitza developed a stable, strong church life. The churches played a central role in the settlement although eventually limited by the Agricultural Union in the 1840s.

In the Molotschna settlement church leadership was firmly established right from the start. Here the division between Frisian and

TABLE II
Molotschna Settlement: *Die Grosse Gemeinde*

Aeltester	Ordained by	Term

Ohrloff-Petershagen Flemish Church
(*Grosse Gemeinde*, 1803-1822)

Aeltester	Ordained by	Term
Jakob Enns Tiegenhagen	Johann Wiebe Chortitza, Flemish	1805-1818
Jakob Fast Halbstadt	Jakob Enns	1818-1821
Bernhard Fast Halbstadt & Tiege	Franz Goertz, Sr. Rudnerweide, Frisian	1821-1824

Die Kleine Gemeinde
(founded 1812)

Klaas Reimer	H. Janzen *Kleine Gemeinde Lehrer*	1812-1837
Abraham Friesen		1838-1847
Johann Friesen	Abraham Friesen	1847-1872

Ohrloff Church

Bernhard Fast	Franz Goertz, Sr.	1824-1860

Lichtenau Church (*Grosse Gemeinde*)
(divided 1841-1842)

Jakob Warkentin	Jacob Dyck, Sr. Chortitza, Flemish	1824-1842 deposed

Margenau-Schoensee Church
(organized June 18, 1842)

Heinrich Wiens Gnadenheim	Christian Schmidt Waldheim, Flemish	1842-1847 exiled
Visiting *Aeltesten*		1847-1861
Bernhard Peters Gnadenheim	Heinrich Peters Pordenau	1861-1887

Lichtenau-Petershagen Church
(organized September 2, 1841)

Duerk Warkentin Petershagen	Heinrich Wiens Margenau-Schoensee	1842-1869

Pordenau Church
(organized September 9, 1842)

Heinrich Toews	Heinrich Wiens Margenau-Schoensee	1842-1868

TABLE III
Molotschna Settlement: The Later Churches

Aeltester	Ordained by	Term
Rudnerweide Frisian Church (immigrated 1820)		
Franz Goertz, Sr. Rudnerweide	Ordained in Prussia	1820-1835
Benjamin Ratzlaff Rudnerweide	Bernhard Fast Ohrloff	1835-1861
Alexanderwohl Old Flemish Church (immigrated 1820)		
Peter Wedel Alexanderwohl	Ordained in Prussia, 1814	1820-1871
Gnadenfeld Old Flemish Church (immigrated 1835-1840)		
Wilhelm Lange Gnadenfeld	Ordained in Prussia, 1810 (1812)	1835-1840
Friedrich Wilhelm Lange Gnadenfeld	Peter Wedel Alexanderwohl	1841-1849 deposed
August Lenzmann Gnadenfeld	Bernhard Fast Ohrloff	1854-1877
Waldheim Old Flemish Church (immigrated 1836)		
Christian Schmidt Gnadenfeld	Benjamin Dirks Ostrog	1842-1866(?) deposed

Flemish churches did not play a significant role since, from the very beginning, both groups decided to cooperate with each other. The major tension in the Molotschna settlement was between the "conservers" and the "progressives." Being progressive was increasingly associated with acceptance of Pietist influences, adoption of a more competitive, open-ended educational system, and the encroachment of Mennonite civil authorities into areas traditionally upon the authority of the church. The *Kleine Gemeinde* stood apart from this conflict. It emphasized traditional Mennonite beliefs like peace and reconciliation, was open to educational innovations, but rejected many of the Pietist influences. By the late 1840s, the church in the

Bergthal settlement was still very young, and most energy was being consumed in getting established. The position this church would take on the issues of education, Pietism and relationship of civil and religious authority would emerge only later.

Despite divisions within the settlements, the new colonies developed a common sense of what it meant to be a Mennonite. A sense of communal identity transcended church differences. Commitment to being the faithful church bound the Mennonite people in New Russia together and gave them a sense of peoplehood.

Notes

1. *Mennonite Encyclopedia,* s.v."Flemish Mennonites;" *Mennonitisches Lexikon,* s.v. "Friesische Mennoniten;" *Doopsgezinde Bijdragen* (1983): 41; *Mennonitische Blätter* (1912): 5.

2. H.G. Mannhardt, *Die Danziger Mennonitengemeinde* (Danzig: Danziger Mennonitengemeinde, 1919), 105, 119, 120.

3. Ibid., 107.

4. *Mennonite Encyclopedia,* s.v. "Schabaelje, Jan Philipsz."

5. See *Mennonite Encyclopedia,* s.v. "Hymnology" for a discussion of Pietist hymns which were incorporated into the *Geistreiches Gesangbuch* of 1752 published by the Polish Mennonite churches. See also Peter Letkemann, "The Hymnody and Choral Music of Mennonites in Russia, 1789-1915" (Ph.D. dissertation, University of Toronto, 1985).

6. Mannhardt, *Die Danziger Mennonitengemeinde,* 121.

7. D.H. Epp, *Die Chortitzer Mennoniten* (Rosenthal bei Chortitz: By the author, 1888), 30.

8. Ibid., 31.

9. Ibid., 32.

10. Ibid., 37.

11. Ibid., 21-23.

12. Ibid., 40.

13. A. Brons, *Ursprung, Entwickelung und Schicksale der altevangelischen Taufgesinnten oder Mennoniten* (Norden: Diedr. Soltan, 1891), 285-286.

14. James Urry, "The Closed and the Open: Social and Religious Change amongst the Mennonites in Russia (1789-1889)" (D.Phil. dissertation, Oxford University, 1978), 78.

15. Epp, *Die Chortitzer Mennoniten,* 35, includes the *Privilegium* which the Russian government extended to Hoeppner.

16. Ibid., 41, 42. The three men were Jacob Wiens, Gerhard Neufeld and Jakob Schoet. The latter name is probably a reference to David Schoet, since no Jacob Schoet is listed by Benjamin Heinrich Unruh in *Die niederländisch-niederdeutschen Hintergründe der mennonitischen Ostwanderungen* (Karlsruhe: By the

author, 1955), 297, but David Schoet (Schuetz) was later a minister in the Frisian group.

17. Peter Hildebrand, *Erste Auswanderung der Mennoniten aus dem danziger Gebiet nach Südrußland* (Halbstadt: P. Neufeld, 1888), 50.

18. Epp, *Chortitzer Mennoniten*, 42.

19. Brons, *Ursprung*, 288; Johan van der Smissen, "Zur Geschichte der ersten Gemeindebildung in den Mennonitenkolonien Rußlands," *Mennonitische Blätter* 3 (March 1856): 18-21.

20. Epp, *Chortitzer Mennoniten*, 43.

21. An extract of this *Privilegium* was published by the Russian charge d'affaires S. de Sokolovsky in Danzig, on March 3, 1788, and reprinted by Epp in *Die Chortitzer Mennoniten*, 16-23. For a discussion of the change in location see Hildebrand, *Erste Auswanderung*, 62f.

22. Urry, "The Closed and the Open," 79. Also, David G. Rempel, "The Mennonite Colonies in New Russia: A Study of their Settlement and Economic Development from 1789-1914" (Ph.D. dissertation, Stanford University, 1933), 72.

23. Nicholas V. Riasanovsky, *A History of Russia*, 3rd ed. (New York: Oxford University Press, 1977), 284; Urry, "The Closed and the Open," 82.

24. Hildebrand, *Auswanderung*, 65, 66.

25. Epp, *Chortitzer Mennoniten*, 52.

26. Jacob Wiens, et al., "Ein Brief aus Chortitz vom Jahre 1789," *Mennonitische Warte* 4 (1938), 20.

27. Ibid.; Unruh, *Die niederländisch-niederdeutschen Hintergründe*, 295; P.M. Friesen, *The Mennonite Brotherhood in Russia* (1789-1910), translated from the German (Fresno, California: Board of Christian Literature, General Conference of Mennonite Brethren Churches, 1978), 165, 891; Hildebrand, *Auswanderung*, 65-66; *Mennonite Encyclopedia*, s.v. "Kronsweide."

28. Hildebrand, *Auswanderung*, 80.

29. van der Smissen, "Zur Geschichte;" Epp, *Chortitzer Mennoniten*, 55.

30. Ibid., 56.

31. Van der Smissen, "Zur Geschichte," *Mennonitische Blätter* 3 (May 1856): 34-37; Ältester Gerhard Wiebe, Diary, Mennonite Heritage Centre Archives, Winnipeg, Manitoba; Epp, *Chortitzer Mennoniten*, 56-57; Brons, *Ursprung*, 289, mistakenly identified Jakob Wiebe as the one who ordained Epp.

32. Epp, *Chortitzer Mennoniten*, 57.

33. Hildebrand, *Auswanderung*, 91f.

34. Epp, *Chortitzer Mennoniten*, 57.

35. Ibid.; Hildebrand, *Auswanderung*, 91-92.

36. Brons, *Ursprung*, 289; Epp, *Chortitzer Mennoniten*, 58 says that the church sent the delegates in 1792.

37. Hildebrand, *Auswanderung*, 92f. His copy of the document of reconciliation, dated June 27, 1794, does not quite agree with the copy in Epp, *Chortitzer Mennoniten*, 60, which is dated simply June 1794.

38. Brons, *Ursprung*, 291; Epp, *Chortitzer Mennoniten*, 61.

39. Epp, *Chortitzer Mennoniten*, 62; Friesen, *Mennonite Brotherhood*, 165.

40. Brons, *Ursprung*, 291.

41. Urry, "The Closed and the Open," 122-123.

42. Ibid., 125-127. Friesen, *Mennonite Brotherhood*, 165 identifies him as Heinrich Janzen.

43. Urry, "The Closed and the Open," 128.

44. Epp, *Chortitzer Mennoniten*, 35.

45. Ibid., 62-63.

46. Hildebrand, *Ursprung*, 100, 101; Epp, *Chortitzer Mennoniten*, 63; Urry, "The Closed and the Open," 130.

47. Epp, *Chortitzer Mennoniten*, 64; Urry, "The Closed and the Open," 130.

48. The text of the *Privilegium* is in Epp, *Chortitzer Mennoniten*, 64.

49. Urry, "The Closed and the Open," 125.

50. Friesen, *Mennonite Brotherhood*, 165.

51. Ibid.

52. Epp, *Chortitzer Mennoniten*, 95; William Schroeder, *The Bergthal Colony*, rev. ed. (Winnipeg, Manitoba: CMBC Publications, 1986). David G. Rempel, "The Mennonite Commonwealth in Russia: A Sketch of its Founding and Endurance, 1789-1919," *Mennonite Quarterly Review* 48 (January 1974), 28-29.

53. *Mennonite Encyclopedia*, s.v. "Braun, Jacob."

54. For a careful analysis and discussion of the educational system in the Chortitza settlement, see Urry, "The Closed and the Open," 343-399.

55. Ibid., 373.

56. *Mennonite Encyclopedia*, s.v. "Chortitza Zentralschule."

57. Friesen, *Mennonite Brotherhood*, 92.

58. H. Goerz, *Die Molotschnaer Ansiedlung: Entstehung, Entwicklung und Untergang* (Steinbach, Manitoba: Echo Verlag, 1950/51), 56.

59. Franz Isaac, *Die Molotschnaer Mennoniten: Ein Beitrag zur Geschichte derselben* (Halbstadt, Taurien: H.J. Braun, 1908), 91. On the cover of the book his name is spelled Isaak, on the title page Isaac.

60. For detailed discussion of the Russian government structures and the relationship of Mennonite local government to these structures, see Urry, "The Closed and the Open," 83f and 139f; and Rempel "The Mennonite Colonies," 36f.

61. Friesen, *Mennonite Brotherhood*, 92; Delbert Plett, *The Golden Years: The Mennonite Kleine Gemeinde in Russia* (1812-1849) (Steinbach: D.F.P. Publications, 1985), 163, 168f.

62. Plett, *The Golden Years*, 168f.

63. Friesen, *Mennonite Brotherhood*, 128.

64. Plett, *The Golden Years*, 163.

65. Isaac, *Molotschnaer Mennoniten*, 91.

66. Goerz, *Molotschnaer Ansiedlung*, 56.

67. Isaac, *Molotschnaer Mennoniten*, 92. Isaac also includes a German version of the *Fürsorgekomitee* order No. 4501 from January 28, 1843.

68. Friesen, *Mennonite Brotherhood*, 93.

69. Plett, *The Golden Years*, 86-91.

70. Friesen, *Mennonite Brotherhood*, 130.

71. Goerz, *Molotschnaer Ansiedlung*, 64; Friesen, *Mennonite Brotherhood*, 96-97.

72. Isaac, *Molotschnaer Mennoniten*, 93.

73. Ibid.; Goerz, *Molotschnaer Ansiedlung*, 65, says 1821.

74. Friesen, *Mennonite Brotherhood*, 131; Isaac, *Molotschnaer Mennoniten*, 93.

75. Goerz, *Molotschnaer Ansiedlung*, 65.

76. Isaac, *Molotschnaer Mennoniten*, 93-94.

77. Friesen, *Mennonite Brotherhood*, 137f.

78. For a discussion of the Bible Society see Urry, "The Closed and the Open," 214. Already in 1819, Jakob Fast had received 500 Bibles and 400 New Testaments from the Bible Society.

79. Regarding Moritz and his mission to the Jews, see Urry, "The Closed and the Open," 231.

80. Friesen, *Mennonite Brotherhood*, 136; Isaac, *Molotschnaer Mennoniten*, 103.

81. Friesen, *Mennonite Brotherhood*, 142; Urry, "The Closed and the Open," 218f.

82. Goerz, *Molotschnaer Ansiedlung*, 59.

83. Isaac, *Molotschnaer Mennoniten*, 106.

84. Ibid., 102-109.

85. Friesen, *Mennonite Brotherhood*, 141f.

86. *Mennonitisches Lexikon*, s.v. "Twisck, Pieter Jansz;" Friesen, *Mennonite Brotherhood*, 133.

87. Goerz, *Molotschnaer Ansiedlung*, 69.

88. Plett, *The Golden Years*, 87-88.

89. Friesen, *Mennonite Brotherhood*, 194.

90. Ibid.

91. Ibid., 101.

92. Goerz, *Molotschnaer Ansiedlung*, 65.

93. Friesen, *Mennonite Brotherhood*, 169; Urry, "The Closed and the Open," 321, 303.

94. Goerz, *Molotschnaer Ansiedlung*, 61.

95. See Urry, "The Closed and the Open," 318f, for a detailed discussion of the controversy leading up to Warkentin's exile.

96. Isaac, *Molotschnaer Mennoniten*, 116-117.

97. The sermon is included in Friesen, *Mennonite Brotherhood*, 135-141.

98. Goerz, *Molotschnaer Ansiedlung*, 66.

Mennonite Education in Russia

Adolf Ens

The Anabaptist understanding of the church as a community whose members have made a personal voluntary commitment to Christ and to each other requires that each member be knowledgable about the faith. From the beginning of the movement, this meant that considerable importance was placed on each member being basically literate. As a minimum, each should be able to read the Bible, hymnbook and catechism in order to be a responsible functioning member of the church.

To ensure such literacy, the Mennonite church believed that it had a prime responsibility to provide schools for the children of its members. By the time of the first immigration to Russia in 1788, this tradition was firmly in place. Therefore, in this sense, the first group of immigrants, with very few exceptions, was literate and quite committed to perpetuating schools for this basic education.

The Pioneering Years 1788-1820

In spite of the fact that many of the first immigrants who settled at Chortitza were from the economically lower class and had few recognized leaders among them, they established schools in every village in the first year or two of settlement.

That these early schools functioned at a very elementary level should not be surprising. Not even Prussia had yet adopted a system of universal public education which might have provided a model for Mennonite schools. Furthermore, the initial immigrant community included no educated elite from whom teachers might be drawn.

More important, the "brotherhood" emphasis of the Mennonite church promoted a kind of egalitarianism which rejected formal education as a way in which some might rise above others in social rank. And finally, the transition from Dutch to High German as the church language had only recently been made in Prussia. As a result, most teachers were not comfortable using German for ordinary communication. Schools were accordingly carried on with *Plattdeutsch* as the main medium of instruction while textbooks (Bible and catechism in addition to a simple primer) were in High German.

Initially the buildings in which school was held were unsuitable, frequently serving simultaneously as a workshop for the teacher in his first occupation as carpenter or harness maker. Facilities were quite limited. Emphasis was placed on discipline and rote memory. In writing, more stress was placed on penmanship than on creativity.

In addition to the basic subject areas of reading, writing and arithmetic, the schools also taught religion, singing and "art." Perhaps the emphasis on penmanship *(Schönschreiben)*, calligraphy and the stylized fraktur decoration of everything from greeting cards *(Wünsche)* to arithmetic book covers does not properly qualify as art. But, like singing, it pointed to the aesthetic in contrast to the rigorously functional approach to the three Rs.

Pupils were divided into three or four levels based on their reading ability. The youngest began with the primer to learn the alphabet and basic phonics. At the next level the catechism served as the basic "text" with stress given to memorization. At the upper levels the emphasis was on reading, beginning with the New Testament and progressing to the entire Bible.[1]

The school year began in October after the completion of harvest work and continued until the beginning of spring seeding in May. All children, both girls and boys, were expected to attend from about their seventh year into their fifteenth. School was in session from 30 to 33 hours per week normally including Saturday mornings. By law the church leaders, bishops and ministers were responsible for the administration of the schools.[2] Village schools were supported financially by a colony-administered tax on land, supplemented by a user fee. The latter was reduced, but not eliminated, for land owners.[3]

The cultural isolation of the Mennonites in the first generations in Russia, together with the economic privations of a pioneering community and a suspicion that too much formal learning might produce undesirable social stratification, led to a stagnation of the limited educational vision brought in by the immigrants. Historian P.M.Friesen argues for this reason that these village schools had no "history."[4]

The satiric caricature, "The School at X," by which the reformer Johann Cornies attempted to shame villages into improving their schools, is undoubtedly an exaggeration. In it the schoolmaster, "pipe clenched between his teeth," sits behind his cluttered table in an "unventilated gloomy room" of his "miserable house" surrounded by some "smudged and grimy books" and the tools of his carpenter's trade. The teacher has no skills, no understanding of the subject matter and no interest in self-improvement. The children "find no pleasure in studying" and, since "each student gets only two or three minutes of instruction" per day, the rest of the time is wasted.[5]

The fact that Cornies still felt that he had to paint such a ghastly picture in 1846, suggests that many village schools did not educate and were indeed gloomy places.[6] There were some schools in which a good teacher made things significantly better. But, as John B. Toews observes, the village teacher was the "servant of the self-contained community and found it difficult to perform above the expectations imposed upon him."[7]

The First Secondary Schools 1820-1842

With the arrival of a new wave of immigrants from Prussia beginning in 1803 came the seeds of new educational life. Not only was this group of settlers economically better off, but it had also been exposed to the Prussian educational system a generation longer than the first group which settled at Chortitza. Furthermore, its ranks included some who had had intimate contact with Pietism. This had the effect, on the one hand, of paving the way for a more individualistic posture than the strongly communitarian Mennonite emphasis fostered, while on the other removing some of the mistrust of higher education. Many of the Mennonite leaders soon considered even educated Pietists as friends, whereas they had always viewed orthodox Lutheran and Catholic Germans with a certain wariness.

It was in the Molotschna village of Ohrloff that the first movement toward secondary education arose. In 1820 the movement crystallized in the formation of the Ohrloff Christian School Association with Johann Cornies as its major leader. Two years later Tobias Voth, recruited from Prussia, opened the first secondary school among Mennonites in Russia.[8] The son of a Mennonite minister in Brenkenhofswalde, Voth was educated in Pietist circles and married a Lutheran girl. He had some years of teaching experience in West Prussia and had passed a government teachers' examination there prior to his appointment in Ohrloff.

The initial response to Voth was very encouraging. Both the day school for younger pupils and the evening school for adults were well attended. In addition Cornies and Voth introduced mission prayer meetings, a literary society and other programs to expand the educational horizons of the people. After seven years, opposition to the school increased and support decreased. Voth left discouraged and Cornies looked for someone more "manly" and perhaps less pietistic.[9]

Far from closing the school, Cornies sought to enlarge its scope. Voth's training and education had been in German. His successor should be able also to teach Russian. Such a person was found in the German Lutheran draft evader, convert to Mennonitism and self-made teacher, Heinrich Heese. In 1829 Cornies induced him to leave his post as secretary of the Chortitza *Gebietsamt* to teach at Ohrloff. By the time he left thirteen years later, two further secondary schools had begun in the Molotschna settlement: the first *Zentralschule* in the village of Halbstadt and a private one on the Steinbach estate.

It is significant that the Halbstadt school, opened in 1835, was founded by the administration of the Molotschna Colony. Until this time the official leadership had concerned itself only with elementary schools. Now it began to take responsibility for teacher training, moving toward a system in which a secondary school would be centrally located (hence the name *Zentralschule*) in each region. In contrast to the school at Ohrloff, which was supported by a School Society, and the one at Steinbach begun by estate owner Peter Schmidt, the Halbstadt school was supported by the local government with public funds received from the renting of surplus colony lands.[10]

By the 1830s the Russian government was beginning to show an interest in the schools of its foreign colonists, at least to the extent of emphasizing that some Russian ought to be taught in them.[11] Few of the village school teachers were able to do this. Those who had studied under Heese at Ohrloff had at least a beginning knowledge of Russian and were able to apply this in their own teaching. This was observed by government officials. When the "Comptoir" of foreign settlers in South Russia at Ekaterinoslav issued permission to found the Halbstadt school, it was likely on the condition that a Russian national be appointed for instruction of the Russian language. In any case, teacher Johann Neufeld had a Russian colleague from the outset, even though "Mennonite authorities could not understand whether and how two teachers should and could teach in one school."[12]

The *Zentralschule* was created as an institution for training teachers for the village schools and secretaries for the administrative office. From the outset a number of orphans and children of poor people were to study here at colony expense each year and in return serve in colony institutions, at an appropriate salary, for as many years as they had studied.

When Heinrich Heese left Ohrloff in 1842, tired of Cornies' exces-

Primary school in Altonau, Molotschna, 1910. The backbone of the Mennonite educational system was the elementary school.

Heinrich Heese (1787-1868), teacher at the Ohrloff secondary school for 12 years and founding principal of the Chortitza Zentralschule.

Photo: Mennonite Heritage Centre Archives

sive demands on his time, he returned to Chortitza and founded the first *Zentralschule* in that colony. Like the one at Halbstadt, the Chortitza school was operated by the colony. And as in Halbstadt, the government permit for the school stipulated that it admit six boys of poor families as wards of the colony.[13]

In spite of sporadic and sometimes only half-hearted support, these secondary schools prepared a growing number of students to become teachers in both the original Mennonite colonies. In contrast to the early village teacher, whose main function was to keep discipline and hear individual pupils read or recite their lessons, these graduates from the secondary school actually taught.[14] This was in sharp contrast to the situation in rural Russian communities where hardly any schools even existed before 1870.[15]

The Cornies Reforms 1843-1870

Johann Cornies, widely recognized by the Russian government for his agricultural innovation and progress, in 1830 became head of the newly created Agricultural Society (literally, "Society for the Furtherance of Forestry, Gardening and Wine Production," later expanded to include "and the Improvement of Agriculture and Industry"). Since he was also the driving force in the Ohrloff School Association, the government in 1843 placed the Molotschna school system under the Agricultural Society and added "Improvement of the School System" to its already long title.[16] A little later the Chortitza school system was also placed under the Society which thus had oversight of

Abram A. Neufeld (1862-1859), influential principal of the Chortitza Zentralschule for 15 years and director of a Realschule in Berdiansk.

Photo: Mennonite Heritage Centre Archives

virtually all Mennonite education in Russia until 1869.[17]

Cornies moved swiftly to bring reform and order into the schools. His "School Method" (General Instructions as to How All Groups in the Village School Shall Be Instructed and Occupied Simultaneously) attempted to ensure that instruction would become more consistent and uniform. It called for daily classes in Scripture study, reading, writing, recitation and composition, arithmetic, geography, penmanship and singing. At the end of the week the Bible work consisted of reading from the Epistles and Gospels for the coming Sunday; the recitation was a review of the material learned that week. No teaching of Russian was yet included.[18]

The eighty-eight "General Rules Concerning Instruction and Treatment of School Children" attempted to spell out a rudimentary philosophy of education and to outline some basic pedagogical principles.[19] The Association also issued instructions for the provision of proper school buildings and equipment, provided guidelines for teacher salaries and instituted examinations for those entering the field of teaching.[20] It grouped villages into districts and appointed two teachers in each district to serve as inspectors *(Ausschußlehrer)*, who reported regularly to the Association on conditions in the schools.

To upgrade the quality of instruction, regular teachers' conferences were introduced in 1850. At the monthly meetings of local chapters, demonstration lessons were presented and discussed.[21] To promote adult education, Cornies organized a readers' club and founded a lending library for the Molotschna Colony. In 1845 it owned 355 volumes, but shortly after Cornies' death it was dismantled.[22]

A different but not less important impact on Mennonite education during this era was made by Heinrich Franz. After passing his teacher's examination at age 20 in Prussia in 1832, Franz taught in elementary schools for a number of years, including an eight-year stint in Gnadenfeld, Molotschna. From 1846 to 1858 he served as Heese's successor at the Chortitza Zentralschule, profoundly influencing a number of students who later became prominent teachers themselves. In 1846 Franz prepared constitutions for the community schools of Chortitza, and five years later assisted in preparing directives for the whole educational system. He wrote a textbook for teaching arithmetic which dominated that aspect of Mennonite schools for half a century, and compiled a book of chorales with cipher notation which "transformed the spiritual singing of Russian Mennonites."[23] Under him and his successor and former student, Heinrich Epp, the Chortitza school became the most prominent in the Mennonite system.[24]

The Agricultural Association, whose primary task had never been education, gradually decreased in influence. With state recognition in 1859 of the *Zentralschulen* as official teacher training institutions for Mennonite teachers, it had achieved a significant goal.[25] In 1869 supervision of the schools ceased to be a responsibility of the Association. In its place, boards of education were elected in the Molotschna and Chortitza colonies.[26]

Building the System 1870-1914

Reforms in the Russian Empire, beginning with the emancipation of serfs in 1861, indicated that the special status of foreign colonies could no longer be taken for granted. A decade later the colonies came under the same jurisdiction as the general institutions of the Empire. The introduction of universal military service and the compulsory use of the Russian language in the schools and in colony administration in the 1870s led to the emigration of about one-third of the Mennonite community. Those remaining sought to retain as much control as possible over their schools. Count Totleben, emissary of the Tsar, encouraged them in 1875 to adjust their curriculum to "the programs of the state schools and not to set lower standards."[27]

The ending of Mennonite exemption from military service in 1874 provided an immediate practical reason for heeding that advice, since the length of the term of the now compulsory state service was reduced from six to four years for graduates of an elementary school and to three years for graduates of the next school category. Mennonites qualified for these reductions only if their schools followed the official curriculum. For elementary schools this included a minimum of eight hours per week of Russian language, reading, and oral and written composition.[28]

In 1870 the colonial and school administration office abolished coeducation at the secondary level "on the grounds that it constituted a danger to morals."[29] Since the *Zentralschulen* had from the outset been open to both girls and boys, this action was another setback for the Mennonite school system. In Molotschna, chairman Andreas Voth of the Molotschna Mennonite School Board responded four years later by opening the first girls' secondary school in his home in Neu Halbstadt. In Chortitza, *Zentralschule* principal A.A. Neufeld organized an association to open and support a similar school, but spent years of fruitless effort trying to get permission to do so. Finally, on the advice of the Odessa Regional Educational Office, application was made for a private institution in the name of one person only. This was approved and the Chortitzer Mädchenschule (girls' school) finally opened in 1895.[30]

In 1881 all schools were placed under the direction of the Ministry of Public Education, a body noted for its hostility to popular education.[31] Changes followed swiftly. Teachers' certificates issued by the Mennonite Board of Education were no longer recognized, forcing

The Maedchenschule *in Ohrloff, Molotschna, founded 1907. When the educational reforms of the 1870s eliminated co-education at secondary level, Mennonites established a number of girls' schools.*

Photo: Mennonite Heritage Centre Archives

all teachers, new and old, to pass a state examination at one of the Russian teacher training institutions. In the Mennonite elementary system, school hours had to be reduced, attendance decreased from eight to a maximum of six years and the curriculum of studies adjusted accordingly. All library purchases were to be approved by the Russian school officials who allowed no German books. Teaching of the Russian language was made compulsory.[32]

The Mennonite education boards, elected in 1869, found their limited powers steadily eroded by the Ministry of Education.[33] Not only were their teachers' certificates no longer valid, they now also lost the right to appoint teachers. Russian officials, who assumed this function even though teachers' salaries continued to be paid by the local communities, placed Russian teachers in Mennonite villages "wherever it could be done without disturbance." The teachers' conference was forbidden. The Molotschna Board replaced the conferences' function by convening "Consultations regarding Religious Instruction," since that area of teaching was left under board control.[34]

In the 1890s the pressure of nationalization mounted. All subjects except religion and German now had to be taught in Russian. In the elementary schools this meant that two-thirds of the teaching took place in the Russian language.[35] To ensure that this would happen, Russian teachers were appointed to many Mennonite schools.[36] By 1895 the situation was such that in some Mennonite village schools only Russian nationals were teaching. The General Conference of the Mennonite churches urged those communities to appoint a second teacher to ensure that the children would also be taught German and religion.[37] P.M. Friesen reports that since 1896 the Halbstadt Zentralschule did not have a Mennonite principal.[38] The Zagradovka Zentralschule, founded in 1895 and built by the colony in good faith without securing its rights in advance, was incorporated as a Russian school and remained so until 1911 with two Russian teachers and one Mennonite.[39]

By the end of the century the Mennonite school boards were virtually powerless. The demise of the most effective of these, the Molotschna Board, was hastened by the retirement in 1896 of two of its most prominent members, Johann K. Klatt and Peter H. Heese.[40]

What was the impact of these government reforms? David G. Rempel suggests that the "immediate and generally bad effects of these reactionary governmental measures were, fortunately, of short duration."[41] He then lists some long-range benefits. First, the constant threat of further curtailment of the schools roused the interest of a large number of hitherto apathetic colonists in education. David Epp's 1903 survey of the Mennonite school scene reflects this renewed interest, listing the opening of new classrooms, the acquisition of visual teaching aids and the reduction of tuition fees as evidence.[42] At the turn of the century more than 90 percent of Russian Mennonites could read and write compared to about 25 percent of the Russian populace generally.[43]

Secondly, the fact that all teacher candidates now had to pass "a rigorous examination before a generally hostile" board representing the Ministry of Education, eventually produced an excellent corps of teachers.[44] By 1912 many of them had become career professionals with long years of service, in contrast to the short-term, high turnover situation of the first fifty years.[45]

Thirdly, the Mennonites realized the need to expand the existing secondary school facilities and to establish new ones for the daughter colonies which sprang up after 1860. Tables I and II list a dozen *Zentralschulen* and four *Mädchenschulen* founded in the various daughter colonies between 1886 and 1914.

Fourthly, leaders recognized the need to upgrade their teacher training institutions. Graduates of the four-year course in the *Zentralschulen* were qualified to receive elementary teaching certificates, but not to teach at the secondary school level. In 1874 Andreas Voth, chairman of the Molotschna School Board, began efforts toward adding a two-year pedagogical class to the course of the Halbstadt *Zentralschule*. Four years later the first class of 12

The teacher training institute in Chortitza, founded 1890, one of two operated by Mennonites in Russia. Photo: Mennonite Heritage Centre Archives

TABLE I
Mennonite Zentralschulen in Russia

Location	Years	Auspices
Ohrloff, Molotschna	1822-1847	society
	1860	
Halbstadt, Molotschna	1835	colony
Steinbach, Molotschna	1838	private
Chortitza, Chortitza	1842-1943	colony
Gnadenfeld, Molotschna	1857-?	private
	1873	colony
Ohrloff, Zagradovka	1886-?	private
	1917-1919	local
Neu Schoensee, Zagradovka	1895-1922	colony
Karassan, Crimea	1905-1925	
Nikolaipol, Iasykovo	1905	
New York, Ignatievo (Bachmut)	1905	local
Alexanderkrone, Molotschna	1906-1913	society
	1933-1941	
Spat, Crimea	1906	society
Schoenfeld, Brazol	1907	
Pretoriia, Orenburg	1907	
Davlekanovo, Ufa	1908	
Lugovsk, Neu Samara	1908	
Kulomzino, Omsk, Siberia	1911-1915	
Neu Osterwick, Chortitza	1912	local
Kuban, Kuban	1913	
Alexandertal, Samara	1917	
Kotliarevka, Memrik	1918	
Dieievka, Orenburg	1920-1923	
Klubnikovo, Orenburg	1920-1926	
Nikolaievka, Ebental, Memrik	1920	
Margenau, Omsk, Siberia	after WWI	
Gnadenheim, Molotschna	after 1917	
Lindenau, Molotschna	after 1917	
Koeppental, Samara	after 1917	semstvo
Alexandertal, Molotschna	?	

enrolled.[46] In Chortitza a similar course was added in 1890.

Fifthly, the ban on coeducational secondary schools from the 1870s through 1905 created a focus on the role of women in Mennonite society that might otherwise not have happened. It required a deliberate effort on the part of the community to make secondary education for girls possible. With the founding of *Mädchenschulen*,

TABLE II
Mennonite Maedchenschulen in Russia

Location	Year	Auspices
Halbstadt, Molotschna	1874	society
Chortitza, Chortitza	1895	private
New York, Ignatievo (Bachmut)	1907	society
Gnadenfeld, Molotschna	1907	society
Tiege (Ohrloff), Molotschna	1907	society
Karassan, Crimea	after 1905	

women teachers received a kind of prominence that might otherwise have been delayed much longer. As teacher (principal) of the first such school in Halbstadt, Sophie Schlenker, a Moravian from Koenigsfelden in Germany, was recruited.[47] In 1910 the principals of all five existing *Mädchenschulen* were women, two of them non-Mennonite. Only the teachers of religion in these schools were usually men, including such prominent leaders as Heinrich Franz, Jr., Benjamin H. Unruh and Jacob H. Janzen.[48]

These benefits did not come about as an intended result of the directives of the Ministry of Education, but rather "against great odds and a usually hostile attitude in the Ministry."[49] The one direct benefit of government reforms came from the requirement that the Russian language be taught at all levels of the Mennonite school system. Until late in the 19th century only an educated elite and the early urbanizers knew the Russian language, creating a potential division of the Mennonite community along undesirable lines. From the turn of the century onward, all Mennonites were reasonably conversant in the language and had at least an introduction to Russian history and literature.[50]

Russia's defeat in the war with Japan, together with internal social and political upheaval, induced Tsar Nicholas II to issue a far-reaching manifesto in October, 1905. Its reforms, granting new freedoms (speech, press, assembly and association) to the Russian people, afforded the Mennonite community a brief period of respite from the pressures of Russification. A Teachers' Association was quickly founded and it took over most of the functions of the by now largely ineffectual school boards. This Association planned curricula and schedules, recommended textbooks and arranged summer schools for teacher upgrading.[51] Until the outbreak of the war in 1914 this body was the main educational force in the Mennonite colonies.

Nine new *Zentralschulen* and four *Mädchenschulen* were founded in quick succession between 1905 and 1910 (See Tables I and II). Since coeducation at the secondary level was now no longer prohibited, the new schools at Spat in the Crimea and Davlekanovo in the Ufa settlement reverted to this earlier Mennonite practice.[52]

To meet the increased demand for qualified secondary school teachers it was clear that the present institutions were inadequate. The *Mädchenschule* in Halbstadt was developed into a girls' *Gymnasium* with eight classes.[53] Attempts to found a liberal arts college or *Realschule* were thwarted by the Ministry of Education. The Mennonite School Association then applied to the Ministry of Commerce for permission to open a business school. In 1907 this was approved and a residential *Kommerzschule* was opened in Halbstadt with an eight-year program. Secondary school graduates could enter class four, the preparatory class for admission to the business school program proper, which consisted of the final four years.[54] Professor Benjamin H. Unruh, graduate of the theological faculty of the University of Basel, was the "soul" of this school.[55]

Beginning with Kornelius B. Unruh and P.M. Friesen in 1871, an ever-increasing number of Mennonite young people also attended teachers' institutes, theological schools and universities in Germany, Switzerland and in a number of cities in Russia.[56] In 1905 and 1906 the Chortitza and Molotschna colonies established special fellowships for prospective teachers who wished to study at Russian pedagogical institutions or universities. In 1914 more than 70 Mennonites were studying in St. Petersburg alone.[57] By 1917 over 130 had graduated from faculties of education (29), engineering and architecture (24), medicine (14), theology (11), law (7), and smaller numbers in forestry, art, agriculture and commerce.[58] Many of them returned to serve as teachers, ministers and other leaders in the colonies. Their influence helped very much to broaden Mennonite horizons and strengthen the school system.

Special Educational Institutions

The village schools provided elementary education for all children except the handicapped. A school for deaf-mutes was developed in Molotschna at the instigation of an evangelical Armenian who had become acquainted with the idea in Switzerland. Abraham Wiebe, Halbstadt Area Administrator, with the support of the church leadership, proposed that such a school be founded in honour of Alexander II's 25-year reign and be named "Maria" after the Lady Empress. Permission was granted in 1881 and four years later the

Graduating class of the Alexanderkrone Handelsschule, Molotschna, 1918. Gerhard Lohrenz, top row, third from left, was one of the graduates.

Photo: Mennonite Heritage Centre Archives

school opened in Tiege in the home of long-time supporter, Gerhard Klassen. Its nine-year course was modelled after the program of the village schools. The first teacher and houseparent was A.G. Ambarzumov, the Armenian who had first suggested the idea.[59]

The "Moriia Society of Evangelical Sisters of Mercy" opened an institution in 1909 for the purpose of training and supporting deaconesses. With Dr. Tavonius of Iurev University teaching the medical subjects, Moriia's three-year training program became the Mennonite school of nursing, accepting up to 40 nursing students per year.[60]

As industrialization in the Mennonite colonies began to attract outside labour, a new set of schools became necessary. The government, at the insistence of the Orthodox State Church, required separate schools for the children of Russian labourers. Facilities for these schools had to be provided by the Mennonite communities. Secular subjects were taught by a Russian teacher of the Orthodox faith, religion by a priest.[61]

A number of less formal avenues of education were also promoted by the Mennonite community. With the introduction of alternative service in forestry work *(Forstei)*, a large number of young men spent several years in camps. As early as 1882 the *Bundeskonferenz* concerned itself with providing library resources for the *Forstei* barracks.[62] In 1907 the conference noted with approval that a *Fortbildungsschule* (secondary school) had been opened in the Anadol Forstei by one of the young men.[63]

Libraries were also promoted in the colonies themselves to encourage continuing education for those who had completed their formal school years. Johann Cornies' library in Ohrloff was a private initiative. By the turn of the century public libraries were appearing in a number of colonies. The one in Chortitza had approximately 700 volumes and an adjoining reading room.[64]

In the absence of regular Bible schools or a seminary, less structured opportunities for biblical and theological teaching were provided by some of the estate owners. Notable among these was David Dick of Apanlee, Molotschna, who regularly invited outside teachers for extended Bible courses for adults. In the summer of 1902, for example, he invited Professor E.F. Stroeter, and hosted some seventy guests, most of them teachers, ministers and other community leaders, for a month-long Bible "course."[65]

After the war some communities were beginning to develop kindergartens. The village of Osterwick, Chortitza, opened one in 1921. Its teacher went to Iasykovo for training, where a kindergarten

The School for the Deaf in Tiege, Molotschna, founded 1891, was one of the special institutions established by Mennonites.

Photo: Mennonite Heritage Centre Archives

was operated by a Mennonite woman who had trained in Germany.[66]

A serious problem facing every person who considered making teaching a life-long profession was how to ensure a means of livelihood after retirement. Even outstanding early teachers like Heinrich Heese (1787-1868) and Kornelius B. Unruh (1849-1910), after retirement from "public" education, were forced to open their own private schools and continue teaching until their death. To remedy this situation the idea of a pension fund was first raised seriously at a general teachers' conference around 1887. Twenty years later it was still not a reality, though now urged by veteran school board member, Ältester Heinrich Unruh, as a "right" of teachers with long years of service.[67]

While a pension system did not materialize, a retreat centre for teachers was established next to "professors' corner" on the south coast of Crimea in 1913.[68]

War and its Aftermath 1914-1926

Anti-German pressures, which had relaxed after 1905, resumed in 1910 and intensified with the outbreak of the war against Germany. In 1915 persons of Russian nationality were to teach all subjects except religion and German. Most of the teachers assigned to the village schools were young Russian ladies, recently graduated from *Gymnasium,* with no understanding of the Mennonite communities. This lasted until the revolution in 1917.[69]

The end of the tsarist regime was marked by a brief period of new freedom. The Teachers' Association, which had been suspended because most Russian teachers were considered revolutionaries by the tsarist government, was allowed to function again. A new wave of founding secondary schools took place (see Tables I and II), while some of the existing *Zentralschulen* (Alexanderkrone and Gnadenfeld) became trade schools (see Table III).

A private Bible school had been operated briefly by Kornelius B. Unruh in Friedensfeld, Zagradovka (1907-09?).[70] But the idea of a school for training ministers for the whole Mennonite church in Russia did not come to fruition, in spite of frequent urging by some leaders. The General Conference of Mennonite churches in Russia at its 1896 sessions favoured the founding of a *Predigerschule* which would be independent of any existing educational institution. A board was elected to draw up a constitution and determine a site for the new school.[71] The pressures of that decade did not favour new educational initiatives. But in 1905 permission to found such a school for ministers was received from the government and a special

TABLE III
Mennonite Special Schools in Russia

Type of School	Location	Year
Teacher Training (Lehrerseminar)	Halbstadt Chortitza	1878 1890
School for the Deaf (Tiege)	Molotschna	1891
Realschule (Private, A.A. Neufeld)	Berdiansk	1905-1909
Business College (Kommerzschule)	Halbstadt	1908
Nurses Training (Moriia)	Halbstadt	1909
Trade School (Handelsschule)	Alexanderkrone Gnadenfeld	1916 ?
Agriculture	Halbstadt	?
Bible (private, Friedensfeld) (Chongrau) (Maiak, Davlekanovo)	Zagradovka Crimea Ufa Orenburg	1907-1909 1918-1924 1923-1926 1923-1927

session of Conference called to proceed with further planning.[72] Three years later the idea was still "a standing question."[73]

After the revolution, when Mennonite control over religious teaching in the *Zentralschulen* became less certain, several Bible schools emerged. Best known was the one founded and led by former missionary Johann Wiens in Chongrau, Crimea. Since this region was not as directly affected by the civil war as were the colonies in Ukraine, it survived from 1918 to 1924.[74] The two Bible schools founded in 1923 in the eastern colonies of Ufa and Orenburg managed to remain open a few years longer.[75]

These were essentially Bible schools with minimal entrance requirements. With an increasing number of ministers receiving training in seminaries or theological faculties in Germany and Switzerland, a Mennonite seminary would likely have emerged if times had remained "normal." With the establishment of the soviet government after the end of the civil war, this was not possible. Instead, as Peter Braun says so dramatically: "With it came a hoar frost which fell on the flourishing educational system of the colonies and blighted it as completely as a night frost would destroy the blossoms of a fruit tree."[76]

Evaluation

What shall be the criteria by which to evaluate the Mennonite educational system in Russia and the intellectual climate which it produced?

Generally the early years are described in very negative terms. John B. Toews considers the era prior to 1860 a "cultural-intellectual desert,"[77] while T.D. Regehr finds that in 1906 many school teachers still had "woefully inadequate qualifications."[78] Like P.M. Friesen, who wrote that the schools prior to the Cornies' reforms had no "history" because there was "no progressive development before the formation of the higher schools,"[79] these evaluations assume that schools are the primary vehicle of education in a community, at least of the kind of education which develops the individual intellect and its ability to think critically.

In contrast to that approach is the description of James Urry. In the Mennonite community in early 19th century Russia, he writes,

> Life and knowledge were essentially pragmatic, learnt by involvement in the activities of subsistence: to do something was to know it, to accept, was all that was required. All other desires to "know" more than the accepted truths were therefore a desire to acknowledge "worldly" facts and a denial of the truths. . . .
>
> If "knowledge" was not something to be learnt solely by teaching, then the concept of "school" and "schooling" was itself limited to ideas concerning training the young in certain skills, rather than revealing to them unknown and varied sources of information.[80]

Thus for the immigrants who came to Russia in 1789 schools were not intended to teach "the general knowledge of faith or the skills of life" — church, home and community taught those — but rather to produce "people who had achieved the same level of knowledge and skill in reading, writing and arithmetic, people who adhered to the same ideals and aims."[81] Given this emphasis on "similitude" and on "socialization into the community," the pre-Cornies schools succeeded in their objective of supporting "the Mennonite vision of the closed order."[82]

The reforms of the two decades around mid-century moved away from this "vision." By the outbreak of World War I, Mennonites had built up an impressive network of schools operating on a different philosophy, one more in keeping with the rest of European society. How successful were they in this enterprise? David G. Rempel finds that by 1914 the Mennonites had built up an "incomparably more . . . remarkable school system" than had the Lutheran and Catholic German colonists in Russia, in spite of considerably inferior numbers.[83] And the latter communities were still ahead of Russian society as a whole in terms of general availability of schools and literacy of the population.

Although fairly large-scale Mennonite settlement in America preceded the first immigration to Russia by a number of generations, Mennonites in North America generally lagged behind their counterparts in Russia in developing post-elementary schools. Hence, both in Canada and in the United States, the arrival of Russian Mennonite immigrants in the 1870s provided a stimulus in the area of education.

Notes

1. Leonhard Froese, "Das pädagogische Kultursystem der mennonitischen Siedlungsgruppe in Rußland" (D.Phil. dissertation, Universitaet zu Goettingen, 1949), 59-60.

2. Peter Braun, "The Educational System of the Mennonite Colonies in South Russia," *Mennonite Quarterly Review* 3 (July 1929): 171; D.P. Enns, "Die mennonitischen Schulen in Rußland," *Mennonitisches Jahrbuch* (1950): 6-7.

3. Enns, "Die mennonitischen Schulen," 8.

4. Peter M. Friesen, *The Mennonite Brotherhood in Russia* (1789-1910) (Fresno, California: Board of Christian Literature, General Conference of Mennonite Brethren Churches, 1978), 775.

5. Ibid., 775-77; Franz Isaak, *Die Molotschnaer Mennoniten: Ein Beitrag zur Geschichte derselben* (Halbstadt: H.J. Braun, 1908), 277-78.

6. Friesen, *Mennonite Brotherhood,* 777. Isaak, *Molotschnaer Mennoniten,* 276, calls it "an objective description" which should "definitely not be called an exaggeration." Jacob Klassen's "account of a school in Bergthal in the 1850s" is less pejorative and probably more objective. See Appendix III in James Urry, "The Closed and the Open: Social and Religious Change amongst the Mennonites in Russia (1789-1889)" (D.Phil. dissertation, Oxford University, 1978), 768-71.

7. John B. Toews, *Czars, Soviets & Mennonites* (Newton, Kansas: Faith and Life Press, 1982), 35.

8. Friesen, *Mennonite Brotherhood,* 689-98; Froese, *Das pädagogische Kultursystem,* 63-65.

9. Friesen, *Mennonite Brotherhood,* 699.

10. Enns, "Die mennonitischen Schulen," 8.

11. Braun, "The Educational System," 172.

12. Friesen, *Mennonite Brotherhood,* 724, 727; H. Goerz, *Die Molotschnaer Ansiedlung: Entstehung, Entwicklung und Untergang* (Steinbach, Manitoba: Echo Verlag, 1950/51), 107-108.

13. Friesen, *Mennonite Brotherhood,* 750; D.H. Epp, *Die Chortitzer Mennoniten* (Steinbach, Manitoba: Mennonitische Post, 1984), 78.

14. Braun, "The Educational System," 172.

15. Enns, "Die mennonitischen Schulen," 10.

16. Friesen, *Mennonite Brotherhood,* 194. David H. Epp, *Johann Cornies: Züge aus seinem Leben und Wirken* (Rosthern, Saskatchewan: Echo Verlag, 1946), 56.

17. Braun, "The Educational System," 173.

18. Ibid., 173-174.

19. Isaak, *Molotschnaer Mennoniten,* 280-89, lists all 88 paragraphs. Epp, *Johann Cornies,* 60-66, omits no. 13. An English translation of 15 of them is found in Friesen, *Mennonite Brotherhood,* 794-96.

20. Braun, "The Educational System," 174-75; Isaak, *Molotschnaer Mennoniten,* 290.

21. Isaak, *Molotschnaer Mennoniten,* 291; Froese, "Das pädagogische Kultursystem," 85.

22. Epp, *Johann Cornies,* 79-80.

23. Friesen, *Mennonite Brotherhood,* 710-12.

24. Froese, "Das pädogogische Kultursystem," 87.

25. E.K. Francis, "The Mennonite Commonwealth in Russia 1789-1914: A Sociological Interpretation," *Mennonite Quarterly Review* 25 (July 1950): 178.

26. Isaak, *Molotschnaer Mennoniten,* 291; Braun, "The Educational System," 175; Friesen, *Mennonite Brotherhood,* 797, 807.

27. Friesen, *Mennonite Brotherhood,* 749.

28. Braun, "The Educational System," 176-77.

29. Friesen, *Mennonite Brotherhood,* 768, 770, and Braun, "The Educational System," 179, date it 1870. See also David G. Rempel, "The Mennonite Commonwealth in Russia: A Sketch of its Founding and Endurance, 1789-1919," *Mennonite Quarterly Review* 48 (January 1974), 41, 44. He attributes this action to the Ministry of Education and dates it 1881.

30. Rempel, "Mennonite Commonwealth," 44.

31. Ibid., 41; Ältester Heinrich Unruh, "Etwas über die Gegenwart und Vergangenheit unserer Schulen," *Mennonitisches Jahrbuch* 1 (1903): 55; Braun, "The Educational System," 176.

32. Braun, "The Educational System," 180-81; Rempel, "Mennonite Commonwealth," 41.

33. Friesen, *Mennonite Brotherhood,* 798, indicates the questionable legal status of the Molotschna board. Epp, *Die Chortitzer Mennoniten,* 80, points out that the board in Chortitza only had provisional status and was still without official confirmation when his book was published in 1889. Ältester Heinrich Unruh still reports the same situation in "Zeitgeschichtliches über Schul- und Bildungsfragen bei uns," *Mennonitisches Jahrbuch* 4 (1906/07): 103.

34. Braun, "The Educational System," 181.

35. Braun, "The Educational System," 181, dates this in 1892; Toews, *Czars, Soviets,* 39, says it took place between 1897 and 1899. See also H. Dirks, "Die

Mennoniten in Rußland," *Mennonitisches Jahrbuch* 1 (1903): 15.

36. J.J. Neudorf, et al., *Osterwick, 1812-1943* (Clearbrook: A. Olfert & Sons, 1973), 50.

37. H. Ediger, comp., *Beschlüsse der von den geistlichen und anderen Vertretern der Mennonitengemeinden Rußlands abgehaltenen Konferenzen für die Jahre 1879 bis 1913* (Berdjansk: H. Ediger, 1914), 62.

38. Friesen, *Mennonite Brotherhood*, 762.

39. Gerhard Lohrenz, *Sagradowka* (Rosthern: Echo Verlag, 1947), 41-42.

40. Friesen, *Mennonite Brotherhood*, 807.

41. Rempel, "Mennonite Commonwealth," 41.

42. D. Epp, "Die Arbeit an unserer Jugend," *Mennonitisches Jahrbuch* 1 (1903): 57-62.

43. T.D. Regehr with the assistance of J.I. Regehr, *For Everything a Season: A History of the Alexanderkrone Zentralschule* (Winnipeg, Manitoba: CMBC Publications, 1988), 9.

44. Rempel, "Mennonite Commonwealth," 42.

45. Kornelius Wiens, "Die Schulen," *Mennonitisches Jahrbuch* 9 (1911/12): 147-53.

46. Friesen, *Mennonite Brotherhood*, 774.

47. Ibid., 770.

48. Ibid., 770-73.

49. Rempel, "Mennonite Commonwealth," 44.

50. Ibid., 43. See Toews, *Czars, Soviets,* 38-40, for a discussion of the impact of this language shift for Mennonite identity.

51. Braun, "The Educational System," 179-80.

52. Friesen, *Mennonite Brotherhood*, 768; H. Goerz, *Die mennonitischen Siedlungen in der Krim* (Winnipeg, Manitoba: Echo Verlag, 1957), 49.

53. Braun, "The Educational System," 180.

54. Rempel, "Mennonite Commonwealth," 44; Friesen, *Mennonite Brotherhood*, 773-75.

55. H. Goerz, *Molotschnaer Ansiedlung,* 160-61.

56. Friesen, *Mennonite Brotherhood*, 717; Toews, *Czars, Soviets,* 36; Rempel, "Mennonite Commonwealth," 42; Enns, "Die mennonitischen Schulen," 15.

57. Regehr, *For Everything a Season,* 17.

58. N.J. Klassen, "Mennonite Intelligentsia in Russia," *Mennonite Life* 24 (April 1969): 52, 59-60.

59. Friesen, *Mennonite Brotherhood*, 810-15.

60. Ibid., 819; *Mennonite Encyclopedia,* s.v. "Morija."

61. Rempel, "Mennonite Commonwealth," 48; Oscar H. Hamm, *Memoirs of Ignatievo in the Light of Historical Change* (Saskatoon, Saskatchewan: Mrs. Ruth F. Hamm, 1984), 166.

62. Ediger, *Beschlüsse,* 6.

63. Ibid., 120.

64. "Bibliotheken," *Mennonitisches Jahrbuch* 1 (1903): 74. At least Memrik, Koeppenthal, Gerhardshof and Kuban also had libraries. *Mennonite Encyclopedia,* s.v. "Kuban."

65. Goerz, *Molotschnaer Mennoniten,* 172-74.

66. Karl Lindemann, *Von den deutschen Kolonisten in Rußland: Erlebnisse*

einer Studienreise 1919-1921 (Stuttgart: Ausland und Heimat Verlags-Aktiengesellschaft, 1924), 26; Neudorf, *Osterwick*, 70.

67. H. Unruh, "Zeitgeschichtliches über Schul- und Bildungsfragen bei uns," *Mennonitisches Jahrbuch* 4 (1906/07): 106-107.

68. Wiens, "Die Schulen," 153; Pet. Braun, "Unser Lehrer-Erholungsheim," *Mennonitisches Jahrbuch* 10 (1913): 142-47.

69. Braun, "The Educational System," 182.

70. [H. Dirks], "Die Geschichte des Mennonitenvölkleins in Rußland während des Jahres 1907," *Mennonitisches Jahrbuch* 5 (1907): 9; Wiens, "Die Schulen," 153; Braun, "Lehrer-Erholungsheim," 142-147; Lohrenz, *Sagradowka*, 42-44.

71. Ediger, *Beschlüsse*, 65.

72. [H. Dirks], "Fortsetzung der Geschichte des Mennonitenvölkleins in Rußland," *Mennonitisches Jahrbuch* 3 (1905/06): 15; Ediger, *Beschlüsse*, 109.

73. H. Unruh, "Zeitgeschichtliches über Schul- und Bildungsfragen bei uns," *Mennonitisches Jahrbuch* 4 (1906/07): 104; [H. Dirks], "Fortsetzung der Geschichte des Mennonitenvölkleins in Rußland," *Mennonitisches Jahrbuch* 6 (1908): 16.

74. H. Goerz, *Krim*, 50-51; Martin Durksen, *Die Krim war unsere Heimat* (Winnipeg, Manitoba: By the author, 1980), 189-90, 209-16; A.A. Toews, *Mennonitische Märtyrer*, vol. 2 (Winnipeg, Manitoba: By the author, 1954), 360-66.

75. Peter P. Dyck, *Orenburg am Ural* (Clearbrook, B.C.: Christian Book Store, 1951), 74-78; Gerhard Hein, ed., *Ufa: The Settlements (Colonies) in Ufa 1894-1938* (Steinbach, Manitoba: Derksen Printers, 1977), 32.

76. Braun, "The Educational System," 182. Brief accounts of two *Zentralschulen* for the inter-war years are Anna Sudermann, "Die Chortitzaer Zentralschule von 1920 bis 1943," unpublished paper, Vol. 1085, Mennonite Heritage Centre Archives, Winnpeg, Manitoba; and Regehr, *For Everything a Season*, 68-120.

77. Toews, *Czars, Soviets*, 35. See also John B. Toews, "Cultural and Intellectual Aspects of the Mennonite Experience in Russia," *Mennonite Quarterly Review* 53 (April 1979): 137-59.

78. Regehr, *For Everything a Season*, 9.

79. Friesen, *Mennonite Brotherhood*, 775.

80. Urry, "The Closed and the Open," 345.

81. Ibid., 344, 347-48.

82. Ibid., 348. Urry, in contrast to Toews, thus finds the educational innovations of the Cornies' reforms and those inspired by Pietism around mid-century less positive. The terms with which he describes the new educational system — elite, progress, competition, individualistic, self-centred concern, achievement — are not wholly positive. Ibid., 363.

83. Rempel, "Mennonite Commonwealth," 44-45.

Mennonite Economic Development in the Russian Mirror

James Urry

In the early 1930s, within a year of each other, two dissertations concerned with Mennonite experience in Russia were submitted for doctorates. The first was written in Germany by a Baltic German, Adolf Ehrt; the second in the United States by a Mennonite, born and educated in Chortitza, David G. Rempel. Although written independently both theses paid particular attention to Mennonite economic development.[1]

Ehrt provided an abstract theoretical account, concentrating on socio-economic developments; Rempel was more historical, more detailed and drew on a wider range of sources. Both authors used Russian literature although at this period bibliographic guides to Russian material were rare and access to Russian sources extremely limited. While both works can be seen as pioneering academic studies of Mennonite economic history, the challenge they presented Mennonites to begin a thorough investigation of their experience in Russia was never taken up. In the early 1930s Ehrt was already deeply involved with right wing emigré groups allied with the Nazi Party and later devoted his efforts to anti-communist propaganda, writing nothing more on the Mennonites. Rempel's dissertation remains unpublished and personal commitments delayed his return to Mennonite studies until after his retirement in the 1960s.[2] In the intervening period Mennonite "historians" reverted to the classic Mennonite sources published before 1914 and the larger Russian context of the Mennonite experience stressed by Ehrt and Rempel was generally neglected.

Since the 1930s great advances have occurred in the research and writing of history, including economic history. In Russian studies economic history has been approached from a variety of perspectives. Soviet historians working within strict ideological constraints, have paid special attention to the role of economic factors in Russia's social and political development.[3] Outside the Soviet Union, Western scholars have also investigated such issues, utilizing older literature, Soviet studies and, in recent years, the rich archival sources available in the U.S.S.R.[4] Not only are the sources for any investigation of Mennonite economic development in Russia therefore now much richer than they were fifty years ago; the social and cultural changes which occurred in Russia after 1800 are also far easier to comprehend. The aim of this chapter is to hint at these changes and to review Mennonite economic developments before 1917 in the light of more recent research.

Russian Economic Development 1789-1917

The period between 1789 when the first Mennonites settled in Russia and the end of the Empire in 1917 was one of great change in Russia and the world. Russia's frontiers expanded, particularly in central Asia, while in the western provinces the Empire was closely involved with the rapidly industrializing states of Western Europe. Within Russia there were major social and political changes. The influence of the state expanded to encompass people in remote regions; this expansion is perhaps most clearly reflected by the growth of government control, especially the bureaucracy. Political power, however, remained centralized in the hands of the tsar and his advisors, at least until the early years of the twentieth century. While internally the country was far less developed than most other European states, economic and social changes became increasingly profound following a period of extensive reforms in the 1860s and 1870s.

At the beginning of World War I Russia was an immense country of over 22 million square kilometres.[5] Rich in potentially exploitable resources it contained a large, ethnically diverse population which had increased rapidly since the eighteenth century. In 1800 Russia's population was 35.5 million, by 1860 it had grown to 74 million, and by 1914 to 160 million. But in spite of its size, resources and population, or perhaps because of them, Russia was, in 1914, still a backward country by Western European standards.

Russian society was essentially agrarian. It was a country of peasants, dependent on small-scale production. Eighty percent of the people lived in rural areas; over 60 percent were employed in agriculture compared with only 40 percent in Germany and less than 20 percent in Britain. Rural society was dominated by peasant households producing food for self-sustenance; the emancipation of the serfs in 1861 had not resulted in any large-scale improvement in peasant conditions. In many areas their situation worsened after 1861. As their numbers increased, the availability of land decreased and government policies restricted peasant development, social mobility and living standards. It has been calculated that by 1905 75 percent of peasant families lived in relative poverty.[6] Other sections of rural society also declined in importance. In 1861 large areas of land were owned by the nobility, but between 1861 and 1914 large estates decreased in area by 45 percent in spite of massive government assistance to such landowners. By 1900 rural Russia was in crisis but the country's economy was still largely dependent on agriculture. In 1913 agriculture accounted for 50 percent of national income and 70 percent of exports.

After 1861, however, industrial output increased, although it was not until after 1880 that growth in this area was sustained. Recent estimates of national income between 1885 and 1913 put the annual growth rate as high as 3.25 percent.[7] Changes in government policy and a massive influx of foreign capital assisted the establishment of modern industries. Railroads were expanded, assisting in the transport of raw materials and the development of heavy industry as well as the export of agriculture produce which helped sustain internal growth. But while urban areas grew in size and the number of large factories employing industrial workers increased, especially in St. Petersburg and Moscow, in 1911 over 77 percent of industrial workers were employed in the manufacture of consumer goods, over two-thirds in cottage workshops in rural areas. By 1914, however, industry accounted for 45 percent of national income. The Russian economy was ranked fifth in the world after the United States, Germany, Britain and France and its rate of growth was a cause for concern to many of its neighbours.

If Russia was economically backward but rapidly developing by 1914, this development was more marked in certain areas of the country than others. One of these areas was southern Russia, in precisely the region where Mennonites had first settled in Russia and where by 1914 they were still largely concentrated: New Russia.[8] New Russia (principally the provinces of Kherson, Ekaterinoslav and Taurida) had been incorporated into the Empire in the late eighteenth century. Agriculture and industry developed so rapidly that by the nineteenth century this region was also called "New America." The population of New Russia rose from just over one million in 1800 to three million in 1863 to nine million in 1914; 80 percent of the population was rural. In agriculture New Russia was among the most advanced regions in Russia. From the early years of the nineteenth century production had been geared to commercial needs, mainly for the export of agricultural produce through the ports of the Black and Azov Seas. Livestock production (sheep for wool, cattle for meat) was eclipsed after 1860 by cereal production as this area became the grain basket of Europe. By 1900 over 70 percent of New Russia was under cultivation, the highest proportion of any Russian region.[9] Most of the commercial farming was carried out on large estates, private landownership being very high in this area of Russia. The major landowners used advanced machinery and employed large numbers of peasants.

New Russia also contained important industrial regions of light and heavy industry, based upon the extensive deposits of coal in the Donetz Basin and iron ore in the Krivoi Rog area. The exploitation of these resources after 1870 was an important factor in Russia's overall economic development. As producers of iron and steel the industries in this region outstripped the older centres in the Urals. By 1913 the southern region of the Empire produced 87 percent of Russia's coal and 74 percent of its iron. The Donetz area alone accounted for 70 percent of the country's coal and 53 percent of pig iron production. Such heavy industry facilitated the development of other enterprises such as engineering workshops which included Mennonite agricultural machine factories. The rapid expansion of the southern rail network to transport coal and iron ore assisted in the movement of other products, including agricultural produce. Processing industries were established at important rail junctions and in urban areas.[10] By 1914 two-fifths of Russia's flour mills and starch factories were concentrated in the southern provinces, a number in Mennonite hands. The urban centres with industrial areas attracted rural peoples, including Mennonites. In 1863 the city of Ekaterinoslav north of Chortitza contained 20,000 people, in 1897 112,000 and by 1914 218,000; Alexandrovsk, which by 1914 had incorporated the Mennonite Chortitza village of Schoenwiese, had a population of 51,000 and was an important industrial centre on the Dniepr River. The province of Ekaterinoslav in fact contained most of the industrial and urban population of New Russia by 1914; about 40 percent of its people lived in urban areas.[11]

All economic indicators clearly show that by 1914 Russia was emerging as a major industrial power and that New Russia, where most Mennonites lived and where their capital was concentrated, was at the forefront of this commercial and industrial development, a development to which Mennonites contributed a minor, but not insignificant, part.

Mennonites and Agriculture

The first Mennonite colonists settled in a New Russia sparsely populated, but not devoid of peoples; indeed it contained a mix of cultural groups involved in a variety of economic pursuits. There were pastoralists like the Tartars who also practised incipient agriculture; there were Little Russian peasants, some serfs, others descendants of Cossack communities now disbanded, who were primarily subsistence cultivators; there were many "foreigners," some like the Mennonites were recent immigrants from more developed areas of Western Europe and accustomed to a semi-commercial way of life. These newer settlers had to adapt to the physical and economic environment of New Russia. For the Mennonites this adaptation in the early pioneer years involved a period of adjustment accompanied by some hardships: the steppe region with its apparently desolate landscape and erratic climate was strikingly different from the delta lowlands they had been acquainted with in Royal Prussia and Danzig. In the long term, however, the previously poorly cultivated land combined with support from a reasonably beneficent government and favourable official policies towards development, allowed Mennonites to utilize their entrepreneurial skills, not only to support a considerable increase in their population but also to considerably improve their standard of living.

The Mennonite population increased rapidly. A high birth rate combined with a continuous flow of new immigrants until the 1850s saw the Mennonite population in New Russia rise from under 2,000 in 1800 to over 10,000 in 1825; 20,000 in the early 1840s; 30,000 by 1860. During the 1850s a number of Mennonites from Prussia settled in the Volga region, but the population gain in this area was offset by the emigration of about 17,000 Mennonites to the Americas during the 1870s. By 1888, however, the Mennonite population in Russia had recovered and exceeded 40,000; by 1897 it was 66,000; by 1910 the figure had risen further to 100,000. By 1914 104,000 Mennonites were scattered all over Russia from Volhynia in the west to Siberia in the east, living in rural colonies, on estates or in urban areas.[12]

The first settlers to Chortitza in 1789 and to Molotschna after 1804 attempted to reproduce the way of life they had known in Prussia. While basic family and community structures and household subsistence patterns were reestablished, it proved impossible to reproduce the larger economic environment they had known in their previous homeland. Unlike Prussia there were no large, developed urban centres to purchase Mennonite goods and produce while communications across the vast steppe were hopelessly inadequate. Many of the tools and forms of tillage proved ill suited to the land and climate, as did many of the crops. With government aid the colonists turned to sheep rearing, mainly for wool, and this became the mainstay of Mennonite commercial agriculture until the 1850s.

Sheep and wool products also became the major export product of New Russia; by 1846 there were over 12 million sheep in southern Russia, including four million pure merinos. As the value of wool became apparent, Mennonite flocks increased from 56,000 sheep in 1825 to 170,000 in 1841; they remained at about this figure until the 1850s when they started to decline. The decrease in sheep numbers was caused by competition from cheap Australian wool which forced down prices. Sheep numbers fell throughout New Russia, but more rapidly in the colonies than on the large estates. By 1886 there were still 33,000 sheep in the Molotschna Colony, but by 1900 almost none.

Sheep raising helped many Mennonites achieve economic security, but by the 1840s only about 40 percent of their income from agricultural produce came from the sale of sheep and wool. As Mennonites were largely self-sufficient in home food production, they already possessed the skills and resources to diversify production. The population of New Russia was growing and communication was being improved. The government, particularly after the establishment of the Ministry of State Domains in 1837, encouraged and aided the colonists to diversify in order to further the economic development of the region and so the colonists could act as model farmers for state peasants.

In the Mennonite colonies Johann Cornies, acting under government instructions, developed an Agricultural Union to direct these developments. Later similar unions were founded in other colonies. Animal stock was improved by careful breeding. Mennonites had always been interested in dairy cattle. Their herds increased steadily in size from 11,000 head in Chortitza and Molotschna in 1825 to 15,000 in 1841 and 20,000 in 1855. The largest increase was in Molotschna where returns from sales of butter and cheese more than doubled between 1839 and 1854. Dairy products remained an important source of income up to 1914. Large scale afforestation was started to provide both firewood for local consumption and fruit for sale; returns from fruit also doubled between 1839 and 1854. Such produce was sold locally but the major commercial crop for export to replace wool was grain, particularly wheat. Between 1839 and 1865 returns from the sale of cereals more than doubled in value; by 1865 60 percent of the total value of sales of agricultural produce came from this source.

The shift from stock breeding to arable farming occurred throughout New Russia, stimulated by the repeal of tariffs against grain imports in Britain and other West European states.[13] Between 1861 and 1888 the area of land sown with wheat increased by 65 percent in Ekaterinoslav and 117 percent in Taurida. Grain trade between southern Russia and Mediterranean ports had existed before 1840. However, after this date trade with Western Europe expanded and port facilities in New Russia were improved to handle increased exports. Between 1860 and 1890 wheat exports increased by 200 percent. Mennonites grew barley, rye and oats mainly for local consumption with wheat being the major export crop. Spring wheat was eventually replaced in the 1870s by a winter-sown variety, the hard red wheat *(Krymka)* which was ideal for milling into bread flour and which sold for high prices. After 1880 the government, desperate for foreign capital to fund industrial expansion, encouraged grain exports. Although this policy had dreadful consequences for many peasants and contributed to the disastrous famines of the early 1890s, for Mennonite producers it proved a boon. By 1890 more than 50 percent of Russia's exports consisted of cereals. The Mennonites introduced new farming methods and mechanized rapidly. Yields however varied from year to year, due mainly to the vagaries of climate but also to poor farming techniques. The red wheat placed a heavy toll on the land's fertility and in the 1890s was largely abandoned for an inferior variety. Between 1850 and 1880 each dessiatina produced between 35 and 40 pood of grain a year, but after 1900 yields improved to between 58 and 65 pood; between 1908 and 1913 70-80 pood per dessiatina was achieved.[14]

The basic farming unit of most Mennonites in the nineteenth century was the family farm, located in a village situated in a colony. Labour was initially based on the domestic household consisting of a married couple, their children, often grandparents and, depending on the developmental cycle of the domestic group, unmarried siblings and sons-in-law yet to establish their own households. The farm household was a structure transferred from Prussia. But the pattern of close-knit households in villages located in exclusive Mennonite colonies was developed in Russia, as were the organs of self-government and the close regulation of local affairs. These were imposed by the Russians.

Although each family farmed as a separate unit, forms of production were constrained by the pattern of land distribution assigned to villages as corporate entities. Distribution of land and the rhythm of agricultural work were agreed to by the farmers at village meetings. There was considerable cooperation in farm work. The agricultural unions issued specific regulations and enforced them in the colonies. As the influence of the unions waned after 1860, the regulations governing farming practices eased. However, joint action continued and colony farmers were not entirely free agents in economic decision-making.

The size of the colony farms varied. Originally all farms were 65 dessiatins in size but after a period of bitter dispute between 1860 and 1880 some of the land was divided into smaller units of 32 and 12 dessiatins. While the smaller "quarter farm" could not produce as much as a "full farm," its owner was still better off than most local peasant farmers who either owned no land or owned only a few dessiatins while many were also constrained within a peasant commune. The shift to arable farming extended and intensified Mennonite use of their plots. Before 1840 in Molotschna only 5 to 10 dessiatins had been cultivated, mainly for self-sustenance; by 1865 this land had increased to 25 dessiatins as commercial crops were sown; by 1888 45 dessiatins were cultivated. Such increased cultivation involved larger labour input. This in turn encouraged the adoption of new techniques and technology.

During the period of pastoral dominance, Mennonites had employed children or hired shepherds, often Nogai Tartars, to herd sheep. In the colonies flocks were combined and farmers devoted their time to small-scale cultivation or to craft work to supplement their incomes. Women and children were essential to farm work, particularly during harvesttime. As cultivation increased and incomes rose, hired labour was also employed; eventually the wives and young children of richer farmers were less involved in field work. In households a female domestic was often employed, especially when children were young. In the early years the maid was often an unmarried Mennonite, sometimes a poor relative, but in time usually Little Russian (that is, Ukrainian) maids were employed.

Increasingly seasonal and full-time farm labourers were used, at first Mennonites from the landless families or imported from poorer settlements in Prussia or Volhynia, but after 1880 mainly local Little Russian peasants. After 1900 migrant seasonal labour came also from central Russia. Between 1842 and 1855 the number of Russian workers in Molotschna increased from 242 to 681 and Mennonite workers decreased from 938 to 737. By 1900 large numbers of workers were employed for the season (May to October) and their numbers were swelled by additional labour at harvesttime. By Russian standards wages were high since there was a shortage of labour in New Russia. However, wages, as a proportion of total costs, were small, especially when compared with Mennonite incomes from farming. The relative cheapness of labour contributed greatly to the steady increase in Mennonite incomes after 1870.

One indication of the expansion and intensification of arable farming was the increase of horses essential for farm work and transport. Horse numbers increased in Chortitza and Molotschna from about 7,000 in 1825 to over 12,000 in 1841 and 18,000 in 1855. Every farm needed six to eight horses to plough, harvest and trans-

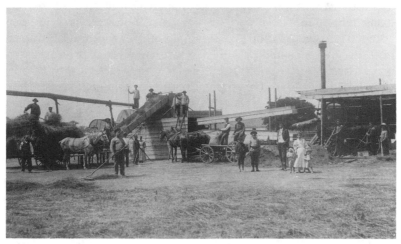

Seeding and harvest time. Agriculture was the basis of economic life of Mennonites in Russia.　　　Photos: Mennonite Heritage Centre Archives

107

port goods. The original light ploughs brought from Prussia proved ill suited to the steppe soils. Consequently new ploughs, some invented or improved by Mennonites, were developed. The most popular was the multi-shared plough *(bukker)* used from the 1850s; from the 1880s onwards a drill-*bukker* allowed ploughing and seeding to occur in a single operation. Other technical improvements included chaff cutters, winnowing and threshing machines. In threshing wheat the flail was replaced by a stone roller, then by a horse-powered thresher after 1840. After the turn of the century threshers powered by steam, diesel and even electricity were used in the colonies. Harvesters first appeared in the 1850s, but were not widely adopted until the 1870s when Mennonite workshops began to produce machines. In a single day a harvester could mow three times the area cut by scythes. By 1914 the use of machinery in farming was widespread even though by contemporary American standards many of the machines were primitive. But new innovations such as binders and small powerful motors for threshing were changing the face of farming.

Arable farming also involved the adoption of new farming practices. Cornies introduced the system of four-field rotation which had been developed in Western Europe by "improving" farmers. He encouraged the use of fertilizers from animal manure which halted the decline of crop yields and even assisted in their improvement. It would be wrong, however, to give the impression that all Mennonite farmers were economic rationalists either in terms of their farming methods or in their response to market conditions. Many were extremely conservative and suspicious of innovations. They persisted in practising antiquated farming methods with a stubbornness born of ignorance and prejudice. It was only when the success of progressive farmers could no longer be ignored that the majority showed interest in improvements. Many old-fashioned farmers persisted in their ways well into the twentieth century when younger and more enlightened farmers succeeded to the control of colony farms.

Early in the nineteenth century a number of progressive farmers left the colonies to establish independent ventures on larger plots on rented or purchased land. Many were entrepreneurs who emerged during the pastoral period, individuals who invested their capital in flocks of sheep and purchased large areas for pasture. By 1860 much of this land had been subdivided among their heirs, but Mennonite landed estates consisting of thousands of dessiatins still existed. This land rapidly increased in value as cereal production replaced pastoralism. Estate agriculture was extensive rather than intensive. Often oxen instead of horses were used and hundreds of peasants were employed, especially at harvesttime. Large modern machines were utilized. From the 1890s expensive steam traction engines were used to power threshers and later for ploughing. Eventually the Mennonite estate owner assumed more the role of an overseer than an active farmer. Following a period of rural disturbances after 1900, many retired to the colonies or to towns and became absentee landlords, using Mennonite managers to run the operations. Besides these large estate owners there were many smaller landowners who owned between 100 and 500 dessiatins, more than the average colonist but less than the estate owners. These people farmed independently or in small communities, utilizing Russian labour and modern machinery.

By 1914, therefore, the Mennonite world, although still predominantly rural, was firmly based on commercial agricultural production. There were important differences in the scale of production and also significant regional variations in the forms of production and degree of economic development. After 1850 Mennonites settled in increasing numbers away from the foundation colonies in New Russia and after 1905 in central Asia and especially Siberia. The majority settled on land purchased by the mother colonies, others on land purchased privately. The new settlers often took time to settle, to adapt to new environments and to repay their debts to the mother colony. As a consequence many were economically backward when compared with the established older settlements. Some of the new colonies were founded in remote, backward areas of Russia such as Orenburg (founded 1894) and especially Terek (1901) in Transcaucasia. These colonies experienced considerable difficulties and had to be supported extensively by their mother colonies. In all new settlements farming had to adapt to local environmental and economic conditions. New crops, grapes for instance, were grown in the Crimean settlements, although Mennonite experience with dairy cattle proved particularly beneficial in many localities. Settlement patterns and community cooperation also changed. In places community was strengthened; in others, as in parts of Siberia where separate homesteads were often established, it was weakened. Regional adaptation and economic diversification in farming had as important implications for the coherence and continuance of the Mennonite commonwealth in Russia in the years before 1914, as did economic changes in the heartland of Mennonite settlement in New Russia.

Mennonites and Industry

Like many rural people Mennonites for a long period were self-sufficient in more than foodstuffs.[15] Women prepared wool and linen thread and wove their own cloth; men knew enough basic carpentry and metal work to satisfy everyday farm needs. But Mennonites had migrated to Russia from a complex rural world in Prussia, one closely connected with urban centres containing various industries and crafts. During the eighteenth century many Mennonites were involved in commerce and manufacture in rural and urban areas, particularly with brewing, milling and the cloth trade. Among the early migrants were not only farmers who possessed specific craft skills, but also experienced artisans specializing in weaving, shoemaking, blacksmithing, carpentry and other trades. While most took up agriculture, many also continued their trades, supplying the needs of fellow brethren and neighbouring non-Mennonites. The household was a unit not only of agricultural but also of craft production. The Russian authorities encouraged farm households to develop cottage industries to supplement their incomes and to assist in the region's development. The most important of these industries established before 1850 was sericulture. Mennonites were encouraged by the authorities to plant mulberry trees, to feed the caterpillars, and were taught how to care for the cocoons, spin silk and produce finished items. The whole family was involved in this work. For some it proved highly successful until cheaper Asian silk reduced its profitability after 1860.

The availability of wool prompted one entrepreneur, Johann Klassen, to found a wool mill around 1810 in Molotschna. Utilizing Mennonite skills the mill contained weaving looms and continued in production until after 1860 although eventually it employed Russian serf labour rather than Mennonites. In later years other workshops and factories were established making use of local skills and resources. When after 1840 new-style houses built of brick became fashionable and were favoured by the Agricultural Union, tile and brick works were constructed in Molotschna using local clay. But most of these establishments belonged to a world of proto-industrial forms of production: small-scale and labour-intensive, producing goods mainly for local consumption as had been the practice in Prussia.[16]

Cornies planned to develop this proto-industrial world so that the colonies could become self-sufficient in most products and the craft industries would provide employment for a growing population who could not be accommodated with land. To this end in 1839 he established an artisan's colony in Neu Halbstadt in Molotschna and attracted craftsmen from Prussia to improve and expand the range of craft skills. But Cornies' artisan colony belonged to an economic world which was already in decline in Western Europe. In the end the small-scale Mennonite craft industry in Russia could not compete with the extensive network of peasant workshops, which were a feature of rural Russia, or with the skills of other artisans, particularly Jews. Mennonite artisans could not sustain their standard of living from trade, at least to maintain pace with farmers' incomes, so many took to farming instead. A few service industries persisted in the colonies, but after 1870 most of the small tradesmen were outsiders. Some artisans however, taking advantage of their technical and entrepreneurial skills, founded specialized workshops to produce equipment to serve the developing agrarian economy of New Russia.

An important area of growth industry in both Chortitza and Molotschna after 1840 involved the construction of heavy-duty farm carts. These carts proved extremely popular in the colonies and among neighbouring peasants and landowners, being sold as far away as Moscow. Production received an added impetus after the Crimean War (1853-1856) during which Mennonites had used their wagons to transport supplies and wounded soldiers. The sturdiness of the carts was widely noted. Wagon manufacturing utilized many established Mennonite skills associated with wood and metal working. The demand for carts forced manufacturers to rationalize production methods, to develop new techniques and eventually to diversify into the production of other kinds of farm machinery.[17]

After 1860 a number of small workshops began to produce agricultural machines: threshing mechanisms, ploughs, harrows and primitive mowing machines. Experience with clock mechanisms led to the development of some technical features of these machines. With the advent of metal casting, large-scale engineering was begun. Many of the machines produced were based on Mennonite inventions but others, including the mowers, were copied from foreign imports, adapted and improved to meet local conditions. The robust mower, the *lobogreika,* proved particularly well suited to the steppe and was produced in large numbers after 1870. It was purchased by colonists, landowners and later by rich peasants. Favourable conditions for mechanized agriculture in New Russia, combined with the large local Mennonite market, encouraged the rapid establishment of the Mennonite agricultural machine industry. Government tariffs against imported foreign machines imposed after 1885 protected manufacturers from foreign competition. Small workshops grew in size and

The Lepp and Wallmann factory complex in Chortitza. Mennonite factories produced agricultural machinery, tile and bricks, clocks and other items.

Photo: Mennonite Heritage Centre Archives

with additional capital, sometimes supplied by richer Mennonite landowners, expanded into factories. One of the pioneer Chortitza industrialists, Peter Lepp, joined with the wealthy family of Wallmann, an association sealed through the intermarriage of their children, to form the firm of Lepp and Wallmann. In 1867 Lepp produced 12 harvesters; by 1888 Lepp and Wallmann were producing 1,200 a year. In 1908 the company's annual production of farm machinery was valued at 900,000 rubles.

Although similar agricultural machinery factories were developed in Molotschna, mainly in Halbstadt and Waldheim, Chortitza was better suited than Molotschna for such industry. It was situated on the Dniepr just south of the provincial capital, Ekaterinoslav and close to the developing industrial city of Alexandrovsk. The river provided an ideal means of transporting supplies to the colony and exporting its produce. Furthermore, after 1870 the colony was connected by rail to sources of coal as well as to developing market centres. New Mennonite factories were founded in daughter colonies and at rail junctions situated near Mennonite settlements such as those in New York, an industrial area of eastern Ekaterinoslav.

The expansion of the Mennonite agricultural machinery industry between 1860 and 1914 was only part of larger Russian developments during the same period.[18] Russian domestic production of agricultural machinery increased in value from 2.4 million rubles in 1876 to 9.6 million in 1894 to 36.2 million in 1908 and 60.5 million rubles in 1913. The number of factories in European Russia (including Poland) increased from 340 in 1875-76 to 400 in 1892 and 775 in 1911. In 1912-13 the industry as a whole consumed 10 million pood of metal, four percent of all rolled iron and steel produced in Russia.[19] By 1908 there were between 30 and 40 Mennonite factories with a combined output valued at about four million rubles a year, or 10 percent of total Russian production by value.

The other area of large-scale Mennonite industrial enterprise was flour milling.[20] Windmills had been built since the first days of settlement. These were later supplemented by water and treadmills. By 1908 there were still over a hundred windmills operating in Chortitza and Molotschna. Mennonite millers rapidly secured a good living in Russia and businesses flourished, especially after the Crimean War when many new mills were built. The Niebuhr family, which settled as millers in Chortitza, was probably the most successful. In the 1860s they imported steam engines to power their mills, introduced other milling innovations and established mills beyond the colonies. Again the building of the railroads assisted in this expansion. Many Mennonites, looking for quick returns, also turned to milling. Some overextended themselves; since flour and grain prices were subject to sudden fluctuations, a number went bankrupt. By 1908 there were 73 motor-powered mills in Molotschna and Chortitza, very conservatively valued for Forestry Service taxation purposes (see below) at over 1.25 million rubles.[21] Chortitza's mills, although only 30 in number, were valued at 0.83 million rubles. Many mills were situated away from the colonies at rail junctions and in larger towns and cities. By 1914 just four Mennonite milling firms valued their annual production at six million rubles, half of which was accounted for by Niebuhr & Co. of Alexandrovsk.

Although machine production and milling were the major areas of Mennonite industrial enterprise by 1908, they were but one aspect of the 576 Mennonite trades and industries registered for taxation purposes by the Forestry Service Commissioners, and valued at 5.5 million rubles. Both the number of industries and their value undoubtedly were grossly underestimated. According to these estimates, however, in Molotschna and Chortitza 92 enterprises were involved in commercial operations ranging from shopkeepers to trade agents, their businesses valued at just under half a million rubles. For a long time Mennonites had been involved in commercial activities, although such people were often despised by the farmers who dominated congregational affairs. Many of the leading Mennonite progressives such as Cornies, who were concerned with the economic development of the colonies, had begun their careers

Milling became an important industry for Russian Mennonites. By the turn of the century practically every village had at least one windmill.

Photo: Mennonite Heritage Centre Archives

as traders.

During the 1840s a number of Mennonites belonging to leading Prussian merchant families migrated to Russia to take advantage of the expanding commercial opportunities in New Russia. Some settled in the Azov Sea port of Berdiansk and became involved with the grain trade. A number of Mennonites in the colonies also bought and sold grain, although by 1914 they had declined in number because of stiff competition, particularly from Jews. Other Mennonites dealt in timber, especially in Chortitza where lumber could be floated down the Dniepr. As incomes in the colonies grew some Mennonites set up shop, but again they faced competition from outsiders, including Old Believers who were shrewd businessmen. In the new colonies and in remote settlements Mennonites became agents for a range of merchandise, including agricultural machinery, some manufactured by Mennonites, some imported. By 1912 there were 83 such agencies in Russia. But Mennonite commercial activity outside the Mennonite world was still in its infancy. The rural peasantry, apart from being poor, still largely depended on locally produced goods or purchased products from wandering peddlers or at local and regional fairs.

The Mennonite Economy

By 1914, although Mennonites were well integrated into the larger Russian economy and were scattered across a large area of the Empire, most were still bound within a distinctive Mennonite universe. This Mennonite world was not only based on the recognition of a common descent or shared religious principles, but also on the pervasive social and economic ties that bound Mennonites together in a web of interdependency.

At the centre of the Mennonite world lay the colonies and at the heart of the colony system lay the mother colonies of Chortitza and Molotschna. The colonies contained the bulk of the Mennonite population and a large part of the capital and resources accumulated during their period of settlement in Russia. Following the land struggles which began in the 1860s it was widely accepted that the colonies were responsible for finding land for their growing populations. Money for such purchases was raised through a system of taxation and by renting reserved areas of land. The funds accumulated until they were needed to purchase additional land and to settle a new generation of colonists. The daughter colonies were responsible for repaying the mother colony for costs involved in the purchase and settlement of the colony once it became established.

Thereafter the colony was expected to be economically independent and to put aside sums for the settlement of its own landless in due course. In practice things were not quite so simple. The prosperity of a daughter settlement depended on its location and the time it took to become established. As land prices in New Russia escalated and the colonists were forced to seek land in less satisfactory areas, the new settlers were often forced to draw on the resources of their mother colony for longer than had been expected. The settlement at Terek is a good example of such a situation. As a matter of fact, the founding of daughter colonies was enormously expensive for the Mennonites. Between 1870 and 1914 the expenditure of such land in real terms must have amounted to tens of millions of rubles.

There were other costly areas of joint responsibility essential to the preservation of Mennonite identity. The most important of these was the Forestry Service, the system implemented from the 1880s onwards as an alternative to military service. The Service was largely funded and administered by Mennonites, with the money being raised by taxes on Mennonite property assessed according to its capital value. In the early years when there were large costs involved in the establishment of the Forestry camps the costs ran to over 100,000 rubles a year. These camp expenses soon dropped to 60,000 rubles but rose again after 1895. By 1907 the cost of maintenance came to about 150,000 rubles a year; of this total taxation raised only 120,000 rubles, mainly because many Mennonites failed to declare the true value of their property. Although assessments were later revised, by 1913 the annual cost of sustaining the Service, including new capital expenditure, had risen to over 300,000 rubles.[22] If it had not been for the valuable property of estate owners and industrialists it is unlikely that the colonists would have been able to maintain the Service.

The colonies were also centres of culture and society. As such they contained many of the cultural institutions essential for the continuation of Mennonite life. Besides the agencies of local and regional government which managed essential services for which Mennonites paid local taxes, most religious congregations were based in the colonies. By 1914 the idea of a paid clergy was emerging; many Mennonites contributed toward the religious education of talented youths. Bible, tract and mission societies (including Mennonite missionaries) were also generously supported.

The most expensive cultural institutions were the schools. By 1914 the Mennonites had developed a complex system of primary and secondary education. New schools were opened to meet the demands of an increasingly well-educated society. Some Mennonites went on to higher education in university and technical institutes, at home and abroad. By 1914 a number of welfare institutions had been founded in the colonies, particularly in Chortitza and Molotschna: hospitals, orphan and old people's homes, a school for the deaf and a mental asylum. The exact cost of the schools and welfare institutions is unknown. However, once again it is clear that without the generous contributions of many wealthy Mennonites, most could not have functioned as they did, and some would never have been begun.

The community contained not only astute businessmen involved in private dealings but also individuals capable of managing large quantities of money for public ends. Banking institutions were a late development in Russia, but Mennonites already had experience with long-term financial transactions. From Prussia they had transferred systems of mutual fire insurance and an Orphans' Office *(Waisenamt)* which administered the estates of widows and orphans. The *Waisenamt* also acted as a credit institution, accepting deposits and providing loans at interest. In Chortitza in 1902-3 the capital of its Orphans' Office was over 1.7 million rubles.

With the development of banking in Russia after 1860 Mennonites took advantage of banking services to invest capital, secure loans and obtain mortgages. It is unclear at present what role this access to new

A store in the settlement of New York.   Photo: Mennonite Heritage Centre Archives

117

forms of credit played in Mennonite economic development. The average colonist for a long time remained suspicious of such institutions, often keeping large sums of cash at home. Many wealthy landowners and industrialists preferred to depend on family and friends rather than on outside sources of finance, and only later did some speculate in stocks and government bonds. By 1914, however, the younger farmers who had succeeded to family land as well as most industrialists and large landowners were more informed about such matters and took advantage of the banking and credit institutions available.

In 1904 the Niebuhr Company opened a bank in Chortitza and later established branches elsewhere. In 1910 the Chortitza *volost'* established a Mutual Credit Union which in 1912 had about 400 members; a similar Union existed in Halbstadt, Molotschna. Such credit unions, along with other specialized cooperative societies mushroomed in Russia after 1908, when legislation against such institutions was relaxed. In 1908 there were 304 mutual credit unions in Russia, by 1914 1,108.[23] In the late 1890s cooperatives were established in many Mennonite settlements and by 1914 they were found in most colonies. By 1914 over 18,000 cooperatives operated in Russia compared with under 5,000 in 1905. The range of Mennonite cooperatives varied greatly. Some were general; others dealt in specific goods such as dairy produce or farm equipment. However, very little is known about their range or mode of operation.[24]

The economic world in which most Mennonites operated in 1914 was therefore large and complex. It reached well beyond their own settlements and made Mennonites subject to economic forces beyond their control. On the whole Mennonites were prosperous and secure.[25] Although not as rich as some Russians, most Mennonites were much better off than neighbouring Little Russian peasants. Colony farmers made up about 70 percent of the Mennonite population and enjoyed a standard of living much higher than most peasants. They owned comfortable homes, well-stocked barns, efficient farm machinery and land which was rising rapidly in value. Moreover, they had the skills and knowledge to secure a prosperous future for themselves and their children. Under two percent of the Mennonite population was really rich, mainly estate owners and industrialists who, though small in number, contributed greatly to the Mennonite community. About 25 percent of Mennonites, however, possessed little or no land, worked as labourers for other Mennonites and had only a basic education with few prospects for change in their situation. By 1914 the rapid pace of economic development within and outside the colony had created social differences in the larger Mennonite community. Furthermore, these differences were being accentuated by regional variations. Those at the top and bottom of Mennonite society were drifting away from the community: wealthy Mennonites into urban areas where many married non-Mennonites; the poorer members, alienated from the community, into the wider society.

In 1914 most colony farmers were secure; since 1908 harvests had been mostly good and profits were high. Government land reforms, however, were encouraging peasants to rationalize their farming methods, a trend which, if it had been continued, would have provided competition to Mennonite farmers. Changes in technology demanded farming on a larger scale than was presently practiced in the colonies, but this challenge lay in the future. Large estate owners were increasingly under pressure from a peasantry which was eager for land and a government which was willing to use the excuse of Mennonite separateness to seize land and to distribute it among peasants who, they feared, threatened their regime.

Those which most felt the cold winds of change by 1914, however, were the industrialists. As Russian industry expanded, particularly after 1908, Mennonite producers of agricultural machinery faced increased competition. For a long time they had been protected by import tariffs, but in 1898 the duty placed on advanced, complex machines had been removed. For a long time this had little effect. Imported machines were complicated and expensive whereas the simple, cheap local products, such as the Mennonites manufactured, were in great demand. But as agricultural prices rose and farming became more commercially viable, the value of advanced imported machinery was recognized and demand for outdated local products declined. The strongest competition came from the American International Harvester Company which, in 1912, opened a large factory outside Moscow to produce modern agricultural machines, especially binders.[26] Some Mennonites producers were soon in financial difficulty while others had to rebuild and reequip their plant. For instance A.I. Koop and Niebuhr modernized and produced binders. In 1912 Koop formed a cartel, called The Harvest, with two non-Mennonite firms, R.T. Elworthy and J.J. Hoehn of Odessa. They joined forces to purchase raw material and market their products.[27] The threat of international industrial capital and the advantages of economies of scale were thus forcing Mennonites to secure their businesses beyond the Mennonite community.

Centrifugal forces were therefore influencing Mennonites on

many levels by 1914. Economic forces affected Mennonite society and threatened its long term viability as a distinct community. But the more immediate threat to the Mennonites in the years before 1914 came from political forces. Mennonite economic success, especially in New Russia, and Mennonite control of land and industry raised the ire of right-wing nationalists; peasants eager for land objected to the large estates and looked with envy at the prosperity of colony farmers; Russian workers in Mennonite factories were becoming increasingly politicized and opposed to bourgeois industrialists.

The Economic Impact of World War I

The conflict which engulfed Europe in the summer of 1914, and which involved Russia in war with Germany and Austro-Hungary, signalled the end of the Mennonite commonwealth in Russia. It took just a little longer for the final curtain to fall.

Some historians have seen one of the causes of the First World War as economic.[28] National rivalry, it is argued, merely reflected more deep-seated conflicts and contradictions inherent in the capitalist system. Groups with vested economic interests allied themselves with the older conservative elite to resist radical forces calling for political, social and economic reform. The tenor of nationalistic rhetoric was thus increased, suppressing internal opposition and expanding the armed forces and the chances for conflict. Whatever the causes of the war, its economic consequences were profound. Of all the European states involved, Russia was perhaps the least prepared and most ill equipped to fight the long war which none of the combatants had foreseen or planned for. In the end Russia was incapable of sustaining war, economically, socially and politically. In early 1914 the old political order was overthrown. Shortly afterwards Russian society and the economic system upon which it was based collapsed.

Mennonites greeted the war with restrained patriotism and some foreboding. Young men volunteered to serve in Red Cross units. By 1917 almost 14,000 Mennonites had enlisted or been conscripted, about half of whom served in the Red Cross and half in the Forestry. This was but a drop in the ocean; by 1917 12 million Russian men, or 40 percent of the male, able-bodied workforce in Russia had been conscripted, mainly from rural areas. Of these 1.8 million had died in battle or were listed as missing with 1.4 million disabled.[29]

Within months of the outbreak of hostilities Mennonite horses and supplies were requisitioned. With the reduction of horses and

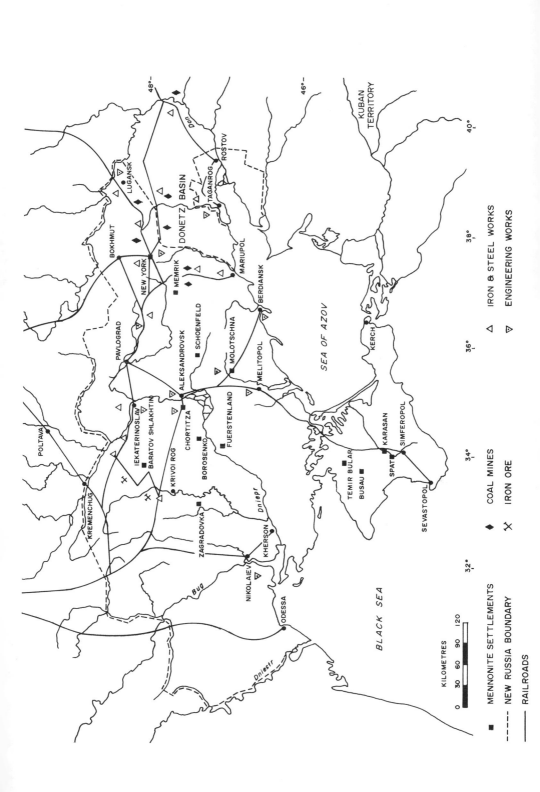

KUBAN
TERRITORY

Don

ROSTOV

LUGANSK

BOKHMUT

TAGANROG

DONETZ BASIN

NEW YORK

MEMRIK

PAVLOGRAD

SCHOENFELD

MARIUPOL

BERDIANSK

IEKATERINOSLAV

BARATOV SHLAKHTIN

ALEKSANDROVSK

MOLOTSCHNA

POLTAVA

CHORTITZA

FUERSTENLAND

MELITOPOL

KREMENCHUG

KRIVOI ROG

BOROSENKO

SEA OF AZOV

KERCH

ZAGRADOVKA

TEMIR BULAR

KARASAN

BUSAU

SPAT

SIMFEROPOL

KHERSON

NIKOLAIEV

SEVASTOPOL

ODESSA

Dniepr

Bug

Dniestr

BLACK SEA

KILOMETRES

0 30 60 90 120

■ MENNONITE SETTLEMENTS   △ IRON & STEEL WORKS

- - - NEW RUSSIA BOUNDARY   ▽ ENGINEERING WORKS

—— RAILROADS   ◆ COAL MINES

                                   ✕ IRON ORE

                                   ■ IRON ORE

48°

46°

40°

38°

36°

34°

32°

peasant labour, production began to fall. The export of grain was prevented by the blockade of the Black Sea, but all grain was demanded for the war effort. Mennonite production of farm machinery was reduced to a trickle and spare parts for existing machines became scarce. Farm production, however, was also affected by a general loss of confidence in the future among Mennonites. In 1914 the duma (parliament) passed legislation intended to expropriate the property of all citizens of enemy descent, including foreign colonists such as the Mennonites. Although never fully implemented, the threat of expropriation, combined with a vicious campaign of propaganda against the colonists which eventually influenced local peasants, had a marked effect in the colonies. Farms were allowed to run down; cultivated areas were reduced; moveable property, including livestock and machinery, was sold.[30] Production dropped, incomes fell, costs increased. By 1917, with increased conscription and inflation, the cost to the community of the Forestry Service alone was running at 100,000 rubles a month.

In the rest of rural Russia the war at first led to an increase in production.[31] In 1914-15 and 1915-16 harvests were good and a number of factors such as military allowances, higher prices for produce and a more rational use of labour, increased peasant incomes. But inflation soon eroded this increase as the government struggled to finance a war that was costing millions of rubles a day. As peasants realized their returns were dropping, they withheld supplies from the market. Food became scarce in urban areas and the government initiated forced requisitions. The peasants reacted by producing less and by hoarding what they had. By 1916-17 agricultural production was 24 percent below 1914 levels. As in the Mennonite colonies, the peasants began to produce mainly for their own subsistence needs.

The demand for war materials provided a massive boost to industry. After initial problems had been overcome, production increased rapidly. Heavy industry expanded and engineering firms, such as the Mennonite agricultural factories, were retooled to produce military supplies, including munitions. Like many other industrialists, Mennonite factory owners did well from the war and used their wealth to exempt themselves from the threats of expropriation facing their colony brethren. As industry expanded, so did its workforce which increased by one-third between 1914 and 1917. Although workers' wages rose, so did prices, particularly in urban areas where most factories were situated. Real wages fell, most dramatically in the period 1916-17. The fall in workers' purchasing power, combined with food shortages caused by peasants reducing production and withholding supplies, as well as by chaos in the transport system, led to industrial unrest, especially in Petrograd. The war was going badly. Confidence in the tsar and his political order had evaporated and early in 1917 he was overthrown by an uprising in Petrograd. But the economic problems did not go away. The Provisional Government's decision to continue the war, causing chaos in city and countryside provided a fertile breeding ground for the promoters of unrest, whether they were nationalistic or Bolshevik. Russia was plunged into civil war.

Rural unrest in New Russia and elsewhere, and eventually the Civil War which devastated much of the countryside, shattered the weakened fabric of Mennonite community life. When peace was eventually restored under Bolshevik control in 1921 the Mennonites rebuilt their shattered lives, but in circumstances very different from those which had prevailed before 1914. The brief respite of the New Economic Policy (1921-28) saw the development of new economic and social forms in the Mennonite communities, but the old prosperity was never restored.

Conclusion

The basic outlines of Mennonite economic development in Russia sketched in this chapter have been known since Ehrt and Rempel wrote their dissertations. What is required now is more research into the details of these developments in New Russia and other areas of the Empire. Work needs to be done on specific aspects of the Mennonite economy and its relation to the larger Russian economy. Official reports and statistics, published and unpublished, undoubtedly contain a mass of information which will require considerable skill to collect, collate and interpret. Prospective researchers will need to be well grounded in economics and history and possess the appropriate language skills. But not too much faith should be placed in such sources — they cannot answer all outstanding questions concerning the relationship between Mennonite economic, social and cultural development in Russia.

While official papers may provide a wider framework for understanding the Mennonite economy, many details of Mennonite life will remain obscure. What was it like to work a farm, run a household, labour in a factory or to manage an estate? How did a family budget its income? What factors lay behind economic decision-making? What was it like to be very rich or very poor? How did the community cope with economic prosperity? These and many other questions concerned with the human dimensions of Mennonite economic development will rarely be mentioned in non-Mennonite sources. Neither is it likely that a great deal will be found in Mennonite sources. However, if the study of Mennonite economic development is to advance beyond statistical commonplace and to move beyond being a mere cataloguing of Mennonite "achievements," such questions must be posed and answers sought. Any interpretation will have to bear in mind, as Ehrt and Rempel indicated, that the Mennonite experience was reflected in a much larger Russian mirror.

Notes

1. Adolf Ehrt, *Das Mennonitentum in Rußland von seiner Einwanderung bis zur Gegenwart* (Langensalza-Berlin-Leipzig: J. Beltz, 1932); David G. Rempel, "The Mennonite Colonies in New Russia: A Study of their Settlement and Economic Development from 1789 to 1914" (Ph.D. dissertation, Stanford University, 1933).

2. Rempel's major published work in this field is "The Mennonite Commonwealth in Russia: A Sketch of Its Founding and Endurance 1789-1919," *Mennonite Quarterly Review* 47 (October 1973): 259-308; 48 (January 1974): 5-54.

3. The major Soviet study available in English is P. Lyashchenko, *A History of the National Economy of Russia* (New York: Macmillan, 1949).

4. Particularly, W.L. Blackwell, *The Beginnings of Russian Industrialization* (Princeton: Princeton University Press, 1968); Olga Crisp, *Studies in the Russian Economy Before 1914* (London: Macmillan, 1976); M.E. Falkus, *The Industrialization of Russia, 1700-1914* (London: Macmillan, 1974); Peter Gatrell, *The Tsarist Economy 1850-1917* (London: Batsford, 1986); Alan S. Milward and S.B. Paul, *The Development of the Economies of Continental Europe 1850-1914* (London: Allen & Unwin, 1977) Chapters 6-7; and the essays in *Cambridge Economic History of Europe* particularly those by Gerschenkron and R. Portal in Volume VI and Crisp in Volume VI, Part 2.

5. Unless otherwise stated Russian and European statistics are derived from the sources noted above or are based on B. R. Mitchell, *European Historical Statistics, 1750-1975* (London: Macmillan, 1980).

6. Teodor Shanin, *Russia as a "Developing Society,"* Volume 1, *The Roots of Otherness: Russia's Turn of Century* (London: Macmillan, 1985), 94-102.

7. Paul R. Gregory, *Russian National Income, 1885-1913* (Cambridge: Cambridge University Press, 1982), 78.

8. The best accounts of the economic development of New Russia before 1861 are in Russian: E. Druzhinina, particularly her *Iuzhnaia Ukraina 1800-1825gg* (Moskva: Akademia Nauk, 1970) and *Iuzhnaia Ukraina v Period Krizisa Feodalizma 1825-1860gg* (Moskva: Akademia Nauk, 1981).

9. George Pavlovsky, *Agricultural Russia on the Eve of the Revolution* (Lon-

don: Routledge & Kegan Paul, 1930), 327.

10. A.M. Solovyova, "The Railway System in the Mining Area of Southern Russia in the Late Nineteenth and Early Twentieth Centuries," *Journal of Transport History* 5 (1984): 66-81.

11. See Roger L. Thiede, "Industry and Urbanization in New Russia from 1860 to 1910" in *The City in Russian History,* ed. Michael F. Hamm (Lexington: University Press of Kentucky, 1976), 125-38.

12. Statistical material on the Mennonites in the following sections, unless otherwise stated, is derived from Ehrt, Rempel or from my thesis, "The Closed and the Open: Social and Religious Change amongst the Mennonites in Russia, 1789-1889" (D.Phil. dissertation, Oxford University, 1978). See also my *None but Saints: The Transformation of Mennonite Life in Russia* (Winnipeg, Manitoba: Hyperion Press, 1989).

13. M.E. Falkus, "Russia and the International Wheat Trade, 1861-1914," *Economica* 33 (1966): 416-29.

14. These figures, and the comments on the decline of the hard red wheat, come from David H. Epp, "The Emergence of German Industry in the South Russian Colonies (1911)," trans. and ed. John B. Toews, *Mennonite Quarterly Review* 55 (October 1981): 289-371.

15. Figures in this section are derived from the sources given in note 12 with the addition of David H. Epp's account (above) and his *Sketches from the Pioneer Years of the Industry in the Mennonite Settlements of South Russia,* trans. J.P. Penner (Leamington, Ontario: Privately Printed, 1972).

16. On proto-industrialization see Peter Kriedte, et al., *Industrialization before Industrialization* (Cambridge: Cambridge University Press, 1977).

17. An anecdotal account of the foundation of Mennonite industry is contained in Epp's *Sketches* and his "Emergence of German Industry."

18. R. Munting, "Mechanization and Dualism in Russian Agriculture," *Journal of European Economic History* 8 (1979): 743-60.

19. P. Gatrell, "Industrial Expansion in Tsarist Russia, 1908-14," *Economic History Review* 35 (1982): 102.

20. Detailed in Epp, "Emergence of German Industry" and Rempel, "Mennonite Commonwealth."

21. These figures and those below for the 1908 Forestry Service have been calculated from P.M. Friesen, *The Mennonite Brotherhood in Russia (1789-1910)* (Fresno, California: Board of Christian Literature, General Conference of Mennonite Brethren Churches, 1978), 866-69.

22. Figures from Lawrence Klippenstein, "Mennonite Pacifism and State Service in Russia: A Case Study in Church-State Relations, 1789-1936" (Ph.D. dissertation, University of Minnesota, 1984), 151, 153, 198.

23. Rempel, "Mennonite Commonwealth," 83-84 discusses Mennonite banking and credit institutions.

24. Material on the Mennonite cooperatives is available, however, in reports in the *Odessaer Zeitung.* On the wider Russian scene see A. Baykalov, "A Brief Outline of the Russian Co-operative Movement," *Slavonic Review* 1 (1922): 130-43 and Crisp, *Studies in the Russian Economy.*

25. On the implications of Mennonite prosperity see my "Through the Eye of a Needle: Wealth and the Mennonite Experience in Imperial Russia," *Journal of*

Mennonite Studies 3 (1985): 7-35.

26. Fred V. Carstensen, *American Enterprise in Foreign Markets: Studies of Singer and International Harvester in Imperial Russia* (Chapel Hill: University of Northern Carolina Press, 1984).

27. Information supplied by the late Hermann Koop of Waterloo, Ontario, April 1974.

28. For various arguments on the causes of the First World War, including economic, see James Joll, *The Origins of the First World War* (London: Longmans, 1984), especially Chapter 6.

29. The economic and social costs of the war were reviewed by a number of authors in the various volumes of the series sponsored by the Carnegie Endowment for International Peace between the mid-1920s and the early 1930s. Although some of their opinions and statistics are today open to question, they are still useful sources.

30. The issue of expropriation and its impact on Mennonites is discussed by David G. Rempel, "The Expropriation of the German Colonists in South Russia during the Great War," *Journal of Modern History* 4 (March 1932): 49-67.

31. The following paragraphs are based largely on the arguments advanced by John L.H. Keep, *The Russian Revolution: A Study in Mass Mobilization* (London: Weidenfeld & Nicolson, 1976), Chapters 3-4 and Norman Stone, *The Eastern Front 1914-1917* (London: Hodder & Stoughton, 1976), Chapter 13.

A House Divided: Russian Mennonite Nonresistance and Emigration in the 1870s

Harry Loewen

In 1874 some 17,000 Russian Mennonites, approximately one-third of the Mennonite population in Russia, began emigrating to Canada and the United States. In North America they were promised religious freedom and given a new homeland. Until fairly recently Mennonite historians such as D.H. Epp, Franz Isaak and P.M. Friesen have told the story of the 1870s migration from the perspective of the more progressive and cultured Mennonites who decided to remain in Russia. Those Mennonites who advocated emigration were regarded by these historians as conservative, culturally backward and even disloyal to their Russian homeland. Now that the sources have become more accessible and are being translated from German into English, younger historians are beginning to challenge and revise the older view of Russian Mennonitism.[1] It is becoming increasingly evident that the earlier historiography was often motivated by political considerations[2] and was biassed in favour of the more acculturated Mennonites in Russia.

In this article I will probe the motives and actions with regard to military conscription in Russia and issues relating to emigration; argue that the majority of Mennonites were not all that serious in their expressed avowals of nonresistance and intentions to emigrate; and indicate that both internal and external factors had prepared for and helped to shape the views of those who decided to stay in Russia and the resolve of those who emigrated.

When in 1870 it became known to the Russian Mennonites that the tsarist government intended to introduce universal military conscription in its Empire, the Mennonites seemed surprised and expressed alarm.[3] Tsar Paul's Charter of Privileges (1800) which guaranteed not only religious freedom for all time but also exemption from military service, was apparently no safeguard against changing times, the nature of developing world events and the fickleness of the Russian emperors. What Russian Mennonites had taken for granted for seventy years was now being challenged by forces outside their control. At stake was not only exemption from military service, but also their rights and policies with regard to education, the German language and control of their colonial affairs.

The new law did not originate independently of socio-political events and developments elsewhere in Europe. Napoleon's campaigns earlier in the nineteenth century and the opposition of nations to the French emperor increased European nationalism and patriotism and created a need for military conscription. With the defeat of Napoleon in 1815 and the creation of the Holy Alliance, Russia was increasingly drawn into European affairs. The Frankfurt Parliament of 1848 registered the drive for equality, representative government and democratic obligations for all German subjects regardless of their status in society. And a united Germany under Chancellor Otto von Bismarck, viewed by Russia as a potential threat, removed all special privileges from minority groups in 1867-68, including military exemption.[4] Add to this Russia's poor performance in the Crimean War (1853-56) and the subsequent rise of Russian nationalism[5] and it becomes obvious why Russia in 1870 introduced policies designed to strengthen its defenses at home and abroad. It was these new policies which were bound to clash with the privileged status of the Russian Mennonites.

With regard to the special status of Mennonites, the Russian government knew that Mennonites elsewhere in Europe were either being forced to abandon their historic principle of nonresistance or were being culturally influenced to renounce it voluntarily. This had happened in the Netherlands as early as the seventeenth and eighteenth centuries, in the western Germanies in the early nineteenth century during the time of Napoleon's advance and in Prussia in the second half of the nineteenth century under Bismarck.[6] The Russian officials no doubt also knew that when the governmental pressures were on, only individuals and smaller groups of Mennonites were willing to leave their homeland for the sake of their conscience. The majority of Mennonites had come to terms with the new realities around them.[7] In Russia itself there were indications that Mennonites did not take their principle of nonresistance all that seriously and that a united action against Russia's new conscription law was only a remote possibility.

And yet, except for some individuals and small groups, Mennonites united in their appeal to the imperial government to honour their almost sacred privileges. Between 1871 and 1873 several delegations were dispatched to Yalta and Petersburg in the hope that the government could be persuaded to retain the special status Mennonites had enjoyed until then.[8] While the question of nonresistance became the central issue in the negotiations which followed, the real concern of the Mennonites was their desire to retain control over such things as education, language and their way of life generally. These issues were so important to the Russian Mennonites that the various groups which decades before and even more recently had fought among themselves over religious, administrative, economic and land questions, put their differences aside and united in a common cause. Yet, as P.M. Friesen observes: "The picture of a harmonious unity between the . . . parties was not a wholesome one. It was the picture of a painful diplomacy between the representatives of . . . antagonistic armies during a temporary cease fire. . . ."[9] While the Russian authorities must have been surprised to see such a concerted effort to change or modify the new law, they nevertheless knew how to deal with the Mennonites.

In their attempt to maintain control over their affairs, including exemption from military service, the Mennonite deputies on their several journeys to the imperial capital referred time and again to their Charter of Privileges and more specifically to their historic peace principle. They were peace-loving people, they said; they could not kill other human beings, not even their enemies whom they would rather embrace than destroy; they could not even serve in departments or units which were connected to the military because it was against their conscience.[10]

The Russians were prepared for these pleas and arguments. On the one hand they smiled at the Mennonites' naive protestations about peace and love; on the other they criticized the Mennonites severely about the contradiction between their profession of faith and their actions.[11] The Russians reminded the deputies that they had shelves full of records in the capital which told the stories of quarrels among Mennonites concerning religious and educational matters and above all of the injustices perpetrated against the land-less among them. The deputies were further told that, after seventy years in Russia, Mennonites still could not speak Russian well, which was a "sin," that they should be prepared to assume some tangible responsibility on behalf of their adopted country and that they should heed more carefully the Gospel's teaching with regard to charity.[12]

Upon examination of the issues between the deputies and the Russian officials in the early 1870s, it becomes evident that the Russian Mennonites seemed to fear the loss of control over their internal affairs more than the loss of their traditional principle of nonresistance. In fact, it becomes rather doubtful, as will be seen, that nonresistance was a deeply felt conviction or widely practised way of life among Mennonites in nineteenth-century Russia.

The Russian officials' reference to rooms full of records about Mennonite quarrels and their criticism of Mennonite lack of charity were of course designed to intimidate the deputies and to blunt their opposition to the new conscription law. In this the Russians achieved their purpose. However, they also managed to reveal to the Mennonites that nonresistance was for many a mere shell whose kernel, if not lost, was certainly no longer healthy. Nonresistance was part of a confession of faith and it was still part of a tradition, but it was no longer a living faith in daily consciousness and life.

Moreover, the Mennonites in all their years in Russia had not developed a consistent policy with regard to military service. In theory they still adhered to the principle of nonresistance but in practice the lines between a strict pacifism and some form of military involvement were rather blurred. During the Napoleonic era there were many who had at least in spirit sided with the war efforts of their government. During the Crimean War (1853-56) there were even more who had actively participated in the *podvod*, that is, the wagon service transporting goods to the fronts and bringing back wounded soldiers. P.M. Friesen later proudly described the active involvement of Mennonites in the Crimean War and the commendations and honours the Mennonites received from the Tsar for their efforts.[13] When the Russian officials reminded the deputies of their past active participation, the Mennonites replied that that had been done voluntarily, whereas the new conscription law demanded compulsory services which was against their conscience.[14] No doubt the Russians noticed that the Mennonites were more concerned about maintaining control over their young men than serving their country in some form.

There is evidence that the great majority of nineteenth-century Russian Mennonites was patriotic and nationalistically minded. Mennonites could not and did not identify fully with Russian culture and people, but they loved their tsars and supported their policies, including their war efforts. Heinrich Heese (1787-1868), a respected teacher and secretary of Johann Cornies (1789-1848), could not find sufficient words to praise Tsar Nicholas I and his military efforts on the one hand and to denounce Russia's enemies on the other. In 1855, at the height of the Crimean War, he wrote to Peter Isaak in Schoenau: The Russian Tsar "will, for the glory of God, have the final victory. Our enemies are despisers of Christ.... Our Prince is serving the Lord, his warriors are believers, God will intervene, and the prayers of the pious will finally have the victory."[15] After the war he wrote: "Tsar Nicholas I . . . diligently promoted the training of the military, and how the bravery of our armies in this murderous war has justified such precaution! Our enemies were very loud with their boasts and threats; the Russians responded with silence. But the French prisoners said: 'The Russians shoot well, and their artillery is superior.' "[16]

P.M. Friesen states that Heese's patriotism was "exaggerated," but he nevertheless admits that the Mennonite community "took the same stance as Heese toward the Crimean War and toward the Russian soldier."[17] He adds: "The Crimean War was regarded . . . as a crusade . . . in which the soldiers, especially the wounded and the sick among them, were viewed as martyrs. Doctrinal considerations concerning nonresistance hardly surfaced; emotions decided."[18] It seems that for Heese, as for many other Russian Mennonites, nonresistance consisted merely in not going to war to kill the enemy. Nonresistance as a heartfelt principle and way of life was strangely absent from a large majority of nineteenth-century Mennonites.

These nationalistic sentiments among the Mennonites found pietistic support from an unexpected quarter during the early 1870s. During their missions to the capital the deputies encountered a friend who became an effective intermediary between themselves and the Russian officials. Theodor Hans, pastor of the Evangelical (Moravian) Brethren congregation in Petersburg, championed the Mennonite cause in the capital and advised the Mennonites how they were to proceed and approach the officials. It is interesting to note that historians such as P.M. Friesen, D.H. Epp and Franz Isaak speak well of the pastor's efforts on their behalf, identifying the pastor's concerns and sentiments with those of the Mennonites.

Friesen includes in his history two lengthy letters written by Theodor Hans to the "elders and assemblies of the Mennonite communities" in which the author not only advises what course to follow but also speaks as one who knows what the will of God is for the Mennonites in Russia. The following excerpts from these letters, written in 1873, are instructive. In the first letter Hans writes:

> The situation into which you have been placed is a far more favorable one than that of your brethren in Germany, who are compelled to serve on the transportation and baggage vehicles in the field. . . . What the [Russian] government is suggesting for you in the present proposal is actually

nothing which would make you party to the evils of war. . . . It gives you a deep concern to see your young men . . . torn from your midst and submitted to a totally strange influence. . . . This concern I share with you . . . [however your] young men will need to be exposed to alien influences [which will no doubt have] a lasting and sanctifying effect . . . you should not automatically decline all government service assignments . . . [nor] take advantage of the right to emigrate. . . . This turns the question of an obligation to emigrate for conscience sake into the question of having the right to emigrate for conscience sake.[19]

In the second letter Hans advises the Mennonites to entrust their cause to "His Majesty the Tsar's good will alone" and not to consider seriously leaving Russia. "Russia needs you and the responsibility which you have received from God for this country is a great one."[20]

Pastor Theodor Hans voiced the wishes of the majority of the Mennonite people. Moreover, in clothing his advice in biblical and brotherly language, Hans provided the Mennonites with sufficient justification and divine sanction for their desire to stay in Russia. It thus became easier for them to come to some mutually beneficial terms with the Russian government.

In spite of the desire of most Mennonites to remain in Russia, a minority of them continued to make preparations for emigration. A twelve-man delegation to North America in 1873 advised that, in view of developments in Russia, emigration was the only way to preserve religious freedom, including exemption from military service and spiritual control over their communities.[21] In an attempt to dissuade the would-be emigrants from their purpose and to strengthen the majority that wished to remain in Russia, "the friendly Tsar Alexander II"[22] sent his special confidante to the Molotschna and Chortitza colonies in April 1974. General von Totleben, of Crimean War fame, in his charming and trust-inspiring ways praised the Russian fatherland, pointed out the uncertainties for Mennonites in America, conveyed the well wishes and love of the Tsar and made what Mennonites considered to be maximum concessions to their conscience.[23]

Totleben offered Mennonites alternative services in factories, fire brigades, hospitals, forestry units and on railways — all civilian departments not under the control of the military. Mennonites opted for the forestry services because here they would be isolated from the rest of Russian society and able to maintain control and discipline over their young men.[24] In a subsequent written response to Totleben, Mennonites expressed gratitude for the government's indulgence toward them and added that they would in future teach the Russian language more effectively and try to discharge their obligations to the state properly. They also added the threat that if in the future the terms with regard to military service were changed they would again consider emigration.[25] The result of Totleben's mission "was an extensive reversal of opinion among the Mennonite people. The brotherhoods in most of the communities were instructed and influenced by the administrations in such a way that the large majority heeded the Tsar's word."[26]

In a poem "dedicated to the most honored hero and patron of the Mennonites: Count von Totleben," Bernhard Harder (1832-1884), preacher and poet, expressed the relief and gratitude of many Mennonites during the crisis of the 1870s: "Confusion reigned and fear abounded,/ but he spoke boldly: 'Children, stay at home,/ the Emperor, so full of grace and wisdom,/ desires that you do not emigrate,/ he will as always care for you.' "[27] This poem is another indication that Harder's "glowing patriotism for Russia,"[28] as P.M. Friesen states, was not limited to individuals like Heinrich Heese, but was widely felt among the Russian Mennonites.[29] It thus comes as no surprise that the majority of Mennonites were not only willing and eager to come to some satisfactory terms with the government but also expressed annoyance and displeasure toward those Mennonites who could not adjust to the new reality in Russia and instead advocated emigration to North America.

There were several leading advocates of emigration. Cornelius Jansen (1822-94) was a prosperous grain merchant and a representative of the Prussian and Mecklenburg Consulate at Berdiansk.[30] He was born in West Prussia and was the nephew of a strict nonresistant elder there, Gerhard Penner of Heubuden, in whose family he had been raised.[31] Leonhard Sudermann (1821-1900) was an elder of the Berdiansk Mennonite Church and a delegate to Petersburg and to North America.[32] Dietrich Gaeddert (1837-1900) led a group of Alexanderwohl immigrants to America in 1874. Isaak Peters (1826-1911) was a teacher and writer in the Molotschna and a zealous advocate of nonresistance and emigration.[33] Because of their open advocacy of emigration, both Cornelius Jansen and Isaak Peters were expelled from Russia.[34] Gerhard Wiebe (1827-1900) was elder of the Bergthal Mennonite Church in Russia and in Manitoba after the emigration. Wiebe was religiously most conservative and held rigorously to nonresistance. He played a significant role in negotiating

Cornelius Jansen (1822-1894) and Aeltester Leonhard Sudermann (1821-1900) of Berdiansk were prominent leaders in the 1870s emigration to the U.S.A.

Photos: Mennonite Heritage Centre Archives

permission for the emigration in 1874.[35]

The more progressive and acculturated Mennonite historians have not been kind toward the advocates of emigration. P.M. Friesen, for example, has an unidentified writer describe "Sudermann, Jansen, Peters and company" as being "incapable of a God-willed and God-permitted closer association with Russian society" and as having "the greatest aversion to culture."[36] Friesen continues to quote his source: "They do not, nor were they capable of appreciating the Tsar's enormous efforts on behalf of his people — particularly also, in the creation of the new military law and all that it entails."[37] The Tsar's efforts were seen as "a relatively evangelical step forward," and the advocates of emigration are dismissed as culturally German-oriented and ignorant of the Russian language, culture and literature.[38] Suspecting their loyalty to Russia and questioning their motives in advocating emigration, Friesen's unidentified writer states that if these "unmanageable, pious foster children" were honest men, they had to leave "in order to preserve their spiritual heritage for their offspring:"

> They were honest men, and they left. Thank God that they left! It was good for them, for their children and for America. . . . They are very industrious farming families which are

enriching Kansas, Nebraska, Dakota, Minnesota, etc. . . . English Canada is also most glad for our orthodox Mennonites because they are good land purchasers and farming people. . . . At the same time, however, the state retained the greatest part of the Mennonite settlers. They allowed themselves to benefit from the wholesome and useful Russian societal and educational circumstances according to the gracious conditions, which astonished the political world, permitted by the monarch of that time and protected by his noble successors.[39]

This lengthy quotation from Friesen (and one suspects that Friesen shared the writer's views) is significant. On the one hand it is an attempt to convince the Slavophiles and the nationalistic critics of the German-speaking settlers in late nineteenth-century Russia that the Mennonites were loyal subjects of the Russian Empire.[40] On the other hand it is an expression of the distance that had developed between the acculturated and the more traditional Mennonites. The 1870s migration to North America registered a divided Russian-Mennonite house.[41]

With regard to the criticism levelled against the advocates of emigration, there is no doubt that they, like most Mennonites in Russia, preferred German to Russian and were more familiar with German ways, culture and history than with Russian. However, the advocates of emigration were also men who lamented the waning of the old Mennonite tradition, took the principle of nonresistance more seriously than the majority of Russian Mennonites and were willing to give up their comforts in Russia for greater freedom of conscience in America.[42] Most of all, while the majority was willing to come to terms with the government and trusted the Tsar's promises, the advocates of emigration remained fearful and distrustful with regard to the future in Russia.

Far from viewing the government's terms as generous offers and considerate of traditional Mennonite principles, men like Gerhard Wiebe expressed grave concerns for the Mennonite brotherhood in Russia and distrust toward tsarist intentions. "Now the time had come," he writes in his *Causes and History of the Emigration,*

when the enemy could prepare to attack the sleepy ones or pull them into his net, for the government had observed us closely for several years, and suddenly it was announced that the Mennonite must participate in state service. When we

135

turned to the government in order to plead for religious freedom, we were told, "Yes, you want freedom, but what of your conduct by now?"[43]

The implied criticism of the "conduct" of Mennonites, especially the religious quarrels and the injustices toward the landless, is obvious.

Contrary to Franz Isaac's assertion that the Bergthal Colony did not participate in the negotiations with the Russian officials,[44] Gerhard Wiebe was chosen by his colony to represent Bergthal at Yalta and in other meetings with Mennonite and Russian officials. At Yalta Wiebe was ordered to appear before the Tsar's adjutant, General Hase, and pressured to agree to the government's terms and to renounce emigration plans. Wiebe asked whether the General could promise that Mennonites would remain exempt from direct military service "for several years or permanently."[45] The General could not make that promise because the Tsar's "hand is this way, tomorrow that way," and he illustrated by turning his hand.[46] The conservative Mennonites were thus not as optimistic about the future as the other deputies.

Not only were the conservatives pressured by the Russian officials to renounce their plans for emigration, but they were also being pressed by their liberal brethren to cooperate and show a united front before the authorities. In 1873 at Alexanderwohl, an all-Mennonite conference had prepared a statement which was to be forwarded to Petersburg. The Bergthal representatives were pressured to sign the statement as well. The statement read:

> We are grateful for all the bounteous benefactions which we enjoy in the Russian Empire, and hope to be able to continue to live under the sceptre of His Majesty in peace and contentment; but we beg His Majesty to shield us as much as possible from military service, according to our conscience, that is, that we will not need to take the sword. And so we depend upon His Majesty's mercy and care, and are confident in our most gracious Czar and Father of our nation, that he will take his distressed children under his protection, and do everything possible for us.[47]

While most conference delegates regarded the statement as an appropriate response to the government's proposals, the Bergthalers rightly saw through the intentions of their fellow Mennonites, namely that they wished to come to some satisfactory terms with the authorities at almost any price. When the Bergthalers did "not sign something so uncertain," the friendship between them and the more liberal Mennonites "now hung only by a thread which was in danger of breaking."[48]

In spring 1874 Mennonites were invited to meet General von Totleben in Halbstadt. Gerhard Wiebe and other conservative elders, unlike the majority of the more liberal Mennonites, remained suspicious of the government's promises. They assessed the situation as follows:

> . . . for four years the government had led us around with a fine thread, never quite letting on what it was we were to undertake, except for the occasional hint. Now they knew that the enemy had already succeeded in dividing us, and that the majority were by now willing to accept some duty. So they came with this decision, perhaps in the hope that a smaller group would follow the larger.[49]

When the advocates of emigration were asked by Totleben what their objection to the government's proposals were, Wiebe reports them as saying: "The church is fearful about the future, and asked us to seek Your Excellency's permission to emigrate."[50]

Near the end of October, 1874, Gerhard Wiebe was ordered to Gronau to appear once more before "someone who has come in the name of the Czar [*sic*]."[51] This representative of the Tsar was kind and condescending toward Wiebe, giving the elder "permission to ask something for yourself and your children."[52] For Wiebe this kindness and offer was a temptation of the devil. His reflection on this occasion expresses well his motives and those of his co-religionists with regard to emigration.

> Now I had been led to the top of a mountain, and shown the riches of this world and Satan also suggested to me what I should ask for: freedom from military service for my children and children's children and also a few thousand dessiatin of land. All this Satan whispered to me and I might have succumbed to his temptation, had not the Lord's hand suddenly grasped me, because time for decision was short, and I still had no answer.[53]

Wiebe and other conservatives did not yield to the "temptation" of an uncertain freedom in the future and a better economic base in

Russia, but requested that their people be allowed to emigrate, a request which was granted. At the end of the interview Wiebe was told by the Tsar's representative: "With such a man as you are, things cannot go well. You will become a despised and rejected man, because the world has never repaid such men otherwise."[54] Indeed,

Heinrich Wiebe (1839-1897), minister in the Bergthal settlement and one of the delegates who negotiated the terms of immigration into Canada in 1873.

Photo: Mennonite Heritage Centre Archives

138

not only the outside world but also the larger Mennonite world in Russia "despised and rejected" those Mennonites who for conscience sake declined the "gracious offers" of the government and instead decided to seek another earthly home elsewhere.

In conclusion, the 1870 military law in Russia, which caused Mennonites to reflect seriously on the religious underpinnings of their existence, was a response to external and internal political factors and developments. Since Mennonites elsewhere in Europe had gradually given in to nationalism and to the pressures of governments with regard to their position of nonresistance, Russia apparently did not expect too much opposition to the new conscription policy from the Russian Mennonites. This assessment of the Mennonite situation was strengthened by the knowledge that Russian Mennonites were pro-Russian during the Napoleonic and Crimean Wars and had been quite willing to serve their adopted country in times of national conflict. By 1870 the acculturation process and internal religious, social and economic developments had undermined the traditional values and changed the ethos of the majority of the Russian Mennonites to the extent that they became quite willing to adjust themselves to the new policies. The protracted efforts on the part of Mennonites to modify the new law were not so much a concern for their traditional nonresistance as a determination to retain at least some control over their existence as a people. The crisis of the 1870s caused the more conservative Mennonites to realize that there was no place and no future for them and their children in a community which had been their home for almost a hundred years. Emigration was the only option for them.

It has been suggested that of all the European Mennonites the Russian Mennonites adhered longest to the principle of nonresistance and that the compromise they worked out with the imperial government was not only the best they could do under the circumstances but was an arrangement which perpetuated nonresistance in intent if not in practice.[55] While there is some truth in this, it may not be beyond the parameters of this paper to point out that the Russian Mennonites continued to serve their country with supplies and other assistance during the Turkish War (1877-78), the Russo-Japanese War (1904-05)[56] and, in World War I, as medical orderlies at the front. When in 1918-19 law and order broke down, many Russian Mennonites organized self-defense *(Selbstschutz)* units to counter the forces of anarchy.[57] It could be argued that the *Selbstschutz* was made possible by a century-long weakening and erosion of an important Mennonite principle of faith.[58] And, sad to say, by World War II there would be few Russian Mennonites, if any, willing to challenge the conscription laws of the Soviet Union and Nazi Germany.[59]

Notes

1. P.M. Friesen, *The Mennonite Brotherhood in Russia (1789-1910)* (Fresno, California: Board of Christian Literature, Conference of Mennonite Brethren Churches, 1978); Gerhard Wiebe, *Causes and History of the Emigration of the Mennonites from Russia to America,* trans. Helen Janzen (Winnipeg, Manitoba: Manitoba Mennonite Historical Society, 1981). The Manitoba Mennonite Historical Society and CMBC Publications are jointly translating and publishing the Echo-Verlag Historical Series. See also the valuable translated sources in Delbert Plett, *History and Events* (Steinbach, Manitoba: D.F.Plett Farms Ltd., 1982) and *The Golden Years: The Mennonite Kleine Gemeinde in Russia (1812-1849)* (Steinbach, Manitoba: D.F.P. Publications, 1985), and John B. Toews, ed. and trans., "Nonresistance and Migration in the 1870s: Two Personal Views," *Mennonite Life* 41 (June 1986): 9-15. James Urry in "The Closed and the Open: Social and Religious Change amongst the Mennonites in Russia (1789-1889) " (D.Phil. dissertation, Oxford University, 1978) was one of the first writers to revise Russian Mennonite history. See also the "Russian Mennonite Immigration Centennial Issue" of *Mennonite Quarterly Review* 48 (October 1974) for valuable articles on this period in Russian Mennonite history.

2. See Harvey L. Dyck, "Russian Servitor and Mennonite Hero: Light and Shadow in Images of Johann Cornies," *Journal of Mennonite Studies* 2 (1984): 9-28.

3. D.H. Epp, *Die Chortitzer Mennoniten: Versuch einer Darstellung des Entwicklungsganges derselben* (Odessa: Selbstverlag des Verfassers, 1889; Neudruck und Verlag von: *Die Mennonitische Post,* Steinbach, and Delbert F. Plett, Steinbach, 1984), 94-96; Franz Isaac, *Die Molotschnaer Mennoniten: Ein Beitrag zur Geschichte derselben* (Halbstadt, Taurien: H. J. Braun, 1908), 295; P.M. Friesen, *Mennonite Brotherhood,* 586.

4. See especially the excellent study by Peter Brock, *Pacifism in Europe to 1914* (Princeton, New Jersey: Princeton University Press, 1972), chapters 6 and 11.

5. On the rise of Russian nationalism and anti-German sentiments, see Harvey L. Dyck, ed. and trans., "Russian Mennonitism and the Challenge of Russian Nationalism, 1889," *Mennonite Quarterly Review* 56 (October 1982): 307-41.

6. Brock, *Pacifism,* 407-41.

7. H.G. Mannhardt, *Die Danziger Mennonitengemeinde: Ihre Entstehung und ihre Geschichte von 1569-1919* (Danzig: Selbstverlag der Danziger Mennonitengemeinde, 1919), 175-80. For an interpretation of nonresistance among the Prussian Mennonites, see John Friesen, "The Relationship of Prussian Mennonites to German Nationalism " in Harry Loewen, ed., *Mennonite Images: Historical, Cultural, and Literary Essays Dealing with Mennonite Issues* (Winnipeg,

Manitoba: Hyperion Press, 1980), 61-72.

8. On the number and names of deputies, see Epp, *Chortitzer Mennoniten*, 99-103; Isaac, *Molotschnaer Mennoniten*, 295-300; and Friesen, *Mennonite Brotherhood*, 586-88.

9. Friesen, *Mennonite Brotherhood*, 1025.

10. Ibid., 587-88; Epp, *Chortitzer Mennoniten*, 99-101.

11. Friesen, *Mennonite Brotherhood*, 588, 1026.

12. Epp, *Chortitzer Mennoniten*, 95-100; Isaac, *Molotschnaer Mennoniten*, 296-300; Friesen, *Mennonite Brotherhood*, 1025-27.

13. Friesen, *Mennonite Brotherhood*, 579-86; cf., James Urry, "The Closed and the Open," and Lawrence Klippenstein, "Mennonites and the Crimean War, 1854-1856," *Journal of Mennonite Studies* 7 (1989): 9-32.

14. Epp, *Chortitzer Mennoniten*, 102.

15. Friesen, *Mennonite Brotherhood*, 702.

16. Ibid., 703.

17. Ibid., 705.

18. Ibid.

19. Ibid., 598-601.

20. Ibid., 602.

21. See Leonhard Sudermann, *Eine Deputationsreise von Russland nach Amerika* (Elkhart, Indiana: Mennonitische Verlagshandlung, 1897).

22. Friesen, *Mennonite Brotherhood*, 590. The royal house was held in high regard by Russian Mennonites. The new laws concerning military service were not seen as emanating from the Tsar but from his powerful advisers. The delegates to Petersburg felt that if they could see the Tsar, the laws would be modified in favour of Mennonites. But this was not to be and even the well-meaning Tsar and Tsarina were powerless to help the Mennonites. See Klaas Peters, *Die Bergtaler Mennoniten und deren Auswanderung aus Russland und Einwanderung in Manitoba* (Hillsboro, Kansas: Mennonite Brethren Publishing House, n.d.), 4-7.

23. On General Totleben's mission and the Mennonites' positive response to him, see Epp, *Chortitzer Mennoniten*, 107-113; Isaac, *Molotschnaer Mennoniten*, 323-25; Friesen, *Mennonite Brotherhood*, 602-08. For the views of the more conservative Mennonites, see Gerhard Wiebe, *Causes and History*, 38-48. See also Brock, *Pacifism*, 436-37, and Urry, "The Closed and the Open," 669-86.

24. Epp, *Chortitzer Mennoniten*, 110.

25. Ibid., 111.

26. Friesen, *Mennonite Brotherhood*, 590-91.

27. Translation by author from Bernhard Harder, *Geistliche Lieder und Gelegenheitsgedichte* (Hamburg: Verlagsanstalt und Druckerei A.-G., 1888), 582. Franz Isaac, *Molotschnaer Mennoniten*, 325, includes another Harder poem dedicated to Totleben. The first stanza reads as follows:

> Du kamst, o edler Mann, uns zu beglücken
> Durch unsers grossen Kaisers Gnadenwort!
> Nun scheidest Du. Und vieler Augen blicken
> Dir tränend nach — weil Du an diesem Ort
> Der Gnadensaat so reichlich ausgestreut
> Und uns geliebt so treu und väterlich!

Wir danken Dir — Und wenn Dein Werk gedeihet —
Gott walt's! so ist's ein süßer Lohn für Dich.

28. Friesen, *Mennonite Brotherhood*, 958.

29. For the possible reasons for Russian Mennonite nationalism and patriotism, see George K. Epp, "Russian Patriotism among the 19th-Century Russian Mennonites," *Journal of Mennonites Studies* 4 (1986): 120-134.

30. See Gustav E. Reimer and G.R. Gaeddert, *Exiled by the Czar: Cornelius Jansen and the Great Mennonite Migration 1874* (Newton, Kansas: Mennonite Publication Office, 1956).

31. Brock, *Pacifism*, 435.

32. See his *Eine Deputationsreise.*

33. On Isaak Peter's writings on nonresistance, see P.M. Friesen, *Die alt-evangelische mennonitische Brüderschaft in Russland (1789-1910) im Rahmen der mennonitischen Gesamtgeschichte* (Halbstadt, Taurien: Verlagsgesellschaft "Raduga," 1911), Teil II, 73-78. Peters knew the history of Christian pacifism from the early church to the Reformation and beyond quite well.

34. Reimer and Gaeddert, *Exiled by the Czar.*

35. See his important story, *Causes and History.* There were other Russian Mennonites who were most concerned about the weakening of the principle of nonresistance among the Prussian and Russian Mennonites. Martin Klaassen, a teacher in Koeppenthal, Am Trakt (Volga region), published a book dealing with this issue: *Geschichte der wehrlosen taufgesinnten Gemeinden von den Zeiten der Apostel bis auf die Gegenwart* (Danzig: Druck von Edwin Groening, 1873). See Walter Klaassen, "A Belated Review: Martin Klaassen's 'Geschichte der Wehrlosen Tauf-Gesinnten Gemeinden' Published in 1873," *Mennonite Quarterly Review* 17 (January 1975): 43-52, for an analysis of M. Klaassen's book. While approximately 17,000 Mennonites emigrated to North America, some Russian Mennonites migrated to south-east Asia to escape the worldliness of their brethren. See Fred Richard Belk, *The Great Trek of the Russian Mennonites to Central Asia 1880-1884* (Scottdale, Pennsylvania and Kitchener, Ontario: Herald Press, 1976).

36. Friesen, *Mennonite Brotherhood*, 592.

37. Ibid., 592-93.

38. Ibid., 593.

39. Ibid., 594. Similar views were expressed by Johann Epp, a minister of a Mennonite congregation at Koeppenthal, Am Trakt (Volga region). See Leonard Gross, ed., "The Coming of the Russian Mennonites to America: An Analysis by Johann Epp, Mennonite Minister in Russia, 1875," *Mennonite Quarterly Review* 48 (October 1974): 460-75.

40. See Dyck, "Russian Servitor,"16-22.

41. Urry, "The Closed and the Open,"685-86.

42. Isaak Peters wrote: "Dieses alles überlegend und in Betracht nehmend, konnten die ersten Auswanderer sich nicht zu der Übernahme des Soldatendienstes für ihre Söhne auch ohne Schwert entschließen, was sie also bewog, gleich ihrer Vorfahren zur Märtyrerzeit, den Wanderstab zu nehmen und ein Asyl sich zu suchen, wo sie ohne Anfechtung ihres Glaubens leben können, und haben noch nie Ursache gehabt, diesen Schritt bereuen zu müssen." P.M. Friesen, *Alt-evangelische mennonitische Brüderschaft*, Teil II, 78.

43. Wiebe, *Causes and History,* 14.

44. Isaac, *Molotschnaer Mennoniten,* 295.

45. Wiebe, *Causes and History,* 28.

46. Ibid.

47. Ibid., 30.

48. Ibid.

49. Ibid., 38.

50. Ibid., 39. The suspicions of the conservative Mennonites concerning the future in Russia came true. According to the testimony of Jacob Y. Shantz before a settlement committee in Ottawa (April 8, 1886), after 1880 it became increasingly difficult for Russian Mennonite young men to leave their country because of the new draft laws. See Sam Steiner, *Victorious Pioneer: The Life of Jacob Y. Shantz* (Winnipeg, Manitoba: Hyperion Press, 1988), 181-203.

51. Wiebe, *Causes and History,* 43.

52. Ibid., 46.

53. Ibid.

54. Ibid., 47.

55. Brock, *Pacifism,* 438-39.

56. Friesen, *Mennonite Brotherhood,* 583-86.

57. John B. Toews, *Czars, Soviets and Mennonites* (Newton, Kansas: Faith and Life Press, 1982).

58. John B. Toews argues convincingly that the *Selbstschutz* was possible because pacifism among Russian Mennonites "was [no longer] a personal conviction based on individual experience and tested by actual confrontations." Pacifism had become institutionalized and was taken for granted as part of the Mennonite privileges in Russia. "The Origins and Activities of the Mennonite *Selbstschutz* in the Ukraine (1918-1919)," *Mennonite Quarterly Review* 46 (January 1972): 12-13. See also Toews' "Nonresistance Reexamined," *Mennonite Life* 29 (Mid-Year, 1974): 8-13.

59. See, however, Hans Rempel, *Waffen der Wehrlosen: Ersatzdienst der Mennoniten in der UdSSR* (Winnipeg, Manitoba: CMBC Publications, 1980) for individual attempts to witness for peace in the Soviet Union and Hitler's Germany. Gerhard Lohrenz, *The Lost Generation and Other Stories* (Winnipeg, Manitoba: Gerhard Lohrenz, 1982), tells stories about Mennonite boys in military uniform. Lohrenz shows that the Mennonite children born between the years 1916 and 1941 belonged to the "lost generation," young people who had experienced want and deprivation and the loss of organized religious life.

The Orthodox church near Rosenthal, Russia (1890) and the oldest Mennonite church in Russia at Chortitza. During the era, 1880-1914, Mennonites were increasingly influenced by Russian culture.

Photos: Peter Gerhard Rempel (1872-1933). Courtesy: *Forever Summer, Forever Sunday*, ed. Hildegard E. Tiessen, John D. Rempel and Paul Tiessen (St. Jacobs, Ontario: Sand Hills Books Inc., 1981)

1880-1914

The era from the 1870s to 1914 has frequently been described as the Golden Age of Mennonite life in Russia. It began with major land reforms, the formation of numerous new Mennonite settlements, and changes in government laws regarding both education and military service and emigration to North America. It ended with the outbreak of World War I.

While this designation — Golden Age — might suggest that community was more perfectly achieved during this era than during any other period of Mennonite life in Russia, it was anything but harmonious, unified and of one purpose. Community seemed as difficult to achieve as during the previous pioneer era. The increasing wealth of the Mennonite people widened the disparity between the rich and the poor. This fact brought greater pressures to bear upon congregational life in which the equality of members was a basic affirmation.

The fragmentation of the Mennonite settlements into Mennonite and Mennonite Brethren congregations resulted in new conflicts and divisions. Religious renewal, which might have become the basis for a new vision for the Mennonite community, seemed instead to leave it further than ever from the goal of unity. A new educated elite developed as young people left to study in Germany, Switzerland and in their own Russian universities, bringing back visions which frequently clashed with the established views of the older generation.

New organizations were created to meet immediate needs; these in turn helped to define Mennonite identity in new ways. A church conference was created which eventually included all Mennonites. Initially designed to coordinate and supervise forestry service as a Mennonite alternative to military service, this all-Mennonite conference helped to define a new sense of unity. In theology, the effects of Pietism gradually became apparent in both Mennonite and Mennonite Brethren churches. As a result of this influence, Mennonites began to look beyond the boundaries of their community. They developed a sense of mission, and sent their missionaries to the Dutch East Indies under the Dutch Mennonite mission program. Mennonite Brethren congregations sent missionaries to India under Baptist organizations. Mennonites also learned to relate to and live with Jews when some of them were selected to form joint agricultural settlements under the so-called Judenplan.

Music was also helpful in creating community. Congregational singing had been part of the Mennonite experience already in

Poland. In the latter half of the nineteenth century new forms of music developed. Four-part harmony, choirs and new Pietist hymns were all part of this expanding tradition. Good choir singing seemed destined to become a characteristic facet of Russian Mennonite life.

The literary arts were slow in developing. The earliest Mennonite writings were designed more often to undergird piety than to probe the soul, or to analyze the life of the people. The first expressions of literature were just beginning to take shape prior to World War I. But a foundation was being laid for greater works later. In the new literature, identity and self-perceptions were being analyzed in ever-widening circles of literary and historical understanding.

Affluence, entry into the business world and studies at Russian cities, led Mennonites to settle in cities. No longer was the village determinative for defining the essense of Russian Mennonite community life. Community was being experienced and expressed in a much wider context as Mennonite businessmen, mayors, intellectuals and missionaries rubbed shoulders with Russians and Ukrainians, and began to be seen as fellow citizens in the great Russian motherland. Mennonites travelled, sent their children abroad for education and began to live the privileged life of the wealthy and powerful in the Russian society. A few even served in the duma (Russian parliament) after 1905.

These developments were all a part of an explosion of Mennonite institution-building in the years prior to World War I. Schools of higher education, hospitals, homes for the mentally-handicapped and the deaf, and banks were built to serve the Mennonite community. It seemed as if the new understanding of community was now to be defined and more firmly undergirded by institutions. It appeared to many, especially to outsiders, that Mennonites had become comfortable, affluent and largely self-sufficient. The poor and the landless played only a marginal role in defining Mennonite community in this era.

This world — comfortable, full of contradictions, wealthy yet precarious, established yet marginalized — was destined to be tested in the whirlwind unleashed by World War I.

Mennonite Churches and Religious Developments in Russia 1850-1914

Abe J. Dueck

The study of religious and ecclesiastical developments among Russian Mennonites in the last half of the nineteenth century and until the beginning of World War I has focused, to a large extent, on the origins of the Mennonite Brethren Church (hereafter MB) and on the various factors related to its origins, especially the impact of Pietism and the presumed decadent condition of the Old Church. Smaller religious groups such as the Templers and the Exodus Church have been studied, as have specific religious concerns such as nonresistance and education. These latter issues were especially determinative with regard to the emigration to North America in the 1870s.

Relatively little, however, has been written about general religious and ecclesiastical developments, especially in the period from about 1870 to 1914. Also, until recently, there have been very few studies of the *Kleine Gemeinde* during the Russian phase after the initial break early in the century. Discussions relating to both the MB and the Old Church (often referred to as the *Kirchengemeinden* or *Kirchliche*) tend to take 1860 as the primary reference point, and hence to obscure some of the distinctive and dynamic factors that characterize the later period. This discussion will therefore seek to correct the imbalance, yet still provide an outline of developments and issues during the period of greatest religious ferment from about 1850 to 1885. Furthermore, although the focus will be on ecclesiastical and religious developments, an attempt will be made to place these in the larger context of societal change. It is perhaps in this area that much work still needs to be done, although the paucity of sources does not permit an adequate assessment of the role of various factors in relation to religious developments. For the earlier part of this era the work of James Urry has helped considerably to place issues in a broader context, not only within Russia but also in relation to changing circumstances in Europe as a whole.[1]

It needs to be recognized at the outset that the Mennonite religious experience became increasingly diverse and complex throughout the century. A previous chapter has already reflected on some of the differences that Mennonite pioneers brought with them from Prussia (Flemish and Frisian groups) and how these settlements evolved in various directions as a consequence of internal dynamics, external influences and new arrivals. It would be difficult to continue to trace the lines of development separately in each settlement because many new settlements emerged, each with a distinctive character and history. More and more Mennonites also lived outside the closed settlements on private estates or in urban areas.

The religious situation among Mennonites in Russia in the latter part of the 19th century continued to evolve and change as a result of various factors, both internal and external. It would be myopic to suggest that one group, such as the Mennonite Brethren, was the primary group responding positively to the forces of change whereas others reacted negatively or remained unchanged and merely carried on earlier religious traditions and practices. While in general terms it might be true that some groups reacted more positively than others to religious influences from elsewhere, the whole of Mennonitism changed dramatically. It is difficult to distinguish which levels of change were effected by internal and which by external factors.

The influence of Pietism in particular was widespread. It was by no means restricted in its impact to such groups as the Brethren and the Templers or the Exodus Church, although it may have been most discernable there. Tobias Voth, the first teacher at Ohrloff, undoubtedly had a long-lasting influence in the colonies. Furthermore some of the congregations that belatedly moved from Prussia to Russia had already imbibed Pietism to a significant degree. Among these the Gnadenfeld group was an especially important factor in the religious ferment of the next several decades. The number of splinter groups coming out of the Gnadenfeld Church, however, tends to shift attention away from religious activity elsewhere.[2] Furthermore, Gnadenfeld Pietism was by no means all channelled into the splinter groups.

The Pietist literature likewise exerted a strong influence on religious life in the Mennonite colonies. The writings of Jung-Stilling, especially the novel *Heimweh*, were fairly widely read. There were also the sermons of Ludwig Hofacker and periodicals such as the *Süddeutsche Warte*. Moreover, several personalities had a direct impact on Russian Mennonites. This included more obscure individuals like the Reformed pastor, Johannes Bonekemper from Rohrbach, as well as the more widely known pastor, Eduard Wuest, who is often regarded as the inspiration for the founding of the MB Church and about whom more will be stated below.

Besides the Pietist influence with its roots in Germany, religious activity which had its immediate sources elsewhere was also significant. James Urry has documented the very significant impact of the British and Foreign Bible Society, specifically the activity of John Melville.[3] The distribution of tracts and other Christian literature became a fairly prominent feature in South Russia, some of it coming from Baptists in Germany. Jakob Reimer claimed to have read Anna Judson's biography as early as 1837.[4] By the 1860s the sermons of Charles H. Spurgeon, the great English Baptist preacher, were being read avidly by some Mennonites.[5] Therefore it seems clear that a general religious transformation was underway among the Russian Mennonites. By no means can those who did not join the reform groups simply be defined by their rejection of the forces of religious change.

The first major religious schism to develop in the latter half of the nineteenth century was that which gave rise to the MB Church. The man whom P.M. Friesen puts at the centre of this development was the Lutheran Pietist from Wuerttemberg, Eduard Hugo Otto Wuest.[6] Friesen refers to Wuest as the second reformer of the Mennonite brotherhood, ranking him next to Menno Simons.[7] Although such a claim must be open to reassessment, there is no doubt that Wuest played a crucial role in Mennonite religious life. Wuest came to Neuhoffnung near the Mennonite colonies in 1845 to become pastor of a separatist German Lutheran congregation. This was only about a year after he had experienced a spiritual crisis and conversion in his own life.[8] By the time Wuest came to Russia and preached his inaugural sermon, the news of his dynamic preaching and joyous message of salvation had already spread, even among Mennonites. A number of them were in fact present to hear his first sermon and were duly impressed.[9] Before long he was also invited to speak at special occasions in some Mennonite churches especially at missions festivals in the Gnadenfeld Church. A group of Mennonite "brethren" began meeting for Bible study and prayer on Saturday afternoons and often invited Wuest as special guest at these occasions.

Not too much time elapsed, however, before some of the religious leaders began to feel concerned or threatened by these developments. Wuest was barred from Mennonite pulpits and was not allowed to address the conventicle groups of the brethren. He continued to attend some meetings, but only to answer questions.

Eduard Wuest (1818-1884), Lutheran pastor and pietist revivalist. His work greatly influenced the formation of the Mennonite Brethren Church.

Photo: Mennonite Heritage Centre Archives

Wuest also began experiencing difficulties in his own church, especially because of some who took his doctrine of free grace to such extremes that it led to various disturbances and moral lapses. Undoubtedly Wuest himself was partly responsible for these developments because of his emphasis on free grace. The final years of his ministry were therefore difficult in many ways. Nevertheless, when he died in 1859, he left many admirers who felt orphaned without him, including a number who eventually became founders of the MB Church.

Although, according to Jacob Bekker, the brethren had observed separate communion quietly several times, it was on a November evening in 1859 that the first open, and therefore defiant, separate communion took place.[10] The news of this spread quickly. Elder August Lenzmann of Gnadenfeld felt compelled to take some action, even though the leader of the communion celebration was not a member of his church. The Gnadenfeld members were called before the church council and admonished. This was followed on December 19 and 27 by several stormy brotherhood meetings where Jakob Reimer and Johann Claassen were particularly singled out for severe criticism. Claassen was asked to leave the session to permit more open discussion. As he prepared to leave someone shouted, "Why don't you call on your associates to follow you?" Claassen responded without hesitation, stating, "Well, brethren, whoever is like-minded, come along." About ten individuals joined Claassen and Reimer and made their exit.[11]

The formal secession of the group took place about one week later on January 6, 1860. Abraham Cornelson was asked to prepare a draft document and, after some discussion, eighteen individuals signed it.[12] This marked the formal beginning of the Mennonite Brethren Church.

The document of secession was relatively brief and has been subject to a variety of assessments. It was certainly not intended as a confession of faith but only as a means of focussing the essential concerns of the Brethren. It was highly critical of the moral and spiritual state of Mennonite churches and was all-inclusive in its denunciation of them. It singled out the "satanic" behaviour at the annual festivals *(Jahrmärkten)* and denounced church leaders for their silence and unwillingness to take action. Other issues that received special mention were baptism on confession of faith, communion as a fellowship of believers only, calling of ministers and practice of the ban. Several references signified their basic agreement with Menno Simons on all issues. Such statements, of course, do not in themselves resolve the issue of their essential Mennonitism. In other respects also the document is only one small piece in the puzzle which contributes to our understanding of the MB movement as well as of the Mennonite community from which it seceded.

In the meantime a renewal movement was simultaneously underway in the Old Colony of Chortitza. Despite significant differences, this renewal movement eventually also fed into the early development of the MB Church.[13] It was first centred in Kronsweide and began about 1853. The sermons of Hofacker were especially instrumental in the early stages of the movement. Extremism manifested itself quickly, however, and soon discredited the movement. A new fellowship centre later emerged at Einlage under the leadership of Abraham and Cornelius Unger and Heinrich Neufeld. Bible study sessions were held regularly. There may also already have been some connections with Baptists or with Baptist literature. The formal beginnings as a separate church, however, did not come until some contacts had been made with Molotschna Brethren in June 1861. The first rebaptism of leaders took place on March 11, 1862.

A hectic sequence of events followed in the months after the secession document had been signed by the Brethren in Molotschna. Essentially these involved attempts by the religious authorities *(Älteste)* in concert with civil authorities (especially David Friesen, the *Oberschulze*) to discredit and suppress the movement. On the part of the Brethren the major efforts involved securing recognition as a legitimate Mennonite religious body, a process which proved even more difficult than with the *Kleine Gemeinde* earlier in the century. Johann Claassen was the man of the hour, for he had the necessary ability, determination, experience and the right connections to deal with various bureaucratic and religio-political hindrances that stood in the way of achieving full recognition. This also involved securing the right to establish a new settlement in the Kuban. Claassen made several lengthy trips to St. Petersburg, and barely escaped apprehension by the Mennonite civil authorities. Undoubtedly, the position taken by the Ohrloff Church was a major factor in the eventual success of Claassen's mission. The reasons why Ohrloff refused to cooperate with the elders of the other churches are themselves partly rooted in events of the previous decades, particularly the barley dispute which had brought the power struggle in the colony to a point of crisis.[14] Thus it is impossible at any stage to separate the purely "religious" components from the larger issues of Mennonite society, including its dealings with government agencies.

The Brethren experienced various degrees of hardship and persecution during the early years. Generally the situation was more severe in Chortitza than in Molotschna, but in both colonies individuals experienced severe physical, economic and social hardship because of their action. Several were imprisoned, including Heinrich Huebert on a false charge of having baptized a Russian girl. Abraham Cornelson lost his teaching position. Shopkeepers were subjected to economic ruin when placed under the ban. Marriages of MBs were not recognized for a time and infants were therefore registered under their mother's maiden names. Daily life was often lived under a great deal of harassment and families were frequently torn by the religious strife.

The darkest blot in the early history of the MB Church was undoubtedly the extremism which manifested itself particularly in the period until 1865. It was referred to as the *Fröhliche Richtung* (Exuberant Movement).[15] As previously noted, extremism was already present before 1860 in Wuest's Lutheran congregation as well as in the awakening at Kronsweide. It is clear that from the beginning the worship styles of the Brethren in the Molotschna were much more spontaneous and exuberant than in the churches from which they had seceded. But relatively mild expressions of joy, such as singing lively songs, shouting and clapping, gradually gave way to more and more radical expressions, including leaping, dancing and the sister kiss. The latter practice, according to Bekker, began as a result of the influence of the Molokans.[16] Serious moral lapses occurred with several individuals. In Chortitza a spiritual despotism also developed, particularly involving Gerhard Wieler and Benjamin Bekker who proclaimed themselves apostles and banned those who dared to oppose them, eventually even banning each other.

As Harry Loewen has argued, the extremism of this early period cannot easily be dismissed as a fringe movement,[17] although MBs have sometimes tried to dismiss it in much the same way that earlier Anabaptist historiography dismissed the Muenster episode as not belonging to Anabaptism proper. Although the majority of MBs certainly were not inclined to the extremism manifested in Wieler, Bekker and Bartel and did not endorse the immoral actions of the few, most of the leaders, including Johann Claassen, were partially caught up in the movement. Initial opposition came especially from individuals like Jakob Reimer and Katharina Claassen. Officially the church finally reached a consensus in opposition to the movement as expressed by their actions during the so-called June reforms of 1865. But this was preceded by much soul-searching by most MBs and was not simply the culmination of a struggle between two opposing groups within the church.

The issue continues to raise serious questions. Loewen's assertion that it is "surprising that this movement . . . could find expression among traditionally conservative . . . stiff . . . sober Mennonites"[18] perhaps ironically offers the best explanation for why it happened. It also seems doubtful that there would have been a great deal more sympathy for the Brethren if extremism had not emerged. The central issue was separation, with all that implied. To some degree, ideological dissent might be tolerated, but the creation of new ecclesiastical structures was intolerable. For the religious and civic authorities the fanaticism obviously created a convenient issue to use in opposing the movement. Nevertheless, the movement of exuberance demonstrated serious weaknesses within the Brethren movement, weaknesses that it undoubtedly shared with many other renewal movements which struggle during the initial stages as they move from rejection to a positive formulation of their own identity. In one sense John B. Toews may be right in pointing to the group's premature institutionalization.[19] In another sense it can be argued that the early movement might have fared better if it had become institutionalized more quickly — that it was precisely its dynamic non-creedal character at the beginning that got it into trouble.

The question of baptism became one of the most problematic issues in the MB Church for the rest of the century and beyond. It should be emphasized that although the document of secession contained a statement regarding the Brethren's concern that believers' baptism was not being practised in the Old Church, there was no move toward rebaptism or toward instituting a new mode. The first baptism, which initially was to involve candidates not previously baptized, was performed in Molotschna on September 23, 1860. This became the occasion at which the issue of mode also arose. Bekker very strongly insists that the question of mode or even the awareness of immersion was not present prior to 1860.[20] According to his report, Claassen called Bekker aside prior to the baptism and gave Bekker a booklet which he had received from the Baptists in St. Petersburg. After contemplating the evidence Bekker was convinced. When the church also agreed, Bekker and Bartel first rebaptized each other by immersion, then baptized the other candidates. The other founding members, however, were not immediately rebaptized by the new mode. Claassen was not rebaptized until 1862. Baptism by immersion was not mandatory for at least three years. It must also be remembered that two issues tended to become intertwined in questions regarding rebaptism: the issue of mode and the issue of whether the first baptism had been based on faith. Although discussions concentrated on the former, feelings that the first baptism had not been based on a vital faith were no doubt often present.

Despite Bekker's insistence that the Brethren had not been aware of immersion prior to the summer of 1860, Urry asserts that discussion had taken place before that time.[21] Peter Klassen refutes this as being without factual basis.[22] Although Urry does not cite the actual evidence, he may have based his claim on Jakob Reimer's report that he had read and become acquainted with various groups who baptized by immersion. Reimer also claimed that he had already discussed the issue with his father before his own baptism years earlier.[23] This evidence does cast some doubt on the accuracy of Bekker's recollection of the situation.

The adoption of a new mode of baptism and the frequent contacts with Baptists by the Chortitza Brethren made them particularly vulnerable as they sought to establish their own identity and as others sought to discredit the movement. Urry asserts that the "brethren had now discovered the criterion of differentiation which would give their movement sacramental distinctiveness."[24] This is probably too strong a statement to apply to the group as a whole even though it might apply to a segment in Chortitza. Whatever it meant to the insiders, it is clear that their opponents were quite willing to exploit the issue against the Brethren.

Along with the baptism issue was the matter of the Brethren's close association with German Baptists. Abraham Unger of Chortitza already had contact prior to 1860 with Johann G. Oncken, the founder of the German Baptists in Hamburg. Unger continued to show his strong Baptist leanings in succeeding years. Then, in 1866 when extremism threatened to destroy the church in Chortitza, August Liebig, another Baptist minister, was invited to come and help bring order. Although he was there for only a short period he made a strong impact on the group and showed the Brethren how to conduct their meetings. In 1869 Oncken came to South Russia and ordained Unger as elder and several others as deacons. Further difficulties in the church resulted in a second call to Liebig in 1871 and a period of ministry which no doubt brought in a variety of Baptist practices, including Sunday School and public prayer in Sunday morning worship services. The greatest problem of identity, however, developed when an official of the government came to the colonies in 1873 on matters pertaining to the military draft law and wanted to know what the relationship of the MBs was to the Baptists.[25] One result of this was that the Einlage group led by Unger sent a report and a confession of faith to the government. The confession turned out to be essentially the Hamburg Baptist Confession with a few additional Mennonite distinctives such as nonresistance. As might have been expected, this gave their opponents further signifi-

The Mennonite Brethren and Russian Baptist Churches, which formed as the result of the same influences, frequently baptized in flowing streams. Both practiced immersion baptism. Photo: Mennonite Heritage Centre Archives

cant evidence in their attempt to discredit the Brethren as Menno-nites.

Molotschna Brethren never accepted the confession. Already in 1862 they had indicated their agreement with the Frisian-Flemish confession of 1660 published by the Rudnerweide Mennonite Church in 1853.[26] The issue was cause for a great deal of further activity and concern. In 1880 the government finally issued a formal statement granting the Brethren recognition as Mennonites.[27] This placed them under the same laws as other Mennonites regarding such matters as forestry service as an alternative to military service. The first definitive confession of faith of the MBs was not issued until many years later in 1902.[28]

The major question which historians have debated concerning the origins of the MB Church is the one regarding the primary causative factors which brought about the new movement. Related to that issue is the question of the essence of the new movement and whether or not the goals of the founders could have been realized from within if the Brethren had been more patient.

Religious factors have usually been regarded as the most signifi-cant, especially by MB historians who have relied heavily on P.M. Friesen's interpretation of the renewal movement. The further ques-tion concerning the extent to which the movement was Anabaptist, Pietist or Baptist in essence has been answered in a variety of ways. In the most recent definitive history of the MB Church, John A. Toews states that "the formative influences which converged in the Menno-nite Brethren Church produced a theology that was true to the Anabaptist vision, was permeated by the spirit of Pietism, and also reflected the polity of the Baptists."[29] The emphasis here is clearly on the essence of the movement being Anabaptist. Toews' view also reflects an era of Anabaptist scholarship which still accepted the Bender school's normative and idealistic view of Anabaptism. Furth-ermore, Anabaptism and Pietism were often viewed as quite antithet-ical. Therefore, the more Pietism was regarded as a factor in the birth of the MB movement, the more discredited the movement became.[30] Recent scholarship has often been more sympathetic to Pietism. Consequently it has viewed the MB movement more positively, even though it has recognized that the two movements have common characteristics.[31] The tendency for scholars to allow ideological commitments to govern their interpretation of the events has also increasingly been exposed. Furthermore, the attempt to distinguish between spirit or form (Pietism) and essence or theology (Anabap-tism), or between internal and external or alien factors may be a somewhat arbitrary approach in trying to understand the movement. Among other things, such attempts tend to beg the question of the character of early nineteenth century Mennonitism as a whole in Russia and of its relationship to its sixteenth century Anabaptist origins and the outside influences which may already have significantly altered its character.

What impact the economic and social situation had on the origins of the MB Church is another major question considered by historians. Most often the debate concerns the question: Can the beginnings of the MB Church be positively correlated with the quest of the landless and the economically deprived for a more equitable status in their community? Attempts to document such a correlation have thus far proved unsuccessful, although some have suggested that the question of origins needs to be distinguished from later developments. Peter Klassen states that "the impetus and early direction of the upheaval came from business and intellectual leaders, but as the movement grew, it attracted those who saw in it the prospect of desired reform, whether they were of the landed or landless elements."[32] It is difficult not to postulate that the two crises which climaxed at almost the same time would not have impinged on each other throughout. It is probable, however, that the economic crisis contributed significantly to the general climate of unrest and therefore made a religious schism more likely, even if the lines of religious strife would eventually be drawn quite differently from the lines of economic and social strife.

A very intriguing interpretation of the MB movement has been put forth by James Urry. Urry sees the movement in the context of a much larger process of change that was taking place in Russian and European society in the nineteenth century. The founding Brethren, according to Urry, were essentially liberal-minded individuals, progressive in attitude not only with respect to religion but in all areas of life.[33] The Brethren saw the world as an acceptable place. In this respect they really stood in the tradition of progressive leaders at Ohrloff and other places. Most of the leaders were brought up in an atmosphere of change, improvement and achievement. Therefore, rather than constituting an economically deprived group, Urry argues that they were educated and skilled people, a large number being either merchants or teachers.[34] They were set apart by education, occupation and outlook.[35] Such an interpretation by no means negates religious factors but puts them into a much larger context.

If there is an emerging consensus today it is probably that there was a coincidence of many factors which contributed to the founding of the MB movement. Therefore most historians resist any reductionist interpretations. Contributing factors included the structures of authority in the colonies, particular personalities trying to preserve their own power, kinship connections, rivalries in the community, economic issues, moral corruption and others, although the dominant one may well have been religious. It is necessary to emphasize continuity and evolution to a greater degree. The elements of continuity and change must be seen both in the Brethren movement and in the Mennonite community from which they seceded.[36]

The Mennonite Brethren movement was by no means the only one to emerge in the latter half of the nineteenth century. A number of smaller schisms occurred. The causes for their emergence often at least partially overlapped with those that gave rise to the MB Church. The Jerusalem Friends or Templers originated in 1863. Leadership of the movement also came from the Gnadenfeld Church. Like the MBs, so also the Templer movement received its impulse from Wuerttemberg Pietism, this time a variety which was inspired by a certain Christoph Hoffmann who called for restoration of the temple at Jerusalem. More offensive to many was the Templer's denial of Christ's divinity and their rejection of the ordinances of baptism and the Lord's Supper. Johannes Lange, who studied in Wuerttemberg, brought these ideas back to the Mennonite community. Some of the individuals, like Nikolai Schmidt who later became attracted to the movement, had close connections with a number of the leaders of the MB movement. Sources such as P.M. Friesen and Jakob Bekker make frequent references to Templers. On occasion MBs and Templers even used the same building for worship, although quite reluctantly.[37]

Mennonite historiography has kept the two movements quite separate and perhaps has paid less attention to the Templer movement than it deserves.[38] Are the connections perhaps more significant than Bekker or Friesen were willing to acknowledge? The animosity of the MBs toward the Templers, quite ironically, was occasioned by the same factor which occasioned the Old Church's animosity toward MBs: they were proselytizing among MBs![39]

The Peters Brethren, also called Breadbreakers because of their insistence on breaking the bread at communion, were a third group to emerge from the Gnadenfeld Church. This group represented an extreme literalism and legalism with regard to their understanding of Scripture and its application to daily life. The founder, Hermann Peters, was himself involved in the extremism of the exuberant movement within the MB Church, being noted especially as one who beat the drum at the religious gatherings.[40] The group seceded from the Gnadenfeld Church in 1865-66. Although it existed for a considerable period of time thereafter, it never became very large. A small group moved to the Crimea and eventually to Omsk in Siberia. Some also came to America in 1874.

A much more intriguing religious development occurred under the leadership of Claas Epp, who became the founder of the so-called Exodus Church *(Auszugsgemeinde).* Because of the dramatic and tragic nature of the early history of this movement and because of the availability of many firsthand accounts and other material, scholars have paid considerably more attention to it than to other movements.[41] Once again one of the significant issues raised by the movement is the question of its essential character: Was it Mennonite or was it something else?[42]

Claas Epp was the increasingly eccentric leader of a trek of wagon trains that left European Russia between 1880 and 1884 to make the arduous journey across the desert and mountain ranges to await the return of the Lord which was expected imminently at an appointed place in Central Asia. Looking to the East as a place of refuge or a place where the final eschatological events would transpire was, of course, not unique to Epp and his followers. These ideas were taken from the Pietists, this time especially from the writings of Heinrich Jung-Stilling. The emergence of these ideas must be seen in the context of the political and social turmoil of the eighteenth and nineteenth centuries, especially as symbolized by the French Revolution. The view of the East as a place of refuge had already inspired earlier migrations from South Germany to southern Russia.

Emphasis on a well-defined eschatology appears to have distinguished the Claas Epp movement quite radically from most other religious movements among the Mennonites in Russia. Most of Epp's followers came from Am Trakt, a relatively recent settlement (1854) of immigrants from Prussia. Hence the dynamics of religious and social turmoil were quite different from those which prevailed in the original settlements in the previous decades. Nevertheless, it should be noted that a significant number of Epp's followers also came from the Molotschna.

Furthermore, this religious movement was clearly affected by the new encroachments of the Russian government, particularly those related to compulsory state service. In this respect it needs to be compared more to the mass emigration of Mennonites from Russia to North America in the 1870s. Many studies of the migration have analyzed the religious factors involved, but the migration has not usually been viewed as a religious movement analogous to those which developed into separate denominational structures.

Finally it should be noted that the Exodus movement of the 1880s tends for obvious reasons to draw attention to one personality, that of Claas Epp. This tendency has perhaps distorted the view of the movement somewhat. Other individuals were involved in significant ways at the beginning but a series of power struggles brought Epp to the forefront. It was he who contributed most to a radicalization of the movement. Those who could not agree with Epp left the group. Eventually Epp designated 1889 as the date for the Lord's return and prepared for the final event by dressing in white ascension robes. His followers gathered around him to watch his ascent but, when nothing happened, Epp revised the date, stating that he had misread the clock in his vision. As Epp became more and more radical, various groups of followers deserted him until he was finally left with only a few adherents. The external hardships which the participants experienced and the trauma of spiritual disillusionment are impossible to describe or imagine. Nevertheless, the story is one which needs to be placed alongside others of the nineteenth century and into the context of the larger Mennonite story.

If, as has been suggested, the MB movement can partly be seen as "1525 Revisited," a similar sense of *deja vu* might be experienced as one reviews the early history of the Exodus Church. Is it perhaps "Muenster Revisited?" With respect to nineteenth century Mennonitism, it is difficult to judge how Mennonite the Exodus movement really was. The answer no doubt depends largely on how integral to the movement the person of Claas Epp is seen to be.

The story of the *Kleine Gemeinde*, the origin of which is discussed in a previous chapter, tends to be omitted from discussion of Russian Mennonitism in the middle part of the century. The fact that the *Kleine Gemeinde* remained a relatively small group, did not participate in any significant way on either side of the conflicts of the 1860s and left the Russian scene entirely in the 1870s are all factors that have led to this neglect. The bias of the major Mennonite historian of the period, P.M. Friesen, may also be a factor.[43] Reference has already been made to the prevalent perception of the *Kleine Gemeinde* in the nineteenth century. In a recent study of the period from 1850 to 1875, Delbert Plett continues his attempt to correct the previous historiography and concludes that the "*Kleine Gemeinde* frequently represented the best of biblical Christianity and thus witnessed to a third major alternative within Russian Mennonitism, one which was most faithful to historic Anabaptism."[44] The *Kleine Gemeinde* failed to win many converts from the other Mennonite groups and itself experienced serious tensions within. One further development was the organization of the Krimmer Mennonite Brethren Church in 1869 by a group which had only had a very brief association with the *Kleine Gemeinde*. Both the *Kleine Gemeinde* and the Krimmer Mennonite Brethren migrated to North America in the 1870s and consequently ceased to be significant factors in Russian Mennonitism.

As indicated earlier, the emigration of the 1870s may need to take its place as a religious movement alongside the various other movements of the period. Ostensibly religious factors were very much at issue, whether or not economic and other factors entered in significant ways.[45] Because particular understandings of Mennonitism were at stake, including the issue of nonresistance, it is clear that the character of Russian Mennonitism must have altered substantially after the departure of large groups to North America.

When viewed as a whole the various religious movements between 1850 and 1885 defy any attempt to relate their origins to a specific set of causative factors. There were obviously certain common elements among many of them, such as the impact of various forms of Pietism and the particular structures of authority that Russian Mennonitism had developed. Perhaps our understanding of Russian Mennonitism in the nineteenth century can be enhanced most if scholarship divests itself of various normative assumptions, even as some about sixteenth century Anabaptism have had to be given up.

It must also be emphasized that the majority of Mennonites remained firm in their allegiance to the Old Church for the remainder of the century. Indeed, according to statistics provided by Mannhardt, more than ninety percent of Mennonites belonged to the *Kirchengemeinden* as late as 1887.[46] These were scattered in many congregations which were not structurally connected before 1883. As the mother churches grew in size and as members moved to new settlements, new congregations were formed which were usually at first affiliated with the mother churches but eventually became independent and elected their own elders and ministers. Thus before the end of the century the Chortitza Flemish church gave rise to independent congregations at Bergthal (1840), Fuerstenland (1864), Borozenko (1865), Nikolaifeld (1869), New Chortitza (1872), New York (1889) and Orenburg (1894).

The Molotschna churches likewise generated various independent congregations. During most of the era they were dominated by the Ohrloff-Halbstadt-Neukirch congregation which included many of the influential ministers and teachers. By 1887 this congregation had four parishes, including Ohrloff, Halbstadt, Neukirch and Herzenberg, all served by one elder, Abraham Goerz. The three major divisions of the *Große Gemeinde* continued to exist: the Margenau Church had established an affiliated congregation at Schoensee; the Lichtenau Church had affiliated congregations at Petershagen, Schoenfeld, Rosenhof and Blumenfeld; the Pordenau Church continued as a single congregation. Likewise the Waldheim, Rudnerweide, Alexanderwohl and Gnadenfeld churches each continued to exist as separate congregations.

New congregations were also established in a variety of new settlements including Koeppenthal (1853), the Crimea (1862), Alexanderthal (1862), Zagradovka (1871) and Memrik (1885).

The number of MB congregations was still small in 1885,[47] with two larger congregations at Rueckenau (Molotschna) and Einlage (Chortitza) and smaller congregations in the Kuban, at Friedensfeld and in the Volga and Don River settlements.[48]

The absence of formal structures tying the individual congregations together meant that churches often varied considerably in character and that the role of the elders *(Ältester)* was a very significant one. Some of the elders presided over very large churches; for example, in Chortitza Elder Heinrich Epp presided over a church of about 3000 or more members in the 1880s.[49] These came from sixteen villages and worshipped in four different buildings. Baptisms were usually conducted once a year and communion celebrated twice a year. At these occasions the elder presided. Each congregation also had a number of ministers or teachers *(Prediger, Lehrer)* and deacons. The Chortitza Church alone had twelve ministers and four deacons in its main congregation around 1887. Many congregations held their regular worship services in the village schools. In Nikolaifeld, for example, there were seven such schools in which services were held. This was a very natural arrangement because the schools continued to be the main centres of religious instruction. Sunday schools were not introduced to most of the Mennonite churches until much later.

Among the elders and ministers who exerted the main influence in that period until 1885 were particularly Elder August Lenzmann and Minister Bernhard Harder. Lenzmann, who was elder in the Gnadenfeld Church during the time of several schisms and who became bitterly opposed to the dissidents, undoubtedly made a major contribution to the life of that church. It was he who baptized

Bernhard Harder (1832-1884), poet, teacher, minister, who promoted reform in the Mennonite community, and his second wife Helena (nee Ewert).

Photo: Mennonite Heritage Centre Archives

Heinrich Dirks (1860) who later became the pioneer Russian missionary and became elder of his home congregation in 1881. Lenzmann rejected many of the Brethren's accusations against the Mennonite Church and provided a perspective which helps correct interpretations communicated by Brethren documents.

Bernhard Harder is characterized by Cornelius Krahn as a man who "did more than anyone else during the second half of the past century to revive the spiritual life of the Mennonites in Russia."[50] Ordained as a minister by the Ohrloff-Halbstadt church in 1860, Harder not only became a gifted preacher and orator but also wrote many poems and songs which were later collected and published by several of his sons. Harder disliked the formalism which characterized the church and was the first to break the tradition of reading sermons. As an admirer of Wuest and himself an itinerant evangelist in later years, he had much in common with the Brethren; nevertheless he refused to join them.

Minister Franz Isaak of the Ohrloff-Petershagen Church, author of *Die Molotschnaer Mennoniten*, devoted much of his energy to creating a mood of tolerance for the separated groups, helping the landless and making representations to the government during the 1870s when exemption from military service was being threatened. Krahn characterizes him as championing "an enlightened, educated and democratic Mennonitism in Russia."[51]

By 1880 the Mennonite religious situation was very complex. While Mennonitism was already polymorphic at the beginning of its

Russian experience, it became even more so as the century progressed. The Old Church of 1850 and the *Kirchengemeinden* of 1880 did not closely resemble the Anabaptism of 1525 or 1536, but neither did the *Kleine Gemeinde* or the MB Church at any stage of their Russian experience. Each might legitimately make certain claims of being the true carriers of the Mennonite religious heritage, but each had been transformed in various ways by forces of which they were scarcely aware and over which they had little control.

The latter decades of the nineteenth century continued to bring further profound changes to the remaining Mennonite communities in Russia, even if the outward manifestations were usually not as dramatic or perceptible as in the early years. Much more scholarly work still needs to be done on this era, especially in the area of church developments.

A number of important structural changes took place in church life after 1860. The *Kirchenkonvent,* an organization of church leaders *(Älteste* and *Lehrer),* never again functioned or tried to function in the way it had in 1860. The fledgling MB Church borrowed a number of practices for its polity from the Baptists while continuing to ward off accusations that it was more Baptist than Mennonite. Records of brotherhood meetings were kept and strict rules of parliamentary procedure were adopted. The various MB churches were organized into a conference *(Bundeskonferenz)* in 1872, the first of the Russian Mennonite groups to do so.

Eleven years later, in 1883, the earlier *Kirchenkonvent* was essentially transformed into a General Conference of Mennonite Churches in Russia ([*Allgemeine*] *Bundeskonferenz der Mennonitengemeinden in Rußland* — hereafter MG).[52] The formation of this conference was preceded by meetings of elders in 1879, where issues relating to forestry service and education were discussed, and a meeting in 1882 which formally decided to create a conference of *Älteste* (elders) and *Lehrer* (teachers or ministers).[53] The theme of the first conference sessions in 1883 in Halbstadt was based on I Thessalonians 5:12-15; the motto proclaimed, "In essentials unity; in nonessentials liberty; and in all things charity." The conference functioned without a constitution and continued as a meeting of elders and ministers *(Lehrstandt)* until early in the next century and was usually referred to as *Allgemeine (Bundes) Konferenz der Vertreter sämtlicher Mennonitengemeinden Rußlands.* In 1906, however, the question was raised whether the Conference could legitimately be called *Allgemein* (general) since the MB Church was not invited.[54] It was decided that henceforth MB representatives should also be invited and that the name should be retained, especially because many concerns such as forestry service and education were common to both groups. However, no concrete action in this regard took place until 1910.

In most respects the two conferences and their congregations were probably very similar in terms of the issues they dealt with and in their religious outlook. However, MG churches tended to have more diversity than MB churches because of the more centralized polity of the latter. The number of churches, the total membership and the geographical distribution of the Mennonite settlements had, of course, increased dramatically by 1914. Approximately forty daughter settlements had been created by 1910, most in European Russia but some in areas beyond. P. M. Friesen estimated the number of MG congregations between 55 and 60 in 1910 and the number of MB congregations between 35 and 40.[55] Many of these had affiliate congregations. The membership of the respective conferences in 1908 was about 26,500 and 4,900.[56] Ministers were not salaried except for itinerant ministers who received small allowances. The

A group of Mennonite men caring for wounded soldiers during the Russo-Japanese War, 1904-1905. One of the main tasks of the Bundeskonferenz, organized in 1882, was to supervise the alternative service program.

Photo: Mennonite Heritage Centre Archives

167

*Heinrich Dirks (1842-1915), first Men-
nonite missionary from Russia to serve
abroad. After a decade in Sumatra, he
returned to Gnadenfeld and became
an important church leader.*

itinerant ministry *(Reisepredigt)* was formally established in the MB
Church at its first General Conference in 1872 and was likewise on
the agenda of the first MG General Conference in 1883. For both
conferences this ministry became an important vehicle for unity.
Detailed reports of the *Reiseprediger's* work were given regularly at
the annual conventions.

Involvement in home and foreign missions was always a major
concern for both conferences.[57] The success of evangelization
among the Russians and the continued "sheep-stealing" from the
MGs created particular difficulties for the MBs. Each conference had
its great pioneer in foreign missions. Heinrich Dirks was the first of
the Russian Mennonites to accept a foreign missions assignment.
Interestingly, as indicated above, he was a member of the Gnadenfeld Church. He left for Sumatra in 1869. The pioneer MB missionaries were the Abraham Friesens who began work in India in 1890.
Detailed reports on mission work were usually given at annual
conventions. Even after his return from Sumatra Heinrich Dirks
continued to represent the cause of missions in the MG churches.

Lay ministry continued to be the norm among all the Mennonite
churches in Russia. This system had advantages as well as disadvan-
tages. Obviously the lack of preparation and training of lay ministers
created serious difficulties. Although the amount of formal training
increased over the years, many ministers lacked the kind of training
that was needed, especially as the educational level of Mennonites as
a whole improved. Consequently, as the century drew to a close,

more and more of the lay ministers were teachers by vocation, whereas in earlier years most of them had come from the wealthier landowners. An increasing number of ministers received some theological education, especially in several European schools. P.M. Friesen assessed the general educational level of an estimated 500 ministers in 1910 and concluded that approximately one-third (160-170) had some kind of theological training. Yet only about 40 of these had seminary-level training.[58] N.J. Klassen compiled a list of eleven theologians and ministers who had received university or seminary education.[59] He indicates that the favourite schools for Mennonites of Russia were the University of Basel, the Evangelical Seminary of Basel, the Barmen Theological Seminary, the Hamburg Baptist Seminary and the Seminary at Neukirchen (Moers).[60] This list, of course, does not include Bible schools such as St. Chrischona.

Many of the ministers who were self-educated read as widely as could be expected and often served their congregations remarkably well. Those who received theological training often brought back emphases which were not necessarily in keeping with Anabaptist-Mennonite theology. As early as the 1880s, many leaders recognized the need for a Mennonite seminary in Russia. Repeatedly this issue appeared on the agenda of the conventions of the MG churches. However, a variety of concerns prevented them from coming to a consensus on this issue; or, when consensus was reached, government restrictions barred the way. To some extent, Bible courses served to fill the vacuum. Also, Bible conferences became very regular events, first in the MB churches (Rueckenau 1875); then in the MG congregations or even as inter-Mennonite events. P.M. Friesen reported that to his knowledge all Molotschna Mennonite congregations had regular Bible conferences in 1910.[61] Speakers from outside the Mennonite community were frequently invited, among them Friedrich W. Baedeker, Jacob Vetter and Ernest Stroeter. Through Baedeker, Stroeter and others, the Plymouth Brethren influence was spread among the Mennonites, especially among the MBs.[62] One of Baedeker's converts was Jakob W. Reimer who preached the dispensationalist message in many areas. Contacts with the Blankenburg Conference in Germany and the St. Chrischona Bible School in Switzerland, both Plymouth Brethren institutions, were frequent. The MG Conference, on the recommendation of Heinrichs Dirks, also approved and gave financial support for the training of missionary candidates at St. Chrischona.[63]

Another issue to which the Mennonites devoted considerable energy was that of social welfare.[64]Among their various welfare institutions were hospitals, a mental health institution, a school for mutes, an orphanage and a deaconess home. While most were not begun as conference projects, they nevertheless testify to some continuity with the sixteenth-century Anabaptist concern for community welfare and mutual aid.[65] Not only did Mennonites provide for their own needy but they also helped victims of famine and war elsewhere.[66]

During the decades between 1885 and 1915, a number of new leaders emerged who had a very significant influence on religious life during that period. Abraham Goerz became elder of the Ohrloff-Halbstadt-Neukirchen church in 1876. By then he was already influential, representing the Mennonites in negotiations with General von Totleben and repeatedly travelling to St. Petersburg on behalf of Mennonites. Later he served on the Molotschna *Kirchenkonvent,* was very active in concerns related to education and also served on the *Kommission für Kirchenangelegenheiten.* Unfortunately, during his period as elder, the church experienced severe tensions and eventually divided into three independent congregations.[67]

Heinrich Dirks, already referred to above, returned from his mission assignment in 1881 to serve as elder in his home congregation of Gnadenfeld.[68] In addition to representing missions and being active as an evangelist, Dirks was very influential among Russian Mennonites as a whole. From 1903 to 1910 he edited the *Mennonitisches Jahrbuch* which carried important articles and information relating to Russian Mennonites. He also published a number of monographs such as *Das Reich Gottes im Lichte der Gleichnisse in Ev. Matth. und Ev. Marci Kap. 4, v. 26-29* (Gnadenfeld, 1892) and *Taufe, Gemeindebeschaffenheit und Abendmahl* (Gross-Tokmak, 1904). Dirks' writings give some indication of the extent of theological awareness among leading Mennonites in Russia.

Another leader among Mennonites was David H. Epp.[69] Besides serving as elder of the Chortitza Mennonite Church for a number of years, Epp was editor with Heinrich A. Ediger of the *Botschafter,* the influential periodical of the MGs from 1905-1914. He also wrote a number of books, including *Die Chortitzer Mennoniten* (1889) for the centennial of the Chortitza Colony, and he served as chairman of the *Kommission für Kirchenangelegenheiten* during the critical years after 1910.

Among MBs, Abraham and Jakob Kroeker (cousins) held a somewhat analogous role as co-founders and editors of the *Friedensstimme,* which was begun in 1903 and continued publication until the outbreak of World War I and for a short period thereafter.[70] The

pensational eschatology. At one point Reimer faced the threat of excommunication from his own church because of his position on open communion. The real founders of the *Allianz Gemeinde,* or Evangelical Mennonite Brethren, as it came to be known, were Peter Schmidt and Abraham Nachtigal. In addition to practising open communion, the church accepted members without regard to mode of baptism and created a somewhat different type of church polity. A similar church, calling itself the Evangelical Mennonite Church, was founded under the leadership of Franz Martens in Altonau, Zagradovka in 1907.[77] The impact of this movement as a whole probably helped to soften relationships between MBs and MGs.

The decade after 1905 was very significant for inter-Mennonite relations, but the factors that impinged on their relationships were often quite different from those of the previous era. Earlier it was particularly the introduction of forestry service and the issue of education which created a need for inter-Mennonite dialogue. The new developments in the Russian state, however, produced further significant changes not only for the Mennonites but also for other religious groups. Early in 1905 a conference of ministers of the Russian government began to consider the introduction of freedom of religion in Russia.[78] On April 17 a new law "On the Establishment of the Principles of Religious Tolerance" was proclaimed. This law partly removed the privileged status of the Russian Orthodox Church. For the first time it became legal to leave the Orthodox Church. This sensitive issue had major implications, especially for the activity of the MB Church which was often accused of "propagandizing." In an 1894 decree the government had tried to restrict the *Stundists* in particular by forbidding them to meet.[79] They were often seen as the most dangerous to the Russian state and church. This 1894 decree was abolished in 1905. Hence, the period from about 1905 to 1909 was a period of tremendous growth for the various evangelical sects.

The newly acquired freedom, however, was very temporary. As early as 1906 some new restrictions were introduced and by 1909 the reactionaries regained the upper hand.[80] In May 1910 new regulations were imposed to try to halt the propagandizing efforts of the sects. Government permission had to be secured for holding church conferences and government approval obtained for the programs and participants. Then on October 4, 1910, a circular "On the Order for Sectarian Meetings" went even further by requiring that every meeting, not only worship services, needed to be approved and police agents had to be present, even at prayer meetings.[81] The problem for Russian Baptists and evangelical sects was compounded by the fact that they were generally considered pacifists and therefore traitors to the country.[82]

Throughout this period Mennonites were very concerned about the preservation of their own religious freedom. Their status under the law was a confusing one. Were they a sect or were they a "confession" like other mainstream religious groups, including Lutherans and Roman Catholics? If the latter was true, then they would be less likely to experience the hostility of the government and the Orthodox Church. Mennonites had one representative, Herman Bergmann, in the third Duma (1907-1912), and later a second, Peter Schroeder, in the fourth Duma (1912-1917).[83] Bergmann regularly brought back information on developments in governmental affairs. This information usually appeared in the Mennonite press *(Botschafter* and *Friedensstimme)*. Letters of concern were also published regularly.[84] Bergmann was expected to speak for the Mennonite people to make sure their religious privileges were protected. Already in 1906 a delegation had been appointed to go to St. Petersburg, but circumstances were constantly changing and nothing very concrete was accomplished. A conference of church leaders from all three Mennonite groups was held in Alexanderwohl on February 7, 1908. Concern was expressed that under the new legislation Mennonites were designated as a sect whereas in the earlier code of laws they had been listed together with other Protestant groups. With regard to propagandizing, the conference stated that Mennonites intended to preach the gospel to all nations. They promised, however, to "abstain from any active propaganda among members of other Christian denominations."[85] An explanatory statement to the government gave a detailed defense of why Mennonites should be considered a confession rather than a sect. The conference also elaborated on the nature of church leadership among Mennonites and further clarified their position in regard to religious propaganda. In 1909 the General Conference decided to submit to the new government regulations concerning the reporting of church activities and to seek government permission for the next convention.[86]

The 1910 General Conference was something of a landmark in terms of cooperation between the MG and MB conferences, although external pressures rather than internal factors were most determinative in bringing about this event. The 1906 MG Conference had decided that henceforth MBs should also be invited, but no significant steps in that direction had been taken in subsequent years. In 1910, however, specific action was taken to ensure MB participation. This conference was also the first one to come fully under the new government regulations requiring approval of the program and participants. The major agenda at the conference concerned the new government legislation. The conference expressed strong concern about various articles which placed Mennonites in an unfavourable position along with the sects. This legislation was regarded as a violation of the privileges granted by Emperor Paul in 1800.[87] A copy of the Charter of Privileges of 1800 was sent to the Minister of the Interior. A church commission was also established to continue negotiations with the government.

Despite the difficult circumstances under which the 1910 conference convened, P.M. Friesen regarded it as an historic occasion:

> Thereby both groups have finally, in the fifty-first year of the existence of the M.B. Church — in a solemn and formal way — each recognized the other as a "Christian Mennonite Church" on one and the same basic confession, especially in the form of the general Mennonite catechism . . . and one and the same governmental legal status. This transpired openly before the authorities and the entire Russian Mennonite brotherhood. More than that, according to the testimony of three prominent "brethren," even the conservative representatives of the M.B. Church have felt at ease, and have found "believers" and brothers in Christ among the officiating Mennonite leaders (elders and ministers). They gathered this from their words and from their exchange with them! In the joint sessions . . . no quarrel or difference of opinion between the two main groups . . . came to the fore. On one lively-debated issue (dramatic presentations . . .), the representatives of both groups (whether present or absent — the latter as partly under indirect attack) were found on either side of the question. That was the form and the spirit of the "General Mennonite Conference" of 1910, and its consequence is obvious. And all this happened in spite of those things which need to be narrated regarding the previously transpired events which threatened the unity of both church groups.[88]

One-third of the delegates at this convention were MBs.

Friesen's optimism was later to be dashed, however. By 1914 significant further steps had been taken to incorporate Russian Mennonites under one common constitution. The earlier *Glaubens-kommission* had been changed in 1912 to *Kommission für Kirch-liche Angelegenheiten der Mennoniten Rußlands* (KfK).[89] Until 1914 very little progress had been made in negotiations with the government. David H. Epp of the MG provided much of the leadership during these difficult years. As editor of the *Botschafter* he frequently argued that Mennonites had every right to be incorporated as a recognized confession.[90] Early in 1914 a vigorous debate began regarding the incorporation of all Mennonites under one constitution and on the question of whether Mennonites were a sect or a confession.[91] The government appeared determined to classify all Mennonites as a sect. It was clear that MBs were a particular liability to the other Mennonites in their efforts to change the government's opinion. The draft constitution prepared by the KfK was the topic of intense discussion in various churches and meetings.[92] Individual churches were to discuss the various articles at brotherhood meetings and bring their recommendations to the August 1914 General Conference.

It soon became evident that all was not well. The "propagandistic spirit" of the MB Church was very much resented. The Chortitza Mennonites in particular did not want to be classified with MBs in any government legislation. Individual churches in various areas responded with considerable hesitation about uniting with MBs in this venture. Repeatedly concerns were expressed regarding the issues of baptism, communion and intermarriage. One church stated that it favoured uniting with the MB Church on condition that some of the grievances would be resolved, including a cessation of propaganda not only in the state church but also in the churches with which MBs intended to unite. If the Mennonite Conference was good enough for MBs to join, then why did MBs continue to proselytize among MGs?[93] Although MB membership was still small in comparison to MG membership, the percentage of MBs had increased significantly since the 1880s, from about nine percent to at least 16 percent of the total.[94] Thus MBs clearly continued to be a serious threat to the other churches.

For P.M. Friesen these events proved to be the most deeply disturbing of his life.[95] Earlier he often had been severely critical of the narrowness of MBs; now he was equally critical of the other side. The realization of his dream of an ecumenical "Old-Evangelical Mennonite Brotherhood in Russia" seemed more remote than ever.

The MB leaders as a whole were deeply worried that their church would be the object of increasing intolerance and might lose its privileges. A special statement was therefore prepared for submission to the authorities. The statement minimized the differences between the two major Mennonite bodies and emphasized historical continuity. Another argument stated that it would be more accurate simply to characterize the one group as "moderate" and the other as "severe" with regard to the practise of church discipline, much like earlier groups among the Mennonites.[96] The basis for separation in 1860, it contended, had not been theological.

P.M. Friesen did not realize that the Mennonites in Russia stood on the verge of another crisis which would change the structure and experience of Mennonitism much more fundamentally than anything he had experienced or could have envisioned. War broke out in the summer of 1914. The General Conference which had been scheduled for August of that year had to be cancelled. New issues imposed themselves on the Mennonite agenda. Nevertheless there were further attempts by the two groups to clarify their relationships to each other. Abraham H. Unruh was present at a meeting just before the October Revolution of 1917. His perception was that "there was not a trace of strife between the representatives of the various churches. The time was ripe to arrive at peace with one another."[97]

By late 1917 it was clear that an era of profound but gradual change was giving way to a new era of traumatic transformation and upheaval. The change and turmoil would be much more drastic than the Mennonites had ever known. In many ways P.M. Friesen's life symbolized the era that was coming to an end. He was born in 1849 at the beginning of the stormy years which gave birth to the MB Church; he joined the MB Church immediately after the period of excesses; his ministry spanned the decades when many sought to heal the wounds of the secession; and he died in 1914, at the close of an era — the close of an era not only for his people but also for the fatherland which he loved so much.

Notes

1. James Urry, "The Closed and the Open: Social and Religious Change amongst the Mennonites in Russia (1789-1889)" (D.Phil. dissertation, Oxford University, 1978).

2. Ibid., 311-12.

3. James Urry, "John Melville and the Mennonites: A British Evangelist in South Russia, 1837-ca. 1875," *Mennonite Quarterly Review* 54 (October 1980): 305-322.

4. Peter M. Friesen, *The Mennonite Brotherhood in Russia (1789-1910)*, translated from the German (Fresno, California: Board of Christian Literature, General Conference of Mennonite Brethren Churches, 1978), 286.

5. Ibid., 538.

6. Although Wuest's overwhelming impact cannot be denied, it should be noted, as John B. Toews indicates, that Wuest was "something of a latecomer to the scene." John B. Toews, "The Russian Origin of the Mennonite Brethren: Some Observations," in *Pilgrims and Strangers: Essays in Mennonite Brethren History*, ed. Paul Toews (Fresno, California: Center for Mennonite Brethren Studies, 1977), 94.

7. Ibid., 211.

8. Abraham Jakob Kroeker, *Pfarrer Eduard Wuest: Der große Erweckungsprediger in den deutschen Kolonien Südrußlands* (Leipzig: H.G. Wallmann, 1903). See also Victor G. Doerksen, "Kirchliche Verwüstung? Eduard Otto Wuest in Wuerttemberg 1844/45," paper presented at the Symposium on Russian Mennonite History, Winnipeg, Manitoba, November 11-12, 1977.

9. The sermon is published in Friesen, *Mennonite Brotherhood*, 213-223.

10. Jacob P. Bekker, *Origin of the Mennonite Brethren Church*, translated from the German by D.E. Pauls and A.E. Janzen (Hillsboro, Kansas: Mennonite Brethren Historical Society of the Midwest, 1973), 39.

11. Ibid., 40; Friesen, *Mennonite Brotherhood*, 229.

12. The original document of secession has been published in German as well as in English translation by a number of authors. See Friesen, *Mennonite Brotherhood*, 213-223. For the German see Franz Isaak, *Die Molotschnaer Mennoniten: Ein Beitrag zur Geschichte derselben* (Halbstadt, Taurien: H.J. Braun, 1908), 174-76.

13. See Friesen, *Mennonite Brotherhood*, 280-324.

14. See Urry, "The Closed and the Open," 43-45; Isaak, *Molotschnaer Mennoniten*, 123-155.

15. For a recent study of this crisis see Harry Loewen, "Echoes of Drumbeats: The Movement of Exuberance among the Mennonite Brethren," *Journal of Mennonite Studies* 3 (1985): 118-127.

16. Bekker, *Origin of the Mennonite Brethren Church*, 97.

17. Loewen, "Echoes of Drumbeats," 124.

18. Ibid., 121.

19. John B. Toews, "Russian Origin," 96-97.

20. Bekker, *Origin*, 70ff.

21. Urry, "The Closed and the Open," 550.

22. Peter J. Klassen, "The Historiography of the Birth of the Mennonite Brethren," in *P.M. Friesen and His History: Understanding Mennonite Brethren Beginnings*, ed. Abraham Friesen (Fresno, California: Center for Mennonite Brethren Studies, 1979), 124.

23. Friesen, *Mennonite Brotherhood*, 286ff.

24. Urry, "The Closed and the Open," 551.

25. Friesen, *Mennonite Brotherhood*, 478f.

26. Ibid., 254.

27. Ibid., 480f.

28. On the development of MB theology, see in particular the study by Abram

J. Klassen, "The Roots and Development of Mennonite Brethren Theology to 1914" (M.A. thesis, Wheaton College, 1966).

29. John A. Toews, *A History of the Mennonite Brethren Church: Pilgrims and Pioneers*, ed. A.J. Klassen (Fresno, California: Board of Christian Literature, General Conference of Mennonite Brethren Churches, 1975), 367.

30. See especially Robert Friedmann, *Mennonite Piety through the Centuries: Its Genius and its Literature* (Goshen, Indiana: The Mennonite Historical Society, 1949).

31. Cornelius J. Dyck states, "Twentieth century Mennonite historiography has made Dutch Anabaptism and Pietism too antithetical. . . ." See Cornelius J. Dyck, "1525 Revisited? A Comparison of Anabaptist and Mennonite Brethren Origins," in *Pilgrims and Strangers*, 69.

32. Klassen, "Historiography," 119.

33. Urry, "The Closed and the Open," 576-86.

34. Ibid., 569.

35. Ibid., 502.

36. John B. Toews, "Russian Origin," 95.

37. Bekker, *Origin of the Mennonite Brethren Church*, 157.

38. Victor Doerksen, "Mennonite Templers in Russia," *Journal of Mennonite Studies* 3 (1985): 132. For more details concerning the movement as well as a number of documents see Isaak, *Die Molotschnaer Mennoniten*, 207-266.

39. Bekker, *Origin*, 157.

40. Friesen, *Mennonite Brotherhood*, 278.

41. See especially the monograph by Fred Belk, *The Great Trek of the Russian Mennonites to Central Asia, 1880-1884* (Scottdale, Pennsylvania: Herald Press, 1976). A vivid firsthand account is given by Franz Bartsch, *Unser Auszug nach Mittelasien* (Halbstadt: H.J. Braun, 1907).

42. See Waldemar Janzen, "The Great Trek: Episode or Paradigm," *Mennonite Quarterly Review* 51 (April 1977): 127-139. See also my response, "Claas Epp and the Great Trek Reconsidered," *Journal of Mennonite Studies* 3 (1985): 138-147.

43. Friesen, *Mennonite Brotherhood*, 457.

44. Delbert Plett, *Storm and Triumph: The Mennonite Kleine Gemeinde (1850-1875)* (Steinbach, Manitoba: D.F.P. Publications, 1986), 334.

45. See for example the study by Gustav E. Reimer and G.R. Gaeddert, *Exiled by the Czar: Cornelius Jansen and the Great Mennonite Migration, 1874* (Newton, Kansas: Mennonite Publication Office, 1956). An interesting account by one of the leaders which focuses on the religious motivation is given by Gerhard Wiebe, *Causes and History of the Emigration of the Mennonites from Russia to America*, translated from the German by Helen Janzen (Winnipeg, Manitoba: Manitoba Mennonite Historical Society, 1981).

46. For a listing of congregations, memberships, elders, etc. see H.G. Mannhardt, *Jahrbuch der altevangelischen oder Mennoniten Gemeinde* (Danzig: Selbstverlag, 1888), 64-78. The listing is not entirely complete. Also, it is not clear from which year the membership statistics are taken, although most are probably from 1887. Some comparisons can be made, for example, with statistics provided for MB congregations by P.M. Friesen, *Mennonite Brotherhood*, 477-514 for the year 1885.

47. For a comprehensive table listing the various settlements, their locations, year of founding, number of villages, area and population see C. Henry Smith, *Story of the Mennonites*, 5th ed., rev. Cornelius Krahn (Newton, Kansas: Faith and Life Press, 1981), 349-52.

48. P.M. Friesen provides a summary of the churches in each of the settlements in *Mennonite Brotherhood*, 477-514.

49. Mannhardt, *Jahrbuch*, 65-66.

50. *Mennonite Encyclopedia*, s.v. "Harder, Bernhard;" Friesen, *Mennonite Brotherhood*, 945-49.

51. *Mennonite Encyclopedia*, s.v. "Isaak, Franz."

52. The resolutions of these conferences have been published by Heinrich Ediger, ed., *Beschlüsse der von den geistlichen und anderen Vertretern der Mennonitengemeinden Rußlands abgehaltenen Konferenzen für die Jahre 1879 bis 1913* (Berdjansk: Verlag von Heinrich Ediger, 1914). Unfortunately the minutes of the Mennonite Brethren Conference have been lost with only a few exceptions.

53. Ediger, ed., *Beschlüsse*, 6.

54. Ibid., 115.

55. Friesen, *Mennonite Brotherhood*, 926.

56. Martin B. Fast, *Meine Reise nach Rußland und zurück* (Scottdale, Pennsylvania: By the author, 1910), 216-235. The source of Fast's statistics are not indicated but they appear to be quite reliable when compared to P.M. Friesen's statistics for 1910. They are helpful also because they provide a more detailed basis for comparisons of the two Mennonite conferences in various areas and in Russia as a whole.

57. Ibid., 659-688. See also the many references in *Beschlüsse* and various articles and reports in the *Botschafter* and *Friedensstimme*.

58. Ibid., 927.

59. N.J. Klassen, "Mennonite Intelligentsia in Russia," *Mennonite Life* 24 (April 1969): 59.

60. Ibid., 54.

61. Friesen, *Mennonite Brotherhood*, 968f.

62. On Stroeter see e.g., Waldemar Gutsche, *Westliche Quellen des russischen Stundismus* (Kassel: J. G. Oncken Verlag, 1956), 60.

63. Ediger, ed., *Beschlüsse*, 53.

64. Friesen, *Mennonite Brotherhood*, 809-831.

65. For a brief evaluation see John B. Toews, *Czars, Soviets and Mennonites* (Newton, Kansas: Faith and Life Press, 1982), 27-30.

66. Friesen, *Mennonite Brotherhood*, 829f.

67. Ibid., 959.

68. Ibid., 659-73; *Mennonite Encyclopedia*, s.v. "Dirks, Heinrich."

69. *Mennonite Encyclopedia*, s.v. "Epp, David Heinrich."

70. *Mennonite Encyclopedia*, s.v. "Kroeker, Abraham Jakob."

71. Franz C. Thiessen, *P.M. Friesen 1849-1914: Personal Recollections* (Winnipeg, Manitoba: Board of Christian Literature, General Conference of Mennonite Brethren Churches, 1974); *Mennonite Encyclopedia*, s.v. "Friesen, Peter Martin."

72. John B. Toews, "Brethren and Old Church Relations in Pre-World War I

Russia: Setting the Stage for Canada," *Journal of Mennonite Studies* 2 (1984): 42-59.

73. Friesen, *Mennonite Brotherhood*, 491-92.

74. Anonymous letter in *Zionsbote*, March 5, 1913, 6.

75. Heinrich Dirks, "Die Mennoniten in Rußland," *Mennonitisches Jahrbuch* (1903): 12-15.

76. Heinrich Dirks, "Fortsetzung der Geschichte des Mennonitenvölkleins in Rußland im Jahre 1905," *Mennonitisches Jahrbuch* (1905/06): 20.

77. John A. Toews, *A History of the Mennonite Brethren Church*, 103f.

78. For a brief review of church and state developments during this period see Gerhard Simon, *Church, State and Opposition in the U.S.S.R.*, translated from German by Kathleen Matchett (London: C. Hurst & Company, 1974), 1-40.

79. Ibid., 31.

80. Walter Sawatsky, *Soviet Evangelicals since World War II* (Kitchener, Ontario: Herald Press, 1981), 36.

81. Ibid.

82. Simon, *Church, State and Opposition*, 37.

83. David G. Rempel, "The Mennonite Commonwealth in Russia: A Sketch of its Founding and Endurance, 1789-1919," *Mennonite Quarterly Review* 48 (January 1974): 53.

84. See e.g., *Zionsbote*, June 7, 1905, 6; September 1, 1909, 4.

85. Friesen, *Mennonite Brotherhood*, 630.

86. Ediger, ed., *Beschlüsse*, 128.

87. Friesen, *Mennonite Brotherhood*, 637.

88. Ibid., 649.

89. Ediger, ed., *Beschlüsse*, 150.

90. *Botschafter*, April 11, 1914, 4; April 18, 1914, 3; April 22, 1914, 3.

91. Almost every issue of the *Botschafter* between April and July carried items on this issue.

92. The draft constitution was published in the *Friedensstimme* as well as the *Botschafter*. See *Friedensstimme*, May 21, 1914, 3-4.

93. *Botschafter*, July 11, 1914, 3.

94. Martin B. Fast, *Meine Reise*, 216-35.

95. Peter M. Friesen, *Konfession oder Sekte?* (Halbstadt: Raduga, 1914), 6ff.

96. Abraham H. Unruh, *Die Geschichte der Mennoniten-Brüdergemeinde 1860-1954* (Hillsboro, Kansas: The General Conference of the Mennonite Brethren Church of North America, 1955), 302.

97. Ibid., 314.

Landlessness in the Old Colony: The *Judenplan* Experiment 1850-1880

Harvey L. Dyck

In 1851 and 1852 some fifty Russian Mennonite landless families from the Chortitza colonies accepted a government offer to settle in a Jewish agricultural settlement as "village overseers" and "model farmers."[1] Thus began one of the most unusual colonization ventures in Russian Mennonite history. Called the *Judenplan,* the six-village settlement was located about a hundred kilometres west of the Mennonite Old Colony on an attractive, fertile, virgin steppeland about ten kilometres square. The *Judenplan* was an exception to the pattern of Mennonites settling together in homogeneous religious-ethnic communities. Yet the experiment illuminates the very same dilemmas and forces that prompted other Russian Mennonite colonization initiatives and should be viewed in this wider setting.

Much of Imperial Russian Mennonite economic and social history revolved around the ownership and use of land. Land was the principal source of livelihood and of status. Possession of land became a measure of personal worth, landlessness a mark of social inferiority. Land acquisition and regulation were also the main raison d'etre of Mennonite village and settlement institutions. From 1789 to 1914 repeated colonization initiatives emerged in response to the urgent needs of a rapidly growing Mennonite population. The resulting ventures profoundly shaped Mennonite society. They also affected the relations of Mennonites to their Ukrainian and Russian peasant neighbours and to the larger Imperial Russian world. It is no exaggeration to say that colonization along the vast but receding grassland steppe frontiers of Imperial Russia became a dominant, underlying theme in Imperial Russian Mennonite history.

However, Mennonite colonization did not evolve without interruptions or problems. Multi-faceted, marked by contention, it passed through three quite distinct phases. From 1789 to the 1840s, virgin crown lands were granted by the Imperial government to Mennonite immigrants from the Vistula Lowlands who established the "mother settlements" of Chortitza and Molotschna and the first "daughter settlement" of Bergthal. By the late 1840s, with some seventy villages and 170,000 dessiatins of land (the equivalent of an area almost fifty kilometres square), these communities had a population of around 25,000.

This first state-dominated phase of Mennonite colonization was followed in the 1850s and 1860s by two decades of uncertainty, experimentation and crisis resulting from widespread landlessness. The *Judenplan* story fits into this age of troubled transition. With crown land in New Russia now scarce and the Imperial government under sharp attack for unduly favouring its German-speaking population, Mennonites fought over a broad spectrum of approaches to the landless question. At one extreme was the notion of directing part of the landless people permanently into the crafts and trades while reducing others to the status of a kind of rural proletariat working for their landed co-religionists. At the other extreme was the socially radical idea of redistributing all lands equally among landed and landless Mennonites families. Finally, in 1866, state arbitration of the landless dispute led to a compromise: acceptance of the principle that the community, using public resources, had a corporate responsibility to provide its members with access to land.[2] Thereafter social tensions gradually lessened, controversy tailed off and a new era of dynamic colonization which lasted until 1914 dawned.

This third period, which might be termed the "daughter colony" movement, saw Chortitza and Molotschna Mennonites, now weaned of their dependence on crown land grants, develop their own organization and the means to push out from their centres. They bought or leased undeveloped gentry estates to turn into daughter settlements for their landless or into privately-owned farms and estates. On average, from 1865 to 1914, they established around six new villages each year.

By the latter date, Mennonite settlements comprised well over four hundred villages and numerous estates in over a dozen provinces and regions in European Russia and Western Siberia. Despite the emigration to North America in the 1870s of about one-third their numbers, Russian Mennonites in 1914 had a total population of about 100,000. The pattern tended to be the same everywhere. Each new homogeneous Mennonite steppe settlement, following the pattern of the mother settlements, consisted of neat, usually one-street treed villages with substantial, largely lookalike buildings, and farmyards, gardens, orchards, churches and schools, set in the midst of common plowlands, pastures and hayfields.[3]

As mentioned, the main deviation from this colonization pattern was the *Judenplan,* a mixed Jewish/Mennonite settlement experiment dating from the 1850s and 1860s. Also state-initiated, the *Judenplan* sheds considerable light on the quandries and choices confronting Mennonite settlement during the period of conflict and transition. Although little has been written about the *Judenplan,* its early development can be traced through contemporary colonist and Russian newspapers, studies of Russian Jewry and, in particular, the informative diaries of Jacob D. Epp (1820-1890). An evocative chronicler of his time, Epp was a Mennonite agriculturalist, lay minister and sometime village teacher in the *Judenplan* from 1852 to 1874[4] (No comparable Jewish eyewitness accounts of the *Judenplan* seem to exist).

Jacob Epp was himself one of the poorer, less distinguished members of a prominent Old Colony family of clerical and lay leaders. His grandfather, David Epp (1750-1802), an elder of the fledgling Chortitza church, helped negotiate the Mennonite Charter of Privileges in 1800. His father, also David Epp (1777-1843), the most influential Chortitza churchman of his day, was well-read and deeply pious.[5] His brothers and brothers-in-law came to occupy leading clerical, teaching, administrative, entrepreneurial and professional positions in the settlement.[6] For the first thirty-one years of his life Jacob Epp lived in the Old Colony. During his childhood and youth in the 1820s and 1830s, the Old Colony was still part of a sparsely populated rugged frontier of colonization, cattle and sheep raising and very slowly expanding grain growing and market economy. The area was, however, in the midst of huge, uncultivated gentry estates averaging more than 15,000 acres each.[7]

The first fleeting glimpses of Jacob Epp date from the years 1837 to 1843. They appear in laconic entries, in a crabbed handwriting, in the rare surviving diary volume of his father.[8] In mid-May 1837, we meet Jacob for the first time making a five-day, fifty kilometre wagon trip with his father and a brother to their rented sheep farm to pay a salt tax.[9] Two years later, as an eighteen-year old, he accompanied his father on an undoubtedly memorable three-week trip to the larger and more prosperous sister settlement of the Molotschna, then embroiled in controversy over the iron-handed leadership of Johann Cornies.[10] Also, as an eighteen-year old, he was baptized and took his first communion.[11] Through this significant rite of passage he entered into full membership in the Mennonite religious and civil community and the responsibilities of adulthood.

After Jacob's marriage in 1841 at the age of twenty, he and his young bride moved into the *Sommerstube* of his parents' home in the village of Chortitza, as was Mennonite custom. The following spring he took over the operation of the rented family sheep farm and there followed, as he wrote, a year of "tranquil happiness."[12] This ended suddenly in 1843 with the unexpected death of his father who, though a prominent minister, was poor and seemingly deep in debt. Within a half year of Jacob's father's death the rented sheep farm was dissolved and the 65-dessiatina family property in the village of Chortitza sold at a three-day public auction. Jacob's impoverished mother and five underaged brothers and sisters were forced to move into a small cottage on a village side street, the so-called *Neue Reihe.*[13] Without a meaningful inheritance or other source of capital, Jacob Epp now joined the growing ranks of the Old Colony landless and came to share their difficult fate.

Young, recently married, poor and with few immediate prospects, Jacob Epp and his wife rented a room in Chortitza village as modest *Einwohner* (leasers). Then in April 1844, as a twenty-three year old novice, in urgent need of making a living since his wife was pregnant with their first child, Jacob Epp hired on as village school teacher on the lovely Dniepr Island of Chortitza. With no formal education beyond the basic literacy provided in his village school, but of a family which valued reading and education, he seems to have established himself quickly as one of a still small group of progressive teachers in the Old Colony.[14] Handicapped by the loss of his left eye at an indeterminate earlier age and shaky in his Russian, but personally warm, open to innovations and interested in the needs of his pupils,[15] Jacob Epp taught school on the Island for eight relatively satisfying years from 1844 to 1852.[16]

As a child of his times, however, Jacob Epp seems never to have considered the low station and poorly paid job of teaching as a lifetime profession. To be a teacher, according to contemporary perceptions, was to be less than fully a man. The social rank of a village school master, as scornful contemporary stereotypes suggested, hardly exceeded that of a village herdsman. Crowded into a small schoolhouse/teacherage with his growing family, the pay he received in money, land use, goods and services was meagre and inadequate. Although he managed to scrape together a little extra as bookkeeper at a few village auctions and briefly as part-time secretary to the Island's village community, Jacob Epp was on the lookout for something better: land and the accompanying status that would raise him to equality with his landholding fellows. He nursed the vain hope that the government would endow the Old Colony with a further crown land grant.

By 1850 the landlessness which Jacob Epp suffered was wide-spread in all of the Mennonite settlements. About sixty percent of all Old Colony households were already without landed property and the situation was deteriorating.[17] The Mennonite population was growing annually by about three percent, two times the Imperial Russian average, doubling every twenty-five years. Also, the amount of allotment-land in the Old Colony was fixed, with land tenure practices expressly prohibiting the fragmentation of the normal Mennonite 65-dessiatina household to create new means of live-lihood.[18]

The landless were themselves differentiated.[19] A handful of those who were more well-to-do and more enterprising bought landed estates and prospered. About a third of the landless — those who owned their own modest home-and-garden plots with a house and a barn in the villages (the so-called *Anwohner* or cottagers) — dabbled in sidelines like peddling, bee-keeping, silk worm culture and linen-weaving while leasing land on nearby gentry estates for sheep and cattle raising and a little grain growing. A further third, mostly cottagers as well, while doing a little farming on the side, took up teaching or engaged in crafts as smiths, cabinet builders, watch-makers and wheelwrights. From this activity, within three decades, would spring a modern farm implement industry.[20]

The last third of the landless, at the bottom of Old Colony society, were generally people, many of them heads of younger families, who, occupying rented quarters as *Einwohner*, worked as day-labourers on the fields of their landed neighbours. As this was the repressive age of Nicholas I and of the equally authoritarian Menno-nite leader Johann Cornies,[21] they quietly chafed at their lot. Yet since landholding, status and identity were vitally interlocked at the time, the *Anwohner* and *Einwohner*, however employed, yearned for a regular land allotment of their own that would give them the rights and station of their more fortunate landed brethren in village and settlement life.

Although Old Colony officials of the day did little to alleviate the problem, landlessness was widely recognized as a timebomb which needed to be defused. In 1851, the first official Old Colony history, written by the well-informed longtime Chortitza secondary school teacher, Heinrich Heese, summarized the dilemma, predicting grave problems if remedies were not found:

> A Mennonite is not especially quick, but he can reason
> and is able and persevering. He is religious according to the

practices of his forebears, quiet, sober and agreeable. In general he has the quality to reach his goal under the careful guidance of his superiors. Short of land himself, his diligence prompts him to lease and work the steppe land of nearby estate owners, to sell agricultural products brought from near and far and to seek a living through the sale of his smithing and woodworking outside of the settlement. But once the estate owners decide to work all of their land, then our community will find itself in a precarious situation because of its rapid natural increase in population. The [landless] cottagers, who now earn a living in the surrounding area, will then be reduced to menial day labourers and the balance between them and the landowners will be destroyed.[22]

Against this cheerless background in the early 1850s, landless Mennonites like Jacob Epp reluctantly settled in the *Judenplan*. The settlement consisted of six villages, each of which would grow to a population of from 400 to 600. Two of the villages, Kamianka and Izluchistaia, dated from the early 19th century. Four, created in the early 1850s, with prefixes "novo," or "new," were named Novo-kovno, Novopodolsk, Novovitebsk and Novozhitomir, after the provinces from which their Jewish settlers had come. Altogether in New Russia a total of thirty-nine such villages were grouped together in several settlements. The *Judenplan*, as were the Mennonite settlements, was administered by the Ministry of State Domains and its subordinate office, the Supervisory Committee in Odessa.

Yoking Jews and Mennonites together in the *Judenplan* was a characteristic experiment of autocratic Russian paternalism in the first half of the 19th century. Direction, superintendence, tutelage and control were its chief watchwords. The program began in the early 1800s when the government established several Jewish agricultural villages with two aims in mind: to relieve population pressures among proletarianized Jews in the northwestern provinces; and to engineer a "more normal" social structure by turning some Jews into peasants.[23] But in the mid-1840s a major government review concluded from the continuing misery of these first Jewish settlements that the program was flawed and needed reform before it could be expanded. The review attributed the poverty of existing Jewish villages to tangled ministerial lines of planning and control; graft and oppression in local village administration; and, perhaps most importantly, the negligence of the state in not teaching the agriculturally inexperienced Jews methods of good farming.[24]

As remedies, it proposed that the Ministry of State Domains be given exclusive administrative control over the Jewish villages and that competent German-speaking colonists from New Russia be recruited as state overseers at the village and settlement levels. Finally, to flesh out the system of tutelary guidance, the government review recommended the appointment of "model settlers" to live in each village. Mennonites were singled out as being ideally suited to serve both as "overseers" and as "model farmers:"

> In every Jewish colony a certain number of qualified Christian farmers should be settled. They would teach the Jewish colonists agriculture and be present at all times with advice and help and so prevent willful or unintended negligence in respect of any aspect of Jewish agriculture. Undoubtedly the German Christian colonists are well qualified to be such teachers and instructors. . . . Among these the Mennonites would be by far the best, for when all is said and done they are genuinely outstanding models of virtuous and industrious people both physically and spiritually. . . . Cornies, the leader of the Mennonites, who exercises superintendence over all of their colonies, should be contacted to see if there is any possibility that members of his community would be willing to settle in the Jewish colonies and take on the task of instructors. This is quite unlikely, however, for the Mennonite treasures his communal existence and his brotherhood highly and would not easily agree to exchange these for material benefits.[25]

There is no evidence that the Old Colony religious and lay leadership debated the potential merits and pitfalls of Mennonites taking up settlement in the *Judenplan*. But Johann Cornies, who from 1846 until his death in 1848 did indeed exercise wide-ranging governmental authority over all Mennonite settlements, embraced the program as one way of relieving demographic pressures in the Old Colony and gave it his endorsement.[26] It was speedily implemented under the direction of the Ministry of State Domains. In 1848 a notice appeared in its monthly German-language journal, *Unterhaltungsblatt für deutsche Ansiedler im südlichen Rußland*, inviting German colonists and Mennonites to apply for positions as village "overseers" and as "model settlers." Prospective "model settlers" were guaranteed the retention of their legal status as "colonists." They were also promised 40-dessiatina grants of good land, long-term tax exemptions and the right to maintain their own schools.[27]

As a village school teacher, Jacob Epp presumably learned of the project from the *Unterhaltungsblatt* which was sent free to each village school. But as the architects of the scheme had foreseen, the strongly community-minded Old Colony Mennonites were at first reluctant to commit themselves to settling anywhere other than in a homogeneous Mennonite village. In 1851 Jacob Epp's older brother Diedrich, one of the Old Colony's best-known cabinetmakers, and three other Old Colony Mennonites were appointed state overseers in the *Judenplan* villages.[28] At his brother's urging, Jacob and his wife, who still felt, as he wrote, a "deep personal aversion" to such a mixed Jewish/Mennonite settlement, twice visited the *Judenplan* to assess prospects firsthand.[29]

They found the settlement, which was surrounded by a few serf hamlets and many large but undeveloped landed gentry estates, advantageously located on land well drained by several tributary rivers and streams of the Dniepr River. Their melodious Turkic and Slavic-sounding names — Saksagan, Kamianka, Sheltaia and Basavluk — appear frequently in Epp's diary. The Old Colony was only a long-day's journey east by horse-drawn wagon. Nearby were the market towns of Sofievka and Krivoi Rog (the latter a booming industrial and iron ore mining town from the 1880s on). Seventy kilometres to the southeast lay the Dniepr port of Nikopol which was slowly evolving as the main entrepot for grain exports from the region via the Black Sea to world markets.

Seven to ten Mennonite "model settler" families lived in each of the six villages. They were joined by about an equal number of landless Mennonites families, most of which leased agricultural land and dwellings from the Jews. Several were merchants or artisans. Over the years, the Mennonite population of the *Judenplan* probably ranged between 100 and 140 families (some 550 to 800 people) with a total Jewish population roughly five or six times this number.[30] The possibility that this critical population mass would allow for the re-creation of normal Old Colony Mennonite community and church life probably clinched Jacob Epp's decision to hazard the move. In spring 1852, after negotiating a teaching position with his Mennonite co-religionists in the village of Novovitebsk, he and his family migrated to the *Judenplan*.[31] They were to remain there for twenty-two years.

Unlike conventional Old Colony one-street villages, Novovitebsk had an unfamiliar configuration as a cluster village. About half a mile square, it was surrounded by pastures and fields. Running along either side of a low marshy area were two main village roads, with several side streets branching off.[32] Along one of these streets, the Mennonite model settlers, including the Epps, lived clumped together as neighbours. Their houses, barns and orchards, Old Colony-style to the last detail, were on one side of the street and their gardens (the so-called "upper garden") on the other.

Laboriously the Epp family dismantled and moved an implement and storage shed from the Old Colony and converted it into a dwelling. They marked off their house-and-garden plot, planted an orchard and garden, helped organize the common pastures and open fields around the newly founded village and painstakingly hand-sowed the first crops.[33] Soon, as Jacob Epp's historian nephew, D.H. Epp, later wrote, in each of the six *Judenplan* villages, the "high pointed gables" of the traditional Russian Mennonite home-and-barn under a single thatched roof could be seen "towering" above the squat, two family Jewish dwellings.[34] In this setting, Jacob Epp and his family took up farming. Supposedly, through example, they tutored unskilled Jewish husbandmen in agriculture. Here also he would bury his first wife and several infant children, remarry and devotedly pastor his community of "landed" and "landless" Mennonite families through difficult times.

Mennonite life on the *Judenplan* deliberately followed well-trodden paths, faithfully reproducing basic Old Colony religious and community institutions and mores. Life revolved around the patriarchal family, Mennonite village schools, and mutual institutions such as the Chortitza Fire Insurance Office and the Orphans' Administration *(Waisenamt)*. Under the direction of the Chortitza elder, Gerhard Dyck, the *Judenplan* Mennonites organized themselves as an affiliate congregation of the Chortitza Flemish Mennonite church. Soon, too, Jacob Epp, scion of the previously mentioned prominent ministerial family, was elected as the first lay minister of the congregation,[35] a position he held until his death. On matters of church policy and discipline, relations with the state and much else, *Judenplan* Mennonites invariably followed the lead of Old Colony religious and secular leaders. Also cementing ties to the "mother settlement" were close trade and business relations and frequent visits back and forth among relatives and friends.

Mirroring the ethnic and religious exclusiveness of the Mennonites was the equally isolated world of the Jews. At least during the first decades of their coexistence on the *Judenplan,* Jews and Mennonites, both products of East European communitarian separateness, related to one another with considerable incomprehension and only grudging tolerance. To be sure, the languages of the Yiddish-speaking Jews and Low German-speaking Mennonites were close enough to allow relatively easy communication. Yet their separate orders of schools, religion, inheritance systems, contrasting occupational orientations and dress and pre-modern beliefs, which emphasized the need for segregated living, severely limited their contacts. Fraternization was discouraged by both sides. Although persisting to this day in I-think-there-was-a-Jewish-great-grand-mother-in-my-family talk among a few Mennonites, Jacob Epp does not record a single close friendship or romantic or sexual liaison between a Jew and a Mennonite on the *Judenplan.*

The Jewish and Mennonite solitudes did of necessity, however, intersect in several areas. Some *Judenplan* Jewish petty craftsmen and merchants leased out their dwellings and lands (many to landless Mennonites from the Old Colony) and moved to urban centres. The bulk of the Jews remaining in the villages seem to have poured their main energies less into field work than into their traditional occupations of the wool and grain trade, money lending, peddling, shopkeeping and innkeeping (Jacob Epp's fiercest ire was reserved for Jewish liquor vendors). Crafts such as tailoring, smithing, shoe-making, saddlery, tanning and tinsmithing were also strongly represented. Although occasionally disputing a deal that might flare up into conflict, Mennonite "model farmers" and Old Colony landless leased some of the Jewish land which had become available and took advantage of the Jewish crafts and trades. In at least one case a Mennonite and a Jew also teamed up as partners in the ownership of a mill, to the displeasure of the Mennonite villagers (and probably Jewish as well).

Jews and Mennonites interacted more actively in areas where administration and landholding were intertwined. Each of the six villages constituted separate administrative and land-regulating entities. Around the villages the plowlands of Jews and Mennonites lay intermingled in communal fields; cattle and sheep grazed on common pastures, requiring a single system of crop and fallow rotation and rules respecting the use of pastures and haylands. The village Jews understandably bristled at the humiliation implicit in the tutelary role assigned Mennonite "model farmers" as mentors. They looked for opportunities to put them in their place. Mennonites, for their part, were resentful when uncultivated or weed-choked Jewish field strips adjoined their own, or the cattle of Ukrainian herdsmen on rented Jewish lands were permitted to roam over their grain and fallow fields.

On occasion, simmering resentments erupted in conflict. Routine quarrels over trampled grain fields, the ownership of runaway cattle, exchanges of insults on the street or injured cattle were usually resolved through discussions among the parties, intervention of the religious leadership or de facto arbitration by the appointed overseers. As a man of probity and deep personal piety, Jacob Epp pastored his sometimes fractious parishioners as best he could, enjoining them to be honest in their dealings, respectful of differences, observant of Sunday as a day of rest and helpful to their neighbours. This befitted them as chosen "models" of enterprise and deportment. Otherwise, as he once reproached a Mennonite smith repairing a plowshare on Sunday, they risked becoming a "mockery to the Jews."[36]

More tangled disputes involving the virtually separate Jewish and Mennonite village administrations, each with its own landowner assemblies and village leadership were, however, less amenable to resolution. The parallel Jewish and Mennonite administrations operated tolerably well where functions were separate, as with inheritances and schools. But where a single administrative system was required, as in the regulation of plow and pasture lands, lines of authority easily became knotted and led to mutual charges of capricious, even vengeful, behaviour. There were complaints and countercomplaints, many addressed to the Supervisory Committee in Odessa. Matters reached their nadir in the early 1870s. The "model settlers" in the *Judenplan* accused the majority Jewish administration of staging confrontations and imposing harsh limitations on the number of their cattle permitted on the common grazing lands as a way of provoking their departure from the settlement.

Among several countermeasures, a two-man *Judenplan* Mennonite delegation, including Jacob Epp on the longest, most exotic trip of his life, elicited from the President of the Supervisory Committee in Odessa verbal and written guarantees of the security of tenure of their landholdings and residence.[37] In the paternalistic bureaucratic idiom of the day, the President assured them that they "could stay where they were forever" and urged them to "return home and, in God's name, work diligently."[38] Such recurring disputes over administration and land use ended finally only in the early 1880s, after the Epps had already left the *Judenplan*. The government ordered that the Jewish and Mennonite plow and pasture lands be separated physically and administratively, removing the main bone of Jewish/Mennonite contention. A decade later a Mennonite observer noted that, after decades of "maladministration" this separation had "freed up creative energies [among the Mennonites], leading to increased productivity."[39] It seems also to have improved relations between Jews and Mennonites.

On a personal level, the Jewish administration in the 1860s repeatedly challenged Jacob Epp's status as "model settler," saying he was the ninth in Novovitebsk, while the norm was only eight.[40] The issue dragged on for years, arousing feelings of insecurity and anxiety. Finally in 1868 (Epp's sixteenth year in the *Judenplan*) on the urging of his administrator brother, Diedrich, he resettled in the neighbouring village of Novopodolsk where his position as "model settler" was uncontested. On the day of his move he wrote resignedly: "For sixteen years I have lived in Novovitebsk, experiencing there much grief and also some joy in good times. Glory be to the Holy Spirit."[41]

Most Mennonite residents seem never to have accepted living in the *Judenplan* as more than a tolerable necessity. Attached to such residence was the stigma of poverty and a loss of self-worth. (Even later, for example, the *Judenplan* was considered a dumping ground for teachers who could not land a position in Old Colony villages.)[42] Normally a paragon of decorum and restraint, Jacob Epp perhaps captured the dominant mood of his fellows in a rare exchange of words with village Jews. The altercation was provoked by a dispute in which the Mennonites denied a charge that one of them had broken the leg of a cow belonging to a Jew:

> The Jews expressed their hatred of us by threatening legal action with the government to force our departure. Several Jews said as much to me this morning. I replied that if the authorities were ever to ask us to move, I would be the first to leave. Nor would I shed a tear, I said. A Jew responded: "Oh, no, we'll ask for permission to move ourselves." And if that were to happen, I replied, no German here would be sorry in the least. At this point several Jews broke out in laughter and suggested that if matters continued in this way, our separation would be a happy one.[43]

Epp and his family periodically made plans to move to an exclusively Mennonite village, a dream which remained their constant goal. Thus prior to settling in the *Judenplan* he had applied for land in the Bergthal Colony where the founding of a new village was rumoured.[44] In 1860, Russia's seizure of the Amur basin raised the

Jacob D. Epp (1820-1890) and his second wife, Judith Epp, nee Dyck (1832-1906), who lived in a Judenplan village. Photo: W.H. Roth, Rosthern (Sask.) Museum

idea of establishing a Mennonite settlement in the Far East. Jacob Epp and his overseer brother, Diedrich, immediately declared their interest in the venture, prompting "all" *Judenplan* Mennonites to speak "enthusiastically about risking such a settlement in God's name."[45] On one occasion, Epp was on the verge of returning to the Old Colony to take over the 65-dessiatina *Wirtschaft* of his second wife's aged parents.[46] And in the early 1870s, he and many other *Judenplan* Mennonites came within a hair of joining the large-scale Old Colony emigration to Manitoba.[47]

But over the years resettlement plans proved unavailing or were rejected by Jacob Epp out of a sense of duty to his church and his community. Thus, as his family came of age, Jacob Epp, like his *Judenplan* fellows, was forced to grapple with the problem of livelihood for his children. Landlessness among Russian Mennonites, including *Judenplan* families, was a recurring phenomenon. This was the logical result of a Russian Mennonite pattern of universal and early first marriages, high birth rates and presumably slowly falling death rates. There was also a pattern of the nuclear family. Newlyweds, after gaining a six-month to one-year start in the parental *Sommerstube* founded new households. Complex, multigenerational families were the exception.

Twice married, the second time to a woman a decade his junior,

Jacob Epp, over a period of thirty years, fathered fifteen children. Eleven survived infancy.[48] To prepare his numerous progeny for an uncertain future, perhaps as landless individuals, he had several of them attend secondary school in the Old Colony and try their hand at teaching. For others of his children he arranged apprenticeships in carpentry, cabinetmaking and wagon construction, or encouraged his sons-in-law in such trades.

In the end, except for one son who took up teaching as a lifetime occupation, all of his children came to depend for their subsistence principally on agriculture. By the late 1860s and early 1870s a number of his children were married and had started their own families or were reaching marriageable age. At first Jacob Epp helped pursue their trades and rented land and accommodations from Jews in the *Judenplan*. He also let them use his implements and draught animals and negotiated sharecrop arrangements on their behalf. Then, however, came the great watershed in the history of Mennonite colonization as the Molotschna and Old Colony administration launched their daughter colony movement. Starting in the late 1860s, the Old Colony administration established a number of multi-village Mennonite settlements on leased or purchased gentry estates within a thirty kilometre radius of the *Judenplan*. These included the settlements of Borozenko, Nepluiev, Baratov and Shlakhtin.[49] A number of private Mennonite *khutors* and estates were also established in the area.

Under these altered circumstances, Jacob Epp assisted several of his married children to acquire land, construct dwellings and barns and otherwise pioneer new villages, first in the leaseland Nepluiev settlement and then in the nearby four-village Baratov-Shlakhtin settlement purchased by the Old Colony for its landless. Within a few years of the start of this process, numerous landless Mennonite families from the *Judenplan* and from the Chortitza and Molotschna settlements, their long ladder wagons piled high with implements, household belongings and children, could be seen travelling the rutted and dusty roads in the environs of the *Judenplan* on their way to such new daughter settlements.

In 1872, observing this phenomenon and with the gift of accurate observation and prophecy, Jacob Epp wrote: "Members of our Mennonite community seem to be scattering themselves to all parts of Russia."[50] Two years later, Epp and his family left the *Judenplan*, joining his married children on a virgin farmstead in the Baratov village of Gnadenthal. Thus ended an Epp presence in the *Judenplan*. Except for a brief period of service as a minister in one of the

Mennonite alternative service forestry camps, he remained in Gnadenthal as landowner and minister until his death in 1890. Soon thereafter his widow and children, with their families, emigrated to Eigenheim, Saskatchewan, to again take up a pioneering life.

Contemporary assessments of the efficacy of the Imperial Russian *Judenplan* experiment varied greatly. For Russian Mennonites the *Judenplan* became a negative example, something to avoid. Until modernity had sunk deeper roots in their communities they were ill-equipped to function comfortably in a pluralist multiethnic and multireligious society. Proud of their agrarian accomplishments, strongly isolationist theologically and out of their tragic martyr past, they strongly preferred what was still within their grasp: familiar, homogeneous, largely self-administered Mennonite settlements. Their aversion toward multiethnic locales should not, however, be confused with discriminatory anti-Jewish feelings or even anti-Semitism. The sources for this study suggest no such feelings among Mennonites on the *Judenplan* in the period 1850 to 1880. There is no evidence in the voluminous daily diaries of Jacob Epp that he or his parishioners engaged in the stereotyping and scapegoating characteristic of modern anti-Semitism.

Clearly, the tutelary hopes which Imperial architects of the *Judenplan*-type agrarian settlements entertained, of turning large numbers of Jews into peasants, were never realized. The Jewish settlements established by the governments of Alexander I and Nicholas I were not very successful nor did they become the centre of an expanding network of Jewish daughter colony settlements. Indeed, in the 1880s, during the period of relentless anti-Jewish discriminatory legislation, anti-Semitic journalists defended the regime's strict limitations on Jewish residence and enterprise by pointing to the "failure" of Jewish agricultural settlements in New Russia.[51] This, they said, was proof of the incapacity of Jews to engage in anything other than exploitive occupations.

To refute such claims, the leading Jewish study of the time, Julius Elk's *Die jüdischen Kolonien in Rußland*, came to the opposite conclusion, arguing:

> The internal communal administration of the [Jewish] colonies experienced a marked improvement. The . . . policy of settling competent Christian instructors in the Jewish colonies was realized and proved itself to be extraordinarily useful. . . . The history of the Russian-Jewish colonies demonstrates conclusively that the Russian Jew, whether he is of

trading or crafts background, can be educated to become a competent agriculturalist in every respect, as long as he is given the time and opportunity to learn and the appropriate legal security.[52]

Although available sources do not provide detailed documentation of the further history of the *Judenplan,* it should be noted that following the earlier mentioned physical and administrative separation of the Jewish and Mennonite croplands and pastures in the 1880s, relations between the Jewish and Mennonite communities improved. Later, during the revolution and civil war, Jews and Mennonites held largely conflicting attitudes toward the main Red and White armed rivals, and went their separate ways.[53] Many *Judenplan* Jews apparently welcomed the Bolshevik victory as a curb on Ukrainian nationalist excesses and a promise of a nondiscriminatory future for themselves. Nevertheless, in the 1920s, as a Mennonite landholder of the time reported, despite limited social fraternization between Jews and Mennonites, their relations were "usually very good."[54] Further archival research in German sources is needed to establish the fate of the Jewish inhabitants of the *Judenplan* during World War II, especially during the Nazi occupation from 1941 to 1943.[55] A Mennonite presence on the *Judenplan* seems to have continued until the mass withdrawal of Mennonites from southern Ukraine with the retreating German armies in the fall of 1943. The present study, which illustrates Mennonite colonization policy from the 1850s to 1870s, can also serve as part of the context for that broader, as yet largely unexplored, subject of Russian Mennonite attitudes toward Jews during late Imperial and early Soviet times.

Notes

1. For the background and early history of Jewish agrarian settlements in Russia, see F. Zakharievich, "Istorikostatisticheskoe opisanie Evreiskikh kolonii Novorossieskovo kraia," *Novorossiiskii kalendar na 1853 god* (1852), 396-416; M. Stanislawski, *Tsar Nicholas I and the Jews: The Transformation of Jewish Society in Russia* (Philadelphia: Jewish Publication Society of America, 1983); Julius Elk, *Die jüdischen Kolonien in Rußland* (Frankfurt a. Main: S. Kaufmann, 1886). For background see also John D. Klier, *The Origins of The "Jewish Question" in Russia, 1772-1825* (Dekalb, Illinois: Northern Illinois University Press, 1986).

2. The history of the landless question among Russian Mennonites, as Peter M. Friesen wrote in 1911, "has still to be written." *The Mennonite Brotherhood in Russia, 1789-1910* (Fresno, California: Board of Christian Literature, General Conference of Mennonite Brethren Churches, 1978), 123. Existing studies deal with the issue almost exclusively in terms of the Molotschna settlement. For an introduction see David G. Rempel, "The Mennonite Colonies in New Russia: A Study of their Settlement and Economic Development from 1789 to 1914" (Ph.D. dissertation, Stanford University, 1933), 179-211.

3. For what is still the best overview of Russian Mennonite history see David G. Rempel, "The Mennonite Commonwealth in Russia: A Sketch of its Founding and Endurance, 1789-1919," *Mennonite Quarterly Review* 47 (October 1973): 259-308; 48 (January 1974): 5-54.

4. See my "Mennonite Community in an Age of Troubled Change: The Diaries of Jacob D. Epp, 1851-1880," *Mennonite Historian* 14 (December 1988): 1-3. The extant diary volumes cover the following years: I (1851-53); IV (1859-1871); V (1871-80), Jacob D. Epp Collection, Mennonite Heritage Centre Archives, Winnipeg, Manitoba. Hereafter cited as *JE* with the date.

5. *Mennonite Encyclopedia*, s.v. "Epp, David;" H. Epp, ed., *Heinrich Epp, Kirchenältester der Mennonitengemeinde zu Chortitza (Südrußland)* (Leipzig: August Pries, 1897).

6. See footnote 4 and D.H. Epp, "Aus der Kindheitsgeschichte der deutschen Industrie in den Kolonien Süd-Rußlands," *Der Botschafter,* August 1, 5, 12 and 15, 1911.

7. Leonard G. Friesen, "New Russia and the Fissuring of Rural Society, 1855-1907" (Ph.D. dissertation, University of Toronto, 1988), 22-53; Ministry of the Interior, *Statistika pozemel'noi sobstvennosti i naselennykh mest evropeiskoi Rossii: Vypusk VIII, Gubernii novorossiiskoi gruppy* (St. Petersburg: Tsentralnii Statisticheskii Komitet, 1885); V.E. Postnikov, *Iuzhno-russkoe krestianskoe khoziastvo* (Moscow: By the author, 1891), 164-5.

8. Diary of David D. Epp, 1837-1843, David D. Epp Collection, Mennonite Heritage Centre Archives, Winnipeg, Manitoba. Hereafter cited as *DDE* and the date.

9. *DDE*, May 17, 1837.

10. *DDE*, January 12-February 2, 1839.

11. *DDE*, May 15, 1839.

12. *JE*, "Background," January 1, 1851.

13. H. Epp, ed., *Heinrich Epp*, 3-4.

14. *JE*, "Introduction," January 1, 1851.

15. A portrait of Jacob Epp as village school teacher has been preserved in a rare, unpublished autobiographical sketch by a former pupil, later brother-in-law and industrial entrepreneur, Kornelius Hildebrand, "Unsere Lebensbeschreibung, 1891," manuscript (photocopy) in possession of the author.

16. Jacob Epp provides rich detail on his last year of teaching on the Island in *JE*, 1851-2. See also, Is. P. Klassen, *Die Insel Chortitza: Stimmungsbilder, Gedanken und Erinnerungen* (Winnipeg, Manitoba: By the author, 1979).

17. Heinrich Heese, "Kurzgefaßte geschichtliche Übersicht der Gründung und des Bestehens der Kolonieen des chortizer Mennonitenbezirkes," *Unterhaltungsblatt für deutsche Ansiedler im südlichen Rußland* (September 1851).

18. A. Klaus, *Nashi kolonii: Opyty i materialy po istorii i statistike inostrannoi kolonizatsii v Rossii* (St. Petersburg: V.V. Nusvalta, 1869); Postnikov, *Iuzhno-russkoe krestianskoe khoziastvo*, 34-68, 295-96.

19. Based on various issues of the *Unterhaltungsblatt* for the years 1846 to 1857.

20. D.H. Epp, "Aus der Kindheitsgeschichte der deutschen Industrie in den Kolonien Süd-Rußlands," *Der Botschafter*, various issues in 1911.

21. David H. Epp, *Johann Cornies: Züge aus seinem Leben und Wirken* (Steinbach, Manitoba: Echo Verlag, 1946) and Harvey L. Dyck, "Light and Shadow in Images of Johann Cornies," *Journal of Mennonite Studies* 2 (1985): 9-41.

22. Heinrich Heese, "Kurzgefaßte geschichtliche Übersicht," 73-77.

23. Stanislawski, *Tsar Nichlas I and the Jews*, 39-40, 43-48, 155-182.

24. Julius Elk, *Die jüdischen Kolonien in Rußland*, 145-91.

25. Ibid., 204.

26. David H. Epp, *Johann Cornies*, 101.

27. "Die Hebräer-Kolonien in Süd-Rußland" and "Aufforderung an deutsche Kolonisten, sich als Musterwirte, Schmiede und Wagner in den Juden-Kolonien niederzulassen," *Unterhaltungsblatt* 3 (March 1848): 20-21.

28. *JE*, March 10, 25, 1851; Diedrich Epp had a long and distinguished career in various supervisory posts in the Jewish agricultural settlements from 1851 to 1900. He received a letter of commendation for distinguished service from the Minister of State Domains in 1861, *Unterhaltungsblatt* 16 (May 1861): 36. His death in 1900 was the occasion for tributes from Jewish friends and admirers, *Mennonite Encyclopedia*, s.v. "Judenplan."

29. *JE*, April 24, July 2, 1851.

30. Mennonite population is an estimate derived from annual birth data included in Jacob Epp's diaries. It assumes that the *Judenplan* Mennonite birth rate was similar to that in the Old Colony, i.e., between four and five percent annually. The total *Judenplan* population in 1853, according to the Tenth Revision, was 3,110. In 1898-99, according to a study by the Jewish Colonization Society, it was 3,317. Leo Bramsohn, "Statistische Untersuchungen über die Lage der Juden in Rußland," in *Jüdische Statistik* by the Verein für jüdische Statistik (Berlin, 1903), 184.

31. *JE*, March 23-27, 1852.

32. Dave Stobbe, "Novovitebsk: A Jewish and Mennonite Village in Russia and its Pattern of Life" (Student paper, Canadian Mennonite Bible College, 1975), Mennonite Heritage Centre Archives, Winnipeg, Manitoba. This informative term paper is based on interviews of Stobbe with his grandfather, a Mennonite resident on the *Judenplan* until the mid-1920s.

33. *JE*, April 6-July 1, 1852.

34. D.H. Epp, *Die Chortitzer Mennoniten: Versuch einer Darstellung des Entwickelungsganges derselben* (Odessa: A. Schultze, 1889), 143-45. D.H. Epp, a nephew of Jacob Epp, often visited the *Judenplan* with his father, Heinrich Epp, who himself was briefly an overseer in the Jewish settlements in the mid-1850s.

35. *JE*, October 18-19, 1852.

36. *JE*, April 11, 1865.

37. *JE*, May 19-June 13, 1870.

38. *JE*, June 13, 1870.

39. D.H. Epp, *Die Chortitzer Mennoniten*, 145.

40. For example, *JE*, April 18, 1867.

41. *JE*, February 29, March 4, 1868.

42. Based on personal recollections of David G. Rempel.

43. *JE*, February 12, 1860.

44. *JE*, February 14, March 4, 1852.

45. *JE*, February 2, March 5, 6, 9, 1860.

46. *JE*, August 17, 29, September 10, 1852.

47. *JE*, December 31, 1872; January 4, 31, September 24, 1873.

48. "Family Journal of Jacob D. Epp" containing genealogical information, a record of service as a minister, harvest yields and occasional poems. Photocopy typescript in possession of author.

49. D.H. Epp, *Die Chortitzer Mennoniten*, 95-96; Jakob Redekopp, *Es war die Heimat . . . Baratow-Schlachtjin* (Filadelfia, Paraguay: By the author, 1966). The Jacob Epp diaries for 1872-74 contain numerous eyewitness entries regarding these various settlements which he also served as minister.

50. *JE*, May 10, 1872.

51. See, for example, K. Slychevskii, "Evreiskiia kolonii," *Russkii vestnik* (April 1890): 201-28.

52. Elk, *Die jüdischen Kolonien in Rußland*, 214.

53. Dave Stobbe, "Novovitebsk."

54. Ibid.

55. In February 1942, the German occupation forced all German-speaking "model settlers" in the *Judenplan* to move together into two villages. Peter (Isaak) Derksen, *Es wurde wieder ruhig: Die Lebensgeschichte eines mennonitischen Predigers aus der Sowjetunion* (Winnipeg, Manitoba: Mennonite Heritage Centre, 1989), 80.

Music among the Mennonites of Russia

Wesley Berg

In the years between the beginning of the Anabaptist movement in the early sixteenth century and the departure of the Mennonites from Poland to Russia in 1789, the music heard in Mennonite churches had undergone many changes. The martyr hymns of the *Ausbund* (1564) continued to be sung only by Swiss and Amish congregations. The Mennonites who had moved to Poland had taken along their Dutch hymnals which some congregations continued to use into the eighteenth century.[1] Most Mennonite congregations, however, used German hymnals borrowed from neighbouring Reformed or Lutheran churches. By the time the migration began the Polish Mennonites had published their own German hymnal and it was this book that accompanied the first settlers to their new home.

As with any of the other arts, a community requires a certain degree of intellectual sophistication, a certain amount of wealth and regular quantities of free time if it is to maintain and develop a musical civilization of any complexity. These requirements were absent in the community that came to Russia in 1789, and musical life in the churches of the first colony seems to have deteriorated quite rapidly.[2] In the absence of hymnals with notated music and of people who could read musical notation, hymns were preserved in the memories of the congregation, these memories stirred and prompted each Sunday by the *Vorsänger* or song leader.[3] As a result, the melodies they were charged with preserving underwent subtle changes over the years. According to George Wiebe, the singing in conservative Canadian congregations in which this tradition has been perpetuated was characterized by a nasal, penetrating tone and a slow tempo necessary to accommodate the many ornamental notes that had been added gradually to the hymn tunes.[4] Recalling his memories as a seven-year-old boy of a church service in the Bergthal colony in 1854, Jacob Klassen wrote, "Endlessly long hymns from the *Gesangbuch* were begun by the *Vorsänger* of the congregation and sung with so many flourishes and embellishments that the melody became completely unrecognizable, and it was impossible, despite my good ear, to retain any of these strange melodies in my memory."[5]

This tradition of unaccompanied unison singing using hymnals without musical notation and a core of melodies perpetuated by means of an oral tradition was carried on in the Chortitza and Bergthal colonies and then by the Old Colony Mennonites in Canada after 1874. In Russia the possibility of musical reform came with the founding of the Molotschna Colony in 1804 and especially with the establishing of the village of Gnadenfeld in 1835. The settlers of the new colony included wealthier and better-educated colonists. Gnadenfeld itself was established by forty families who had been associated with and influenced by the Moravian Brethren in Brandenburg. John B. Toews suggests that this village "provided a potential cultural and spiritual redemption for the Russian Mennonites."[6]

The Musical Reforms of Heinrich Franz

In Gnadenfeld the signs of reform first became evident a mere two years after the village had been established. Heinrich Franz, a young Prussian Mennonite school teacher, came to teach in Gnadenfeld in 1835. Franz's reaction to the singing he heard was similar to that of Heinrich Heese, another school teacher in the colony, who wrote, "O that our Lord Jesus Christ would no longer be greeted with such distorted singing in our churches, from which even the angels turn away in offense."[7] Franz wrote in the foreword to his *Choralbuch*, "That the holy art of singing has lost much of its beauty, clarity and correctness, preserved and propagated as it is, solely by ear, needs no proof — experience shows us. In 1837 a good friend and I began to assemble the hymns of the *Gesangbuch* in order to do my small part in improving singing first in my school and through it in the church services of the congregation in which I had been placed as a teacher, so that they might regain their original purity and consistency."[8]

The main purpose of the *Choralbuch* was the restoration of the *Gesangbuch* melodies to their original form, stripped of all the melodic accretions that had accumulated over the years. Instead of staff notation Franz used numbers or *Ziffern*, a system of notation that had its origins with Rousseau in France, with subsequent refinements by Galin, Paris and Chev in France and by B.C.L. Natorp in Germany.[9] Franz's system used Natorp's symbols for pitch notation; symbols for the notation of rhythm were a combination of French elements and features unique to the Mennonite teacher.[10]

The result was a notational system of considerable flexibility, simple enough to permit school children to learn the hymns of the *Gesangbuch* with ease, yet sophisticated enough to allow choir directors to transcribe Mendelssohn oratorios or Handel's "Hallelujah Chorus" into *Ziffern* for performance by their choirs. Its great advantage was the reduction of the complexities of staff notation, with its twelve major and twelve minor keys, to one major and one minor key with a moveable tonal centre, permitting its mastery by relatively unsophisticated singers in a short time. It was not suitable for instrumental music and was eventually superseded by staff notation for those Mennonites who came to North America, but it continues to be used by many congregations in Canada, Mexico, Paraguay and the Soviet Union.

Franz's *Choralbuch* circulated in manuscript form for 23 years until its publication in 1860. Its influence became apparent even before it had been published. In 1846 Johann Cornies suggested that singing hymns from the *Gesangbuch* according to *Ziffern* should be a regular part of the curriculum in Mennonite schools.[11] The first Russian edition of the *Geistreiches Gesangbuch* had appeared in 1844. The second edition of 1854 included a list of tunes that corresponded exactly with the 163 tunes of Franz's book, suggesting that the *Choralbuch* had quickly become the standard to which all other publications had to correspond.[12]

One might think that the ease with which it was now possible to learn the hymns would have recommended the new method to Mennonite parents but, like any other innovation, it was viewed with suspicion at first. Jakob Epp, a minister in the *Judenplan*, wrote in a diary entry of January 18, 1860, that a fellow minister, one Isaac Klassen, was very upset and compared the new way of singing to the work of the anti-Christ.[13] By 1870, however, he was able to report that "singing in ciphers, which caused considerable unrest here, has now been introduced and accepted everywhere, and the quarrelling and bickering have ended."[14] In 1863 Jakob Toews reported that crowds of curious people, some from other colonies, came to attend the public examinations of the Chortitza and Molotschna teacher training schools primarily to hear the four-part singing that was practised in those schools.[15] Although it might not yet have reached all the colonies, a revolution in the way Mennonites sang their chorales had clearly taken place, and the training of teachers in the new method ensured that the revolution would spread.

Mennonite Brethren, Gospel Hymns and Choirs

The year the Franz *Choralbuch* was published also witnessed the beginning of a second revolution in music among Russian Mennonites. The founding of the Mennonite Brethren Church in 1860 led to far-reaching and radical changes in Mennonite music-making. In its search for a warmer, more fervent expression of faith, it was probably inevitable that the hymnody and singing style of the parent Mennonite group would be found wanting, even if the conflict between the two groups had been less bitter. Some of the initial musical manifestations of the new spirit proved to be too radical, as can be seen in one of the statements from the June Reforms of 1865.

> The wild expressions of joy, such as dancing, were unanimously declared as not pleasing to the Lord; the drum (actually a tambourine) was not to be used any longer since it had caused much offence. Music that had been used in an unseemly, loud, and provocative manner was to be performed in a pleasing and harmonious manner instead. The joy in the Lord should not be prohibited, but everyone was to behave in a manner that edifies.[16]

While the excesses of the "Fröhliche Richtung" were soon brought under control and a more characteristic Mennonite decorum was reinstated, the Brethren introduced a number of important changes. In place of the *Geistreiches Gesangbuch* they used *Glaubensstimme der Gemeine des Herrn,* the hymnal of the German Baptists. This hymnal contained many of the same chorales they already knew, though in the simpler form which was already becoming familiar through the Franz *Choralbuch.*[17] After 1875 the Brethren found an even more congenial repertoire of hymns in *Frohe Botschaft in Liedern,* compiled by Ernst Gebhardt, a Methodist minister. *Frohe Botschaft* contained very few chorales. Gebhardt emphasized the spiritual folk songs of the Pietist movement and German translations of American gospel hymns instead.

Abandoning the *Gesangbuch* and its traditional melodies also meant abandoning the *Vorsänger* and his traditional role. At first ministers led congregational singing by lining out the hymns. After 1870 the Mennonite Brethren followed the Gnadenfeld pattern and introduced choirs into their congregations. Choral singing had been a natural outgrowth of music instruction in the schools, which centred around learning the hymns of the *Gesangbuch.* The 1860 edition of the *Choralbuch* was in four parts. Obviously the collection was intended to make choral singing possible, and the first documentary evidence for part-singing among Mennonites in Russia dates from 1860.[18] Choral singing moved from the school choir to the village choir, with young teachers organizing these groups to meet

The Chortitza community choir on an excursion.

Photo: Mennonite Heritage Centre Archives

the needs of the young people of the villages in which they taught. Soon choral singing moved into Mennonite Brethren churches.

In 1866 it was said that "not one church amongst fifty M.B. congregations in Russia . . . uses music in the regular services (although in some private meetings and for special festivities some choirs made up of the music groups of the younger members of the local church do participate)."[19] Two decades later church choirs had become common in Mennonite Brethren congregations. Here the influence of the village of Gnadenfeld can undoubtedly be seen. Choirs had been heard at mission festivals in Gnadenfeld as early as the 1840s under Elder F.W. Lange.[20] The practice would therefore not have been unfamiliar to the founders of the new church. It is also significant that in the main Mennonite group, the *Kirchliche Gemeinde*, only the church in Gnadenfeld seems to have had a choir in the 1890s.

In addition to providing a wholesome outlet for young people's energies within the church, the choir in Mennonite Brethren churches also led the congregation in its singing and taught it the

207

new hymns. By the early 1890s articles on choirs and choral music began to appear in Mennonite newspapers, and in 1893 Mennonite choirs and choir directors gathered in Rueckenau, a village in the Molotschna Colony, for the first of many choral festivals and workshops. A detailed record of the festival that took place in the same village the next year has been preserved in a letter from Friedrich Schweiger, the director of the Russian Choral Association, who had been invited to serve as guest conductor.[21] Eleven choirs were in attendance, all from Mennonite Brethren churches with the exception of the choir from Gnadenfeld. More than 2000 persons attended the event, where they heard individual choirs, the mass choir and addresses by various ministers. Schweiger commented on the good congregational singing, the sight-reading ability of the choir members, the good quality of their voices and the enthusiasm with which both choirs and congregation sang.

The most urgent problem now facing Mennonite Brethren church leaders interested in the musical development of their congregations was the training of choir directors. The musical education acquired in Mennonite schools was designed to equip the student to become a useful member of the congregation but fell far short of the sophistication needed to train a choir. In the initial stages, at least, Mennonite musicians looked to an association of choral groups known as the Christlicher Sängerbund for models, guidance and instructional materials.

The Christlicher Sängerbund had been formed in Germany in 1879. The first Mennonite choir joined in 1881.[22] By 1907 there were 31 Mennonite choirs listed as members of the Sängerbund, although 23 choirs withdrew in 1908, probably because of anti-German pressures developing in Russia at the time.[23] In 1898 the annual Mennonite Brethren conference authorized the formation of a branch of the Christlicher Sängerbund in the colonies. As a result the Südrußischer Sängervereinigung was formed as one of many affiliated regional associations.[24] One of the most important benefits of belonging to the Sängerbund was its periodical, *Sängergruß*. *Sängergruß* contained articles of a general inspirational nature, articles about music, choral singing and conducting, reports from festivals and workshops, and supplements containing printed music.[25] The Mennonite colonies were too isolated to be able to have many direct contacts with other members of the Sängerbund, except for infrequent visits by men like Schweiger. However, *Sängergruß* kept them in touch with developments elsewhere, provided information about collections of choral music available in Germany, and was also a valuable source of instructional materials and printed music.

Although direct contacts were infrequent, several visits by young men of the Mennonite colonies to Zyrardow in Poland, the head-quarters of the Russian affiliate of the Sängerbund and the home of Friedrich Schweiger, proved to be extremely important. Bernhard Dueck travelled to Zyrardow to attend a conductors' workshop led by Friedrich Schweiger in January 1894.[26] In May of that same year Schweiger made his visit to Rueckenau. During Schweiger's visits to several congregations before the festival he had also been impressed with a young choral conductor in Andreasfeld named Aron Sawatzky. Sawatzky had been elected choir director of the Andreasfeld Menno-nite Brethren Church in 1893. In the winter of 1895 the congregation sent him to Zyrardow to participate in a workshop led by Schwei-ger.[27] Several others who also travelled to Poland were F. Froese and Wilhelm Dyck. Dyck later served as president of the Südrußischer Sängervereinigung for more than a decade.

For the first decade after the Rueckenau festival, these men served as the main instigators and leaders of the choral movement in the Mennonite colonies. Dueck was especially active, having organized the first choral conductors' workshop among the Mennonites in Friedensfeld in the last week of 1894. He had been elected to the position of choir director in Friedensfeld in 1892 and presided over a large range of activities in the next ten years. His choir participated in Sunday morning services, of course, but also sang at funerals and weddings, ministered to the ill and went carolling at Christmas. The choir also visited congregations in other areas, serving as a source of inspiration and as a role model for other choirs.[28] Aron Sawatzky soon became well-known as a workshop leader and composer of choral pieces in the gospel hymn style. Around 1900 he published a booklet entitled *Gesangschule in Noten und Ziffern für christliche Sänger und Dirigenten.*[29] In 1903 he emigrated to Saskatchewan where he soon became the leading workshop leader on the prairies.[30]

Congregational and Choral Music

By the turn of the century the congregational and choral music sung in Russian Mennonite churches presented a picture of consid-erable variety and complexity. The Mennonite Brethren had begun by using the Baptist hymnal, *Glaubensstimme,* and had then moved on to Gebhardt's *Frohe Botschaft.* In 1890, Isaak Born, a choral conductor from Lichtfelde in the Molotschna Colony began to pub-lish a booklet entitled *Heimatklänge.* This publication contained the

A choir from the Grigorievka settlement district.

Photo: Mennonite Heritage Centre Archives

hymns made popular by Mennonite Brethren choirs, thus making them available for congregational use. In 1903, *Neue Glaubensstimme, Frohe Botschaft* and *Heimatklänge* were bound in one volume to produce the *Drei-Band*, the unofficial Mennonite Brethren hymnal in Russia.[31]

The *Kirchliche Gemeinde* continued to use the *Geistreiches Gesangbuch*, the hymnal they had brought with them from Poland, for more than a century. The first edition of 1767 contained 150 Psalms drawn from Lobwasser's *Psalter* in addition to 505 hymns. Three hundred and twelve of the hymns were borrowed from Lutheran or Reformed sources; 108 were translations of Dutch hymns. Among the remaining songs were a number that Peter Letkemann has identified as original Mennonite hymns.[32] During the first half of the nineteenth century the hymnal changed as most of the Psalms were eliminated and more hymns added. In 1892 the Conference of Mennonites in Russia published *Gesangbuch zum gottesdienstlichen und häuslichen Gebrauch in den Mennoniten-Gemeinden Rußlands*, containing 725 hymn texts. Only 182 of these were taken over from the *Geistreiches Gesangbuch*. Some texts were by Mennonite poets like Bernhard Harder; many new texts were from Pietist and Baptist sources, making it very similar in content to *Glaubensstimme*.[33] The hymns were to be sung to 115 tunes, only five of which were not in the Franz *Choralbuch*.

In 1897 Wilhelm Neufeld and Kornelius Wiens produced a new *Choralbuch* in which the tunes in Franz's book that were no longer being used were discarded. While Franz had made a great contribution with his collection, it is also clear from various harmonizations containing many part-writing errors that he had not received more than a rudimentary musical training; the new book provided better harmonizations for most of the hymns that Franz had harmonized.[34] The Neufeld-Wiens *Choralbuch* went through several editions until it was superseded by a new one produced in 1914. After examining these books and their sources in considerable detail, Letkemann points to two hymns that he was unable to find in any other sources and suggests that they are probably original Russian Mennonite creations. The first is "O daß mein Herz ein Altar wär," from the Neufeld-Wiens *Choralbuch*. The second is "So lange Jesus bleibt der Herr," from the supplement or *Anhang* of the *Choralbuch* of 1914.[35]

Although church choirs sang from the various hymnals as they led the congregational singing and taught the congregation new hymns, any choir director knows that a choir participating regularly in worship services soon develops a voracious appetite for printed music. In addition there were village choirs, school choirs, male choirs and choral societies (often known as *Liebhaberchöre*) that also had to be supplied with music. Russian Mennonite choir directors faced a special problem in that their singers sang only *Ziffern*. They could therefore not simply acquire collections of choral music from Germany. All their music had to be transcribed laboriously from notes into *Ziffern*.

Before long, collections of choral music in *Ziffern* began to appear. The first was *Chor-Gesänge: Eine Sammlung von geistlichen lieblichen Liedern,* edited and published in 1883 in Muntau (Molotschna) by J. Reimer and B. Peters.[36] Another was entitled *Liederstrauß*, compiled by Heinrich Janz and published in 1886. The most important collection of choral music was undoubtedly Isaak Born's *Liederperlen*. Beginning in July 1889 Born began to publish monthly instalments of a collection entitled *Sängerfreund.*[37] In 1891 he changed the name to *Liederperlen*. Eight volumes of *Liederperlen* had been published by the end of 1914, although Born had withdrawn from the work in 1903.

About forty percent of the music in *Liederperlen* was in the gospel hymn style of the Moody-Sankey revival movement. These were German translations of hymns by writers like Sankey, McGranaham and Bliss, simple hymns intended by their creators to be sung at mass revival meetings. Their most common characteristics are major keys, simple harmonies emphasizing the tonic and dominant, slow rates of chord change, dotted rhythms and compound metres and refrains. A second group, the gospel anthem, contains pieces that are like the gospel hymns but more complex, with prose texts, changes of texture and tempo, and independent instrumental accompaniments. Letkemann points to "Der Friedensfürst" as an example of a gospel anthem that is still sung in some Mennonite churches.[38] The third group of choral songs found in Russian Mennonite collections was drawn from the large body of pieces written by German and Swiss composers like Franz Abt, Konradin Kreutzer, Friedrich Silcher, Hans Naegeli and Bernhard Klein for the amateur choral societies established in Germany and Switzerland in the first half of the nineteenth century. A few compositions by Mennonite composers — Heinrich Janz, Aron Sawatzky, Wilhelm Neufeld, Bernhard Dueck and Isaak Wiens — were also included.[39]

Virtually the entire repertoire of Mennonite choirs and congregations came either from Germany or from the United States by way of Germany. Letkemann has identified only twenty-two Russian compositions in the seventeen choral anthologies produced by Mennonites. Of these, one-third are prayers for the tsar.[40] After 1900 the Russian language was the official language of instruction in schools. There was an increasing appreciation on the part of many well-educated Mennonites for Russian literature and culture as well. Nevertheless, "the Russian Mennonite soul of 1908 was still German."[41] Nowhere is this more clearly shown than in the music that Mennonite choirs sang.

Folk Music

Although it is clear that most Mennonite music-making revolved around the church, it would be a mistake to assume that secular music was non-existent. Unlike music for the church, folk songs were not collected, written down and published, but they did exist. Mennonites sang German folk songs, of course, readily available in collections like the ones assembled by Heim. One can also find occasional, fleeting references to singing in the vernacular *Plautdietsch* (Low German) in contemporary reports. The most convincing and detailed evidence for the latter activity is found in several publications that are based on research done recently among Canadian Mennonites with Russian Mennonite roots.[42] The song in Peacock's collection entitled "De Büa enn de Prädja," for example, is an "anticlerical allegory" contrasting the "simple bucolic bliss of the Mennonite way of life" with the intrusion of a preacher who represents the Church of Rome.[43] Many of the nursery rhymes and maxims in Friesen's *The Windmill Turning* are familiar to Mennonites who came to Canada from the Soviet Union after World War II. And according to Doreen Klassen, 30 of 130 songs in her early collection originated in Russia.[44] Most of these are children's songs.

Developments to World War I

A survey of the five years before the outbreak of World War I reveals many examples of how music among the Mennonites of Russia had developed since 1860, the year Heinrich Franz's *Choralbuch* was published and the Mennonite Brethren Church appeared. Choirs were now found in virtually all Mennonite Brethren churches, although only the *Kirchliche Gemeinde* congregations in Gnadenfeld and Halbstadt had established regular choirs. Published collections of photographs contain pictures of church and village choirs, as well as male choirs.[45] The village of Chortitza had a brass band made up of factory workers.[46] Periodicals published by Mennonites carried advertisements for pianos and harmoniums, the major schools all had music teachers, and amateur orchestras could be found in many villages.[47]

As in other areas of intellectual and cultural life, there were signs of increasing sophistication. Perhaps the most significant evidence of this can be found in the activities of Kornelius G. Neufeld. Born in

In addition to choirs, instrumental groups also sprang up in some communities.
Photo: Mennonite Heritage Centre Archives

The Liebhaberchor *in the Davlekanovo settlement, 1912.*

Photo: Courtesy Mrs. H.F. Klassen

Alexanderkrone, Molotschna in 1871, Neufeld became a school teacher. Like a large number of young Mennonite men at the turn of the century, he studied abroad in Switzerland and England, where he heard many of the great musical masterworks. On his return he became one of the leading workshop leaders in the colonies. One of his most important contributions was the publication of a journal directed at Mennonite musicians, *Aufwärts: Blätter für Sänger und Dirigenten und für Liebhaber des christlichen Gesanges*. Only two volumes appeared, and only the first volume (1909) concerns itself with music, but this volume is a valuable and fascinating source of information about musical activities in the Mennonite colonies.[48] Neufeld's colleague at Davlekanovo was Franz C. Thiessen, who was responsible for introducing Mennonites in Russia and in Canada to large choral works like Mendelssohn's *St. Paul* and *Elijah*.

World War I to the Present

The ravages of war and revolution eliminated all possibilities for further growth during the next decade. It was not until 1923 that musical activity on a scale approaching that of the pre-war period was possible. As soon as life became secure enough to make cultural

214

activities feasible, choirs and choir festivals experienced an astonishing revival.[49] One of the most significant events of the 1920s was a choral workshop and festival that took place in January 1926 at Lichtenau in the Molotschna. The correspondent to *Der Bote* summed up the occasion and the musical activities of the period in general with these words:

> In the Molotschna Colony and in the Gnadenfeld district choir and congregational singing are flourishing. Choirs exist in every village, and where they do not, it is hoped that they soon will. The shortage of good conductors who have received at least some training is one difficulty that still prevents progress in most places. In order to deal with this difficulty, a workshop has been planned for some time as a continuation of the two-day gathering in Rudnerweide last year, and as a further development of the practices of the Mennonite Brethren before the war.[50]

Choral singing seems to have filled a special need in the 1920s. It is quite likely that gathering as a group to sing together or to listen to a choir sing was less likely to be frowned on and forbidden by government officials than gathering for a formal worship service. It was also a way of keeping young people within the fold, just as it had been for the Mennonite Brethren in the 1870s. The difference now was that Mennonite young people were being educated by a government that preached atheism and the threat to their faith was much greater than it ever had been. Even as choirs and choral festivals multiplied, however, and the task of training music leaders was taken up again, the storm clouds began to gather. By 1929 the harsh measures Stalin was taking to enforce collectivization of farms and the purges of church and civic leaders that accompanied this process had severely disrupted organized religious life.

By the mid-1930s most evangelical churches had been closed and religious activities of any kind, especially on the part of children, severely restricted.[51] The possession of religious books like Bibles or hymnals was strictly forbidden. As a result, even the singing of hymns was both dangerous and difficult, and singing in choirs was virtually impossible.[52] George Sawatzky recalls that it was only after the German occupation in 1941 that choirs were heard once more in the colonies.[53] Church services were now possible but there were very few hymnals. People therefore sang hymns that they had once known and could still remember. The German occupation did not

215

last very long, of course, and life was once more a matter simply of survival, both for those Mennonites who retreated with the German army and for those who had been moved eastward before the Germans arrived.

Since the end of World War II, the story of about two-thirds of the Mennonites in the Soviet Union is closely identified with the story of the All-Union Council of Evangelical Christian-Baptists (AUCECB).[54] Although the subject warrants special study, one can get a general impression of their musical practices from Walter Sawatsky's study of Soviet evangelicals since World War II. Like the Mennonites of the 1920s, the members of this group place a great deal of emphasis on music and singing and use choirs at least partly as substitutes for conventional youth programs. Because special youth meetings are illegal, the carefully planned rehearsals of a volunteer youth choir are used to instruct and edify young people in AUCECB congregations.[55]

For many years the training of competent musical leaders was hindered by the absence of a theological seminary. This situation has improved in the last twenty years. In 1968 a seminary which offered courses by correspondence was established; in 1974 courses in music were begun; and in 1979 a three-year course for church musicians was established. In addition, *Bratskii Vestnik,* the AUCECB journal, introduced a special section entitled "Music and Singing" in 1978.[56] Here church musicians can find new songs and theoretical articles about music.[57] The hymns sung in AUCECB congregations present an interesting mixture of translated German and English gospel hymns from the nineteenth-century revival movements, hymns written by Soviet composers in that same style and hymns with a marked Slavic character by a number of Soviet composers.[58]

According to Sawatsky, the hymnody of the remaining group of Mennonites not associated with the AUCECB is just as interesting. The German language is predominant and about half of the music used is still printed in *Ziffern.*[59] The *Drei-Band* continues to be used and more recently a selection of hymns from the *Drei-Band* has been published. Visitors to a Mennonite church in Karaganda report that the congregation sang hymns from sheets containing only the text, while the choir sang from hand-written manuscripts.[60] The choir director was obviously competent and the choir well-trained, using *Ziffern* in their rehearsals. Their impression of the choir's singing is consistent with other reports: Mennonite choirs in the Soviet Union sing with accuracy, conviction and infectious enthusiasm, though often without the refinement to which many North American congregations have become accustomed.

And so the story goes on. As opportunities for advanced education for evangelicals within the Soviet Union improve, so will the general level of singing and music. In the past ten years a number of North American Mennonite musicians and musical groups have been able to visit the Soviet Union, the most notable example being the work undertaken by George and Esther Wiebe during a sabbatical from their work at Canadian Mennonite Bible College. As Wiebe, Sawatsky and other visitors are quick to point out, however, the learning that takes place as these contacts increase will flow both ways. One important truth cannot be forgotten: Several times in this century Mennonites in the Soviet Union have demonstrated that music and singing are powerful allies in the fight to survive in the face of oppression and in the struggle to keep the faith.

Notes

1. Peter Letkemann, "The Hymnody and Choral Music of Mennonites in Russia, 1789-1915" (Ph.D. dissertation, University of Toronto, 1985), 72.

2. For a detailed survey of the development of Russian Mennonite hymnody and choral music to 1915, see Letkemann, "Hymnody." For a more general survey of the period from 1789 to 1928, see Wesley Berg, *From Russia with Music: A Study of the Mennonite Choral Singing Tradition in Canada* (Winnipeg, Manitoba: Hyperion Press, 1985), 13-39.

3. *Mennonite Encyclopedia*, s.v. "Chorister."

4. George Wiebe, "The Hymnody of the Conference of Mennonites in Canada" (M.A. thesis, University of Southern California, 1962), 71. See also Charles Burkhart, "The Church Music of the Old Amish and the Old Colony Mennonites," *Mennonite Quarterly Review* 27 (January 1953): 42-45, and "Music of the Old Colony Mennonites, *Mennonite Life* 7 (January 1952): 20-21, 47; and George Pullen Jackson, "The Strange Music of the Old Order Amish," *Musical Quarterly* 31 (July 1945): 275-288.

5. Jacob Abraham Klassen, "Autodidakt: Erinnerungen aus meinem Leben," typescript, Centre for Mennonite Brethren Studies, Winnipeg, Manitoba.

6. John B. Toews, "Cultural and Intellectual Aspects of the Mennonite Experience in Russia," *Mennonite Quarterly Review* 53 (April 1979): 139.

7. P.M. Friesen, *The Mennonite Brotherhood in Russia (1789-1910)*, trans. J.B. Toews, et. al. (Fresno, California: Board of Christian Literature, General Conference of Mennonite Brethren Churches, 1978), 111.

8. The four-part version of the Franz *Choralbuch* was published by Breitkopf und Haertel in 1860. In 1865 a version containing only the melody line was

produced. It is this version that continues to be used by conservative congregations in Canada, Mexico and Paraguay.

9. See Letkemann, "Hymnody," 133-151, for a survey of the history of this notational system. For the conflict between Russian Mennonites using *Ziffern* and North American Mennonites using staff notation in the 1920s and 1930s, see Wesley Berg, "Gesangbuch, Ziffern and Deutschtum: A Study of the Life and Work of J.P. Claszen, Mennonite Hymnologist," *Journal of Mennonite Studies* 4 (1986): 13-15.

10. See Letkemann, "Hymnody," 152-155, for details of the Franz *Ziffernsystem*.

11. David H. Epp, *Johann Cornies: Züge aus seinem Leben und Wirken* (Rosthern, Saskatchewan: Echo Verlag, 1946), 75.

12. Letkemann, "Hymnody," 56-57.

13. Cited in Letkemann, "Hymnody," 178.

14. Ibid., 180.

15. Ibid., 239-40.

16. Friesen, *Mennonite Brotherhood*, 276.

17. The Franz *Choralbuch* was in two parts, the first presenting the chorales of the *Gesangbuch*, the second a supplement containing 112 melodies taken from various late eighteenth and early nineteenth-century sources. The most important source was *Glaubensstimme* from which Franz used 47 tunes. Letkemann, "Hymnody," 302.

18. Ibid., 180.

19. Friesen, *Mennonite Brotherhood*, 443.

20. Letkemann, "Hymnody," 221, 357.

21. Friedrich Schweiger, "Ein Besuch unter den Sängern in Rußland," *Zionsbote*, September 26, 1894, 3-4. See Berg, *From Russia with Music*, 22-23, for a more comprehensive summary.

22. Letkemann, "Hymnody," 405.

23. Ibid., 418.

24. Ibid., 417.

25. Ibid., 404.

26. Bernhard Dueck, "Die erste Reise eines Dirigenten aus Südrußland nach Polen," *Sängergruß* 16 (May 1894): 37-38. Cited in Letkemann, "Hymnody," 409.

27. A.G. Sawatzky, "Von meiner Reise nach Polen," *Zionsbote*, April 24, 1895, 2-3.

28. D.D. Braun, Jr. "Ein Jubiläums-Sängerfest," *Zionsbote*, April 16, 1902, 1-2.

29. See Letkemann, "Hymnody," 458, for a brief description of its contents.

30. His work there is described in Berg, *From Russia with Music*, 47-54.

31. Letkemann, "Hymnody," 328-30.

32. Ibid., 79.

33. Ibid., 331.

34. Ibid., 269-70.

35. Ibid., 338, 345.

36. Ibid., 379.

37. Ibid., 431.

38. Ibid., 439.

39. See Letkemann, "Hymnody," 455-69, for a discussion of these pieces.

40. Ibid., 470.

41. John B. Toews, *Czars, Soviets and Mennonites* (Newton, Kansas: Faith and Life Press, 1982), 42.

42. See especially Kenneth Peacock, *Twenty Ethnic Songs from Western Canada,* Bulletin no.211, Anthropological Series no. 76, (Ottawa: National Museum of Canada, 1966): 48-62;Victor Carl Friesen, *The Windmill Turning: Nursery Rhymes, Maxims, and Other Expressions of Western Canadian Mennonites* (Edmonton, Alberta: University of Alberta Press, 1988); and Doreen Klassen, *Singing Mennonite: Low German Songs of the Mennonites* (Winnipeg, Manitoba: University of Manitoba Press, 1989).

43. Peacock, *Twenty Ethnic Folk Songs,* 49, 52-53.

44. Interview with Doreen Klassen, January 8, 1989.

45. See, for example, Walter Quiring and Helen Bartel, *Als ihre Zeit erfüllet war: 150 Jahre Bewährung in Rußland,* 3d ed. (Kitchener, Ontario: A. Klassen, 1974), 38, 53, 63, 69; N.J. Kroeker, *First Mennonite Villages in Russia, 1789-1943: Khortitsa-Rosental* (Vancouver, B.C.: N.J. Kroeker, 1981), 242-43; and Berg, *From Russia with Music,* 35.

46. Kroeker, *First Villages,* 241.

47. Quiring, *Als ihre Zeit,* 53.

48. For a survey of the contents of the first volume see Berg, *From Russia with Music,* 31-34.

49. These are documented in the pages of *Unser Blatt,* the publication of the Commission for Congregational Affairs of the General Conference of Mennonite Churches in Russia, published from 1925-28.

50. "Aus der alten Heimat: Die Dirigentenwoche in Lichtenau," *Der Bote,* March 17, 1926, 5.

51. Walter Sawatsky, *Soviet Evangelicals since World War II* (Kitchener, Ontario: Herald Press, 1981), 46-48;Toews, *Czars, Soviets and Mennonites,* 169.

52. Interview with Kornelius Krahn, December 24, 1988.

53. Interview with George Sawatzky, December 20, 1988.

54. Interview with Walter Sawatsky, December 22, 1988.

55. Sawatsky, *Soviet Evangelicals,* 70.

56. Ibid., 426.

57. Ibid., 330.

58. Ibid., 110.

59. Interview with Walter Sawatsky, December 22, 1988.

60. Interview with Lola Neufeld, January 7, 1989.

The Print Culture of the Russian Mennonites 1870-1930[1]

Al Reimer

The print culture of the Russian Mennonites is generally regarded as the least developed aspect of Russian Mennonite society. Even P.M. Friesen, who was ebullient about the cultural development of his people, begins his chapter on Mennonite publications in Russia with the apology that it "turns out to be short and modest."[2] He concludes his survey with the assessment that the "whole work of distributing the Russian Mennonite literature and writings has begun remarkably late. It is extremely modest for a hundred-year existence of the Mennonites in Russia in relatively great affluence and high, though agriculturally-based, culture."[3] Altogether Friesen lists 46 book titles as of 1910, a total that does seem low on the face of it for a period of over a century.[4] However, Friesen's bleak generalization is misleading when we consider that over 80 percent of Russian Mennonite publications came out in the period 1870-1920. In other words, it seems safe to say that the Mennonites of Russia were developing their print culture at an impressive rate in the closing decades of the Mennonite commonwealth.

The usual reasons given for the paucity of Mennonite publications in the first half of the century are that the original settlers in Russia were culturally primitive to start with and that they were too busy carving out a place for themselves on the Russian steppes to bother much with books and periodicals or the writing of them, except for a few traditional devotional books. According to John B. Toews, Russian Mennonite society before 1860 was "a cultural-intellectual desert."[5] Perhaps an even more important factor was that the early Mennonites brought no literary heritage of their own with them, nor even a literary language. In a sense they were "between" languages, having left Dutch behind in Prussia and not yet feeling entirely secure in the High German they had adopted as a church and cultural language. And the *Plautdietsch* they spoke daily was not a written language for them at all. Finally, the Mennonite school system during those early decades was too weak to produce many readers or book buyers, and certainly not writers.

Yet even in that early period there was a lively interest in religious books, papers and pamphlets, and such materials were obtained on a regular basis from Prussia. While P.M. Friesen is probably right in stating that the first Russian Mennonite publication to be printed on Russian soil was the old Prussian *Gesangbuch,* tenth edition overall, first edition in Russia (Odessa: 1844),[6] Delbert Plett has recently shown that the first book published by Russian Mennonites was a German translation of Peter Peters' *Spiegel der Gierigkeit,* printed (almost certainly) in Germany in 1827.[7] This was followed in 1834 by Peter von Riesen's revision of Menno Simons' three-volume *Fundamentbuch* (Danzig, 1834), again published by the Kleine Gemeinde, an important work which contained Menno's most important teachings and writings.[8] A third publication of the small breakaway church was *Einfache Erklärung* (Danzig, 1845), a brief but well-reasoned theological and polemical defense of the Kleine Gemeinde by its then elder Abraham Friesen.[9]

That the despised Kleine Gemeinde, criticized and maligned from its earliest years as anti-educational and unprogressive, led the way in book publications is an irony of nineteenth-century Russian-Mennonite history. In the 1860s the Kleine Gemeinde published another major series of religious reprints: J.P. Schabelje's *Die wandelnde Seele* (Stuttgart, 1860); *Das kleine Märtyrerbuch* (Stuttgart, 1863); and Peter Peters' *Ausgewählte Schriften* (Stuttgart, 1865). The subjects of these early Kleine Gemeinde publications indicate a desire to keep alive and strengthen the traditional currents of Anabaptist-Mennonite faith and belief. Far from being a means of disseminating new ideas and increasing cultural-intellectual sophistication, these publications were specifically designed to reinforce Mennonite religious traditionalism, to act as a bulwark against new-fashioned ways of thinking and new modes of faith. Viewed in the most positive light, as Plett views them, they were intended to take readers back to their true Anabaptist roots.[10]

By comparison, the other Mennonite churches in Russia published very little during this early period. In addition to the old *Gesangbuch* already mentioned, there were, according to Friesen, two religious works: *Konfession oder kurzes und einfältiges Glaubensbekenntnis derer so man nennt die vereinigte Flämische, Friesische und Hochdeutsche Taufgesinnte Mennonitengemeinde* (Odessa, 1853); and *Katechismus oder kurze und einfältige Unterweisung aus der Heiligen Schrift, in Frage und Antwort, für die Kinder zum Gebrauch in den Schulen* (no specific place or date given). Two other popular books published for use in schools during this period were Heinrich Franz's *Aufgabe für's Tafelrechnen* (Odessa, 1853) and his immensely popular *Choralbuch* (Leipzig, 1860). There was also an attempt at Mennonite history in *Kurze älteste Geschichte der Taufgesinnten (Mennoniten genannt)* (Odessa, 1852).[11] What might be considered the beginning of periodical literature for Russian Mennonites was the appearance in 1846 of the monthly *Unterhaltungsblatt für deutsche Ansiedler im südlichen Rußland*, an agrarian journal read by many Mennonites.[12]

Apart from this meagre list there was nothing else by way of publication in this early period. The colonies had not yet had time to develop a proper historical self-awareness, and of literary writing there is no trace to be found before 1870.

1870-1900

The closing decades of the nineteenth century saw a dramatic leap forward in the material and cultural lives of Russian Mennonites. The Russian government's new policy of Russification, including the gradual adoption of Russian as the language of instruction in schools, provided part of the impetus, to be sure, but most of the economic and cultural progress was self-generated. The increasing prosperity of the colonies led inevitably to greater cultural sophistication as Mennonites began to look up from their isolated settlements to the larger world beyond. More and more Mennonites began reading German language papers like the *Odessaer Zeitung* and the *St. Petersburger Zeitung*, as well as foreign periodicals like the Danzig-published *Mennonitische Blätter* and the *Mennonitische Rundschau* from America. A few even began to subscribe to Russian papers and periodicals. The Mennonites of Russia were also beginning to read more books — mostly non-Mennonite books and for the most part of a religious or edificatory nature — but they also welcomed the Mennonite publications that began to appear more frequently during this period.[13] The first lending libraries were being established and while there were as yet few bookstores in the colonies, colporteurs had been taking their book wares from village to village since at least the 1850s.[14] And in 1887 Peter J. Neufeld established the first Russian Mennonite printery in Neu Halbstadt, the establishment that later became the important publishing house Raduga.[15]

Nowhere was this cultural evolution more evident and more promising for the future than in the Mennonite school system. By the seventies and eighties there were university-trained teachers like

P.M. Friesen, J.J. Braeul, Kornelius Unruh and A.A. Neufeld whose advanced pedagogical methods and sophisticated intellectual approaches influenced successive generations of students in progressive *Zentralschulen* such as those in Halbstadt, Ohrloff and Chortitza.[16] Paradoxically, while these well-trained teachers were fluent in Russian and capable of teaching it, they also returned from their Swiss and German universities with a love for German language and literature, a love they passed on to their students.[17] Regularly held teachers' conferences further helped to homogenize curricula and energize the educational ethos, thus helping to foster a Mennonite school experience that could accommodate both Russian and German patterns of thought and literary expression within the accepted parameters of Mennonite culture.[18]

School texts designed expressly for German and Mennonite students in Russia were slow in coming, but they did gradually replace earlier texts printed in Germany. As early as 1870, G. Rempel brought out his *Leitfaden zum Unterricht in der Geographie für die deutschen Schulen Südrußlands* (Odessa, 1870). The growing interest in church history was reflected in a new school text written by W. Neufeld, P. Riediger and K. Unruh: *Leitfaden zur Kirchengeschichte für mennonitische und lutherische Elementarschulen in Rußland* (Neuhalbstadt, 1895).[19] For the first time Mennonite students had a text that stressed the Russian setting and cultural atmosphere. Indeed, this was the reader (in its several editions) that moulded the reading tastes of the last Mennonite generation before the breakup of the Mennonite commonwealth. Kornelius Unruh brought out several other important texts before the end of the century: a brief German grammar for elementary schools, *Kratkaya Nemetskaya Grammatika* (Berdiansk, 1898) and *Leitfaden für den Religionsunterricht* (Halbstadt, 1899), a text that was reprinted as late as 1913. Unruh brought out several more texts after the turn of the century and deserves to be remembered as the most productive Mennonite pedagogue of his time. Two other educators wrote preliminary accounts of Mennonite schools and education during this period: Abraham Goerz in *Die Schulen in den Mennoniten-Kolonien der Molotschna im südlichen Rußland* (Berdjansk, 1882) and A.A. Neufeld in *Die Chortitzer Centralschule 1842-1892* (Berdjansk, 1893).

The approaching centennial year 1889 stimulated a new interest in the Russian Mennonite past. In 1887 Jakob Toews translated Alexander A. Klaus's *Nashi Kolonii,*[20] first published in 1869, a history of foreign colonization in Russia, as *Unsere Kolonien: Studien und Materialen zur Geschichte und Statistik der ausländischen Kolonisa-*

tion in Rußland (Odessa, 1887). While Klaus's history dealt only in part with the Mennonite colonies, the book was eagerly read by Mennonites and gave them fresh pride in their achievements.[21] Two specifically Mennonite histories appeared in time for the centennial celebrations: Peter Hildebrandt's *Erste Auswanderung der Mennoniten aus dem Danziger Gebiet nach Südrußland* (Halbstadt, 1888) and David H. Epp's *Die Chortitzaer Mennoniten: Versuch einer Darstellung des Entwickelungsganges derselben* (Rosenthal, 1889). The Hildebrandt booklet covered the original migration to Chortitza and the early period of settlement.[22] Epp's history of the Old Colony was more comprehensive but suffers from having been written by an author untutored in historiography.[23] To these historical works we can add a commemorative little biography of the prominent elder of the Old Colony, Heinrich Epp (1827-1896): *Heinrich Epp Kirchenältester* (Leipzig, 1897). It consists of a brief account of Elder Epp's life and career by his son Heinrich H. Epp, as well as three funeral orations by the elder's ministerial colleagues and one of his own sermons. This odd little book was almost certainly the first attempt at biography in the colonies.

As might be expected, religious and polemical publications again exceed other types of books during this period. In 1873 Martin Klaassen published his *Geschichte der wehrlosen taufgesinnten Gemeinden von der Zeit der Apostel bis auf die Gegenwart* (Danzig, 1873), a history of the Anabaptist-Mennonites based mainly on the *Martyrs' Mirror*.[24] The book was designed, according to the author, to "reawaken and quicken the lost consciousness of our church-historical destiny among the congregations here."[25] As a church-sponsored history based on limited source materials, Klaassen's book can be more properly regarded as a religious-polemical work (Mennonites had recently lost their special status of military exemption) than as a work of historiography.

The 1870s also saw the publication of two "prophetic" books, one of which had a direct bearing on the ill-fated Mennonite exodus to Turkestan in 1880. The book was Claas Epp's *Die entsiegelte Weissagung des Propheten Daniel und die Deutung der Offenbarung Jesu Christi* (Neusalz, 1878), published at Epp's own expense. It went through three editions and enabled Epp to recruit the necessary followers for his visionary refuge in Central Asia in preparation for the Second Coming.[26] Several years earlier another "prophetic" book had been published by the Kleine Gemeinde, its last in Russia: a reprint of Peter Jansz Twisk's *Das Friedenreich Christi oder Auslegung des 20. Kapitels in Offenbarung St. Johannis* (Odessa, 1875).[27]

Twisk (1565-1636) was a second-generation Dutch Anabaptist and a staunch follower of Menno Simons and Dirk Phillips. One of the earliest publications by the Mennonite Brethren was *Glaubens-bekenntnis und Verfassung der gläubig getauften und vereinigten Mennoniten-Brüdergemeinde im südlichen Rußland* (Einlage, 1876). In the early nineties, Heinrich Dirks, the well-known missionary, preacher and editor, published two religious booklets out of Gnadenfeld in the Molotschna: *Ist es recht, daß man sich noch einmal taufen läßt?* (Gnadenfeld, 1891); and *Das Reich Gottes im Lichte der Gleichnisse* (Gnadenfeld, 1892). These were followed by David H. Epp's popular instructional booklet *Kurze Erklärung und Erläuterungen zum Katechismus* (Odessa, 1896), which went to several editions and was translated into Russian. In 1899 Friedrich Lange published *Geschichte des Tempels* (Jerusalem, 1899), an account of the Temple Church in the founding of which he and his brothers Johannes and Benjamin had played significant roles. In addition to these religious publications there were several more hymnbooks, including a second edition of Franz's *Choralbuch* (Leipzig, 1880), followed by Heinrich Janz's *Liederstrauß* (Halbstadt, 1886) and Isaac Born's very popular collections of hymns and gospel songs *Liederperlen* (Halbstadt, 1889) and *Heimatklänge* (Halbstadt, 1900).[28]

In a class by themselves were the polemical pamphlets of the Russian Mennonite radical and political activist, Abraham Thiessen, who energetically and courageously fought the cause of the landless Russian Mennonites against the Mennonite landowners, for which he was exiled to Central Russia from 1874 to 1876. His pamphlets, revolutionary in tone and argument, consist of *Ein Brief nur für die Mennoniten im berdjanischen Kreise* (Odessa, 1872); *Ein Rätsel, oder die Frage: weshalb war ich vom Jahre 1874 bis 1876 in Verbannung?* (Zuerich, 1876); *Die Lage der deutschen Kolonisten in Rußland* (Leipzig, 1876); and *Die Agrarwirren bei den Mennoniten in Südrußland* (Berlin, 1887).[29]

Even the poetic muse made her first decorous appearance during these closing decades. The first book to appear was Bernhard Harder's *Geistliche Lieder und Gelegenheitsgedichte* (Hamburg, 1888), a posthumous collection prepared and edited by Heinrich Franz in memory of the famed preacher and revivalist. The bulk of the collection consists of conventional hymns and religious verse, but some of the occasional poems contain flashes of genuine poetic inspiration. A "purer" poet than Harder was the refined and erudite Old Colony teacher, Gerhard Loewen (1863-1946), whose collection of lyric, nature and religious verse was published as *Feldblumen* (Halbstadt, 1895).[30] Just before the turn of the century Johann Joh. Loewen published *Herzenstöne für schlichte Christenherzen: Eine reichhaltige Sammlung von Gelegenheitsgedichten* (Halbstadt, 1899), a collection of religious and secular verse.[31] Two other poets who had their work published "in various periodicals in Russia and abroad" during the period were Bernhard Peter Fast and Martin Fast.[32]

The only Mennonite fiction I have been able to discover in this period is Jacob Toews' "Die Steppe im Winter," a series of three short stories or, more accurately, prose sketches, published in twenty-two instalments in the *Odessaer Zeitung* in 1886-1887.[33] In their rambling form and casual conversational method and tone, these plotless genre sketches are reminiscent of Turgenev's famous *Sportsman's Sketches.* The first two sketches have Mennonite settings and characters, while the much longer third sketch is set in Odessa and the German *Kolonisten* villages in the area. All three are very realistic in treatment and in the two Mennnonite sketches the dialogue between the Mennonite characters is entirely in *Plautdietsch.* The Mennonites and the Russian peasants are favourably depicted, but the Jewish settlers and their villages are portrayed with a strong anti-Semitic bias, while the *Kolonisten* are also depicted, somewhat condescendingly, as inferior economically and culturally to the Mennonites. Toews is a good writer and his descriptions of landscape, places and social conditions are very competently done. Unfortunately, his mode of realistic fiction was not fully adopted by later Mennonite writers of fiction like J.H. Janzen and Peter B. Harder, who tended towards the melodramatic and didactic. Earlier in the 1880s the *Odessaer Zeitung* also carried several contributions in which there were attempts to write in a form of *Plaudietsch* that reads like a rough imitation of Fritz Reuter's Mecklenburg Platt.[34] The most interesting of these Low German pieces is a little satire on *De gode ohle Tiet* in which two arch-conservative oldtimers gravely deplore modern education and the foppish young men which the new-fangled *Zentralschulen* are producing.[35] Regrettably, these early experiments in the writing of Low German petered out quickly and were presumably not resumed until J.H. Janzen began writing his Low German playlets a generation later.

1900-1930
The first decade of the new century brought a tremendous upsurge in both the quantity and quality of print culture in Menno-

nite Russia. As we have seen, the Mennonite educational system was being continually improved and beginning to turn out literate adults of increasing sophistication and intellectual curiosity. By 1904, for example, there were 143 subscribers to the *Odessaer Zeitung* in the Molotschna and at least 68 in the Old Colony. Overall, the roughly 25,000 Mennonites of the Molotschna subscribed to 226 papers and periodicals for a total of 2,367 subscriptions. The figures for the Old Colony, with a population of about 15,000, were 85 periodicals for a total of 1,211 subscriptions.[36] When we consider also that it was the custom for papers and journals to be passed around from family to family we can readily appreciate how widespread the reading of periodical literature had become in the Mennonite colonies, at least in the two oldest mother settlements.

School libraries continued to grow in numbers and holdings, and lending libraries were to be found in the larger villages and even on the *Forstei* stations. In 1903, for example, the library in the town of Chortitza contained about 700 volumes with about 100 subscribers. Even the more remote Memrik Colony had a library of several hundred volumes.[37] It is difficult to ascertain the exact number of bookstores, printers and/or publishers in the Mennonite colonies during the early years of the century, but there must have been a dozen or more bookstores or bookdealers and at least four printers and/or publishers. As noted, the first print shop was established by Peter J. Neufeld in Neu Halbstadt in 1887. In 1904 Neufeld sold his firm to H.J. Braun who in 1908, along with his partners Abraham J. Kroeker, Jakob Kroeker and J.S. Prochanov, established the Raduga ("Rainbow") publishing firm. This became a flourishing enterprise that formed the heart of Mennonite publishing in Russia. Other Mennonite publishers in Russia were H.A. Ediger in Berdiansk, Hermann A. Lenzmann in Tokmak and Peter Janzen and J. and P. Reimer in Gnadenfeld.

The most immediate and dramatic contributing factor in the rapid growth of print culture in this period was the emergence of a Mennonite periodical press. It began in 1897 with the founding of Abraham Kroeker's *Christlicher Familienkalender,* an almanac of Christian character containing general information (i.e., non-statistical) about Mennonite life in the colonies. The *Familienkalender* appeared annually through 1915, was suspended in 1916 and 1917 but brought back in 1918 and 1919, after which it ceased operations permanently. It was immensely popular with Russian Mennonite (as well as some non-Mennonite) readers, and reached a peak circulation of 15,000. From the beginning the *Familienkalender* carried an extensive and diversified advertising section that took up to a third and more of the available space.

The enterprising Abraham Kroeker and his cousin Jakob Kroeker also published *Christliches Jahrbuch zur Belehrung und Unterhaltung* from 1902-05. It carried religious and literary articles, but in spite of its name it was not an informational and statistical handbook either. After an initial success this publication proved to be short-lived. It was followed by *Mennonitisches Jahrbuch,* an annual publication that ran from 1904-1914 and which focused specifically on events and achievements in the Mennonite colonies. The *Jahrbuch* was edited by Elder Heinrich Dirks until 1911, when David H. Epp took over as editor under the auspices of the Conference of Mennonites. Not the least important aspect of these almanacs were the numerous advertisements they carried for a wide assortment of other periodicals, papers and books which were thus brought to the attention of prospective Mennonite readers.

Important as the almanacs were, however, their overall impact probably did not equal that of the two Mennonite newspapers *Die Friedensstimme* and *Der Botschafter,* founded in 1903 and 1905 respectively. *Friedensstimme* was founded by Abraham and Jakob Kroeker, with the former serving as editor for its entire lifespan. Because of Russian censorship restrictions, the paper was published in Berlin as a bi-monthly for the first three years.[38] The long-range publishing was extremely costly and resulted in a loss for the co-owners. After months of negotiating with the Russian government, the partners finally received permission in late 1905 to publish their paper in Halbstadt. From 1906-1908 *Friedensstimme* appeared as a weekly, after which it appeared twice weekly in a 16-24 page tabloid form until 1914, when it was forced to suspend operations because of the proscription against the use of German in wartime Russia. In the "golden years" before World War I the paper had a press run of over 6,000 copies and had Mennonite subscribers all over Russia. On May 13, 1917, Kroeker revived his paper under the politically expedient name of *Nachrichten des "Volksfreund."* From August 12 to October 28, 1917, the name was changed to Molotschna *Flugblatt,* then again became *Volksfreund* until July 2, 1918, when under the protection of the German army of occupation Kroeker was once again able to use the name *Friedensstimme.* In early 1920 the paper again became *Volksfreund* until its demise with the October 10, 1920, issue.

In a late issue of *Friedensstimme* — no. 59, October 12, 1918 — Kroeker wrote a brief history of his paper and outlined its philosophy and character. Founded as a general publication for Christian families, *Friedensstimme,* he notes, gradually developed into a newspaper, but without losing its Christian character. Kroeker obviously takes pride in the fact that his is the only Mennonite paper still alive and trying to serve the shattered Mennonite commonwealth.[39] Leonhard Friesen has pointed out that politically the paper was "slightly to the left of the political centre on the Russian spectrum."[40] In a cultural sense, however, it was quite conservative, more conservative in cultural outlook than *Der Botschafter.* All in all, *Friedensstimme,* had an honourable history as an influential newspaper that served not only the Mennonite Brethren but the Mennonite constituency in general. It was the first Mennonite paper in Russia and the longest to remain in the field.

The second paper established in Mennonite Russia was *Der Botschafter,* which was published twice weekly from 1905-1914 in a five-column, six- (sometimes eight-) page newspaper format that included domestic and foreign news, a regular section on Mennonite churches and congregational activities, a *feuilleton* or leisure column, containing everything from religious meditations to serialized fiction, plus a lavish advertising section that by 1914 usually took up to two or even more pages of each issue. Published briefly at first in Ekaterinoslav, then in Berdiansk by the prominent businessman, J.J. Thiessen, it was more secular in orientation than *Friedensstimme,* reflecting as it did the Mennonite landowning and business establishment with its somewhat right of centre stance.[41] Under the capable editorship of founding editor David H. Epp, later joined by H.A. Ediger as co-editor, this lively little newspaper accurately reflected the impressive economic and cultural strides the Mennonites of Russia were making in the years leading up to World War I. The advertising section, promoting everything from imported luxury soap and perfume to luxury bathrooms (with flushing toilets), central heating and imported boat motors, motorcycles and motor cars (Opels, Fords, etc.), made blatant appeals to Mennonite readers to avail themselves of the "good life" made possible by the latest technology and obviously within the means of *Botschafter* readers.

In 1909 Kornelius G. Neufeld of Davlekanovo, Ufa, founded the monthly magazine *Aufwärts,* whose subtitle, *Blätter für Sänger und Dirigenten und für Liebhaber des christlichen Gesanges,* indicated that the periodical was designed to promote the art of choral singing in Mennonite churches. In the second volume, however, Neufeld broadened his approach and changed *Aufwärts* into a magazine for young people which included articles on history, science, poems and a column titled "Lose Blätter" for which Peter B. Harder wrote short stories and genre sketches. *Aufwärts* contained 32 pages and was published in Leipzig. Unfortunately, the ambitious Neufeld soon felt the financial burden of printing his magazine abroad and was forced to give it up in 1911 after only 24 issues.

The last periodical to be published during this period was *Unser Blatt*, which ran from 1925 to 1928 during the relaxed period of the New Economic Policy (NEP) just before Stalin tightened his grip on the Soviet Union. *Unser Blatt* was a monthly publication officially sponsored by the Allgemeine Bundeskonferenz der Mennoniten-gemeinden in Moscow in an attempt to foster spiritual unity and cultural consolidation among the scattered and demoralized Mennonites. The editor was the brilliant but ill-fated Alexander H. Ediger of Schoensee in the Molotschna.[42] The paper was plagued throughout its brief life by the censors and gave up the ghost with the June 1928 issue. A parallel publication to *Unser Blatt* was *Der praktische Landwirt*, a monthly journal published by the All-Russian Mennonite Agricultural Association from May 15, 1925, to December, 1926.

As already indicated, the centennial celebrations of 1889 had generated a new historical awareness in the Mennonite colonies.[43] An even more significant stimulus that led the Russian Mennonites to assess themselves and their history in a series of historical works was the revolution of 1905.[44] Eager to dispel the impression given in the Russian press that Mennonite society was "parasitical," Mennonites began writing histories and biographies describing their contributions to their adopted country.[45] The spate of historical works began in 1907 with A. Goerz's *Ein Beitrag zur Geschichte des Forstdienstes der Mennoniten in Rußland* (Gross Tokmak, 1907) and Franz Bartsch's *Unser Auszug nach Mittelasien* (Halbstadt, 1907), the heart-breaking story of Claas Epp's ill-fated trek to Central Asia in 1880. The following year saw the publication of Franz Isaak's carefully documented *Die Molotschnaer Mennoniten: Ein Beitrag zur Geschichte derselben* (Halbstadt, 1908), still an important source for Russian Mennonite history. The incredibly industrious David H. Epp followed with three works: his biography, *Johann Cornies: Züge aus seinem Leben und Wirken* (Ekaterinoslav, 1909); *Die Memriker Ansiedlung: Zum 25-jährigen Bestehen derselben im Herbst 1910* (Berdjansk, 1910); and his brief biography, *Heinrich Heese und seine Zeit* (serialized in *Der Botschafter* in 1910). Epp's biography of Cornies is impressionistic and hagiographic, but served the purpose of justifying Mennonite society as represented by its most important leader. Most of Epp's books were first serialized in *Der Botschafter*, and due to the war some of his "historical" works were never issued in book form. Finally, there was P.M. Friesen' mammoth *Die alt-evangelische mennonitische Brüderschaft in Rußland (1789-1910) im Rahmen der mennonitischen Gesamtgeschichte* (Halbstadt, 1911), a richly documented but somewhat pietistically oriented history of the Mennonites in Russia which had been commissioned 25 years earlier as a "brief" history of the first quarter century of the Mennonite Brethren movement.[46] In the final analysis, Friesen's book, quite apart from its undoubted merit as a work of historiography, was a masterful apologia for the "Mennonite Brotherhood in Russia."[47]

Publications of a religious or devotional nature are too numerous during this period to list individually. In addition to the religious material carried by Mennonite periodicals, they regularly advertised all manner of religious books and pamphlets by non-Mennonites and Mennonites published in Germany as well as in Russia. Heinrich Dirks published several more volumes of his own sermons: *Der Christ wie er sein soll* (Gnadenfeld, 1900) and *Predigt über Taufe, Abendmahl* (Gross Tokmak, 1904). Jakob Kroeker published a collection of sermons under the title *Im Heiligtum des Vaterunsers* (Gnadenfeld, 1889), as well as several other works listed by P.M. Friesen.[48]

The first work of fiction published in book form was J.H. Janzen's *Denn meine Augen haben deinen Heiland gesehen* (Halbstadt, n.d.), a collection of twelve didactic short stories that was well received and that inspired a future writer like Arnold Dyck.[49] In 1913 Peter B. Harder published in book form *Lose Blätter* (Davlekanovo, 1913), the stories he had written for *Aufwärts* in 1909-10. That same year Harder also brought out the first Mennonite novel published on Russian soil, *Schicksale: oder die lutherische Cousine* (Davlekanovo, 1913).[50] A sequel to this novel — *Onkel Andreas und die Frie-denshöfer* — was advertised in 1914 as being "in the press" in Germany.[51]

J.H. Janzen also wrote three one-act plays in *Plautdietsch: De Bildung* (Halbstadt, 1912), *De Enbildung* (Halbstadt, 1913) and *Daut Schultebott* (Tiege, n.d.). These Low German plays introduced a comic tradition in that colourful language which Arnold Dyck raised to a masterful level with his much greater comic works in *Plautdietsch* here in Canada. J.H. Janzen's older brother, Johannes Heinrich Janzen, was by all reports a gifted artist and writer who specialized in children's stories. His enchanting narrative poem *Das Märchen vom Weihnachtsmann* was published (with his illustrations) in the Molotschna in 1924, republished in Canada by J.H.

Jacob H. Janzen (1878-1950), one of the first writers of fiction and drama among Mennonites in Russia.   Photo: Mennonite Heritage Centre Archives

Janzen (1938) and republished once more in a handsome edition edited by Dr. Waldemar Janzen of Canadian Mennonite Bible College in Winnipeg (1975). In his "Nachwort" to this edition Dr. Janzen observes that by and large the work of Russian Mennonite writers was of a didactic and instructional nature — *Gebrauchsliteratur* — and raises the question of whether the pure literary fancy of a Johannes Janzen gave promise of a new kind of literary blossom in the Russian Mennonite garden had it not been nipped in the bud by war and revolution.[52]

The question remains hypothetical, but there were definite signs in the decade before World War I that Russian Mennonite writing was gaining as rapidly in quality as it did in quantity. Even P.M. Friesen, who began his chapter on Russian Mennonite publications with an apology for its brevity, sounded a note of optimism when he contemplated the future: "Consequently, to the youthful Mennonite literature belongs a future of unlimited possibilities for growth and self-improvement."[53] Circumstances would not permit that future to be realized in Russia, but the print culture that developed there was in large measure preserved and transported to other lands by the Russian Mennonites who emigrated in the twenties. The momentum that had been gathering in Russia was checked there but continued here in Canada and, to a lesser extent, in the United States and Germany in the thirties and forties.[54]

Although P.M. Friesen did not know it in 1910, his apology was premature and unnecessary. That a relatively small sect of Anabaptist-Mennonites lacking any tradition of book culture had, after establishing themselves as an agrarian society in Russia over the span of a century, developed such a promising print culture called for praise rather than apology. With its ever-improving and expanding school system, the Mennonites of Russia were ensuring themselves of a literate community which in the final decades of the Mennonite commonwealth was giving every sign that a literate people will demand and get the kind of indigenous print culture it needs and deserves. Even the literary talent, which requires a rich cultural humus if it is to thrive, was beginning to emerge, and the self-criticism required in good literature would also have developed if time had permitted. It is interesting to speculate that had the Revolution not come the Russian Mennonites might have begun to create within the next generation a literature in Russian, just as they began to create one in English a generation after arriving in Canada in the twenties.

Notes

1. Included for discussion in this paper are all works written and "published" by Mennonites in Russia regardless of where those works were printed, but not works dealing with the Russian Mennonite experience outside of Russia, even if their authors were Russian Mennonites. I wish to thank James Urry for generously sharing with me some of the research references he had tracked down in this area.

2. P.M. Friesen, *The Mennonite Brotherhood in Russia (1789-1910)* (Fresno, California: Board of Christian Literature, General Conference of Mennonite Brethren Churches, 1978), 831.

3. Ibid., 841.

4. Friesen's list is not quite complete even for his own time. Adolf Ehrt in *Das Mennonitentum in Russland* (Langensalza: Beltz, 1932), writing at the end of our period, gives the total number of books and periodicals as 52. My own total in this paper comes to just under 70 titles, and I have not listed everything.

5. John B. Toews, *Czars, Soviets and Mennonites* (Newton, Kansas: Faith and Life Press, 1982), 35.

6. Friesen, *Mennonite Brotherhood*, 831.

7. Delbert Plett, *The Golden Years: The Mennonite Kleine Gemeinde in Russia (1812-1849)* (Steinbach: D.F.P. Publications, 1985), 320.

8. Ibid., 321.

9. Ibid., 324. The full title of Friesen's treatise was *Eine einfache Erklärung über einige Glaubenssätze der sogenannten Kleinen Gemeinde: Wohlmeinend aufgesetzt von einem treuen Diener am Worte des Herrn im Jahre 1845.*

10. Plett, *The Golden Years,* 318 and chapter 17 passim.

11. The first historical account of the Old Colony was a brief report by Heinrich Heese submitted to the Guardians Committee in July, 1848, as a supplement to similar reports written on each individual village of the settlement. In 1857 Johann Peters was also asked to write a brief account of the history of the first settlement in Russia. See David G. Rempel, "An Introduction to Russian Mennonite Historiography," *Mennonite Quarterly Review* 48 (October 1974): 411-12, note 4.

12. Johann Cornies and other prominent Mennonites were contributors to the *Unterhaltungsblatt.* It ran until 1862 when it was replaced by the *Odessaer Zeitung,* which became even more popular with Mennonite readers and contributors.

13. In the last of a series of articles on the Volga Mennonites published in *Odessaer Zeitung,* 283 (December 16/28, 1989), there is a note on reading and books: "Überall fanden wir bei den Mennoniten Bibeln . . . und irgend ein religiöses Blatt. Hier gibt es ganze Bibliotheken mit belletristischen und wissenschaftlichen Werken, ganz abgesehen von den verschiedensten deutschen Kalendern und Zeitungen. Von Zeitungen fanden wir häufig die 'Petersburger Zeitung' . . . eine Reihe von Romanen und Novellen Coopers, Walter Scotts, Hoffmann u.a. . . . Man sieht, die Mennoniten interessieren sich für alles, was über sie im Auslande und bei uns geschrieben wird."

14. See Isaac P. Fast, *Züge aus meinem Leben* (Winnipeg, Manitoba: A.J. Fast, 1932), 12-13.

15. See *Zur Erinnerung an das 25-jährige Bestehen der ersten mennonitischen Druckerei in Rußland* (Halbstadt: N.p., 1912).

16. John B. Toews, "Cultural and Intellectual Aspects of the Mennonite Experience in Russia," *Mennonite Quarterly Review* 53 (April 1979): 150.

17. Ibid., 154.

18. Toews sees these trends as eventually leading to the kind of comfortable cultural and literary provincialism that precluded any real development of imaginative literature and art, but the cultural dynamism and rapid expansion of print culture in the decades before World War I would seem to indicate otherwise. Ibid., 152-159.

19. According to P.M. Friesen, this German textbook "was accepted only with great difficulty" because "it was believed that this reader would supplant the Bible." *Mennonite Brotherhood,* 806 and 1036, note 76. The merits of the reader were thoroughly analyzed in a series of articles in *Odessaer Zeitung,* November 20, 23, 24 and 29, 1895.

20. The full title was *Nashi Kolonii: Opyty i Materialy po Istorii i statistike Inostrannoi kolonizatsii v Rossii* (St. Petersburg: V.V. Nusvalta, 1869).

21. See Rempel, "Russian Mennonite Historiography," 417.

22. For a fuller account of this book and its author see Rempel, 418. The book was reprinted most recently in *Zwei Dokumente: Quellen zum Geschichtsstudium der Mennoniten in Rußland* (Winnipeg, Manitoba: Echo-Verlag, 1965).

23. Rempel, "Russian Mennonite Historiography," 421-22.

24. For an analysis of this book see Walter Klaassen's "A Belated Review: Martin Klaassen's 'Geschichte der wehrlosen taufgesinnten Gemeinden' Published in 1873," *Mennonite Quarterly Review* 49 (January 1975): 43-52.

25. Ibid., 43.

26. For a full account of Epp's book and the expedition see Fred Richard Belk's *The Great Trek of the Russian Mennonites to Central Asia 1880-1884* (Scottdale, Pennsylvania: Herald Press, 1976).

27. Delbert Plett unravels the tangled history of this publication in *Storm and Triumph* (Steinbach, Manitoba: D.F.P. Publications, 1986), chapter 18.

28. See Wesley Berg, *From Russia with Music* (Winnipeg, Manitoba: Hyperion Press, 1985), chapter 1, for the early history of Mennonite choral singing and music publishing in Russia.

29. For a detailed account of Thiessen's fascinating career see Plett, *Storm and Triumph,* 131-144.

30. Loewen kept writing poetry after migrating to Canada and published a revised and expanded edition of *Feldblumen* (Steinbach, Manitoba: Verlag von Arnold Dyck, 1946).

31. I am indebted to the poet's grandson, Dr. Harry Loewen, Chair of Mennonite Studies, University of Winnipeg, for bringing this volume to my attention.

32. P.M. Friesen, *Mennonite Brotherhood,* 834.

33. *Odessaer Zeitung,* 273-293 (December 3/15, 1886 — December 30/January 11, 1886-87). This is the same Jakob Toews who translated *Nashi Kolonii;* see p. 224-225 above.

34. Ibid., 12 (January 16/28, 1883); 40 (February 18, March 1, 1884); 74 (April 3/15, 1883); 103 (May 6/18, 1884); 138 (June 24/July 6, 1883).

35. Ibid., 103 (May 6/18, 1884): 2-3.

36. The figures for the Old Colony are incomplete and do not include German and Russian newspapers. A further breakdown of these statistics reveals that readers in the Molotschna subscribed to 183 German papers and periodicals for a total of 2,180 subscribers while 42 papers and periodicals in Russian were taken for a total of 186 subscribers. The overall figures given for German papers and periodicals subscribed to in the Old Colony are 110 for 1,403 subscribers. In general, religious periodicals were more popular in the Molotschna — 91 periodicals for 1,420 subscribers, compared with 25 for 693 in the Old Colony. On the other hand, entertainment and fashion magazines were more numerous in the Old Colony than in Molotschna. See *Odessaer Zeitung* (May 21/June 3, 1904): 2-3; (July 13/26), 1904; July 14/27, 1904; and October 14/27, 1904).

37. See report on "Bibliotheken" in *Mennonitsches Jahrbuch* (1903): 73-74.

38. No issues from the initial Berlin period of 1903-1905 of *Friedensstimme* are known to exist.

39. Abraham J. Kroeker was indeed an intrepid and uncommonly dedicated Christian journalist whose full heroic story has yet to be told.

40. Leonhard Friesen, "Mennonites in Russia and the Revolution of 1905: Experiences, Perceptions and Responses," *Mennonite Quarterly Review* 62 (January 1988): 45-46.

41. Ibid., 46.

42. Ediger was a university-educated teacher and minister of remarkable talents and character. He was a fine musician and became the leading choir director in Molotschna. Convinced that his leadership was needed in the new Russia, he refused to emigrate in the twenties and was later arrested and swallowed up in the gulag in the thirties.

43. This phenomenon was repeated in Canada during the centennial year 1974, which also acted as an impetus for a spate of historical and literary writing that has grown into an ever-widening stream since then.

44. For a fine interpretation of this period of Russian-Mennonite history see Leonhard Friesen, "Mennonites in Russia," 42-45.

45. Ibid., 52.

46. Friesen's history has become more popular than ever since being translated into English in 1978 (see note 2 above).

47. On this point see Rempel, "Russian Mennonite Historiography," 432, and L. Friesen, "Mennonites in Russia," 53.

48. P.M. Friesen, *Mennonite Brotherhood*, 834.

49. See Arnold Dyck, "Jacob H. Janzen — Writer," *Mennonite Life* 6 (July, 1951): 33.

50. For a fuller discussion of these early Russian-Mennonite works of fiction see my article "The Russian-Mennonite Experience in Fiction" in *Mennonite Images: Historical, Cultural, and Literary Essays Dealing with Mennonite Issues,* ed. Harry Loewen (Winnipeg, Manitoba: Hyperion Press, 1981), 223-227.

51. See *Christlicher Familienkalender* (1914): 217. According to Heinrich Goerz, Harder's second novel never appeared because World War I intervened, followed by Harder's early death in 1923. H. Goerz, *Die Molotschnaer Ansiedlung: Entstehung, Entwicklung und Untergang* (Steinbach, Manitoba: Echo-Verlag, 1951), 167.

52. Waldemar Janzen, "Nachwort" to Johannes Heinrich Janzen, *Das Märchen vom Weihnachtsmann* (Winnipeg, Manitoba: CMBC Publications, 1975), 30.

53. P.M. Friesen, *Mennonite Brotherhood*, 841.

54. Even in the Soviet Union, although we still know very little about Mennonite writing in Russia after the Revolution and the emigration in the twenties, some writing and publishing did continue, apparently, as evidenced in the case of David Schellenberg, who published poems, songs and even a trilogy of novels in the early thirties. See also the Soviet German newspaper, *Neues Leben;* various issues of the periodical, *Heimatliche Weiten,* which began publication in 1981; and *Anthologie der sowjet-deutschen Literatur,* in 3 Bänden (Alma-Ata, 1981-82).

Urban Mennonites in Russia

George K. Epp

Russian Mennonites liked to think of themselves as a *Bauernvolk*, a people of rural background, for whom farming was the dream of generations. Their reputation as innovative farmers had been established. They liked their *Bauernvolk* image. Rural life seemed to offer the simple, ideal life-style which was compatible with their theology. That ideal was very much on the mind of the 17,000 Mennonites who left Russia in the 1870s; it was again the dream of more than 20,000 who followed that first wave of emigration to North America; and, although less pronounced, it was still on the mind of many that left after 1945.

This could leave the impression that in the past, especially in Russia, Mennonites were a strictly rural people for whom agriculture was the only acceptable occupation. That, however, has never been quite true. This paper will attempt to shed some light on the history of a substantial number of Mennonites in Russia who chose to live in urban centres.

The First Urban Mennonites in Russia

The major factor influencing the four waves of Mennonite immigration into Russia, between 1789 and 1890, was the abundance of land in the scarcely populated steppes of Ukraine. Many of the immigrants in the first group of settlers were landless children of farmers. Although many of them had learned a trade, their ties to the land were very strong. The promise of a plot of land was enough incentive for them to risk the journey into an unknown future. What the Russian government liked about these settlers was their desire for land, although the government never did make it mandatory for any settlers to become farmers. The *Privilegium* (letter of special privileges granted to immigrants) stated specifically that all settlers, including the Mennonites, were free to settle on land or in cities and follow the trade of their choice. Bartsch and Hoeppner, the two delegates who were sent to inspect the proposed settlement land in south Russia, pressed this point with the authorities in St. Petersburg when they presented their petition to the government. Paragraph 5 of the petition asked for the right "to build factories and other necessary enterprises in the cities and villages of the Ekaterinoslav and Taurida provinces. . . ."[1] This privilege was granted. Some of the early settlers took advantage of this right and chose to settle in the city of Ekaterinoslav. Like farmers, they too were exempt from paying taxes for ten years but they forfeited the allotment of land to which only farmers were entitled.

The first Mennonite to establish himself in a Russian city was Heinrich Thiessen. He settled in Ekaterinoslav in 1805 where he built a treadmill and a vinegar processing plant. When Heinrich Heese arrived in that city in 1808, he found hospitality in the home of the Thiessens.[2] The Thiessens' business which, according to D.H. Epp, specialized in flour and vinegar for 106 years, was the oldest commercial enterprise of the city of Ekaterinoslav and of the whole province. Thiessen probably chose Ekaterinoslav over Alexandrovsk because his business instinct told him that in Alexandrovsk he would eventually have strong competition. Already in 1801 a mill had been established in Chortitza right next to Alexandrovsk.[3] Heinrich Thiessen came to Ekaterinoslav at the same time as Heinrich Cornies, David Schroeder, Heinrich Toews and Jakob Epp. Twenty years later young Heinrich Heese II and Abram Hamm arrived there as students. However, Mennonites did not move into the city in large numbers. In 1889 only nine families, a total of 50 persons, lived in the city of Ekaterinoslav.[4]

The city of Berdiansk was the closest commercial centre for Mennonites in New Russia. It was incorporated in 1837 and developed into a significant port by Graf Vorontsov, the governor of Taurida province. Berdiansk thus became the major export centre for Mennonite wheat and also the first Russian city with a Mennonite suburb. The city had designated some of its land for a small gardening community. When the designated fifty plots of three-quarter dessiatins each were not taken up by Russians and Ukrainians, Graf Vorontsov instructed the city to offer the land to Mennonite settlers from the Molotschna Colony.[5] The location of Berdiansk on the Sea of Azov must have been very attractive to some of the new settlers from the Danzig area because 50 families were quickly found. In 1841 the garden plots on the east side of Berdiansk were settled by Mennonites. In addition to the 50 garden plots the community also received two centrally located lots for a school and a church building. Under the leadership of Abraham and Leonhard Sudermann this community prospered right from the beginning and became known as the

Niemetskaia sloboda (German suburb). By 1850 at least 50 families, a total of approximately 200 people, lived in Berdiansk.

Among the early Mennonite settlements in Russia, Schoenwiese, the only Chortitza Colony village located on the east bank of the Dniepr, held a unique place. The original 17 families, who in 1797 were given land just south of the town of Alexandrovsk, liked their beautiful meadow *(schöne Wiese)* and its proximity to the town. However, in contrast to the Ekaterinoslav and Berdiansk settlers, the Schoenwiese settlers never did want to be city dwellers. They were farmers who enjoyed being close to market in the town of Alexandrovsk, from which they were separated only by a small tributary of the Dniepr, the Moskovka. The city of Alexandrovsk developed before their eyes. They only had to cross the bridge to sell their produce. However, this ideal location would some day leave these farmers no choice. They would be incorporated into the growing city and, even in the early years, could not escape its influence. They had more contacts with the Ukrainian city population than any other villagers. In spite of its determination to live its Mennonite village life, Schoenwiese, which the Russians called Moskovka, soon turned out to be a "different" village. However, incorporation into the city was not forced on the community until the twentieth century.

The Impact of Industrialization and Education

In retrospect it is difficult to see how a successful farming community could have hoped to perpetuate a strictly rural life-style for all members of the group. However, their success seemed to convince them that in the villages, Mennonite youth could be involved in "useful employment," that is, feeding the world, and also be provided with the happy life, as the villagers understood it. But the Mennonite colonies were not monastic communities. Mennonite immigrants were a relatively daring and adventurous group. A closer look at the early immigrants reveals quite a number of fascinating characters. Some, like Heinrich Heese, were recent converts from the Lutheran faith. These new converts were less bound by tradition. Heese arrived in 1808; by 1809 he had found employment with a Russian family of nobility so he could learn Russian. It would seem that early settlers in general were not averse to mobility and did not hesitate to move into the city. The Thiessens, Cornies, Schroeders, Toews and Epps could apparently settle in Ekaterinoslav without fear that they would be ostracized by the larger Mennonite community.

The trend toward more mobility and a willingness to leave the villages ran parallel to the development of industry and education.

The first windmill in Chortitza (1801), Thiessen's treadmill in Ekaterinoslav (1805), Sudermann's treadmill in Berdiansk (1841), and the many windmills which eventually could be found in almost every Mennonite village, were all signs of a gradual industrialization process. It was also obvious that there was an interrelationship between agricultural success, industrial development, education and urbanization. Agriculture demanded the presence of mills which in turn invited more productivity, especially when in the 1830s the port of Berdiansk opened the door for exports. More aggressive agriculture demanded more and better mills; better mills called for better agricultural machinery to supply the mills; and mills and the growing industry demanded educated personnel. It is difficult to say which aspect of this development was more important, but it is clear that one could not have developed without the other.

The breakthrough of education among Mennonites in Russia in the last quarter of the nineteenth century sent literally hundreds of young Mennonites to reputable schools in Russia and Europe. The number of farmers who sent their children to universities grew. In 1917, 32 percent of university graduates had a farming background; in addition 33 percent came from the lower middle class (teachers, ministers, employees of various enterprises) whose roots were in the farming community.[6] Also, by 1917, Mennonite schools had an abundance of university-trained teachers, at least 18 practising Mennonite physicians, nine lawyers and 34 engineers whose expertise served the flourishing industry.[7] Without this pool of educated human resources, the impressive achievements of Mennonite industry at the beginning of the twentieth century would have been impossible. As it was, 73 motor- and steam-driven mills and 105 smaller mills comprised a 51.8 percent share in the milling industry of Ukraine; twenty-six Mennonite factories produced 10 percent of all agricultural implements in southern Russia (Ukraine) and about 6.5 percent of the total Russian production.[8] These achievements of Mennonite industrial enterprises would not have been possible in isolation. Agriculture, industry and education went hand in hand.

The inevitable by-product of this success was a movement away from the community and the beginning of a Russification process. Mennonite millers, who controlled 51.8 percent of the milling industry in Ukraine, had to move out of their colonies to towns where their skill was in demand. Between 1850 and 1917 there was a Mennonite miller in most leading Russian centres. The millers first chose the Russian or Ukrainian cities and towns around the Mennonite colonies: Ekaterinoslav, Berdiansk, Melitopol, Orekhov, Pologi, Nikopol,

Millerovo and Iusovka. Early in the twentieth century they followed the new railroad into Siberia. The families involved in such enterprises sent their children to Mennonite schools or to Europe to make sure they would not lose their identity.

There is reason to believe, however, that in the long run separation from the community took its toll. Their children grew up among Ukrainians (they would say Russians) and gradually lost a feeling for the religious community from which they were separated most of their life. A classic case was the family of a Mennonite miller who, together with his young wife, established a successful milling operation in a town in southern Ukraine. They intended to earn enough money so that they could move back into a Mennonite colony where they hoped to buy a comfortable property. Their children went to Mennonite schools, but before the parents were ready to move back into the colony one son married a girl of Greek background, one married a Russian girl, one married a Jewish girl and the daughter married a Ukrainian. Only one of these couples found its way into the Mennonite community, was baptized and established a positive relationship with the Mennonite church.[9]

It is not surprising that the church began to warn against adventures far away from the supporting community. It seemed apparent that the value system of those living in isolation from the community gradually changed, sometimes drastically, even where ties with the Mennonite community were maintained more successfully.

Many also considered education a mixed blessing. Would it not destroy the strong Mennonite community spirit? Until late into the 1860s, Mennonite parents in general refused to let their children study in schools that were not under Mennonite control. The government increasingly put on pressure, in part because young Mennonites did not learn enough Russian in Mennonite schools, and also because integration of all minority groups and total Russianization had become government policy. In 1869 the governor of South Russia, Count Kozebue, instructed Mennonites and German settlers to send representatives to Odessa to discuss the improvement of education in the colonies.[10] These representatives were told to follow the lines of the new school reforms, namely to introduce Russian instruction in all schools, and to establish three annual "Alexander Scholarships" for Mennonite students to attend Russian *Gymnasiums* and universities. Two scholarships were for Molotschna students and one for a Chortitza student. The first students from the Molotschna to benefit from these scholarships were the sons of the *Dorfschulze* from Molotschna, Johann and Jakob Esau, and Wilhelm

Penner from Chortitza. The three recipients of these scholarships turned out to be worthy candidates for the honour, although, as Johann Esau relates in a brief autobiographical sketch, the selection process was simple because there were so few candidates.[11] The two Esau boys were not at all averse to studying in a distant city, and their father, the *Schulze,* also felt obligated to send his boys, because the government demanded that students be sent to a Russian *Gymnasium.* When they returned to the colonies, they quickly earned a reputation. Penner became a teacher at the *Zentralschule,* Johann Esau became a very successful engineer and administrator, and Jakob Esau became the first Mennonite physician in Russia.

From the 1870s on a growing stream of Mennonite students attended Russian and European universities and other schools of higher learning. The estimated number of Mennonite university graduates in Russia between 1880 and 1917 was somewhere between 150 and 200, a percentage far above the Russian average. Those graduates present an interesting record.[12] In the first twenty-five years of Mennonite participation in university education, only 67 percent of the students married Mennonite partners, 12 percent married partners belonging to non-Mennonite evangelical churches, 21 percent married partners belonging to the Russian Orthodox church and 16 percent moved to the city.[13] This trend probably would have continued and the number of mixed marriages actually

Mennonite students in St. Petersburg with a visiting minister, 1889.

Photo: Courtesy Esau family

would have increased if the catastrophic events of 1917 had not ended all normal development in the Mennonite communities.

Important Mennonite Urban Communities

Berdiansk was the first Russian city where Mennonites became involved in society in a significant way. The 50 families which settled in the *Niemetskaia sloboda* of Berdiansk quickly became an influential factor in the city. In a short time many of these city dwellers became involved in commercial enterprises.[14] Abram Sudermann built the first treadmill in that city. The most influential grain merchant was Cornelius Jansen, who settled in Berdiansk in 1850 and was the Prussian consul there from 1859 to 1862(?). Abram Sudermann, a minister, immediately after his arrival from Danzig in 1841, began organizing a Mennonite church, which affiliated with the Gnadenfeld congregation until 1865. During Leonhard Sudermann's leadership, from 1865 to 1876, the Mennonite church in Berdiansk became independent, but after Sudermann's departure to America it again affiliated with the Molotschna church. The Mennonite congregation of the *Niemetskaia sloboda* also built its own school.[15]

Later, probably in the 1860s when land for another suburb was distributed, Mennonites were again among those who took advantage of a generous offer by the city of Berdiansk. A number settled in the new suburb, Makorty. Heinrich Ediger, who was city counsellor for many years, mayor of Berdiansk for several years (1900-?) and Danish Consul (?-1918), lived in Makorty and was responsible for establishing a school there. Ediger was named the first curator of the new Pushkin School in the Makorty suburb.[16] There is no doubt that Mennonites in Berdiansk had a high profile, were well accepted by the Russian-Ukrainian community and made a significant contribution to the political and social life of that city.

During the Crimean War (1853-1856) life in both of the Berdiansk suburbs was disrupted when the whole Mennonite community had to take refuge in the villages of the Molotschna Colony. After a year they returned and the community continued to thrive.[17]

Leonhard Sudermann and Cornelius Jansen were good friends of the evangelical pastor, Eduard Wuest. One can get a sense of Wuest's influence on the Berdiansk community by looking at Jansen's library, which included titles like Milton's *Paradise Lost*, Kierkegaard's *Letters*, Menno's *Fundamentbuch* and a collection of Hofacker's sermons.[18] Jansen was involved in distributing Christian literature at his own cost, 1800 rubles worth, between 1864 and 1873.[19] We have to conclude that the Berdiansk church, under the leadership of its

Ältester Leonhard Sudermann and layman Cornelius Jansen was evangelical and certainly more sophisticated than the rest of the churches in the Russian Mennonite colonies of that time. Serious disruption and instability were experienced by the community when its leaders decided to emigrate in the 1870s. Both Jansen and Sudermann decided to leave Russia and make a new start in the United States. In spite of this the Mennonite community in Berdiansk continued to grow. By 1909 it recorded 109 tax-paying members. This roughly corresponded to the number of households.[20]

Heinrich Ediger, publisher and co-editor of *Der Botschafter* after its transfer from Ekaterinoslav, was one of the strong new leaders in the Mennonite community. Furthermore, he was a strong voice in the councils of the city. It is not surprising that this community would also play a significant role in the affairs of the Molotschna Colony. Berdiansk was the major grain exporting centre for Molotschna farmers. The Sudermanns, Jansen, and later Ediger and other men from the Berdiansk community were often consulted on business matters. Ties between the Molotschna Colony and the Berdiansk Mennonite community remained fairly strong, in spite of differences in life-style and sophistication.

Until 1918 the Mennonite community in Berdiansk thrived. Available records indicate that it had an excellent relationship with its Russian, Ukrainian and Greek neighbours. During the civil war, the community suffered the fate of the rest of the Mennonite commonwealth in Russia.

Although Berdiansk and Ekaterinoslav in Taurida province had the largest urban Mennonite communities in Russia, there were a number of other smaller and larger cities in which Mennonites established themselves and in whose cultural and political life they eventually played a significant role. The town of Orekhov, founded in 1796 and incorporated in 1801, was located about 50 kilometres southeast of Alexandrovsk and almost the same distance from Halbstadt. In the 1860s several families from Schoenwiese moved to Orekhov. Ivan Andreievich Janzen built two steam mills there and encouraged other Mennonites to do the same. Soon another smaller Janzen *Mühle* (not related to Ivan Andreievich) and the Krueger factory which produced agricultural implements were established. By 1874 this small Mennonite community in Orekhov acted according to good Mennonite tradition and built a school and a church. Since the Mennonite community was not very large, Lutheran neighbours in that city joined the Mennonites. Both the school and church services were run jointly. Years later, a resident of Orekhov who had emigrated to Canada recalled, "We were used to thinking of our-selves as the German community of Orekhov. I do not remember that we ever used the term, Mennonite community."[21] However, for major festivities the community split up to celebrate in the respective home churches in the colonies. Most of the Orekhov Mennonites would go to Schoenwiese for those events. The drama presentations and the choirs in Schoenwiese were worth it, and of course the young people had to meet prospective Mennonite partners.[22]

The town of Orekhov had a population of 10,000. The total number of the *niemtsy* (Germans, a term applied to all foreigners) was less than 200. Because of the small numbers the relationship between these *niemtsy* and the Ukrainian population was good. In 1874, relatively soon after his arrival, Ivan Andreievich Janzen was elected mayor of Orekhov; he was reelected for consecutive terms until he retired in 1899.[23] Orekhov must have liked Janzen since they kept him on as mayor for 25 years in spite of the growing national-ism. Undoubtedly he knew the Russian language well and thus was able to move freely among the population without constantly reminding them of his foreign background. Of course they may have elected Janzen precisely because he was an "honest *niemets.*"

Toward the end of the 1880s two Mennonite colonies, Naumenko (1888) and Zamoilovka (1889), were established in the southern part of Kharkov province. The four villages of the Naumenko settle-ment were grouped around the railroad town of Barvenkovo, which had a population of 14,000. The villagers of the Naumenko Colony were from the Mennonite Brethren community of Einlage. The enterprising Mennonite businessmen in Barvenkovo came from Chortitza and Molotschna. At first the Mennonite community in Barvenkovo faced difficulties with local authorities. However, even-tually relations improved. Mennonites established four steam mills, two smaller mills, one agricultural implement factory and two large dealerships for imported machinery. They built a meeting house for the Mennonite Brethren. They also operated their own elementary school and a successful School of Commerce in cooperation with their Russian neighbours. Both schools offered instruction in Ger-man and in Russian. According to the *Mennonitisches Lexikon (ML)*, the Mennonite population of Barvenkovo in 1914 was 216.[24] Student records, which list 44 students in the elementary school, plus a number of students attending the School of Commerce, would lead one to believe that the total number of Mennonites living in Barven-kovo could have been higher than stated in the *ML*.

The Barvenkovo community and the whole Naumenko Colony

suffered because ties with the mother church were not close. Part of the problem was distance (approximately 350 kilometres). Lack of strong leadership may also have been a factor. By the beginning of the twentieth century colony life experienced marked cultural and religious decline.[25] Russification must certainly have become a serious problem in the Barvenkovo community, just as it had in Orekhov. However, the close cultural ties which the Mennonites in Orekhov maintained with the Chortitza Colony (Schoenwiese) had offset the trend toward Russification there.

Another significant and very promising Mennonite urban community was established at the beginning of the twentieth century in the important railroad town of Millerovo. At that time the population of Millerovo was probably just over 10,000. The first Mennonites to move to Millerovo were David Klassen, W.I. Dyck, W. Friesen, J. Nickel and J. Siemens. The group formed the so-called *Donskoie Tovarishchestvo* (Don Corporation) and, in 1903, built the first large steam mill in that region. In 1904, the Martens, De Fehr, Dyck Implement Factory, which employed 300 workers, was founded.[26] Very soon three more mills were built by Mennonites. The community thrived. Most of the Millerovo Mennonites were from the Einlage Mennonite Brethren Church, but a small group was of *Kirchliche* Mennonite background. The whole community benefitted from the strong leadership which W.I. Dyck gave to church life. A meeting house was built and the Mennonite Brethren church, affiliated with the Einlage church, was founded. Like in Orekhov, the church and school were shared by the whole German community which consisted of Mennonite Brethren, *Kirchliche* Mennonites, Lutherans and Baptists. C. A. DeFehr related that they thought of themselves as the German community of Millerovo.[27] By 1919 the membership of the Mennonite Brethren church in Millerovo was 140; the total Mennonite population was probably over 300. During the Civil War (1919) a considerable number of Millerovo Mennonites went to the Kuban region. In 1926 231 Mennonites still lived in Millerovo and vicinity, but soon thereafter most of the Mennonite Brethren families emigrated to Canada. There is no information available on Mennonites in Millerovo after 1927. The community probably ceased to exist soon afterwards.

Aside from these larger Mennonite urban communities numerous smaller Mennonite groups resided in Russian towns and cities. Records are available for only a few. Melitopol in Taurida province, geographically close to the Molotschna Colony, attracted Mennonite businessmen relatively early. The group was never very large but,

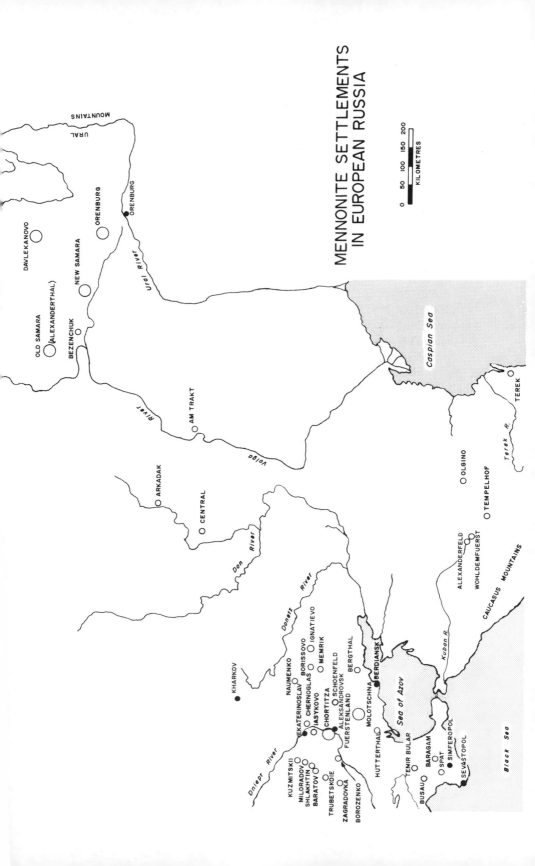

MENNONITE SETTLEMENTS
IN EUROPEAN RUSSIA

with the support of Mennonite estate owners of the district, it had its own church building. The last Russian-Mennonite *Bundeskonferenz* (General Conference of all Mennonites churches) was held in Melitopol on October 5-9, 1926.[28]

Another city where the Mennonite presence was significant, not because of high numbers but because of its importance for the larger community as a commercial centre, was Nikopol on the Dniepr. Several Mennonite mills had been established in this city. Johann Wieler's private school was also well known. The small Mennonite community offered a good contact point for Mennonite travellers.

Just north of the Molotschna Colony was the Russian town, Pologi. It was only about 50 kilometres from the nearest Mennonite village. Therefore it was one of the Russian towns where Mennonite millers found a ready market for their skills. Best known was the Albrecht mill. The Mennonite community here was small and depended on the Molotschna Colony for its spiritual nourishment.[29]

Mennonites who settled in the Crimea very soon found their way into Simferopol which was close to their settlements. By the early twentieth century even Sevastopol had a small Mennonite community. However, Sevastopol, like a number of other major Russian centres, attracted Mennonite students rather than business people. P.M. Friesen reported in the *Zionsbote*, May 19, 1902, that, together with his own children, 17 students were residing in the Friesen home, and 20 persons were participating in the regular worship services.

In the late nineteenth and early twentieth centuries, Mennonites moved east and settled in several urban centres in Siberia. In 1897 Peter J. and Justina Wiens from Schoenau, Molotschna, established a commercial enterprise in Omsk, selling agricultural machinery to the rapidly expanding farming sector of the region. Early in the twentieth century Mennonite farmers were attracted to the Omsk region and several moved into the city. Soon Omsk had a Mennonite elementary school, but it did not survive very long because of the changing political climate. However, Omsk played a significant role in the life of the young Mennonite community in Siberia. In 1924 the *Mennoverband* was organized in Omsk to represent Mennonite interests.[30]

At about the same time two more Mennonite colonies were established in south-western Siberia, the Pavlodar and the Slavgorod settlements, with 13 and 59 villages respectively. These settlements usually assumed the names of the cities around which they had settled. The cities provided the markets for their agricultural produce. Therefore it was also natural that some Mennonites would move into these market centres. Several Mennonite families established themselves in Pavlodar. Although the community was never large, it nevertheless played a major role for the area settlers. The Driedger-Voth House of Agricultural Implements, the two large mills of Goerzen and Thiessen, and the *Auffahrtshöfe* (cheap lodging for farmers who came into town with horse and wagon) of Schartner and Schmidt were almost indispensable for the Mennonite farmers.[31] In the city of Slavgorod the Mennonite population had grown to 254 by 1921. In 1923 this city became a centre for the relief efforts of the American Mennonite Relief Organization; in 1924 it became the seat of the Slavgorod section of the *Verband Deutscher Bürger Rußlands* (Union of Russian Citizens of German Lineage).[32] The activities of this Union were soon suspended.

In addition to the towns and cities which attracted Mennonite industrialists and merchants, the major Russian educational centres attracted Mennonite students. A list of Russian-Mennonite university graduates, compiled by N.J. Klassen, Peter Klassen and Heinrich Goerz, shows that Mennonites actually studied in nine of the better Russian universities, most often in St. Petersburg, Moscow, Kharkov and Odessa. The list of Mennonite students indicates that at least eight graduated from the University of Kharkov, eight from the University of Odessa, 17 from the University of Moscow and 27 from the university and other institutions of higher learning in St. Petersburg (Leningrad).[33] Although there were never large Mennonite communities in these cities, a growing number of Mennonites felt quite comfortable in large urban centres which offered theatre, ballet and other sophisticated cultural attractions. During World War I, and especially after the Revolution, a number of Mennonites settled in Moscow, Odessa and Kharkov. However, with the new political reality their presence in those cities was of no consequence to the larger Mennonite community.

The Shift in Economic and Cultural Factors

The Molotschna Colony seemed to have every advantage over the smaller and, in the early stage, less prosperous Chortitza Colony. However, in retrospect one should not be surprised that, with the advance of industrialization, the scale would eventually tip in favour of the Colony located on the Dniepr River. Even at the early stage of industrialization, Mennonite millers seemed to prefer a location near the Dniepr. But in the late 1860s, when regular boat service was established between Alexandrovsk (Zaporozh'e), Nikopol, Kherson and Odessa, the last advantage of the Molotschna Colony — the shorter distance to the major port for grain export — was eliminated. Odessa gained in importance, and the Chortitza Colony had the advantage of a cheap water transportation system. By 1875 the incredibly fast development of a major industrial centre in the Chortitza Colony had surpassed developments in the Molotschna Colony.[34] The aggressive phase of industrialization had begun.

In this context it seems necessary to stress once more the correlation between all aspects of an agricultural people's development. The economic success of the farming community was the foundation for the industrialization process which, not by accident led to the beginning of the milling industry. The success of the milling industry made the diversification of industrialization possible, and that success freed resources for the impressive educational achievements of the Russian Mennonites. How closely the economic success and education are related can best be demonstrated by the startling figures of N.J. Klassen's research on Russian Mennonite university graduates between 1890 and 1914.

First of all it is a well-known fact that, in the nineteenth and early twentieth century, university graduates hardly ever included sons and daughters of farmers. Yet among the 133 Mennonite graduates between 1890 and 1917, 32 percent were farmers' children; and 33 percent came from families of teachers, ministers and employees who were also from farming backgrounds.[35] One could argue that among Mennonites, over 60 percent of university graduates were of farm background. However, even if only 32 percent of the graduates were village children, that is a unique statistic in the European history of that particular period. The correlation between various aspects of regional development are also demonstrated by Klassen's statistics. Twenty eight percent of the graduates came from the smaller Chortitza Colony (18 villages), while only 31 percent came from the Molotschna Colony which had three times as many villages (55). This is even more surprising when we consider that, during the first half of the nineteenth century, the Molotschna Colony had attained a significant head start in education. However, most revealing is the fact that 16 percent of the graduates came from urban Mennonite communities.

Two Unique Urban Communities

Schoenwiese

The Mennonite villagers of Schoenwiese had no intention of becoming city dwellers. Schoenwiese was one of the smallest villages only because land for a larger farming community was not available. But at the beginning of the twentieth century D.H. Epp called it the "Minneapolis of the Colonies." Gradual change in the village began in 1834 when the villagers convinced the Vogt brothers, who were on the move from Danzig to the Molotschna, to stay in Schoenwiese as weavers. In spring 1840, the young Hermann Niebuhr was impressed with the milling business of Schoenwiese. By the end of the 1840s Peter Bock of Schoenwiese had established himself as a master mill builder; by 1860 he employed 40 people.[36] In 1863 Schoenwiese added a brewery to its growing industry. Its builder and owner, Heinrich Janzen, developed the brewery into a very successful business. *Brua Jaunzes* were important members of Schoenwiese society. Johann Janzen, son of the founder of the Janzen brewery, reports in the family records that the last traces of rural economy in Schoenwiese disappeared at the beginning of the twentieth century: "By 1904 there were five large mills, three large factories manufacturing agricultural machinery, the beer brewery, several stores, a bank and various office buildings, all in Mennonite hands. Industry displaced agriculture."[37]

Change had come slowly but had not gone unnoticed by the city fathers of Alexandrovsk, who had watched the thriving community from across the Moskovka. In June, 1911, after a long struggle to incorporate Schoenwiese into the city, the Schoenwiese "villagers" were forced to accept the decision of the ministerial council in St. Petersburg. Schoenwiese officially became what in reality it had been almost from the day of its inception, a suburb of Alexandrovsk.

This change was not immediately evident because life went on as it had before, although taxes were modified somewhat to the disadvantage of those who could easily absorb them. The good Schoenwiese elementary school, the two-year *Fortbildungsschule,* the beautiful Schoenwiese church and the Schoenwiese Mennonite society continued as before. The *Leppovsky Pereulok* (Lepp Street) was the Russian street built by Lepp and Wallmann for their workers. Any worker could apply for a lot on this street. Land and lumber were provided by the factory free of charge.[38] Hildebrandt and Pries built a hospital for their workers where treatment was unconditional and free of charge.[39] To what extent the three companies, Hildebrandt and Pries, Koop, and Lepp and Wallmann cooperated to synchronize their social security program is not known, but it would be reasonable to assume that some common efforts existed among them.

In many ways Schoenwiese had become the progressive industrial suburb of the city of Alexandrovsk. After the Revolution the three

Mennonite factories were taken over by the government and amalgamated into a giant factory called *Communar*. In 1925 the *Communar*, still under the leadership of the Mennonite engineers Dyck, Hamm, Pauls and Thiessen, produced the first combine in the Soviet Union. In 1927 they all received the Order of Lenin for their contribution to Soviet industry and agriculture. However, in the early years of the Stalin era all four men, along with thousands of other Mennonites, disappeared in the Siberian camps.

Ekaterinoslav

Ekaterinoslav was the first city to receive Mennonite settlers in the early nineteenth century. Despite its relative isolation from the larger rural community, the small urban community remained very Mennonite in its outlook. In 1889 the nine families of this community persuaded D.H. Epp to become their teacher and minister. In the course of another decade the population of the Mennonite community in Ekaterinoslav had grown to 158 persons. A larger school-church was erected, the program expanded and three teachers hired. Numerous Mennonite mills controlled by the Thiessen, Heese, Fast and Toews families were flourishing. Whereas Heinrich Thiessen's

The Jacob Toews family in the city of Ekaterinoslav, ca. 1910.

Photo: Courtesy Esau family

first mill, built in 1805, had a daily output of eight sacks of flour, the large mills now each produced 800 to 1000 sacks a day.

This milling industry gave the Mennonite community its early economic strength. Soon it would also become an intellectual centre in the true sense of that word. The idea for establishing a Mennonite mental health centre germinated in this urban community and was realized eventually at Bethania in the Chortitza Colony. The idea of the *Mädchenschule* (girls' *Gymnasium*) in Chortitza was born here. Also, a number of projects that never went beyond the dreaming stage but were totally realistic were all conceived in this community. One example is the projected hydro-electric station near Einlage, which was proposed and actively pursued by engineer Johann Esau and his Ukrainian friend, Iurgevich.

At the beginning of the twentieth century the Mennonite community expanded rapidly. Plans were underway to build a church and to further expand the school. However, this process was brought to an end abruptly in 1914 when the First World War began. Between 1895 and 1918 the outstanding personality in the urban community of Ekaterinoslav was Johann Esau, whose contribution went far beyond the Mennonite community. Yet Esau was a man who always remained very much dedicated to his church. He deserves special attention in the context of our study.

Profile of One Urban Mennonite Family

Young Heinrich Heese and Abram Hamm were two exceptional boys who came to Ekaterinoslav in the early 1820s in search of better educational facilities. They would find no imitators until 1869, a year which would become synonymous with a new beginning in Mennonite education.

In 1869 the Russian government put considerable pressure on the Mennonite colonies to implement the school reform regulations advocated by Alexander II. Crown Prince Alexander III even visited the Molotschna Colony. As an expression of loyalty, the colonies promised to establish three "Alexander Scholarships" in honour of the crown prince, two for Molotschna and one for Chortitza. As mentioned earlier it was hard to find takers for the two scholarships in the Molotschna. Only the *Dorfschulze* of Halbstadt, Jakob Esau, was willing to send his sons to study in Ekaterinoslav. The two Esau boys, Johann and Jakob, first studied at the *Gymnasium* (high school) in Ekaterinoslav, then pursued their studies at the universities of Riga and Kiev. Johann came back from Riga with a degree in engineering, while Jakob graduated from the Kiev Medical School. In

1884 they reported to the Molotschna Colony, but were released from any obligation because there was no work for them there. As a result, both of these first university graduates from the Molotschna ended up in Chortitza. Jakob became the colony physician; Johann very soon became chief engineer of the Lepp-Wallmann factory. During their fifteen years of studies — for Johann an additional five years of practical experience in Sevastopol and Baku — the two village boys had learned their trade well. They spoke flawless Russian, as it was spoken only in educated Russian circles.

By 1894 Dr. Jakob Esau had established a private eye clinic and a small hospital in Ekaterinoslav. Johann Esau had started a new factory on the outskirts of that city. In 1895 he sold the factory to a Belgian company but continued as director of the expanding enterprise. At the beginning of the century Johann Esau became involved in city politics. In 1904, a year after the Honourary Hereditary Citizenship award had been bestowed on him, he became Chief Administrator of Maintenance and Operations, in 1905 mayor of Ekaterinoslav. Reelected for a four-year term in 1906, he went to Paris to get a loan of five million gold rubles which made it possible to modernize the city. The first major project undertaken was a new pumping station for the city's water supply. The old pumping station took water from the river below the city, using a contaminated water supply and thereby inviting frequent epidemics of typhoid. The new pumping station was far above the city and finally gave Ekaterinoslav a safe water supply. Esau then proceeded to build a new sewer system, a new water supply system, a new streetcar line to connect all points of the city and a new markethall. During his term as mayor, Ekaterinoslav also established several girls' *Gymnasiums*. With all of these improvements during Esau's relatively short term in office, not only did the city's income increase sharply, but also the mayor's reputation rose steadily.

Johann Esau's other achievements included his participation in 1906 on the Stolypin Commission. This involved preparing documents for the duma concerning reforms of rural and urban administration. In the same year he was awarded the Order of St. Stanislav, third class.

In 1909 Johann Esau was not reelected as mayor of Ekaterinoslav. The political wind began to change with growing anti-German feeling. It is therefore surprising that two cities, Kharkov and Baku, approached Esau about becoming mayor in those cities. Esau declined the Kharkov invitation immediately. But Baku was planning a giant water supply project which lured the engineer to that city. He

joined the delegation from Baku to investigate the prospect. However, the presence of three factions in Baku — a minority Russian
group and strong Armenian and Tatar factions — did not bode well
for working relations. Therefore, he declined and returned to Ekaterinoslav. Here an invitation from Prince Urusov awaited him: to
accept the directorship of the South Russian Exhibition which was to
be held in Ekaterinoslav in 1910. The exhibition was a great success
and Esau was awarded the Order of St. Anne, third class.

In the summer of 1914 Esau was busy in Yalta. He and his partner,
Chaiev, an engineer from St. Petersburg, had just completed a deal
concerning property on which a new railway station was to be built.
News of the war sent Esau home. Prince Urusov again had a task for
him. He invited Esau to accept responsibility for the Red Cross work
of the whole southern region, which included the Ukraine, the
Caucasus, the Black Sea area and Rumania. The task was enormous.
The Russian army had soldiers but no medical units to serve along an
enormously long front. Esau recalls: "We had to put together 60
transport units and 10 to 20 hospital trains, get 3000 horses from
Siberia, material from Moscow and some from Japan. . . . We had to
equip new hospitals and supply depots. . . ." And very soon two Red
Cross transport ships had to be manned and equipped.[40] It was a
challenge to serve his country and his people "who had become
second class citizens" in that country. At Esau's request, Prince
Urusov got 2000 Mennonite men to serve directly under Esau's
command. To these Mennonite men Esau gave credit for the reputation of the southern Red Cross administration. Esau's son, Paul,
became Quartermaster of the "Athene," one of the two Red Cross
ships on which he served with distinction throughout the war. When
the war was over, Johann Esau recalls, all trains were to report back,
"but only one (of twenty) arrived, like a miracle in that confusion.
This train was commanded by a Mennonite doctor, and not a single
item was missing on that train."[41]

In 1918, Esau found a way to leave Russia. Eventually he and his
family settled in California, where his two children became highly
respected American citizens. Paul served as an engineer until his
retirement. Katherine, after completing her university studies in
Berlin and at Berkeley, became professor of botany at Berkeley.[42]

Conclusion

At the turn of the century only one percent of the Mennonite
population in Russia was urban, yet Mennonites made significant
contributions not only to their own Mennonite communities but

also to the civic life in the towns and cities where they lived. By 1900 they were active as justices of peace, city counsellors, administrators of important city departments and even as mayors of such significant centres as Ekaterinoslav, Berdiansk and Orekhov.

Urban Mennonites had established a healthy relationship with their Ukrainian and Russian neighbours.[43] The many instances in which Mennonite candidates were elected to high positions in the city administration are indicative of a high degree of acceptance. Urban Mennonites seem to have developed a better relationship with their native neighbours than did the rural Mennonite population. This should not be surprising, since Mennonites in the urban setting were a small minority, had daily contacts with their neighbours and had achieved a higher educational level.

Finally, the trends established by industrialization and education indicate that urbanization among the Russian Mennonites increased in the early twentieth century because the rural community could not have absorbed the growing number of well-educated people whose interest in agriculture was marginal. As land became more scarce, this trend eventually could have been considered a blessing. However, before the concept of a Christian *Bauernvölklein* could be threatened, the history of the Russian Mennonite commonwealth would come to an abrupt end.

Notes

1. D.H. Epp, *Die Chortitzer Mennoniten* (Odessa: A. Schultze, 1889), 27.

2. Heinrich Heese, "Die Biographie und Erlebnisse von Heinrich Heese (I)," unpublished manuscript, 1867, courtesy of Alice Schmidt; also D.H. Epp, *Heinrich Heese;* Nikolai Regehr, *Johann Philipp Wiebe: Zwei Vordermänner des Südrussischen Mennonitentums* (Steinbach, Manitoba: Echo Verlag, 1952), 12-13.

3. D.H. Epp, "The Emergence of German Industry in the South Russian Colonies,"trans. and ed. John B. Toews, *Mennonite Quarterly Review* 55 (October 1981): 314.

4. *Mennonite Encyclopedia,* s.v. "Ekaterinoslav."

5. Heinrich Ediger, *Erinnerungen* (Berdjansk: By the author, 1927), 6-7.

6. N.J. Klassen, "Mennonite Intelligentsia in Russia," *Mennonite Life* 24 (April 1969): 54.

7. Ibid.

8. C. Henry Smith, rev. Cornelius Krahn, *Story of the Mennonites* (Newton, Kansas: Faith and Life Press, 1981), 305-307.

9. Names withheld at the request of relatives.

10. P.M. Friesen, *Die alt-evangelische mennonitische Brüderschaft in Rußland 1789-1910* (Halbstadt: Raduga, 1911), 605.

11. Johann Esau, "Erinnerungen," unpublished manuscript courtesy of Paul and Esther Esau; also in *Der Bote,* September 15, 22, 29, 1970.

12. N.J. Klassen, "Mennonite Intelligentsia," 59-60.

13. Ibid., 54.

14. Heinrich Ediger, *Erinnerungen,* 7.

15. Gustav E. Reimer and G. R. Gaeddert, *Exiled by the Czar* (Newton, Kansas: Mennonite Publication Office, 1956), 8.

16. Heinrich Ediger, *Erinnerungen,* 8.

17. Ibid., 9-10.

18. Reimer and Gaeddert, *Exiled by the Czar,* 30.

19. Ibid., 27.

20. *Mennonite Encyclopedia,* s.v. "Berdyansk."

21. Interview with Olga Lepp, September 10, 1986.

22. Ibid.

23. Ibid.

24. *Mennonitisches Lexikon,* s.v. "Barwenkowo."

25. *Mennonite Encyclopedia,* s.v. "Kharkov."

26. C.A. De Fehr, *Memories of My Life* (Winnipeg, Manitoba: By the author, 1967), 21.

27. Ibid., 19.

28. *Mennonite Encyclopedia,* s.v. "Melitopol."

29. Interview with Abram Albrecht, September 9, 1986.

30. Peter Rahn, *Mennoniten in der Umgebung von Omsk* (Winnipeg, Manitoba: Christian Press, 1975), 211-212.

31. Gerhard Fast, *In den Steppen Sibiriens* (Rosthern, Saskatchewan: By the author, 1957), 152.

32. *Mennonite Encyclopedia,* s.v. "Slavgorod Mennonite Settlement."

33. N.J. Klassen, "Mennonite Intelligentsia," 59-60.

34. P.M. Friesen, *Alt-evangelische mennonitische Brüderschaft,* 693.

35. N.J. Klassen, "Mennonite Intelligentsia," 54.

36. D.H. Epp, "The Emergence of German Industry," 354.

37. Janzen Family Records, courtesy of Margaret Janzen. Schoenwiese was the only Mennonite village which changed its rural image. Halbstadt, Chortitza and Rosenthal also had factories, but the larger segment of the Mennonite population continued to be farmers, and their life style did not change significantly. Tourists agree that even today these communities have a somewhat rural character.

38. Interview with Olga Lepp, September 10, 1986.

39. N.J. Kroeker, *First Mennonite Villages in Russia, 1789-1943: Khortitsa-Rosental* (Vancouver, B.C.: By the author, 1981), 92.

40. Johann Esau, "Erinnerungen."

41. Ibid.

42. Dr. Katherine Esau holds two honourary degrees from California universities; she has 159 scholarly publications to her credit. In the 1970s she was honoured as one of the most outstanding American women.

43. P.M. Friesen, *Alt-evangelische mennonitische Brüderschaft,* 697-698.

1914-1988

World War I shook Mennonite perceptions of themselves. They were abruptly reminded that they were still foreigners in Russia. Ultimately education, wealth and social status could no longer protect them from their government's wrath when Germany and Russia went to war against each other. Very quickly it became evident that even after a hundred and thirty years in Russia, Mennonites were still perceived simply as Germans. As the war dragged on, Mennonites tried to show their loyalty to Russia by serving faithfully in the forestry camps and the Red Cross medical corps. The strident anti-German and anti-Mennonite attitude of the tsarist government severely tested the fragile identification with Russia which had formed during the Golden Age.

The October Revolution which toppled the Kerensky regime introduced the kind of terror and lawlessness that Mennonites only a short time earlier could not have imagined possible. For Ukraine half a year of German occupation followed soon after the Revolution. This interlude of foreign occupation provided a ready and very attractive alternative for Mennonites whose identity with Russia had begun to crumble. After all, they spoke German and had studied German literature in their schools. A certain sense of oneness with Germany came into being almost overnight.

A much more serious challenge to Mennonite self-perceptions occurred when the German army withdrew. Now suddenly completely vulnerable, Mennonites had to ask themselves whether they were in fact a community of peace, and if so, what such a characterization meant in this situation of personal danger and threat of destruction. Some of the larger settlements, such as Molotschna, chose armed defense. Others did not form self-defense units. The question whether peace was a way of life for all situations, or only for times of tranquility and prosperity would remain alive for many years to come. The fact that some Mennonites did resort to arms in 1918 and 1919 became a liability which later generations in the Soviet Union would have to deal with again and again.

After the civil war ended and it became clear that Ukraine would become part of the new Soviet Federation, many people saw emigration as their only hope. The community which they had struggled to create in Russia had, they sensed, been irretrievably lost. Their institutions, economic possibilities, and perhaps most importantly, a kind of inner connection with the country had vanished almost overnight.

Especially for the well-to-do it seemed that community could only be reestablished in some other country. Thus, about 22,000 people emigrated, most of them to Canada and some also to Paraguay, Brazil, Mexico and the United States. Many of these had been leaders in their communities back home.

Those who stayed in the Soviet Union did so for a variety of reasons. Some did not have the opportunity to emigrate. Others believed that in the new political order it would be possible once again to establish faithful and strong communities. Some of the Mennonite intellectuals came to understand the pathos of the long-suffering Russian peasants. They hoped that this new Soviet order would now set right the ancient wrongs and in the process create a world in which Mennonite community could be reconstructed again.

All these hopes and ideals came to naught in the 1930s. The possibilities for community which emerged were far different from anything anyone could have imagined. Community had to be created on the collective farm. Church life gradually ground to a halt as all leaders, religious and others, were slowly but surely sent into exile. Education continued, sometimes in the same schools and even with Mennonite teachers, but the schools no longer served the function of undergirding Mennonite community. The new learning became a threat and a bane, a system from which those who wanted to remain Mennonite were being forcibly excluded. The elaborate system of institutions collapsed and community was created in the relationship of suffering people to one another. Physically many still lived in the villages and buildings in which community had been created before the war. However, the old communities were gone, and in their place suppressed people were struggling to create something new.

Physical links with the past were almost entirely lost during World War II. Many Mennonites in Ukraine were evacuated to destinations in Siberia, northern Russia and in the various Asiatic republics. Some fled west with the retreating German armies. Two-thirds of these were overtaken by the Red Army, repatriated and settled in Siberia or in Central Asia. Their main experiences now were dislocation, separation, hunger, pain and death along with dominant feelings of fear, anxiety and a sense of loss. The quest for community seemed to be only a dream at best.

After Stalin died, Mennonites as well as many others, were released from their prison terms or from their locations of forced labour, allowing new communities to form. These were located not in Molotschna or Chortitza, but in Karaganda, Frunze, Alma Ata and Dzhambul. The shape of the new Mennonite community was very different from that of the Golden Age. In many respects, however, the people recaptured a strong sense of togetherness once again. This new Mennonite community had been tested by persecution.

The people had figuratively and literally wandered in the wilderness, and had now come to experience something much better. This was community based on the commitment of people to each other and to God. It had only a minimum of institutional support.

During the past two decades many Mennonites again decided to emigrate. A large number of the people who have left had obtained places of leadership in the new settlements of Central Asia. Now another generation of leaders has been removed. Once again the question of what kind of community will remain has become acute.

Mennonite search for community in Russia has been ongoing for two hundred years. The search was complicated and redirected time and again by inner Mennonite tensions, government laws, revolutions, wars, changing political systems, exile, persecution and repeated emigrations. Stability and continuity always seemed to be fleeting. Change and anxiety were constant companions.

In the late 1980s the Russian Mennonite community is experiencing a major emigration. Whether Mennonites in the U.S.S.R. will discover that elusive community for which they have been searching, or whether their very existence may come to an end, remains to be seen.

Early Communism and Russian Mennonite Peoplehood

John B. Toews

In tsarist days the Russian Mennonite battle for freedom of faith and separate peoplehood was fought on a modest scale. For well over half a century the Mennonite sense of well-being rested upon the *Privilegium* granted by Catherine II. The average villager probably saw it as an inviolable right, granted in perpetuity. The sudden demand for universal state service in the early 1870s caught the constituency off guard and generated widespread consternation.

Ultimately the defense of Mennonite peoplehood focused on two diverse strategies. The first related to the emigration of one-third of the population to North America. For some, who sold their Russian lands at ludicrous prices, it was a journey of faith. Others were attracted by cheap land. In later decades most migrants viewed the episode as a flight for conscience' sake, as an action essential to the preservation of Mennonite peoplehood. Those who remained in Russia gradually evolved a second strategy.

By 1874, thanks to the clever diplomacy of General von Totleben, a clarification of Mennonite obligations to the state had emerged.[1] Ultimately the demand for civilian state service meant direct interaction with Russian society. Its implementation implied eventual cultural and structural assimilation. Autonomous Mennonite institutions constituted the only defense against such a threat. Vigorous petitioning created a special agency to supervise the state service which found its major expression in the *Forstei* (forestry service).[2]

As Russification pressures intensified during subsequent years Russian Mennonites fortified their sense of peoplehood by erecting a broad spectrum of welfare, medical and educational institutions. By 1917 the various settlements counted two teachers' colleges, a business school and a considerable number of high schools which drew their students from hundreds of village schools. An active social conscience found expression in hospitals, old age homes, an orphanage, a school for mutes, a deaconess home and a mental institution. At some stage in their life most Mennonites actively participated in various levels of this organizational structure and in the process strengthened their sense of peoplehood. Ultimately the Mennonite institutional response to tsarist nationalist policy promoted an unprecedented sense of unity that broke down many of the religious and geographic barriers which at times had plagued the colonies in the past.

Intertwined with the growth of institutionalism was the recovery of a somewhat dormant but basic Mennonite belief: nonresistance. When the conscription question was finally settled in 1880, the Russian government exempted Mennonites from military service but insisted that their young men serve in an alternative fashion, namely in forestry work. A historic pacifism, inward looking and crystallized for more than half a century, broke out of its shell. Nonresistance became a more positive principle associated with obligations and duties. A creedal tradition once more found practical application.

Russian Mennonites managed to cope with late nineteenth century Russification policies which insisted that the Russian language become the compulsory medium of instruction in all schools. Normally such a broad exposure to the Russian environment posed the danger of religious and cultural assimilation. This was not the case here. Russian teaching in the schools was implemented by a Mennonite intelligentsia trained in Russia and abroad, well able to administer Russian language and culture in tolerable dosages. Ironically as long as Russification remained a constant pressure — and it continued unabated until 1917 — Mennonite identity became stronger. The Mennonite world remained largely self-contained and self-perpetuating but was substantially stronger than its predecessor in the mid-nineteenth century. A sense of peoplehood flourished with only a minimal need to control the relationship of members with the surrounding Russian society. This setting responded to both stability and change though, like any social system, it was not capable of dealing with outright revolution.

By 1914 Russian Mennonites exhibited a collective and individual sense of solidarity rarely duplicated in Anabaptist-Mennonite history. A sense of confidence and hope catapulted many Mennonites to amazing levels of cultural and educational achievement. While many entered urban professional life, there was minimal intelligentsia loss to the outside world. A precise cultural-religious identity, which is an essential component of ethnicity, not only absorbed the increased circulation of books, periodicals and newspapers but also became creative by turning its pen to poetry, novels and history.

With the unexpected outbreak of World War I many Russian

Mennonites demonstrated how comfortable they were with their own traditions and their nation by entering national forestry camps and joining the Red Cross medical service in large numbers. The War brought unexpected assaults upon the Mennonite sense of well-being. There was the inevitable hate campaign against the German minority in Russia which not only permeated the public press but also found expression in the prohibition of the German language in public assemblies and the press in November 1914. Property liquidation laws, decreed in 1915, sought to force the German colonists in Russia to dispose of their lands in eight months. Fortunately the overthrow of the tsar and the establishment of Kerensky's Provisional Government with its lenient minority policies prevented further deterioration of their status. Under the Provisional Government the Russian Mennonites again felt secure, at least judging by the broad agenda of the All-Mennonite Congress which met in Ohrloff on August 14-18, 1917.³ The Mennonites had wide-ranging plans for cultural, religious and economic improvement. They looked to the future with optimism.

In a sense the discussions at the Ohrloff Congress reflected the impact of World War I upon Russian Mennonites. Never before had the community responded so broadly. Figuratively speaking, Mennonites left the forests and came to the battlefields as healers. While the young men were at the front, their elders not only paid their

World War I Red Cross unit which included both Mennonites and Russian nationals.   Photo: Mennonite Heritage Centre Archives

267

expenses but made contributions to the Red Cross, cared for soldiers' families near their settlements and even maintained field
hospitals. All the while they continued to bear the costs of the
forestry service. Perhaps a new kind of Mennonite emerged from this
experience. Confronted by the cataclysmic suffering of the Russian
nation they became less concerned about fine-tuning the Mennonite
belief system, about life style or about their exact relation to the state.
Instead they were broadly committed to alleviating the suffering
caused by war.

They were not only devoted to works of mercy but also to the
pursuit of justice. Scattered over the length and breadth of Russia
they saw the darker side of the tsarist system with its exploitation and
repression. The political structure which brought prosperity and
freedom to the Mennonites crushed others. Some of the young
responded in anger. They returned from their alternative service
terms advocating reform and change. Their radical visions surprised
some of their elders at Ohrloff. A few spoke of the nationalization of
land while others argued that Christianity supported socialism.

There were also Mennonites who were disillusioned. They
pointed to the mounting hostility against the German presence in
Russia. The land liquidation laws, the prohibition of the German
language, the attacks in the press — theirs was a disconcerting
legacy. The delegates at Ohrloff found it difficult to believe that
Russians would view them as an alien and potentially disloyal minority. Surely if the Provisional Government knew of the repeated
violations against German minority rights, it would make amends.
After all, its decrees on minority rights also assured Mennonites a
place in the new Russia. Unfortunately the government which promised equality and justice was not destined to last.

Mennonite ways and values, however adaptable in the past, found
it difficult to surmount the demands of the Bolshevik Revolution of
1917. The first encounter with the new political structure in South
Russia began during February 1918, when many of the Mennonite
volosts came under the jurisdiction of local soviets (councils of
workers and peasants). Mennonite self-government, which had
lasted for more than a century, now came to an abrupt end. These
soviets consisted largely of the economically underprivileged who
frequently exploited their new legal and political powers to better
their status.

The new structure, initially of brief duration, foreshadowed the
economic, social and political system under which Mennonites
eventually lived. By early 1922 communism had come to stay,

Nestor Makhno (1889-1934), the anarchist who symbolized the terror and destruction of the civil war and revolution. Photo: Mennonite Heritage Centre Archives

anarchy, civil war and famine notwithstanding. In Ukraine Mennonites were vulnerable to the charges that they were supporters of the counter-revolution, thanks in part to their particular geographic and cultural setting as well as to the political events transpiring between 1918 and 1922.

During this period Mennonites had little control over the chaos which ravished their settlements in Ukraine. The region was not only the major theatre for the clash between Red and White armies. It had also to contend with the anarchist bands which operated on the fringes of the ever-moving fronts. One such movement led by Nestor Makhno proved a fatal temptation to the Mennonite settlements exposed to his brigandage. Widespread robbery, rape and murder induced them to organize self-defence units *(Selbstschutz)*. The largest of these contingents in the Molotschna combined with Lutheran and Catholic colonists, knowingly or unknowingly, to fight the Red Army for several days. In the end an appeal to mitigating circumstances mattered little. The Mennonites, in a region saturated with counter-resurgency, had resisted the Bolshevik cause. The action was remembered in government circles decades after the debacle.

In southern Ukraine civil war and banditry soon reduced affluent and confident settlements to poverty and dependence. Forced requisitioning by various armies during the civil war as well as grain seizures by government officials afterward left no reserves. Red Army quartering, lasting from November 1920 until March 1922 increased the burden. Even nature took vengeance on the sorely oppressed. Drought conditions in Ukraine contributed to a massive famine in 1921-22. Many colonists were saved from starvation only by the timely arrival of aid sent by the recently organized American Mennonite Relief.

With the establishment of Bolshevik control in Ukraine a reasonable degree of civil stability returned to the Mennonite settlements. Several major questions now emerged. Was it possible for the Mennonites to retain a sense of identity or would they face forced assimilation? How would nationalization and the redivision of land influence the Mennonite settlements? The most pressing immediate problem, survival, became crucial late in 1920 and early in 1921, when the first great famine of the Soviet era struck Ukraine. In spite of such disheartening circumstances Mennonites aggressively sought a solution for their difficulties. Before long an agency was created to negotiate with the Bolshevik government. Its activities encompassed two areas considered absolutely necessary to Mennonite survival: religious and economic independence.

By 1921 Ukrainian Mennonites became increasingly apprehensive about the possible induction of Mennonite young men, traditionally pacifists, into the Red Army. In the hope of bringing this problem to the attention of the central authorities, a special All-Mennonite Conference was called at Alexanderwohl, Molotschna, on February 19, 1921. Its convocation resulted in the formation of a new union known as the *Verband der Gemeinden und Gruppen des Süden Rußlands.* A shortened form, *Verband der Mennoniten Süd-Rußlands* (Union of South Russian Mennonites), was commonly applied to the agency.[4] Once ratified by the Ukrainian government the organization became known as the *Verband der Bürger Holländischer Herkunft* (VBHH) (Union of Citizens of Dutch Lineage).[5] The organization was granted a broad range of economic concessions. Commercially it had the right to deal in any raw materials or manufactured goods essential to its program. It could participate in any financial and credit operation and even draw on foreign capital if necessary. Agriculturally it could initiate cooperatives, maintain storage facilities, utilize existing transportation systems and exploit certain lands for experimental purposes. Industrially, the VBHH could begin the production of items as needed for the success of its program. In the social sphere it was given a free hand in the operation of benevolent and cultural institutions.

The ratified VBHH charter was of deep significance to Mennonites in Ukraine. It distinguished them as the first foreign minority to obtain such broad privileges. The potential economic importance of the charter was far-reaching. Mennonites were allowed to continue independent farming, though their landholdings were reduced to a maximum of 32 dessiatins. In their agricultural operations they were free to pursue such commercial contacts as were most profitable at home and abroad. Schools and benevolent institutions generally remained under the control of the *Verband*. In addition the organization was free to associate with other groups of similar character. Its executive officers were elected by its constituency. There was no forced integration with Russians or with any other minority group in the vicinity. In brief, with the ratification of the VBHH charter Ukrainian Mennonites were provided with a unique opportunity to survive as an economic and cultural group.

Mennonites outside Ukraine were equally aggressive in seeking an economic base amid the new circumstances. After prolonged negotiations, Mennonite groups from widely separated areas in Russia received permission from the Presidium of the Central Executive Committee in Moscow to inaugurate an agency similar to the VBHH. Ratified in May 1923, the *Allrussischer Mennonitischer Landwirtschaftlicher Verband* (All-Russian Mennonite Agricultural Union) was to work towards restoring the Mennonite settlements in the RSFSR to their former level of economic prosperity.[6] Viewed in retrospect, the activities of the VBHH in Ukraine best illustrated the economic strategy adopted by the Mennonites in seeking to come to terms with the Soviet government. For the majority of Mennonites, the most crucial economic issue related to landholding, though in a somewhat detached, almost clinical sense. Such a stance resulted from the widespread interest in emigration which had emerged as early as 1921. It was clear that whatever portion of the Mennonite population chose or was able to leave, a sizeable segment would remain behind. These needed an economic base to sustain them. In the event that Mennonites were unable to emigrate the question of landholding became even more important. The VBHH charter provided a legal springboard to test whether a Mennonite future based on landholding was possible in the new Russia.

As early as July 1921, the VBHH chairman managed to discuss the question of the Mennonite future with P.G. Smidovich of the Central Executive Committee in Moscow. The interview resulted in a memorandum which was dispatched by the Central Executive Committee in Moscow to the Commissariat of Agriculture in Kharkov stipulating that every effort be made to preserve the historic centres of Mennonite culture in Ukraine. The Ukrainian government proved cooperative and no further land division was attempted during 1921. Not unrelated to this forbearance was the termination of War Communism and the introduction of the Lenin's New Economic Policy (NEP) in March 1921. In the hope of encouraging agrarian redevelopment the Commissariat of Agriculture promised the colonies every consideration even to the point of entertaining any economic projects the Mennonite *Verband* suggested.

Responding to the new liberality of the Kharkov regime, the *Verband* congress meeting in Margenau, Molotschna on January 3-4, 1922, endorsed a resolution advocating the redivision of all land still in Mennonite possession among all the Mennonites in Ukraine, including also refugees and landless.[7] Why such a proposal? Most of the Margenau delegates hoped that its official sanction would end the widespread demands for Mennonite land made by the neighbouring Russian population. Simultaneously this ensured the continuation of an ethnic solidarity within Mennonitism. The Margenau proposals naturally aimed at maintaining a Mennonite identity and were excessively optimistic. Already by March 1922, it was clear that Mennonites would receive no special landholding exemptions. Landless Mennonites were eligible for the maximum land parcel allowed in each province and in most of Ukraine. Although preliminary assurances spoke of at least 32.5 dessiatins, this amounted to only 21 dessiatins. The landholding issue raised another problem.

On April 11, 1922, the VBHH chairman was invited to attend a

Mennonite emigrants bound for Canada board the train in southern Russia.

Photo: Mennonite Heritage Centre Archives

meeting of the executive council of the agricultural commissariat.[8] The encounter suggested that, provided all members of the community be assured an equal share, colonies with moderate landholdings could remain intact. Those with excessive land, however, had to forfeit this for the settlement of landless Russians. The threat of forced structural assimilation severely threatened the Mennonite sense of group identity. When another VBHH Congress met in Landskrone, Molotschna on May 29-31, 1922, delegates appeared to censure the government's agrarian policy by insisting that Mennonites needed all their present lands if they were to maintain their productive norms.[9] This apparent economic concern reflected a much deeper crisis. Land reallotment as it was being implemented by mid-1922 was in the hands of district authorities, who had little regard for established norms or legal procedures. It seemed certain that one-half to three-quarters of Mennonite holdings would be transferred to Russian settlers.[10]

This land transfer policy, and not economic loss, was the most critical factor in the break-up of traditional Mennonite agricultural patterns. Though landless Mennonites were eligible to apply for lands made available by the redistribution, most of the excess land went to other nationalities.[11] Frequently, not only the land between Mennonite villages, but also land directly connected with residence within a Mennonite village was taken over by Russian settlers.[12] Such graphic developments made it abundantly clear that the forced economic change directly affected the social and religious structure of Russian Mennonitism. The last barrier capable of halting ethnic dissolution — group control of interaction with the outside world — was rapidly deteriorating. At least one desperate and, in retrospect, rather risky action stemmed from this concern. At the beginning of November 1922, Mennonite leaders submitted a special petition to the Central Executive Committee in Moscow requesting that the Mennonite colonies be allowed 65 or 50 dessiatins per farm.[13] Not surprisingly the Soviet government remained firm in its resolve to limit the size of Mennonite farms to a maximum of 32 dessiatins. Mennonite sensitivity to the land question expressed itself at the VBHH Congress meeting in Marienort, Kalinovo, Donetz Province on March 1, 3 and 4, 1924, when a special resolution was dispatched to government authorities re implementing the land division.[14] The resolution was once more representative of prevailing Mennonite anxieties, but did little to change the fact that the cultural-economic pattern of Mennonite life would have to rest on a reduced land quantum. By 1925 there were even suggestions that agriculture based on private initiative and control was obsolete.

Mennonite ethnicity was certainly threatened by the economic perspectives which the October Revolution of 1917 produced. Unlike earlier periods of economic change, developments after 1917 demanded incredible adaptability within a very short time period. The first months of Bolshevik rule witnessed chaotic attempts to implement nationalization. It was the ensuing civil war, however, which almost totally destroyed the prevailing economic order. As stated earlier, War Communism with its highly centralized control finally gave way to the New Economic Policy in March 1921. Mennonite interest in economic reconstruction and the government endorsement it received coincided with the New Economic Policy period. As a prerequisite for reconstruction *Verband* leaders sought for a minimal land area totally under Mennonite control.

Such sensitivity was not an irrational insistence on the right of private enterprise in a socialistic economy. It aimed rather at maintaining group coherence in the face of forced assimilation brought about by the settlement of landless Russian peasants within Mennonite villages. The increasingly open interaction with Russian society up to 1917 had posed little danger because of a sophisticated and all-embracing Mennonite institutionalism. By 1921 a deep-seated cultural attrition held sway. Russian society began to penetrate the Mennonite social and cultural structures by intermingling economically. Under these circumstances Mennonite ethnicity was left without its traditional defences. Whether always clearly articulated or not, it was this sensitivity which constituted a major formative force in the Mennonite migration.

A Molotschna settler, addressing himself to a representative of the American Mennonite Relief, then active in Russia, summarized the dilemma:

> You have learned to know us somewhat. But do you fully understand us? Oh, we hardly understand ourselves, we hardly recognize ourselves: are we this or is it a bad dream? . . . Tell our brethren abroad we are sick from head to foot. There were too many events which tumbled us headlong over one another, too many sad experiences. Our nerves could not endure it, we became apathetic. We are innerly torn apart, we are aware of our own contradictions, we feel insecure, we become sceptical. There is no will to work, no pulling oneself together for a happy, blessing bestowing activity. . . . We have almost lost faith in a worthwhile future.

We see it on our farms, on our homes and dispositions: no hand moves to improve anything. We have given ourselves over to indifference. Hunger and poverty have weakened us morally and physically; there is no longer any backbone, no manly confrontation with this paltriness and its ethical results. Life appears empty.[15]

The school teacher and the minister constituted another major force in the struggle for Mennonite religious-cultural survival. The schools were especially hard hit during the course of World War I and the revolutionary period which followed. In 1914 mobilization removed many teachers from the schools, though the majority remained operational because retired teachers went back to work. The conscripted teachers had just begun to return home in 1917 when the October Revolution erupted. There was little systematic instruction in subsequent years. By 1922 the new order initiated two changes which seriously affected Mennonite schools. The first prohibited religious instruction in the schools; the second decreed that a teacher could not simultaneously be a minister. In addition special exams, designed to expose the religiously inclined, eliminated many others.[16] The 1920s emigration, which at first allowed only the landless and those without property to leave, further decimated the teaching ranks.

Forced collectivization, with its many arrests and exiles, did not affect the school as seriously as might be expected. The First Five Year Plan was not aimed at the intelligentsia but at the propertied elements in the village. The school in fact made an amazing comeback during the early 1930s. Communist officials viewed the school as a key means of influencing the young and made every effort to raise the prevailing standards. The propagandistic potential of the school possibly explains the high level of tolerance and autonomy extended to Mennonites schools. Generally the subject matter was broadened, the number of teachers was increased and books were acquired for local libraries. All teachers were of course expected to subscribe to party views on methodology and curriculum and to participate actively in the socialist reconstruction of society. Constrained by official pressure and by the need to survive, some Mennonite teachers acquiesced. Still others embraced the new order and became active proponents of its values. Mennonite teachers spearheading anti-religious crusades in the village were not unknown.[17]

There was one surprising school concession, at least in Chortitza and Molotschna: German remained the chief language of instruction until 1937 and in some cases until 1938. The presence of German-speaking teachers naturally gave some hope of cultural survival. Compulsory school attendance was enforced for ages 8 to 14. While the number of grades taught in some village schools was reduced, grade levels in neighbouring villages were often raised. Children in Burwalde, for example, who wished to go beyond the fourth class had to travel seven kilometres to Nieder Chortitza. In this instance difficulties arose when the collective refused to supply transportation. Most villages appreciated the cultural benefit of German instruction and did not object to compulsory school attendance. Many of the reports, however, complain about parental inability to adequately nourish and clothe the children. Within the school itself the problems generally related to a lack of instructional supplies, not poorly trained teachers. Qualified teachers, German and Mennonite, were apparently not in short supply. Neuendorf in Chortitza reported: "Eight German teachers work in the school, all of whom have the necessary pedagogical training. Four of them have worked at the school for more than twenty years and received their training during tsarist times. The other four received their training in Soviet schools and have worked from three to five years."[18] Cultural continuity through the schools was also bolstered by the teacher training program attached to the Chortitza High School which used German as the language of instruction until 1938 and produced a substantial number of teachers for village schools.[19]

The years 1937-38 brought two radical changes to the Chortitza school system. The languages of instruction became Russian and Ukrainian, while German was reduced to a special subject studied at class level four or five. The shift apparently had widespread implications. Many of the village reports suggest that the younger children, raised in Low German-speaking homes, could not understand their teachers. A second change involved the importation of Russian teachers into Mennonite villages and the placement of German teachers in Russian villages. The shift back to German and the expulsion of Russian teachers after the German occupation of Chortitza seems almost as radical as the 1937-38 shift. Only one non-German teacher was listed in 16 village reports in 1942. German, as the Mennonite medium of culture, received no concessions after the German troops withdrew in 1943. By then Mennonite colonies in Ukraine were in their last stages of dissolution.

The questionnaires used by "Kommando Dr. Stumpp" not only focused on the school but also on Chortitza cultural-intellectual activities between 1930 and 1940.[20] The material suggests that two new elements entered Chortitza cultural life between 1930 and 1940: the cinema and books in the Russian language. The emergence of the cinema was one aspect of the "socialist realism" which dominated Soviet literature and art by about 1932. Stalin's political dictatorship demanded ideological uniformity and film became a valuable propagandistic device in achieving this goal. If some of the reports can be trusted, Chortitza residents became enthusiastic movie patrons. Certain villages were served by mobile film units as often as every ten days, others owned their own projector. There were two movie theatres, one at Chortitza seating 170, the second at Einlage seating 240.

Rather large local libraries were established in every village, many of them containing 200 or even up to 600 volumes. Some questionnaire respondents insisted they were rarely used because of highly political or complex scientific content. These village libraries no longer existed by 1942. The Neuenburg report states that the books were burned by the retreating Red Army, while in Chortitza this service was performed by German occupation troops. It might be reasonable to assume that the predominantly Bolshevik material was offensive to the equally doctrinaire Nazi cultural agents accompanying the German armies.

In the 1930s a significant cultural shift affected most Mennonite settlements: there was little German reading material available. This decline began in the 1920s when the publication of virtually all German religious periodicals was forbidden. The *Christlicher Familienkalender* published its final volume in 1919 while the newspaper, *Friedensstimme*, printed its last issues in October 1920. Thanks to the effort of the All-Mennonite Conference in Moscow in 1925, a new periodical, *Unser Blatt*, appeared in October of that year, but was already forced to stop publication in 1928. By this time religious materials from Germany had not reached the Mennonite colonies for more than a decade. Little German material was available in the village libraries of the 1930s. About fifteen percent of the books in the Adelsheim library were in German, while in Burwalde only a few old German periodicals remained. There was little else to ensure cultural continuity. Most of the German material in the homes was destroyed by owners because the secret police viewed any foreign literature as proof of espionage. The only acceptable German paper during the 1930s was probably the *Deutsche Zentral-Zeitung* published in Moscow.[21] In the questionnaire a number of villages also reported receiving the *Deutsch-Ukrainische Zeitung*. Another potential periodical, *Brücke zur Heimat*, begun in 1943 and published by the German Ministry for the Occupied Eastern Regions, appeared too late to be of much use in Ukraine.[22]

A long-standing ingredient of Mennonite cultural-religious awareness related to the church and its leadership. The All-Mennonite Conferences of the 1920s made a determined effort to ensure the continuation of religious freedom. In May 1924 a special petition was addressed to the Soviet government which called for unrestricted freedom of worship, Mennonite exemption from military service, freedom to hold special Bible courses, the right to distribute Christian literature, permission to build new churches and an end to special taxes levied on churches. Delegates attending the All-Mennonite Conference at Melitopol on October 5-9, 1926, learned that Soviet officials had granted several of the concessions requested in 1924.[23] Generally the prevailing mood indicated greater religious freedom. It proved an illusory calm. In the years to come Stalin's political entrenchment terminated most of the earlier concessions. By 1928 religious leaders lived in constant fear of arrest and exile.

In its initial two years the First Five Year Plan, at least in the Mennonite villages, concentrated almost exclusively on the elimination of the kulak. Though direct pressures eased after the publication of Stalin's "Dizziness from Success," more subtle strategies now emerged. There was still some concern with the wealthier elements within the village but from mid-1930 onward the campaign focused on the destruction or neutralization of the ideological religious leadership of the village. The demise of the church was ensured by the prohibition of its teaching ministry, the exile of its leaders and the closure of its buildings.

A letter from Neu Halbstadt dated February 5, 1931, described the basic proceedings:

> In Halbstadt there are no ministers. Elder Abram A. Klassen and Gerhard Harder were assessed 1200 and 900 rubles respectively, which they naturally could not pay. For this they were imprisoned in Halbstadt for one month and no one was allowed to visit them.
>
> Recently the former elder has been sentenced to five years imprisonment and a further five years banishment from Ukraine. He has also been fined 3000 rubles. Gerhard Harder is very ill in the Muntau hospital. Heinrich Harder got assistance, paid and has left so that Halbstadt has no ministers. The ministers have all been expelled from the Artel, and in some instances are not only without bread but without clothes.[24]

A former Halbstadt resident and Mennonite minister described the same situation when he wrote on January 20, 1931:[25]

> Our situation is becoming more critical. The ministers all have to leave. . . . They are assessed sums which they cannot pay, then they are imprisoned and everything is taken from the families. In our former home the old minister Gerhard Harder and the elder Abram A. Klassen are in prison. The dear old brother is not always fully conscious. Heinrich Harder has sold his last cow and paid. He then left so that there was no Sunday service either in the church or in the hall. The last ministers of the Word plan to leave these days. I cannot work because of my health and my sons have asked me not to begin because it is impossible to hold that position for long. . . . In this manner the churches are robbed of all their workers. The newly elected do not accept the position out of fear. I have always believed, "The Lord will help" (Isaiah 41:14) and believe that today, but I am in the dark as to how I can trust God entirely and completely that he will lead further. For the future nothing can be expected except demoralization, hunger and death. . . . Many have no bread for the summer. A pood of flour can cost between 22 and 25 rubles. One can't think of buying clothes. Many farm homes are being torn down. . . . In Alt-Samara 20 ministers are imprisoned. . . . Thirty-seven families are in exile in Archangel.[25]

The exile of ministers and elders during 1930-31 did not bring an immediate end to religious life. Several elements helped sustain church life, at least for a while. The universal policy of transforming churches into club houses seems to have progressed slowly in Chortitza, and some churches remained open until 1935. In other instances serious Christians gathered in private homes or local halls. Even after the churches were closed some sense of continuity may have been sustained through choir singing. Almost all the village reports record the presence of choirs prior to collectivization and at least six indicate that choirs sang during the time of the First Five Year Plan. In two instances the choirs sang until the churches closed in 1935. Though not directly related to church life, the presence of string and brass ensembles throughout the 1930s also helped to maintain a sense of community continuity.

During the early 1930s the traditional role of the laity in the life of the Mennonite church did much to sustain piety in the virtual absence of leadership and formal services. Whatever its weaknesses, congregational democracy in the Russian Mennonite tradition generated an acute sense of individual responsibility for public welfare. This sense of personal participation in the life of the community midst a village setting ensured a commitment capable of transcending loss of leadership or building. Committed to the elimination of religion generally, Soviet authorities lashed out at every manifestation of the old piety, barring Christian festivals and forbidding any religious functions at funerals and weddings. Judging from the Chortitza village reports the absence of special celebrations proved most devastating to the ongoing life of the religious community.

The forceful expulsion of religious leaders as well as the decline of the school initiated a process, less obvious and external, yet more deadly because it touched the very soul. A Mennonite elder from the Molotschna alluded to the prevailing mood in a letter of October 20, 1930:

> The practitioners of those feared three letters, GPU or Cheka, work so efficiently that all remain calm. It is a terrible calm. . . . The flames of this, in the final analysis insane system, consume everything: happiness and prosperity; peace and joy; the will and strength to work; the last remnants of personal freedom and independence. It is often hell on earth and here I do not think primarily of the disenfranchised, the despised and exiled. Under certain circumstances these can be courageous and innerly strong in spite of everything. Frequently those who out of blindness or necessity have given themselves to the system experience it as hell.[26]

There was no longer any basis for hope in the future. Earlier revolution and civil war had passed; War Communism had led to the New Economic Policy. There was religious and educational revival, at least until 1926; for some there had been a choice of economic reconstruction in Russia or emigration abroad. Hope for emigration glimmered briefly at the gates of Moscow in 1929. By the end of 1930 the majority felt that current political events ensured the extinction of the Mennonite peoplehood they had known in the past.

It was not as though the churches or schools were being closed. The real problem related to the forced alteration of lifestyle and school curriculum. As a January 10, 1931, letter explained:

The schools are in a terrible condition. The issue is not, as at teachers' conferences, pedagogy and methodology, but collectivization, the five year plan, pioneer activity and in recent times anti-religious propaganda. On Christmas Eve, for example, anti-religious programs had to be given in all schools. . . . Those who resisted lost their jobs within the next month; all teachers are to show their political colours and join atheistic clubs. . . . This time the nation was without Christmas. Nothing but mocking poems in the papers and anti-religious evenings in the schools signified the holidays. . . .

One thing is certain . . . spiritual and moral crippling is afflicting old and young. Since all opposition is squelched we are rushing towards religious decay. . . . Truthfulness, honesty, trustworthiness, love, peace, unity, gentleness, humility, chastity, good intentions towards one another, obedience to parents . . . these are not only ignored, but regularly trodden into the mud. . . .[27]

Religion and its values were intertwined with the very fabric of the Mennonite soul. Its presence in church and school influenced family and society customs and morals. By 1931 it was apparent that continuity was impossible: the majority of ministers had been exiled and the school was totally controlled by the state. A letter of February 5, 1931, stated the problem succinctly: ". . . because no counteraction is possible, our youth is rapidly inclining towards unbelief. . . . The number of atheists among the teachers has become large."[28] By 1935-36 young Mennonites were devoid of their past and incapable of forging a future identity. Even the last defensive bastion, the family, now drew nurture only from itself. It operated not only under religious and cultural but economic handicaps as well. Its ability to function as a self-contained economic unity was hampered when foodstuffs were paid out in allotted rations for services rendered to the collective. Increased assessments and requisitions exhausted private reserves and discouraged further productivity. The activists, special brigades and non-Mennonites who were brought into the villages to force collectivization further strained the family unit.

One level of Mennonite consciousness, nonresistance, proved amazingly durable during the late twenties and early thirties. The Soviet military law of September 18, 1925, allowed exemptions for religious reasons, provided these were granted by the district courts. For the majority of Mennonites the continuity of nonresistance now depended on the courts. In many colonies they were reluctant to grant alternative service status after 1926. An exception to this was the Chortitza settlement where the local minister, Aron Toews, still won court exemption for the majority of Mennonite draftees as late as 1929. During 1930-31 these worked on the construction of the Dniepr power station, a new railway crossing on the Island of Khortitza and the demolition of the old railway bridge near Einlage.[29]

In the course of the First Five Year Plan another development affected the Mennonite conscientious objector. Forced collectivization disenfranchised the children of kulaks and clerics, making them politically unreliable elements, ineligible for draft into the Red Army. These became the so-called *Tylovoye Opoltshenieie,* a type of two- or three-year reservist supervised by the Ministry of War. Though subject to military organization and discipline, the reservists primarily engaged in various kinds of civil activity including coal mining, heavy industry, stone quarrying and forestry work. In 1932 the alternative service was joined to the *Trud* army. This work force, composed mainly of the sons of Russian kulaks and clergymen, was dispatched to various areas of Ukraine, the forests of Siberia or the coal mines of the Far East. One group which left for the Vladivostok region on December 26, 1932, consisted of some 250 Mennonites and 500 disenfranchised Russians.[30] Generally the term of service was two or three years.

By 1935 no courts granted exemption from military service for religious reasons. Fortunately the idea of the civil reservist was retained, though for negative reasons. The practice of sustaining a large work force enabled the state to get useful service from its politically unreliable elements and proved of special significance during the war years as a means of utilizing the suspect German minority. The civilian work force as it existed during the late thirties and early forties certainly did not represent any state concession to the Mennonite nonresistance as had the Military Law of 1925. The structure nevertheless allowed the majority of young men to serve the state without shedding blood.

Did nonresistance have any meaning in the circumstances of the 1930s and 1940s? After 1932 the presence of Mennonites in Soviet work brigades did not reflect a government recognition of nonresistance nor were they particularly conscious of performing an applied peace witness similar to the pre-revolutionary forestry service. Their work in forests and coal mines was simply the end result of Soviet policies calculated to generate societal changes of vast magnitude. These "free workers" had other less fortunate Mennonite associates

— those arrested at the height of the great terror and sent to work in prison camps. Neither group was capable of nurturing the concept of nonresistance due to the absence of traditional community ties as well as the lack of ministers and religious services.

Some Perspectives

From the very beginning tsarist colonization policies effectively separated Mennonites from other German colonists and from the Russian population. In the century which followed neither the demand for state service nor the expanded economic activity involving new settlements and new technologies seriously threatened Mennonite isolation. The expansion of intellectual and spiritual horizons was likewise a controlled process. Periodic crises like the Russification policies of Alexander III or the Revolution of 1905 passed rather quickly. Though the anti-German politics associated with World War I generated considerable uneasiness, the February Revolution of 1917 momentarily alleviated these fears. Virtually every pillar supporting Mennonite identity remained intact until 1917.

Until the Bolshevik Revolution of 1917 there was no significant change in the structural setting of Mennonite peoplehood with its village and land-holding patterns, its right of self-government and its right to expansion in new, closed colonies. The stable political scene was augmented by Mennonite control of the schools. Most were staffed by Mennonite teachers with amazingly uniform values. The bond between school and church was readily forged since many teachers were also ministers in the local congregations. Such a setting not only produced a steady affirmation of traditional religious values but fostered a steady cultural identification with Germany. The flow of foreign newspapers and periodicals continued until the outbreak of World War I. The Mennonite press with its *Botschafter, Friedensstimme, Christliches Jahrbuch, Christlicher Familienkalender* and *Mennonitisches Jahrbuch* bonded the widely dispersed Mennonite settlements with its religious nurture and information flow. Whether travelling or migrating anywhere in Russia, the Mennonite encountered familiar societal and village patterns. The sense of commonality encompassed economics, religion, social practices, food and of course Low German, the prevailing lingua franca.

While cataclysmic from the standpoint of its ideological radicalism and use of force, the first stage of Bolshevik rule made only moderate demands for change: smaller farms and the elimination of the religious school teacher. Unofficially the pressure was more encompassing: the famine of 1921-22; the inductions into the Red Army; the general opposition towards religion. Most of the values and practices associated with Mennonite community nevertheless remained intact. Until Stalin's consolidation of power in 1927-28, Mennonite economic, religious and cultural concerns remained somewhat negotiable.

The First Five Year plan with its forced collectivization, tight control of the schools and prohibition of all religious activities or publications seemed to mark the end of traditional Mennonitism in Russia. While most settlements remained identifiably Mennonite during the 1930s the Mennonite soul encountered an increasingly fragmented world. The liturgy and interaction formerly associated with weddings and funerals or Easter, Pentecost and Christmas celebrations ceased when such gatherings were prohibited. Some aspect of the old piety survived as cultural trappings — the choirs, orchestras and bands — but the words and melodies of faith did not resound. It did not seem to matter that German had been the language of faith and Low German the language of everyday life. Both now spoke words associated with the priorities of collectivization. Yet for some Low German became the language of identity, comfort and even faith. The isolation of exile or imprisonment during the Stalinistic terror was often broken by the presence of a fellow Mennonite, uttering words quite foreign to the ears of the all-pervasive state. No one had really thought of this tongue as an ideal prison language. It also had the potential for reviving old memories of faith and peoplehood, of sustaining a lingering awareness of old homelands and old values.

Mennonites in Ukrainian settlements together with other Germans were forcibly deported to eastern Russia when Hitler invaded Russia in 1941. Many of these would spend the next decade and a half as members of forced labour battalions restricted to specific regions. In 1955 freedom came on one condition: no return to former homelands. Was the past of any importance to the deportee or camp survivor in the new setting? Apparently a sense of collective belonging survived fifteen or twenty years of family and community separation. Within a few short years large numbers of Mennonites gathered in the urban centres of eastern Russia. Those with religious conviction and faith banded together to form new churches.

What emerged was not radically different from what had been. Memories of the old liturgies and songs, the old celebrations and sermons figured heavily in the emerging structures and practices. Those who affirmed faith, whether of Mennonite Brethren or *Kirch-*

liche persuasion, usually defined their parameters according to what they had known. The new people of God proved surprisingly orthodox. Persecution and hardship, while creating a faithful remnant, had narrowed the lines of demarcation. Some insisted they could be Baptist and Mennonite, others preferred to be *Kirchliche* and Mennonite Brethren once again. Even the old language and the old liturgical modes were regarded as essential. The *Kirchliche* revived catechism instruction while the Mennonite Brethren spoke of conversion. Each insisted on its own baptismal mode.

What had happened? Had persecution generated heroes of the faith who were so stalwart and rigorous as to be inflexible, or were these new people of God overwhelmed by insecurity? Perhaps it was the latter. How was the new church to be organized? How could people of diverse backgrounds function harmoniously? Virtually no one had theological training or leadership experience. Under such circumstance it was best to cling to the known, to old memories and old patterns.

Notes

1. See J. Sudermann, "The Origin of Mennonite State Service in Russia, 1870-1880," *Mennonite Quarterly Review* 17 (January 1943): 34-42.

2. A good documentary survey can be found in A. Goerz, *Ein Beitrag zur Geschichte des Forstdienstes der Mennoniten in Rußland* (Groß Tokmak: H. Lenzmann, 1907).

3. J.B. Toews, ed., *The Mennonites in Russia, 1917-1930: Selected Documents* (Winnipeg, Manitoba: Christian Press, 1975), 449-480.

4. For records relating to the conference consult, "Die Wehrlosigkeit der Mennoniten in Rußland nach dem ersten Weltkriege," in Memoirs, B.B. Janz Archiv, Centre for Mennonite Brethren Studies, Winnipeg, Manitoba; also in the same file, "Die Gründung des Verbandes in Alexanderwohl" (cited hereafter as BBJ).

5. "Statuten des Verbandes der Bürger Holländischer Herkunft in der Ukraine," A.A. Friesen Collection, Mennonite Library and Archives, North Newton, Kansas (cited hereafter as AAF).

6. C.F. Klassen, F. Isaak and P.F. Froese, "Bericht über die Entstehung des Allrussischen Mennonitischen Landwirtschaftlichen Verbandes." AAF. See also in same file, "Protokoll der ersten Vertreterversammlung des Allrussischen Mennonitischen Landwirtschaftlichen Vereins zu Alexandertal, Gouvernement Samara, am 10. Oktober 1923."

7. "Protokoll der allgemeinen Versammlung der Bevollmächtigten des Mennonitischen Verbandes in Südrußland aus dem Saporoger Gouvernement am 3.

und 4. Januar, 1922 in Margenau, 3." AAF.

8. B.B. Janz to the Studienkommission, April 7, 1922, 5; B.B. Janz to the Studienkommission, Kharkov, April 27, 1922, 8. AAF.

9. "Protokoll der General-Versammlung der Vertreter des VBHH in der Ukraine, Landskrone am 29., 30. und 31. Mai 1922." AAF.

10. B.B. Janz to the Studienkommission, July 25-August 4, 1922, 5. See also B.B. Janz to the Studienkommission, Kharkov, September 13, 1922. AAF.

11. B.B. Janz to the Studienkommission, April 16, 1924. AAF.

12. B.B. Janz to the Executive of the AMLV, February 10, 1924. BBJ.

13. B.B. Janz to the "Verwaltung des VBHH in der Ukraine, Tiege-Ohrloff," Moscow, November 9, 1922, 2,3. The CEC passed the document on to the Federal Committee of Lands, which insisted that the division of Mennonite land be done according to existing laws, but that Mennonite refugees be allowed to share in the redistribution (Excerpt from Minute No. 41 of the Presidium of the Federal Committee for Lands, November 1922. AAF.). This decision was then communicated to the Commissariat of Agriculture (Federal Committee to the People's Commissariat of Agriculture of the USSR, November 24, 1922. AAF).

14. "Protokoll der Vertreterversammlung des Verbandes der Bürger Holländischer Herkunft in der Ukraine am 1. 3. und 4. Marz 1924 in Marienort (Kalinovo) Donetz Gouv.," 9, 10. AAF.

15. D. Claassen to C.E. Krehbiel, Halbstadt, January 1, 1923 in C.E. Krehbiel Collection, Mennonite Library and Archives, North Newton, Kansas, File 47.

16. See, for example, K. Peters "Jekaterinoslawer Dorfschule, 1925." AAF.

17. "Alexanderkrone, Halbstadt Wolost," *Der Bote*, March 19, 1930, 4.

18. Captured German War Documents (CGWD), Library of Congress, Box 150.

19. A. Sudermann, "Die Chortitzer Zentralschule im Zeitraum von 1842-1942," in the Chortitza questionnaire. CGWD, Box 148. Also interview with Mrs. H. Thiessen, Calgary, Alberta, a 1933 graduate, August 13, 1979.

20. The various village reports on which the discussion is based are contained in CGWD, Boxes 146, 148, 150, 152. The reports for Nikolaifeld, Nieder-Chortitza and Rosenbach were missing in the xeroxed material sent to me by the Library of Congress.

21. One article reported that "enthusiastic" Chortitza collectivists visited Moscow. *Deutsche Zentral-Zeitung*, February 18, 1932, 2.

22. A copy of Vol. I, No. 1 (January 1943) is contained in file R 6, vol. 117 of the Bundesarchiv, Koblenz.

23. "Protokoll der All-Ukrainischen Konferenz der Vertreter der Mennonitengemeinden in der USSR in Melitopol vom 5.-9. Oktober 1926." AAF.

24. B.H. Unruh, "Bericht XXIIIA,"March 3, 1931, 5 in Mennonitische Flüchtlingsfürsorge Archiv, Weierhof b. Marnheim, Germany (cited hereafter as MFA). For more information on Abram A. Klassen see Aron A. Toews, *Mennonitische Märtyrer* (Winnipeg, Manitoba: Christian Press, 1949), I, 205-207. Old and ailing, Klassen apparently died in a cattle car enroute to northern exile. Gerhard Harder subsequently died in the Muntau Hospital. H.B. Janz, "Prediger Gerhard Harder," *Der Bote*, March 25, 1931, 2. The article also makes reference to the disappearance of Heinrich Harder, the minister of the Mennonite Brethren Church in Halbstadt.

25. B.H. Unruh, "Bericht XXIIIA," March 3, 1931, 4-5. MFA.

26. For example in Adelsheim. CGWD, Box 148; and in Blumengart. CGWD, Box 146.

27. B.H. Unruh, "Bericht XX," November 20, 1930. MFA.

28. B.H. Unruh, "Bericht XXIII," February 3, 1931. MFA. A case study in the erosion of Mennonite identity in the village of Ohrloff can be found in J.B. Toews, ed. and trans., *Letters from Susan: A Woman's View of the Russian Mennonite Experience (1928-1941)*, C.H. Wedel Historical Series, vol. 4 (North Newton, Kansas: Bethel College, 1988).

29. B.H. Unruh, "Bericht XXIIIA," March 3, 1931, 5. MFA. See also Aron P. Toews, *Siberian Diary of Aron P. Toews with a Biography by Olga Rempel*, trans. Esther Klaassen Bergen, ed. Lawrence Klippenstein (Winnipeg, Manitoba: CMBC Publications, 1984).

30. Hans Rempel, *Waffen der Wehrlosen: Ersatzdienst der Mennoniten in der UdSSR* (Winnipeg, Manitoba: CMBC Publications, 1980), 122-123.

Survival and Identity in the Soviet Era

Victor G. Doerksen

The Mennonite story has been narrated and interpreted in many different ways and from very diverse perspectives. After the cataclysmic events of war and revolution, of chaos and gradual establishment of the new Soviet reality, it is natural to ask: How does the Mennonite story continue in the Soviet Union? Is there a "zero point," a hiatus in the history of the Mennonites? If so, when did it occur and how does the story go on from that point?

Of course, many of the Mennonites who remained in Russia believed, especially in the early years, that in some form their lives, their communities and their churches would continue to function. Otherwise they would not have stayed as long as they did. Indeed, there were some who believed that an improved life lay ahead, and during the time of the New Economic Policy they were not all that wrong. Yet, we know now how drastic the dispersal and attempted destruction of that very entity — the Mennonite world in Russia — was. Those who have attempted to record the "history" of the postwar period have found that there was indeed a break in the institutional history. For a time there was no Mennonite church as such, but there were scattered Mennonites who sought to survive, as human beings, as Christians and as Mennonites.

The records of these scattered groups and individuals constitute a different, if not a new kind of "history" — different because they do not record the "official" history of a duly constituted church or other organized group, and because they are written from a different, perhaps radically different, perspective: that of the dislocated member, usually a woman. The men who had always been the family representatives in the church group had been taken away. Those who remained were women, old and disabled men and children. When women set about recording their experiences during these hard times, they did not give accounts of facts and statistics, as would be found in annual church reports; instead they gave concrete descriptions of living conditions, of what people suffered in body as well as in spirit. This is not to say that such women writers were unaware of the spiritual dimensions, but only that even such matters appeared in a very concrete context. The following texts illustrate how a period in which organizational structures had been dismantled and were in ruins was chronicled by individuals and family groups who were attempting to keep body and soul together.

The book, *A Wilderness Journey* by Heinrich and Gerhard Woelk, is an attempt at telling the story of the Mennonite Brethren Church in the Soviet Union between 1925 and 1980. Because ordinary church records did not exist for much of the period in question, the Woelks had to gather accounts written by various individuals. Some of these narratives were of necessity observed and written by women and all by participants in those events:

> In 1941 the terrible war between Russia and Germany broke out. The last remaining men were torn from their families. Most of them were marked as enemies of the people or as socially dangerous types and they were sent into the forests of the Urals of West and North Siberia and to the tundra of the high north. Sverdlovsk, Ivdel, Vorkuta, Norilsk, Magadan and many other places known as "ends of the earth" are silent witnesses to the suffering and sacrifices of our century. Only a few, very few, ever returned.
>
> Others, mainly the young people, but also older women, were inducted into the "work army" *(Trudarmee)*. Here our women, poorly dressed, had to fell trees in deep snow, just like the men.
>
> And the families with children and old people were hurriedly dispersed into the whole broad Asiatic area (Middle Asia and Siberia). Pains were taken to separate German families and to spread them into a wide diaspora throughout Russia: in each of the villages of Kazakhstan, Kirghizia, Russia or Tadzhikistan only two or three families were allowed to settle. Then came strict supervision by the local militia, which forbade all meetings and disallowed leaving the home village. In larger towns the families were limited to their own particular area.
>
> Only the families of the colonies of Orenburg, Omsk and Slavgorod were not torn from their homes. They were considered to be far enough into the interior but the men here were all taken away too.
>
> The deportation of families from the villages of the Ukrainian colonies did not fully succeed, since the troops of

the German army advanced too rapidly and soon made evacuation impossible. These villages then remained in German occupation during 1941-43. Spiritual life was rekindled, congregations regrouped. The Word of God was proclaimed and sinners were pointed to Jesus. When the German army retreated, the German colonists went along with them in a great trek to the west. But they were overtaken by the Russian army in Poland, Czechoslovakia and Germany and taken back into Russia in 1945. Not many succeeded in escaping. Those who did were separated from their families. Those who were returned to Russia were sent to hot Ajikastan [*sic*], where eggs can be fried on the sand, or to bitterly cold Eastern Siberia, where human breath freezes immediately, or into the forests of the Komi people and many other places. The principle of separation was followed here too: two or three families were brought into a village and all persons over 16 had to report monthly to the militia and sign a declaration that they would not leave the place, otherwise they would be liable for up to 20 years of imprisonment. It amounted to imprisonment of a whole

Wagon train of Mennonites on the trek from Gnadenfeld to Poland, 1943.

Photo: Mennonite Heritage Centre Archives

291

people forever or "for all times," as the government documents had it. Again an "eternity" for our people. How long
would this one last?[1]

The decades between the Revolution of 1917 and the 1980s may
well have seemed like an eternity to the many Mennonites scattered
in a vast diaspora throughout the Soviet Union. In terms of their
experience as a people the year 1956 may well be decisive. Before
that date separation without prospect of reunification pervaded the
Mennonite experience. The dominant image of the wilderness —
typically biblical but also uncannily realistic — suggested the bleak-
est of prospects. Hundreds, perhaps thousands, succumbed to the
hardships. Some were able to establish contact with relatives or
friends within the Soviet Union or in other countries; many doubt-
less could not. The year 1956 was a turning point. Some of the
limitations and restrictions on residence in a particular area were
lifted. Immediately the scattered members began to gather, not back
to the fertile Ukraine or the lush Caucasus, but to the places where
the authorities wanted them in any case: Kazakhstan and Siberia,
frontier areas which were in need of development, whether as
"virgin soil upturned" or for their mineral resources. In a centre like
Karaganda, a city pockmarked by coal mine shafts, these "Germans"
were welcome. Helene Woelk tells a story of a pilgrimage from one
coal town to another:

> When the war broke out we lived in the town of Krasnogo-
> rovka in the Donetz coal district. We and several other
> families had fled there in the years 1932-33 due to the
> persecutions in our home villages. Now, at the outbreak of
> war, there was no safe place left anywhere in the Ukraine and
> we anticipated the future with trembling. We did not have to
> wait long. Our son Gerhard was born into these difficult
> times on August 10. Barely two weeks after this, on Sep-
> tember 3, 1941, a militia vehicle pulled into our yard. We
> understood at once what this meant, and we were not
> wrong. First the militia made a thorough search of the whole
> house. Then they declared my husband to be arrested, put
> him into the truck and . . . they drove off without pity. Where
> should I go? And what should I do with my family, in my
> weak and delicate condition?
> Then began the worst period of my life, the most difficult
> in all respects — spiritually, mentally and physically. We

were left alone. A heavy burden was laid on me and threatened to crush me. Heinrich, my husband, had been taken away. Forever? I saw him driven away. Evening had come.... My heart cried to God but I could not find comfort. All about me was emptiness and desolation. I covered my eyes with my hands and went back into the house. What happened then I do not know. . . . When I opened my eyes again I saw my children: Heinz (11) and Helenchen (7), standing at the bed calling "Mama!" At the foot stood our grandfather (my dear old father, Papa Fleming, 71 years old), crying.

Then I heard crying from the next room and this brought me back to full consciousness. Now I knew everything: my littlest one (3 weeks old) was crying and he should not cry. I pulled myself together and comforted him. I now felt the weight of loneliness but also the responsibility for these four, dear people on my shoulders. Papa prayed and I felt strengthened.

Strength! Father, hear me!

I need strength to bear the load. . . .

. . . So some three weeks passed. Then the militia came and told us that we should be ready to be evacuated in 24 hours. But the Lord gave strength and presence of mind. Three good neighbors came to me and offered to help. We weren't ready in 24 hours, but in three days we were. Each family was allowed to take 100 kilograms, but because my father had many good friends in the town (he had worked as a teacher in a school in the last years), we were allowed 100 kilograms for each person. A goat was butchered, three sacks filled with potatoes, three sacks filled with bedding, and then some clothing (we heard we were heading north and it was the end of September), cookware and other necessities of life. I went back to take leave of what had been our home. But what lay ahead? I cannot describe my feelings and don't really want to. The pain of parting arose in me along with the question that pursued me day and night: "Where is my Heinrich?" . . .

. . . At Roya Station we waited for three days and nights for an opportunity to be loaded into freight cars; people and belongings under the open sky. Only women with small children were allowed to take refuge in a house.

I want to record one event of these days: our Heinz had been a favorite of his teacher in school. He saw her walking past from the place where we had to wait and she saw him as well and called to him. The boy jumped up and ran to her in glee. But the militia drove him back. How he cried! I could not answer his question: Why? Helenchen, who was seven, didn't understand the seriousness of the situation and she sat patiently with her grandfather and observed everything that happened around her. It was hardest for grandfather to endure all of this. He felt his age and lack of strength, saw the family for which he felt himself responsible. He cried aloud and I had to comfort him. And who was my comforter? He who says: "I will not leave you nor forsake you."

Finally in the third night (it was pitch black, for lamps were not allowed because the front was so close) a freight train approached, which was to take us along. But who would load our things onto the train, since we were without manpower? I still don't know how it was done, but the things were loaded, thrown in somehow, and on top of them, we people, large and small, old and young. It was a long train, but consisted only of women, children and old people.

Pitch black night! The front very near. The doors were closed and the train silently started on its way. Where was it going? For the first night we cowered on our belongings. When day came, every family found its own things. There were some forty persons in our car. When the train stopped at a station, the few men looked for boards and soon two levels were constructed in the car and some order established. Thus each family received its own humble place. The train stopped very seldom. When it did, Heinz and I ran to find hot water. We had taken sugar and bread with us and that was our food for 31 days. Our situation deteriorated very quickly because the lice descended on us and how could we defend ourselves against them? There were only two small, high windows and only those close by had a chance of doing battle with the lice. The others had none and the problem became very great. This made me very anxious about my two-month old boy. It was hard to watch him being tortured by these pests and to be quite helpless! Once the train stood still long enough for me to wash all his things. But we were never told how long the train would stand and thus could not know whether we could undertake any such projects. During these 31 days I lay down very seldom. The nights seemed endless. How happy I was that I had taken along a package of Christmas candles. By this light I found comfort in God's Word. Then I went to my "big" children and kissed them goodnight, for they needed comfort too. No evening passed when I did not remind them: "Pray for our father!" We could not imagine what awaited us.

I will describe one difficult experience: At one station where our train was standing we heard that an adjacent train was filled with prisoners from the city of Stalino. That is where my husband Heinrich had been taken. I went out into the night. I soon found the train and saw the following: A car was open and armed soldiers stood around the door. A pail of soup was brought and passed in. I looked and searched; could Heinrich be among them? By lantern light the soldiers could not see me, but I could see everything. The pail did not come back for a long time. Then a soldier took off his coat and, with his pistol at the ready, he jumped in. Soon I heard heart-rending sounds, loud crying by a man and the short: O *Bozhe moi!* (Oh my God!). Then all was quiet within. The soldier jumped out with the pail and the door was closed. By the light of the lantern the soldier showed his blood-covered hand with a devilish laugh. That was too much for me, for I thought of Heinrich being in the car. . . .

I will mention one more trial and that will suffice. Again the train stopped and I jumped off along with old Mr. Basler and two women. But the train moved off again and left us behind. I cried out to God, out loud. We ran. I lost a shoe. The old man could not run any more. I ran as though I could overtake the train and — really — the train stopped. . . . When I got back to my family my father looked at me gratefully and my children whispered in my ear: "We prayed very hard." . . .

Our food supplies dwindled. Finally we reached our destination on November 5. The train stopped in the steppe. We got out. The wind was icy. Everyone picked up their things. Oxcarts were waiting for us. Where had we arrived? The men who had come to fetch us could barely speak Russian. But we didn't ask long; we were all happy to leave the train. We were brought to a Kazakh village. . . .

. . . Now ordinary life began for us again. At first I thought I would not be able to stand it, but the Lord strengthened his weak child. The Kazakhs had food but lacked clothing. They decided to exploit our weak position and provide themselves with our clothing and bedding. For this they were clever enough. They gathered us together and let us know that they would not give us any work (i.e., no earnings) until we exchanged our things with them. So we were forced, from the outset, to live on the little they would give us for these items. But what could we do? We couldn't let our children go hungry and we had to eat.

Housing was very poor. Our whole family was given a small space which had previously been a storage room.

Now we had to try to make our way. Because we were not given jobs in the commune, we were forced to look for other ways of earning something. We cleaned houses for the Kazakhs, turned their handmills, knitted for them and did other odd jobs. But the pay was very skimpy.

And how did we spend our Sundays? The Kazakhs are Muslims and do not observe Sunday. I had taken along Bibles and Testaments, so I told the children Bible stories. In this lonely situation I felt the need of the fellowship of believers. Our sense of loneliness increased and Papa and I tried to comfort one another. Oh, my poor Papa! Quietly and patiently he bore these spiritual and physical privations in his old age. . . .

Then came death. Heinrich Harder was the first. Poor food to which he was not accustomed, the depressing circumstances, the absence of the most essential necessities for old people and hopeless longing — all these were more than his weak spirit could bear. He went home, our minister Heinrich Harder, the former leader of the M. B. Church of Halbstadt, his Master called him away. Onkel (Uncle) Harder's suffering under the circumstances had been noticeable; once such a cheerful, smiling individual, he became more and more serious. He often came to see father; they understood one another. But it grieved him to see his daughter, Njuta Buller, who was expecting a child.

One morning, it was April 10, 1942, Njuta came to tell us that her father had died that night and that her mother didn't want to close his eyes. I went along with her. What a sad picture! Onkel Harder lay on the floor and his wife kneeled next to him murmuring disconnected words. . . . I kneeled beside her and gently tried to persuade her to close her husband's eyes. . . . Then my father came, washed and dressed the body, covering it with a white sheet. I reported the death to the village council. This gave rise to the new question for them: where to bury the body. The corpse of a Christian would desecrate a Muslim cemetery. Then the body of Onkel Harder was carried out into the steppe where a grave had been hurriedly dug. There were no coffins here. Following Muslim custom, a niche was carved out at the bottom of the grave and there the body was placed and covered with earth. Njuta insisted on accompanying the body to the burial. The men didn't want to permit it, since according to their customs no woman should touch or accompany a dead person. . . . Tante Harder was in shock and afterward never regained her full faculties. But the heavenly Father knows his children and all their weaknesses. He will find his own, they will hear his voice and arise from their graves. Even if that is a lonely grave on the wide steppes of Kazakhstan. . . .

Tante Harder lived for another nine months and then the Lord reached into these pitiful circumstances and released her poor, weak spirit. One morning Njuta found her mother dead, beyond hunger, cold and all manner of suffering. That was January 7, 1943. Outside there was a terrible storm with bitter cold. The men could not dig a grave. Wrapped in a blanket the body was carried out, laid against a wall in an old cemetery and covered with earthen bricks. The wind covered everything with snow. . . .[2]

Although these are not the voices of professional historians, there is no doubt that a history is being witnessed to here. These are voices "crying in the wilderness" as in other, more distant periods of human history. These few tales may be multiplied many times over in order to comprehend the scale and scope of a process of destruction and dislocation which could only be defended like other revolutionary movements in which, it was believed, the existing structures must be eliminated before a new order could be put in place. In the face of such ideological reasoning the human aspects of the existing order have no chance. People in such situations become the victims of history; they are sacrificed for principles and purposes which they do not understand.

What is truly remarkable in the face of this unprecedented uprooting of a "Russian Mennonite world" is the fact that, after those prolonged hardships, after years and decades of separation and every kind of suffering, these people in many cases located relatives and friends, established contacts within and outside the Soviet Union and moved, if possible, to areas where they could congregate once again. These centres were no longer the fertile steppes where they had felt so much at home; they now gathered in the areas to which they had been exiled: Siberia, Kazakhstan and such. Here they had to befriend, or at least come to terms with, alien cultures as well as with harsh geography. In view of all that they have suffered and overcome, both physically and spiritually, it is no wonder that Mennonites of the Soviet Union are as industrious and ingenious as ever in their history and that their faith is fervent and more attached than ever to the notion of life as a journey to a better land.

Notes

1. Heinrich and Gerhard Woelk, *A Wilderness Journey: Glimpses of the Mennonite Brethren Church in Russia, 1925-1980*, trans. Victor G. Doerksen (Fresno, California: Center for M.B. Studies, Mennonite Brethren Biblical Seminary, 1982), 25-26.
2. Ibid., 28-34.

From Russian to Soviet Mennonites 1941-1988

Walter Sawatsky

To say that Russian Mennonite history in the twentieth century was eventful is surely to understate reality. Indeed most writing has focused on the tumultuous events: World War I, the revolution of 1917, the famine, the terror of Makhno, the collectivization of 1929-30, World War II — to name only the most striking. Which one had the greatest impact? Which brought the greatest tragedy? Often neglected in the discussion is a consideration of the degree to which a sustained process accounts for change. The primary intention of this chapter is not so much to recount events but to examine the long process which brought about change for Mennonites in Russia after the Second World War.

A major assumption in this essay is that during the twentieth century the so-called "Russian" Mennonites have become soviet-ized, irreversibly so. A related assumption is that the Soviet regime is not temporary, that it will be the governing form for the foreseeable future, and that badly needed reforms of the system may be revolutionary in substance but will be without bloodshed. Indeed the program of *perestroika* which was begun in April 1985 has initiated a major process of transformation and rethinking in virtually all spheres of Soviet life.[1] To recognize that fact probably requires the reader to adopt a different attitude toward present-day believing Soviet Mennonites than may well have been the case in the past. Instead of praying for strength to survive catastrophe and persecution until there is freedom, or else praying and working for salvation through emigration, one must assume that the majority of Soviet Mennonites will remain in the Soviet Union indefinitely. Will they be Mennonite there, or will most choose to abandon that identity as irrelevant? That the Christian faith will continue to flourish in the Soviet Union is no longer in doubt.

Soviet Mennonites today have a different understanding of themselves as Christian believers than they had before the revolution. Also, their sense of peoplehood has changed. To illustrate: the religious history of the Soviet Mennonites cannot be separated easily from the general story of Soviet evangelicals. The Mennonite story has the same uniquely Soviet features which are present among Baptists and Pentecostals. They also sense the difference with their counterparts in the Soviet Union.[2] Secondly, with regard to peoplehood, it was customary during the nineteenth century to speak of "colonists" and "Mennonites" because the Mennonite-German colonists impressed officials and observers as being noticeably different from the other German colonists in New Russia. Indeed the Mennonites did keep to themselves. Since World War II in particular, the Soviet Mennonite story is so interwoven with that of other Soviet Germans, that their common experience provides the framework for this presentation. Today, when Soviet Mennonite believers refer to themselves, they often say *Dietsche* when they mean Mennonite, and *Niemtsy-mennonity* when they are also including German Baptists or Lutherans. The identity question has served as a topic for more than one Soviet writer on the subject.[3]

The contemporary era must begin with World War II. For Mennonites, that war brought tragedy; ultimately, for those fated to survive, it brought newness: newness of place names, of church forms, and newness of options for the future. The war began on June 22, 1941, when the German army launched "Operation Barbarossa," invading Russia, advancing very quickly to the gates of Moscow, and even forcing the evacuation of the government to Ulianovsk (which, by the way, was not far from the Volga colonies). On August 28, 1941, the Supreme Soviet of the U.S.S.R. issued an order that all Germans in the autonomous Volga German Republic were to be evacuated eastward to the regions of Novosibirsk, Omsk, the Altai, Kazakhstan and other contiguous localities.[4] This had apparently been a prepared contingency plan, was already being acted upon before the announcement and was to be applied to all Germans, including those in Ukraine and the Caucasus. For Mennonites, as for other Germans, in total about one million persons in 1941, it meant that those living east of the Dniepr were almost all deported eastward. Those further west were still awaiting transport when the German troops arrived. For them a two-year period of German rule followed. This period came to an end with the forced trek westward during which many perished.

The survivors were placed in settlements in the Warthegau (Posnan region of Poland) with males as young as 16 forced at gunpoint to serve in the German army. Many were also given German Reichspassports. With the collapse of the German army and the advance of the Soviet army which overtook them these Germans were deported to the vast northern and eastern regions of the U.S.S.R. where they spent the next decade in a special deportation regime. Others were repatriated from other parts of post-war Germany, thanks to the cooperation of the British and the Americans with the Russians.[5] Thus it turned out that the Nazi drive to the East resulted in a worse fate for the Soviet Germans than they had experienced so far.[6]

The post-war experience of all Soviet Germans can be divided into four phases. This periodization applies to the Mennonites with minor modifications:

1945-55. Under the Deportation Regime
1956-64. On the Road to Rehabilitation
1964-72. Reestablishment as Mennonites and as Germans
1972-88. Soviet Assimilation and Emigration

Since Mennonite faith institutions were in collapse soon after 1930, followed shortly by the breakup of communities, the memory of the past quickly dimmed. The anti-German, anti-Mennonite and anti-religious propaganda which stressed their unfair share of wealth and privilege and their misuse of power — including the Mennonite recourse to armed self-defence — soon taught them to think differently about their earlier so-called "golden age." The Old Testament judgement speeches seemed to be the appropriate way to make sense of what was happening. Throughout the post-war period, Soviet Germans were never able to free themselves fully from the stigma of being Germans and, by implication, fascists at the same time.

The Deportation Regime 1945-55

The special regime, known as *Spetskomandantura,* applied to all three categories of Soviet Germans: the local Germans who had not been uprooted, the repatriated Germans and those from the Labour Army *(Trud Armee).*[7] There were significant numbers of Mennonites in each. Moreover, as was the case for other Soviet Germans, for other repatriates and for other Soviet citizens, many of their leaders were in prison camps. Some of them had been captive since the thirties, others received 10- to 25-year sentences for having been forced to serve in the Nazi army, or for having worked with the German occupation forces, or merely for having been in the West. The small minority that survived and was released rejoined family and fellowship after Stalin's death — one of the stopovers on the road to rehabilitation.

At the same time there were leading figures among the Mennonites, as well as among other groups, with whom the bureaucracy caught up only in the middle of the Deportation Regime period. Some of these were sent off to prison on Nazi charges. For others arrest for a religious cause resulted in additional charges of collaboration with the Germans and Americans. There is insufficient space to go into much detail, but for our purposes it is important to remember that Mennonites under the Deportation Regime were largely leaderless. The typical family consisted of a mother and children, some of the latter near adulthood, who wondered where the husband or some of the other children were. Also a disproportionately large number of orphaned German children was kept in state orphanages.[8]

The initial deportation decree of 1941 was arbitrary, failing to specify a legal basis and, contrary to Soviet law, extending the charge of treason collectively. A subsequent secret decree of November 26, 1948, provided the administrative organs making references to Article 58 of the Soviet Criminal Code, sections 1a, 1b, 1c and 1d, as well as Article 19 which spoke of "intent to commit treason" and "preparation" for the same.[9] The 1948 decree also made clear that the deportation punishment was to be permanent. Punishments, according to the code, included deportation for 10 to 25 years or even imposition of the death penalty. In one sense then, the punishment for all Soviet Germans was to put them in forced labour camps, three types of which had been established by the Forced Labour Code of August 1, 1933.[10] But a special board was set up to handle the deportations and within the Ministry of the Interior (MVD) the NKVD (Narodnyi Komissariat Vnutrennikh Del, or the People's Commissariat of Internal Affairs) established the Main Directorate of Deportations *(Glavnoe pereselencheskoe upravlenie)*. This directorate had "representatives in every large town and village and an officer posted in every enterprise and large office."[11]

Following are some implications for Mennonites and other Germans under this regime:

1. The immediate and automatic loss of all civil rights.
2. Splitting up of families, especially from 1942-45 when men and all able-bodied women without children younger than age three were put in the Labour Army, producing also numerous children lost to orphanages. Separations were also caused by the arbitrary rounding up of people in the West where the war had broken up families.
3. Deprivation of freedom to travel and to conduct corres-

pondence. That also involved economic difficulties.

4. Placement outside the educational network of secondary and higher education, sometimes even outside the elementary education network. That resulted in a generation of children born after the mid-thirties with a high percentage of illiteracy, as well as the overall "almost total obliteration of [its] national culture."[12]

Having received a special deported-nationalities identity card, all Germans were required to report to the NKVD Deportation Main Directorate, the *Spetskomandantura,* twice a month initially, then monthly during the second stage and, beginning in 1954, only annually.[13]

A technique to hasten the collectivization of the land, initiated in 1929, was the deportation of all kulaks to Siberia and Central Asia. Kulaks (the word meant fist) were those peasant farmers with above average landholdings who had shown noticeable entrepreneurial spirit during the efforts at agricultural reform at the turn of the century. Since Mennonites were so wealthy, many of them fell into this category. But during collectivization, the designation of kulak became an arbitrary term used to facilitate the removal of all leaders, potential resisters to forced collectivization and even persons who simply had the bad luck of falling victim to someone's whim.[14] These kulaks were often forced to settle in wilderness territories in the Far North, in Siberia, in Central Asia and in the frozen wastes of northeast Siberia. Common locations were Arkhangelsk, Vologda, Kotlas, Narym, Krasnoiarsk, numbered settlements between Petropavlovsk and Lake Balkash. Alternately, they were sent to work in mines near Magnitogorsk, Medvezhoie and Karaganda. Those who survived were later able to help new deportees who were familiar with local conditions by then. The total number of deported kulaks is estimated to have been between 10 to 13 million, of which a quarter to one-third, "predominantly children,"[15] perished.

In 1945 approximately 500,000 of the Soviet Germans in 1945 were still living in their original homes in the Orenburg settlements near the Urals, in Western Siberia and in the Asiatic republics. As Soviet power had extended eastward, their land had been reorganized into *kolkhozy* (collective farms) or *sovkhozy* (state farms). Often even the new administrators were still German-speaking, though now loyal to Marxism-Leninism. These persons were put under the *Spetskomandantura* and issued new identity cards that required bi-weekly reporting, but they usually kept their jobs. Most

This scene of Mennonite women in Rosenthal, Chortitza, working on a collective farm in 1934, expresses the pathos of Mennonites in the Soviet Union during the Stalin era.   Photo: Mennonite Heritage Centre Archives

of them were peasants in the agricultural sector. Their religious and cultural institutions had been eliminated during the Stalin purges, especially during the great anti-religious campaign of 1929-33.

The story of religious life in these areas is episodic. Despite the fact that infrequent moments of worship became a bit more frequent after Stalin's death in 1953, the dominant impression is that most people were preoccupied with long work hours, the quest for food and the fear of punishment for any religious practice.[16] A German visitor to Orenburg in 1954 found the morale "depressive," the worst condition of German colonies anywhere. Yet from the perspective of retaining the residues of peoplehood, this category of Soviet Germans and Mennonites was the best off.

The second category of Soviet Germans was the repatriated group. Specialists distinguish between those who moved to existing places of residence, either to settlements of local Germans or to those in new industrial centres; and those who were sent to new areas in the wilderness of the forests north of Vologda or among nomadic Asiatic tribes. These Germans did not experience improvements in their conditions until after 1948. In fact, the pitiable economic situation of Soviet Germans did not begin to change significantly until the years 1953 to 1955[17].

In his semi-autobiographical novel, Walter Wedel spoke for many when he described the feelings and situation of his group as it reached the end of the rail line: "just another twenty kilometres to go."[18] Indeed, his group of mothers with young children and two weak, old men could only now leave the badly heated boxcar which had been their travelling prison for the past month and a half. At least they had survived. The two-day trek through deep snow and the temporary wooden barracks at the end were additional troubles to overcome. Then came the backbreaking labour of felling trees, hauling logs and trying to stay alive on floating logs which threatened to jam when their legs and feet scarcely did their bidding because of extended exposure to the elements. Survivors remember hunger as the most painful hardship to endure. Intense preoccupation with food dominated their thinking and even their consideration of God at least through 1948.

Worship opportunities were rare. Many already felt helpless in their personal sense of God, then discovered that things could get even worse. The weakened ones became ill, yet received no medicine. A 23-year old woman, Tina Ens, for example, developed an infection in her legs, gradually lost the strength for movement, then finally was able to get to a hospital 200 kilometres away. Her condition worsened anyway and eventually she died. Relatives asked the authorities to have her buried since they were not able to do so. But in spring a worker informed the family that the frozen body, along with many others, still had not been buried.[19]

Recent memoirs constantly refer to God as a source of strength in suffering. For some it was the spiritual rootedness of a grandma that was a model for survival. For others it was Onkel Aron Thiessen or Elder Johann Penner who spoke the word of support when nothing seemed to point to God anymore. Franz Petrovich Thiessen, age 32 in 1952, was an experienced prisoner, but when he came to the forced labour camp at IA/1 near Dushanbe, Tadzhikistan, he encountered such a difficult situation that he did not see how he could survive another day. But later that same day he met Elder Johann Penner who encouraged him to trust in God. Penner was transported elsewhere a day later, but Thiessen had recovered the sense of God's presence.[20]

Elder Johann Penner had been ordained in 1941. After the war he began seeking out lonely settlements of Mennonites, inviting the people back to faith, baptizing secretly and, after 1956, even trying to organize a Mennonite church. In his prime he was remembered as someone with a charismatic quality that drew people to him. He was physically large and strong, and continued to practice his black-smith's trade when possible.

In the third category of Germans were those who served in the Labour Army, both male and female, and continued in similar work after the war under the Deportation Regime.[21] Some of them were placed into the mines of the Ural region. A large number became mine workers in and around Karaganda, Kazakhstan — a delayed blessing of sorts being the possibility of an early pension for women and men, age 50 and 55, because of the heavy labour which made "coal miner's lung" a permanent condition. Still others were sent to Central Asia to dig out the Chu Canal by hand. There are numerous cases of families where husband or son finally managed to get permission for other family members to move to his place of labour, but as a general rule reuniting of families came after 1955.

Two religious developments deserve to be highlighted for this period. Those Mennonites who found themselves in cities such as Novosibirsk, Karaganda, Frunze, Alma Ata, Slavgorod and others, discovered that Evangelical Christian-Baptists had been permitted to reopen and register churches.[22] Many young Mennonites heard their first sermon and experienced their personal conversion at such a fellowship. They were baptized and joined the membership, secure in the knowledge of fellowship in Christ, even though the language was Russian. Later, as more Germans congregated in these cities, such believers sometimes developed divided loyalties between their fellow Baptists and fellow Mennonites.

There were, of course, many incidents of the state repressing religious expression including renewed imprisonment of preachers after 1949, 1952 and 1957. One such incident, not yet widely known, involved the arrest and trial of between 17 and 30 Mennonites, and could be labelled the largest trial of Mennonite believers after World War II.[23] The story contains twists involving even American Menno-nites. On August 30, 1951, eight persons — all Mennonite and four of them preachers — were arrested in Taboshar, a secret uranium mining settlement 60 kilometres from Leninabad, Tadzhikistanskaia SSR. This was followed by the arrest of at least nine more persons on April 26, 1952. All were convicted and sentenced for treason, based on Article 58 1a, to 25 years of forced labour plus an additional five years without citizenship rights. The four leaders, chief among them the leader of the Mennonite fellowship which had begun in 1946, Dietrich Klassen, and the younger leader, Heinrich Wiens, received the death penalty. In the end, only Wiens was actually executed, shot on September 23, 1952.

Wiens and Klassen in particular were accused of spying for the Americans under the guise of religion. They had been prisoners of war (POWs) in America, after having been part of the trek to Germany and having been forced to serve in the German army. At the Buettner POW camp in America they had been visited by plain-coated American Mennonites.[24] Klassen, who had studied theology in America, was also accused of being trained by the Central Intelligence Agency (CIA). In any case, their trial now served as a domestic aspect of the Cold War, a pattern that was to repeat itself later, even if not in such drastic fashion. All the other prisoners had been forcibly repatriated from POW camps in Germany and Austria.

One participant felt that this response was precipitated by an additional factor, at least at the second trial: this group had submitted an application for registration as a Mennonite church fellowship back in 1949. With the arrests, most of the religious literature was also taken, although not even all four preachers had owned Bibles. Nevertheless, Wiens' father-in-law, Nikolai Regehr, now took over the leadership of the fellowship, retaining it till he died in 1971. But it was primarily the women who made certain that worship continued, even though they also had had their limited personal property confiscated when their husbands were sentenced. Most of the persons who were sentenced were freed by the middle of 1956. One such person lived through the experience of being freed from the 25-year sentence early in 1956, only to get another 25-year sentence the next day because of his religious membership. That one was finally dismissed by a special commission in July 1956, an expression of the de-Stalinization policy now underway.

An episode from the short life of Heinrich Wiens is worth preserving. At age 33 he was shot for treasonable religious activity. After having served several years of his 25-year sentence, Franz P. Thiessen was working with a small labour camp brigade applying paint and stucco to new buildings under construction. At noon he took the liberty to go off to a separate room for a short rest and for personal prayer. Soon he noticed that a young Afghani, who had a strange deep scar circling his head, was also slipping away. One day he decided to follow him and discovered the Afghani on his knees saying the Lord's Prayer in German! It turned out that the Afghani had shared a cell on death row with Heinrich Wiens. Although only 32, Wiens' hair had turned prematurely white, and he had appeared like a saint to the others. Wiens had taught the Afghani how to pray, to sing "Gott ist die Liebe" and to recite some Bible verses. The story of Heinrich Wiens' witness began to circulate (with minor variations) and became one more inspiring testimony of a faith worth dying for.

The Road to Rehabilitation or The Great Search 1955-1964

The official disappearance of Soviet Germans, including Menno-nites, began to come to an end. In December 1955, following the visit of German Chancellor Konrad Adenauer, the Supreme Soviet of the U.S.S.R. issued a decree which abolished the Deportation Regime. The decree merely stated that "in consideration of the fact that the restrictions on the legal status of the Germans and their families in different regions of the state are no longer necessary, they are hereby abolished."[25] It had been preceded by an amnesty decree on September 17, 1955, freeing many persons accused of collaborat-ing with the occupying authorities and reducing the sentences of others. A supplementary amnesty decree was published a year later.

The end of the *Spetskomandantura* era meant that the search for relatives could begin in earnest. It also meant that written corres-pondence with relatives abroad could be resumed. With organized help from the Red Cross in Hamburg, persons within the Soviet Union began finding each other. Thanks to the amazing work of the Mennonite Central Committee (MCC) *Suchdienst* in Frankfurt, which began in 1957, more then 10,000 persons were found.[26] Furthermore, it now became possible for Germans to move to other localities for the sake of a better climate or to join relatives. Another consideration for moving was the fact that less isolated locations would permit children to go to secondary schools or even to enter vocational institutes. However, in these locations Mennonite young men were eligible for military service, and most of them subse-quently did begin to serve.

The end of this era also brought other limitations. First of all, the Soviet Germans had to sign a promise that they would never ever return to their old homes in Ukraine. Nor did the decree provide an actual rehabilitation. That change was to take time and would become another significant moment in international relations. Hence, this era became the period of the great search: for family, for peoplehood, for church fellowship and for citizenship.

New communities of Mennonites now began to emerge. Some of the small settlements such as Nitva, Novaia Lialia and various Vologda forest camps were abandoned. The Mennonites settled around the Kazakhstan capital city of Alma Ata instead. Others joined relatives in and around Karaganda, or in other cities such as Tselinograd, Kustanai, Aktiubinsk, Pavlodar and Semipalatinsk. Still others sought out the Kirgiz Republic, settling along the transport route from Frunze to Przhevalsk. That added the names of Tokmak, Krasnaia Rechka, Kant, Stantsia Ivanovka and Romanovka to the new Mennonite localities. Seldom were new locations sought out. Usually other relatives or fellow Mennonites had already come there involuntarily, some even voluntarily as was true for the Siberian settlements and the Rot Front (Bergthal) settlement (1929) near Frunze.

This internal migration plus the release of prisoners, including preachers who had been active before the war, led to a spiritual revival. Enterprising men such as Johann Penner, Heinrich H. Voth and Aron Thiessen from the *Kirchliche* Mennonites began to travel and hold secret worship services. Mennonite Brethren such as Abram Koop, Cornelius Woelk and Peter Engbrecht, to name a few, also visited and preached. Sometimes these visits resulted in dramatic conversion experiences. Often too it was merely new access to at least a portion of the Word of God, or the experience of some Christian singing which led to spiritual rebirth and renewal. The known stories of witness and faith could easily fill a book. The point to make here is that a few bridges for passing on the faith were being built. Older leaders, who still remembered what it meant to be Christian and Mennonite, could teach men [*sic*] who had grown to adulthood under the Deportation Regime, who knew nothing of the past. They taught them how to organize and lead churches. Some of those teachers taught leadership and organizational skills by personal example or private conversation. Others, such as Jacob Rempel of Orenburg (later Rot Front, Kirgizia) who had been to Bible school, could teach Bible and doctrine through systematic private lectures.

From the beginning the Mennonite Brethren were in a more advantageous situation than were the Church Mennonites.[27] Little more than language distinguished the Mennonite Brethren from other evangelicals. Also, many of their leaders had joined existing congregations to form the All-Union Council of Evangelical Christian-Baptists (AUCECB) after 1944. Other leaders had learned practical ecumenism in prison. Differences were irrelevant as long as the chief concern was to be able to worship regularly and to preach the message of salvation. There are many reports from the mid-fifties about inter-Mennonite and inter-evangelical fellowships. Soon, however, leadership conflicts and doctrinal nuances began to force divisions between Mennonites and Mennonite Brethren; in a few places, especially Karaganda, between Brethren and Baptists.

Relationships with Mennonites abroad, especially with those in the United States and Canada, became possible again in 1956.[28] The initiative came from North America, with Harold S. Bender as President of the Mennonite World Conference and David B. Wiens from Canada visiting the Soviet Union. They made contact with some former Mennonite leaders who came to their hotel in Moscow. At the end of the visit, Bender wrote a letter to the Council for the Affairs of Religious Cults (CARC) requesting official state recognition of the Mennonites.[29] Secondly, he urged the AUCECB leadership to provide an umbrella of protection for the Mennonites until they could obtain this recognition. An immediate result was imprisonment for some of the persons contacted. The AUCECB did urge its congregations to also accept Church Mennonites for communion (1964). German language worship services also became possible in AUCECB churches after 1958. They were even reported positively in the official journal.[30]

This foreign contact was renewed in subsequent visits which were usually sponsored by MCC. Orie Miller visited in 1958; a four-man delegation followed in 1960.[31] In 1962 MCC also helped host an AUCECB delegation which included the Mennonite, Viktor Kriger. However, between 1960 and 1966 no Mennonite delegation visited the Soviet Union. Thus, North American Mennonites failed to be in touch during the crucial years of the anti-religious campaign when the Baptists were split into two denominations and when the Mennonites joined the AUCECB. Subsequently, contact by visitation became more regular. The visitors also became more informed about what was happening in the Soviet situation and in church alignments there.

Church Mennonite leaders who had met with Bender did try to organize churches. This included unsuccessful efforts to secure legal recognition as local Mennonite congregations, which failed. It included attempts in January 1957 to bring together in Solikamsk, Permskaia Oblast, existing elders and leading ministers to form a common organization or at least to speak with a common voice.[32] To that the authorities responded with prison sentences. Therefore, to the present day there is no legal central organizing body for the Mennonites, although informal talks continue.

More important for the decade of the sixties was the experience of Mennonite Brethren within the larger evangelical world. A concomitant of the de-Stalinization efforts after 1956 was the rapid growth in numbers of religiously active people. The Khrushchev regime responded with a major anti-religious program, which quickly became administratively heavy-handed. The years 1959-64 are known as the second worst period for believers with one-half of the recently reopened churches once again being closed. An especially problematic feature of the campaign was the effort to enlist the assistance of the church leadership in restraining church activity. The Moscow leadership of the AUCECB was constrained to issue a more restrictive constitution which it sent to regional superintendents (Senior Presbyters) with a Letter of Instruction (1960). That produced conformity in many congregations concerning such actions as preventing children from attending worship and removing some activist preachers and deacons. It also resulted in a resistance movement which made active and creative use of *samizdat* (illegal self-publishing) to circulate its views. Between 1960 and 1965 support for this *Initsiativniki* movement grew until nearly half of the evangelicals were supporting it.[33]

Driving evangelicals into illegal underground activity was hardly the aim of the government's effort, but that was the result, in spite of the imprisonment of numerous *Initsiativniki* leaders. Thus the authorities could be persuaded in 1963 to assent to an All-Union Conference of AUCECB delegates. One of the means to counter the public image of splintering within the AUCECB was to invite a new body of evangelicals, namely the "Brethren Mennonites," to join. In 1963 this was largely a staged event. Heinrich K. Allert, unknown to most Mennonites, told the Evangelical Christian-Baptist assembly of delegates that since there were no significant differences between them, the Mennonites would like to join the AUCECB. During the next three years, joining the AUCECB became a matter for discussion in Mennonite regions. At the All-Union Congress in 1966 this union became more official when 74 representatives reported their readiness to join. At that time a statement of agreement between the AUCECB and the Mennonites was affirmed.[34]

Details of the agreement were made public only gradually, so that the union of Mennonites with the AUCECB, usually dated to 1963, is more the story of a generally successful wooing of the Mennonite bride after the marital bans were already announced. Initially, about 16,500 Mennonites were said to have joined. Mennonite representative Viktor Kriger was claiming 18,000 by 1968. Then the number increased to 20,000. During the eighties the AUCECB has regularly claimed that around 30,000 "German Brethren Mennonites" belong to the Union.

Soviet Mennonites 1964-72

Soviet Germans, including Mennonites, profited from Nikita Khrushchev's efforts after the Berlin Crisis to prepare the way for his visit to West Germany. On August 29, 1964, a decree of the Supreme Soviet rehabilitated all Soviet Germans morally and politically. This change in the deportation decree of August 28, 1941, began by saying that "life has shown that mistaken and unfounded accusations were the result of arbitrary action in the conditions of Stalin's cult of personality".[35] The decree further stated that "during the war years, the decisive majority of the German population together with the Soviet people contributed in fact by its toil to the victory of the Soviet Union over Nazi Germany, and since the war the Germans have actively cooperated in communist construction."[36]

As a means of rehabilitation the decree's chief value was moral and political although it was only published in the official gazette on December 28, 1964, and in *Neues Leben* in German on January 20, 1965. That is, the general public was not informed through the press. The rehabilitation also resulted in some economic and cultural assistance to the Soviet Germans in the form of language schools, radio programs and German language publications, chiefly through Alma Ata, the capital of Kazakhstan where the majority of Germans now lived. But it was not full rehabilitation, since the Volga Republic was not reestablished nor were the Germans granted the right to move back to their former lands.

However, with the official stigma removed, Soviet Germans, including Mennonites, could now go about demonstrating their qualities as good Soviet citizens. Statistically this soon became evident with the percentage of Germans in higher education reaching normal levels by the beginning of the 1970s.[37] One expert reported that in 1967, 81.5 percent of the Germans owned one cow, compared with 60 percent of the general population; and 67 percent of the Germans "live in new houses that they have built themselves since 1955," obviously also a higher number than the national average.[38]

Western Mennonites who read the lists of prisoners' names circulated after 1964 by the courageous women who organized the Council of Prisoners' Relatives (CPR), took note of the typical Russian Mennonite names that frequently appeared. In the first place that included Georgi P. Vins (Wiens) who does indeed have Mennonite relatives but whose father had already chosen to join the German Baptists before the Revolution of 1917.[39] But there were other persons sent to prison whose local congregations were German-speaking. These were Soviet evangelical congregations located in former Mennonite colonies, especially in the Slavgorod and Altai regions, or persons from the new post-war Mennonite and German settlement areas who had chosen to support the reformers.

The most prominent such ex-Mennonite was Kornelius K. Kreker (Kroeker) of Novosibirsk who was elected to the Council of Churches of Evangelical Christian Baptists (CCECB) leadership council of 17 persons.[40] Many other "Mennonites" were active in regional leadership as superintendents, as local pastors and as travelling evangelists. The latter included Peter D. Peters who is easily the most revered of the young fiery preachers totally dedicated to Christ.[41] A disproportionately large number has also been arrested for working in the secret printing press, which may reflect the traditional Mennonite emphasis on the need for personal Bible study.[42]

The *Initsiativniki* movement became a separate denomination when it organized in 1965 as the Council of Churches of Evangelical Christian Baptists (CCECB), but it has remained an illegal body.[43] Repeated requests for legal recognition were rejected by the authorities, except for one national congress which was held legally in Tula in 1969. General evangelical support for these reformers grew until by 1966 nearly half of the former AUCECB supporters were behind them. But significant steps in self-reform of the AUCECB between 1966 and 1969, as well as an image of unnecessary intransigence which some of the CCECB leaders projected, subsequently have caused a steady drop in support. The stalemate between the state and the evangelicals after 1970 meant a drop in harassment during worship services and a gradual increase in church registrations. However, this did not apply to the CCECB churches. With the deportation of their imprisoned General Secretary, Georgi P. Vins, in 1979, state pressure through the imprisonment of leaders increased again. Further support was lost due to persecution fatigue by some supporters, but also due to leadership conflict as President Kriuchkov became increasingly arbitrary in his leadership style.[44]

This reform movement was of significant relevance to the Mennonites for two reasons. It included many Mennonites, more accurately ex-Mennonite supporters. Secondly, the CCECB became a negative model of confrontationist behaviour for the larger body of Mennonites. Yet the continued CCECB challenge to the state forced the latter into making concessions to alternative and more moderate evangelical groups. One such concession was the possibility of legal recognition as a local autonomous Mennonite congregation.

How "Mennonite" were these persons in the CCECB? From a denominational point of view, they had left the Mennonites to join the Baptists, a pattern also common in North America. That meant that they had rejected Mennonite distinctives such as nonresistance and non-swearing of the oath. Upon questioning, such persons frequently explained that to be Mennonite meant to smoke and to drink and to speak Low German; however those "Low Germans" who had had a personal conversion experience were now Baptist by confession of faith, even though ethnically they were still Mennonite.

That answer became a problem for some when they became aware that there were practising Mennonite Christians who had the same conversion experience and habits of life as they. For those emigrating to West Germany in the 1970s, this dilemma became acutely confusing. Some chose to join German Baptist congregations; others sought out Mennonite Brethren churches; still others congregated in large enough numbers to form a separate congregation. The latter had formed their own Brethren-Baptist Conference by 1976, maintaining self-conscious ties to the CCECB in the Soviet Union through their *Missionswerk Friedensstimme*. They developed a variety of pragmatic relationships to the surrounding Baptist and Mennonite churches. Others began to form separate Mennonite Brethren congregations. Relationships were also complicated by the intensification of family ties to Mennonites in Canada. Many of the close relatives were now in key Mennonite leadership positions and also had the potential for providing financial aid.

Another way to test their "Mennoniteness" was to inquire into their faith and theology. Several Soviet scholars pointed to the fact that the *Initsiativniki* might not technically be Mennonite, but the roots of its members' radical Christianity did go back to the Anabaptists of the 16th century.[45] These writers also mentioned the tendency of 20th century Soviet Mennonites to join the *Initsiativniki*. It is striking to note that most of the known conscientious objectors to military service are from the CCECB, and that this group is particularly sensitive to the oath of allegiance which soldiers need to swear upon induction. Presently, there are no congregations in the Soviet Union that are officially registered as Mennonite which include the nonresistant distinctive in their constitution.[46] Obviously this raises the question to which we must return: What is the meaning or content of the word "Mennonite"?

For the majority of contemporary practising Mennonites in the Soviet Union, something in the confrontational style of the CCECB did not suit their understanding of being the "Quiet in the Land." One illustration was their evaluation of specific prisoners of conscience whom they knew personally as having abrasive personalities or as being motivated by pride to claim the designation of "martyr." As one individual put it, Mennonites believed it was better to suffer imprisonment silently, not making the names known with public letters, and to show that one cared for the soul of the persecutor.

A sign that the Mennonites were now more nearly rehabilitated was the registration in 1967 of the Mennonite Brethren Church of Karaganda as an autonomous local congregation. The Mennonite congregation in Novosibirsk was given de facto recognition almost at the same time, whereas in the republic of Kirgizia, the Mennonite congregation in Tokmak became legally registered. These congregations had existed for some time already and their requests for legalization had been pending for years. What the precise reasons for granting autonomous registration were can be attributed to a composite of factors, but the general rehabilitation of the Soviet Germans after 1964 was an obvious prerequisite.

The Karaganda congregation traced its beginnings back to 1956 or to 1960, to a time when the Karaganda Baptist Church ceased meeting officially because of the Khrushchev campaign.[47] Numerous groups began meeting in homes in scattered parts of the city. Within a few years the Karaganda Baptist Church was publically active again, with a mostly German-speaking congregation under the leadership of Abraham Friesen. Other Mennonite leaders, some of them new arrivals, wanted a specifically Mennonite church, at least one which rejected the use of the Russian language in worship. Perhaps personality conflicts were also present among the leaders. At any rate Willi Matthies, associate elder of the congregation, went to the Council of Religious Affairs offices in Moscow in 1966 at the time of the AUCECB Congress. At that time, other congregations with many Germans and Mennonites officially joined the AUCECB. The Soviet official suggested to Matthies that they might register autonomously as Mennonites. Official approval came in May 1967. Matthies made a dramatic and surprise announcement to the AUCECB leadership at a special meeting called by the latter to discuss how to improve relationships with the Brethren Mennonites.

The Mennonites in Kirgizia did not receive such pressures from the AUCECB to join. Their practice of baptism by effusion remained an inflexible barrier. In Tokmak they were meeting in Baptist facilities during off-hours. The Baptists had been forced by state authorities to make room, but this arrangement was unsatisfactory for establishing a full church life. Heinrich Heese, a deacon, made the trip to Moscow with Elder Johann Penner. They submitted a special Mennonite constitution in Russian translation with their application for separate legal registration. Official approval finally came in 1967. They were now permitted to meet in separate quarters in a converted private house.

The Challenge of Being Soviet Mennonites 1972-86

The most recent stage in the Soviet Mennonite experience can be dated to another political action which affected all Soviet Germans. This was a decree of the Supreme Presidium on November 3, 1972, concerning "Abolition of the restriction on choice of place of residence that were imposed in the past with regard to various categories of citizens."[48] The decree was not published but a directive to the Ministries of Justice and of the Interior from the Procurator General's office on November 9, 1972, entitled *Prikaz general' nogo prokurora,* No. 54, spelled out its implications in three clauses. First, it abolished the restrictions on choice of residence as laid down December 13, 1955, for Germans and also one of September 1956 which applied to Greeks, Turks and "persons of enemy nationalities without civil status." Secondly, it stated that the Soviet Germans' rights of choice of residence were equal to that of other citizens. These were dependent on existing legislation for work arrangements and identity certificates. Finally, the supervision was entrusted to the Ministries of Justice and of the Interior.

The most significant element in this new and complete rehabilitation or full integration of Soviet Germans into Soviet citizenship was the question of how the ministries would administer it. By withholding permission to accept new applications for residence in the southern Ukraine, because of an effort to distribute the working population more rationally — a common practice in Europe — the ministries curtailed movement back. Indeed, the authorities remained committed not to return their old residences to the Soviet Germans because of the uprooting and the hard feelings this would cause for the new residents, many of whom had been assigned to those sequestered homes by governmental fiat decades ago. Nevertheless, this decree did make it possible for many Soviet Germans and Mennonites to move to the Baltic republics and for a smaller number to move to Moldavia. The Baltic area was culturally more European. Since new workers were not as much in demand, it became easier for Soviet Germans living in these areas to obtain permission to leave the Soviet Union for reunification with family members in West Germany. Between about 1973 and 1986 when this "emigration" ceased, about 67,000 Germans had emigrated.[49] Of this number, 13,000 were Mennonites or of Mennonite origin making this the fourth largest Mennonite emigration movement.

This relative "freedom of movement" was a primary factor which influenced even the religious developments of the Mennonites. Not only was the emigration option once again very relevant for how Mennonite leaders approached their future as Soviet Mennonites. It now also became a factor in the development of the CCECB, and, therefore in the shaping of the AUCECB and its relationship to the Soviet German Baptists and Mennonites.

Between 1974 and 1978 it became evident that Soviet authorities were seeking to weaken the leadership of the CCECB by offering them the emigration option. Georgi Vins himself was approached about finding relatives abroad that would send him the needed *vyzov* or invitation form. He refused. Other activist pastors were also approached about the emigration option. Frequently the authorities warned them that the choice would be between lengthy and repeated prison sentences or emigration. Soon local congregational leaders advised such pastors that they might be more effective in helping from abroad and encouraged emigration. Rather quickly a long list of such aggressive leaders found themselves in West Germany. Included were David D. Klassen, Jacob Esau, Ewald Hauff, Gerhard Hamm, Abram Hamm, Nikolai Klassen, Jacob Loewen, Walter Penner, Diedrich Wiens and many more. Today these leaders are the "missionaries" in West Germany, working on behalf of believers in the Soviet Union.

In a less explicit sense, persons in church leadership in AUCECB churches, as well as in independent Mennonite churches, often discovered that they received the permission to emigrate rather readily, compared with the average successful applicant who had been rejected at least ten times and had suffered various job discriminations in the process. The motivations for such church leaders to move to West Germany were diverse and no doubt ambiguous. Certainly the attraction of rejoining family was a common one.

Another was the prospect of freely expressing one's religious belief, especially of ending the discrimination against their children in school. A very common motivation, which also caused some guilt, was the emotional fatigue and spiritual burnout which had been caused by the very strained atmosphere within which they had tried to provide spiritual and administrative leadership to their congregations in the Soviet Union. They left to get a breather, but how would those congregations survive?

Generally speaking, since only about five percent of the Soviet Germans were able to leave, enough persons remained to fill the ranks. The estimated total population of believing Mennonites was scarcely affected because of the high birth rate among Mennonites. Sociologically speaking, although without the desired raw data to support it, one can say that the leaders who left were generally untrained, self-taught preachers and pastors who could be replaced by electing someone else. Further, as the gradual integration of the Soviet Germans made itself felt, more of the younger persons who were now elected to church office came with some post-secondary school education and with greater language competency in Russian. Of course, these younger leaders usually showed less confidence in speaking German.

The Church Mennonites' post-war public history as organized congregations falls primarily into this latter period when they had received full citizenship. A process that is less easy to document by events and decrees was the gradual sovietization of their members, most notably those under age forty. There was no golden era from the past that they could remember, nor a time when they had been the more dominant Mennonite church in terms of membership size, institutions and trained leaders. Groups of people who had fellowshipped together in the special settlements of the Deportation Regime often moved to the new settlements in Central Asia and Kazakhstan. In the seventies, they and other groups could now hope to obtain one of three forms of official church status.

A few, such as Novosibirsk and Tokmak, obtained legal status as a registered local religious society. A goodly number were registered indirectly by being added to the membership list of an AUCECB congregation, or to a Lutheran or Methodist congregation in the Baltic republics. As far as atheist propaganda statistics were concerned, this guaranteed that no increase of churches needed to be registered. For the State Council of Religious Affairs, it meant that such subgroups were the responsibility of the legal signatories of the larger church of evangelicals. Internally, that church would treat the

daughter group as a subunit which was meeting in a home in a village some miles away. The group might also meet in the same building during off-hours with minimal spiritual contact with the main church.

A further kind of arrangement that became more common was that of allowing a Church Mennonite congregation such as Romanovka and Krasnaia Rechka to be registered under the Church Mennonite congregation in Tokmak, but to grant it all the de facto rights of independence such as a meeting place and independently elected leadership. Still another variation was to give the group verbal permission to exist as an independent congregation with leaders keeping state officials regularly informed, yet without obtaining the actual certificate of registration. The latter was certainly risky, but in the context of Soviet experience, the registered congregations always assumed that their rights could quickly be erased and the appropriate paper work would follow, if necessary.

Nevertheless, particularly since the more liberalized revision of Soviet legislation on religion (1975 revision as compared to the secret one of 1962), there has been a slow increase in the number of publicly existing Mennonite congregations.[50] In 1986 ten such congregations were known to exist in the Orenburg region, plus twelve

The Kirchliche *Mennonite Church in Tokmak, Kirghizia, June 1988.*

Photo: Peter H. Rempel

elsewhere, for a total of 2446 members.[51] The precise statistics account for only a portion of the 10 to 15,000 Mennonites generally assumed to exist in the Soviet Union today.

Those Mennonites that were part of the AUCECB were seldom counted very accurately. Up to 49 congregations have been mentioned as being predominantly German. These represent up to 30,000 individual believers. After 1967, the leaders of the one independently registered Mennonite Brethren congregation in Karaganda began to foster ties to potential sister groups. One such group in the suburb of Novo Pavlovka just outside Frunze, Kirgizia, did indeed obtain official registration a decade later in 1977.[52] Two other groups, Nartan (Caucasus) and Razdol'naia (Moldavia) which consisted largely of families from the Karaganda church, were dissolved after a few years when those families had emigrated.[53]

During the second half of this era, a curious arrangement developed in the Orenburg region. This had been a Mennonite settlement since the turn of the century. The residents were not uprooted in 1941, although the males and many females served in the Labour Army. After the war these settlements received many new Mennonite residents from elsewhere. All were now required to report according to the Deportation Regime regulations. Although the post-war period was a time of religious renewal accompanied by the organization of church life, Orenburg region came to be known as a place of especially severe religious persecution.[54] No doubt the effectiveness of state-inspired restraints on religious practice was due also to the fact that local administrators also spoke Low German and understood the mentality of the people they were to restrain.

In 1977 a congregation was finally registered in the village of Donskoe with Daniel Janzen elected as leader.[55] This fellowship had existed for some years, with registration application pending since 1972. That was true also of many others congregations, such as the one at Suzannovo, where children had been the most consistent in meeting for prayer regularly. After many futile efforts, Donskoe members finally were able to erect a place of worship which was officially dedicated in October 1978. Other congregations followed in both the lower and upper villages, the majority of them Mennonite Brethren. Some were also Church Mennonites. By the mid 1980s, this area had become a showplace of religious progress.[56]

Officially, at the end of 1986 there were 14 Mennonite Brethren congregations with 1,600 members in the former Orenburg colony.[57] In addition there were nine congregations representing 1,140 members in Neu Samara, including the Donskoe church with 430

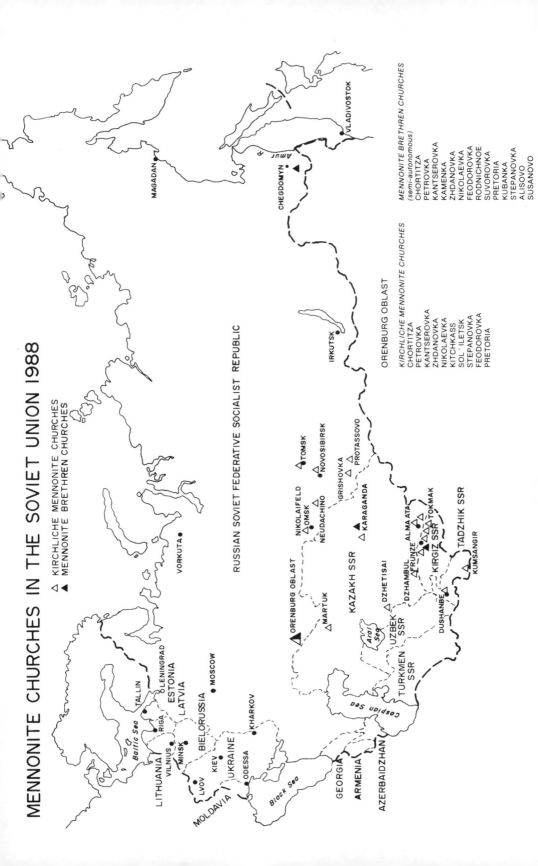

MENNONITE CHURCHES IN THE SOVIET UNION 1988

△ KIRCHLICHE MENNONITE CHURCHES
▲ MENNONITE BRETHREN CHURCHES

RUSSIAN SOVIET FEDERATIVE SOCIALIST REPUBLIC

ORENBURG OBLAST

KIRCHLICHE MENNONITE CHURCHES
CHORTITZA
PETROVKA
KANTSEROVKA
ZHDANOVKA
NIKOLAEVKA
KITCHKASS
SOL' ILETSK
STEPANOVKA
FEODOROVKA
PRETORIA

MENNONITE BRETHREN CHURCHES
(semi-autonomous)
CHORTITZA
PETROVKA
KANTSEROVKA
KAMENKA
ZHDANOVKA
NIKOLAEVKA
FEODOROVKA
RODNICHNOE
SUVOROVKA
PRETORIA
KUBANKA
STEPANOVKA
ALISOVO
SUSANOVO

MAGADAN
VLADIVOSTOK
CHEGDOMYN
Amur R.
IRKUTSK
TOMSK
NOVOSIBIRSK
NIKOLAIFELD
OMSK
NEUDACHINO
IGRISHOVKA
PROTASSOVO
KARAGANDA
ALMA ATA
FRUNZE
TOKMAK
KIRGIZ SSR
KUMSANGIR
TADZHIK SSR
DUSHANBE
DZHETISAI
DZHAMBUL
UZBEK SSR
KAZAKH SSR
ORENBURG OBLAST
MARTUK
Aral Sea
TURKMEN SSR
Caspian Sea
VORKUTA
MOSCOW
LENINGRAD
TALLIN
ESTONIA
RIGA
LATVIA
Baltic Sea
LITHUANIA
VILNIUS
MINSK
BIELORUSSIA
LVOV
KIEV
UKRAINE
ODESSA
KHARKOV
MOLDAVIA
Black Sea
GEORGIA
ARMENIA
AZERBAIDZHAN

members.[58] Further, the larger city congregations in Orenburg city and Orsk had about 190 out of a total membership of 270 who were Mennonite. This represents a total of approximately 3,000 Mennonite Brethren members.

A few cautionary comments are in order with regard to interpreting these statistics. First of all, they are based on recent reports to Mennonite World Conference officials. But, like statistics reported earlier, the categories for indicating official status vary with the source. The special feature for Orenburg, for which we suddenly have the greatest detail compared to years of virtually no information, is that these churches are not clearly registered as independent Mennonite Brethren. Technically they appear to represent a special category. Since at least 1966, men like Daniel Janzen have attended AUCECB congresses nationally and regionally, but the Orenburg churches consider themselves as holding fraternal status, not full membership in the AUCECB. Thus, for example, they choose not to regard themselves as part of the World Council of Churches (WCC), even though the AUCECB joined the WCC in 1962. AUCECB officials, however, include them also when claiming 30,000 Mennonites, along with Mennonites in the Slavgorod and Altai region where as yet few of the churches are officially registered.

In preparation for the Strasbourg Mennonite World Conference in 1984, a small MCC delegation first visited Orenburg. Daniel Janzen and Diedrich Thiessen, the latter from the Kitchkas Church Mennonite congregation, were delegates to the Strasbourg meeting. In both cases these visits were facilitated by the AUCECB. Several subsequent visits have taken place, including those of private individuals who were invited by the AUCECB to visit Orenburg. In this case it should be pointed out that the individuals in question were Canadian Mennonite Brethren leaders, even if they were not officially sent by that conference.[59]

Finally we turn to the largest group of Mennonites in the Soviet Union. These are the ones who belong to an inter-evangelical body technically known as the All-Union Council of Evangelical Christians, Baptists, Pentecostals and Mennonites. That title was shortened immediately. It became customary to speak of "Evangelical Christian Baptists" in order to indicate a new fused body. In popular parlance they are known as Baptists, the dominant group that has also established the strongest ties abroad. The AUCECB has been a full and active member of the Baptist World Alliance since 1955, even more integrally of the European Baptist Federation since 1958. Following the internal reforms in the mid-sixties, the AUCECB began sending delegates to the World Pentecostal Fellowship. Finally in 1978, a delegation attended a Mennonite World Conference for the first time.

After 1966, Mennonites began to gain influence in the AUCECB. Immediately two persons, Jacob Fast of Novosibirsk, the assistant pastor for the large German contingent there, and Viktor Kriger of Moscow, became the Mennonite spokesmen. Kriger remained in Moscow in 1964 after having completed military service and became a staff member responsible for maintaining contacts with Germans/ Mennonites throughout the Soviet Union. Both Fast and Kriger were elected to the All-Union Council in 1969, the latter as candidate member. In 1974 Fast was reelected to the Council and also to the more powerful 10-member Presidium that met monthly. Kriger, for personal reasons, did not let his name stand for election. He did retain his job in Moscow, although his focus shifted to assisting the union president in administrative duties. Traugott Quiring of Dushanbe was elected instead as candidate member. Within two years Quiring had not only joined the All-Union Council as full member, but became the first regional Senior Presbyter who was German/Mennonite. In his case, he was responsible for three republics in Soviet Central Asia with about 4,000 members, somewhat over half of them German.

This Mennonite role in the central leadership was part of the understanding that had been worked out by 1966, an arrangement that was referred to in subsequent elections. But these persons also enjoyed wide respect, usually being among those individuals elected to national office with the highest percentage of votes.[60] Nevertheless, at the 1979 national Congress of the AUCECB, delegates voiced more strongly their wishes for special attention to German/Mennonite concerns. Included were requests for Bibles and song books in German, which were granted only in small numbers by state authorities. In addition Fast, who was reelected to the Presidium, was asked to move to Moscow, and Quiring became a candidate member of the Presidium.[61] As part of a broader effort to improve the services of the Union to churches in the largest republic of all, the RSFSR, a super Senior Presbyter was appointed in 1979 together with two associates, one of them the Pentecostal, Peter Shatrov, the other Jacob Fast. These two now were entrusted with a more influential administrative base to assist their respective constituencies. It is surely not coincidental that in the eighties so many congregations in the Orenburg region were registered, or that buildings were constructed, achievements that usually required church bureaucratic assistance. That has not been true, however, for Mennonites in the Slavgorod area.

All these developments proceeded in the context of the large emigration movement to West Germany. Many more than could do so were eager to emigrate. The AUCECB journal, *Bratskii Vestnik*, made frequent references to emigration in an effort to discourage it.[62] Increasing German/Mennonite staff leadership as described above, as well as choosing assistant Senior Presbyters in Kazakhstan who were German, were further responses to help Germans stay. Indeed, one might say that the greatest concessions came to that group of Mennonites in the Orenburg region which had the fewest of its number emigrating.

The emigration did have its effect. Gradually the churches in Alma Ata, Frunze, Novosibirsk and Slavgorod lost several of their regular preachers and their best choir leaders. The leaders named above were persons who had deliberately chosen to remain, who saw their calling to be in the Soviet Union. But for a variety of reasons, Traugott Quiring finally applied for permission to join his family in West Germany, no longer having any family members in Central Asia. After several years of personal humiliation he left in early 1985. A year later Jacob Fast was forced to resign from all positions on moral grounds, certainly a major blow not only to him personally but to the overall leadership of the Mennonites and the AUCECB.

Mennonite leadership in the AUCECB entered a period of flux and strain. Quiring and Fast were succeeded by Peter Ens (Orenburg) and Emil Baumbach (Karaganda). Three assistant superintendents who were of German Baptist rather than Mennonite origin were appointed in Kazakhstan. At the same time a younger man, Johann P. Dyck of Karaganda, was employed by the AUCECB to be Referent or specialist for Mennonites and functioned as staff assistant to Baumbach. Dyck rose rapidly to prominence as respected historian and thinker, not only for Mennonites but for the entire AUCECB. It is interesting to note that it is Dyck and the other representatives of the German/Mennonites who have shown the greatest interest in Anabaptist history and thought. Unfortunately, in July 1988 Baumbach too was excommunicated for adultery, leaving Ens as sole representative of the Mennonites on the AUCECB Presidium, assisted now by a half dozen ministers elected locally.

A Persisting Identity Crisis

Christians have always believed that faith in Christ would never disappear in the Soviet Union. Most knowledgeable Soviet officials also have made the tacit assumption that Christianity will be around well into the next century. However, whether the Mennonite denomination will still exist after the year 2000 is much less certain. There are those who assume that the disappearance of Mennonite self-identity is only a matter of time, that Mennonites cannot survive the process of acculturation and the influence of atheism. Others wonder whether the demands of Christian unity and the adjustments for the sake of mission in the Soviet Union make the persistence of a Mennonite denomination desirable. Complicating the process is the persistent confusion about identity.

How, if at all, do Soviet Mennonites approach the question of the future? One indicator is the way in which recent anniversaries have been celebrated. For example, soon after the 1984 centenary obser-vations for the first Baptist Union in 1884 when Mennonite evangelist Johann Wieler was elected president, the Mennonites within the AUCECB organized their own celebration to commemorate 125 years since the beginning of the Mennonite Brethren in 1860. The speeches surveying the history and speaking to the present emphas-ized the interlocking nature of this story with that of the Baptists, at times to the point of distortion.[63] Further, the event was celebrated without inviting any Mennonites from abroad.

Church Mennonites, on the other hand, have not held such cele-brations, although someone may think of remembering 1989 as marking two centuries since Mennonites came to Russia. Instead one reads discussions in the West on the question, Can culture cradle faith? That reflects the assumption, still held more strongly by Church Mennonites, that retaining the German language in worship, as well as resisting ethnic integration through marriage, will help preserve the Mennonite faith.[64] Yet gradually local congregations have taken a formal position to begin to practice immersion baptism, thereby removing the barrier to fraternal acceptance by Mennonite Brethren and Baptists. Gradually also, translation from German to Russian becomes necessary in order for those under 40 years of age to be able to understand. Visitors continue to report that the median age for Church Mennonites is higher than for the Baptists — the young people go to the latter.

Several Mennonite World Conference visits in 1986 and 1987, focusing more on the Orenburg than on the usual Alma Ata and Frunze area, report confusing readings of the situation. In contrast to the emphasis in Heinrich Woelk's book that the Orenburg Brethren were independent and not Baptist, this delegation noted the very close relationship between Baptists and Mennonite Brethren in

Orenburg, the difference being little more than the name and the mother tongue. Further they reported many deep feelings of estrangement between Church Mennonites and Brethren Mennonites. Moreover, with regard to Anabaptist/Mennonite distinctives, one observer noted that the "nonresistance stance, a major factor in precipitating the migration to Russia, has essentially been lost." That is mainly due to state restrictions. But in the latest reports observers still state that "both leadership and lay members lack adequate or even minimal resource materials."[65]

This is a time for rethinking possible solutions. What is the Mennonites' future as Soviet Germans? Recent experts suggest that there are three possible solutions to the German national problem, if German ethnicity is to be preserved. The least likely option is the territorial solution such as establishing a new Volga Republic. More probable is the extraterritorial solution whereby the state would facilitate some sense of identity through culture, with German at least as a second language. Thirdly, there is the emigration option. The latter has been a persistent hope but with only five percent of the Soviet Germans managing to emigrate, the primary issue is, "What happens to those who remain?"[66]

What possible options have they as believers? What will be their status as a minority in that society? Will they strive to be Anabaptist in orientation, or will they be evangelical, and what is the difference? Ten years ago there was talk of an overarching federal structure for the diverse free church or evangelical groups in the Soviet Union. More recently, the achievements of Pentecostals, Lutherans and Adventists suggest the slight possibility that national denominational structures will be able to relate to sister denominations abroad.

The latter raises the question of the meaning and implications of Mennonite relations to fellow believers abroad. For a long time it was felt that Harold Bender's well-intentioned efforts in 1956, like the efforts in 1930, had resulted in greater difficulties for individual Mennonites in the Soviet Union, including interrogations, fines and imprisonments. Intensive interrogations of Mennonite hosts after foreign delegations leave are still the norm today. Yet major events and decisions taken by Soviet Mennonites have come at those times when foreign Mennonite links were the most tenuous, like before 1956, or between 1960 and 1966, or in even more recent developments. In short, foreign Mennonites learned about major decisions after the fact; they had no direct influence.

Restrictions for travel are not the only barrier to communication. For decades, communication was possible through the common use of German. As both North American and Soviet Mennonites abandon the German, it becomes more evident how few Mennonites in the Soviet Union are learning English and how few in North America are learning Russian. Now is probably the time to be anxious about the lack of will for relating to one another.

No doubt, the future is shaped by the way in which the story of the past is told. This effort at telling the story from the perspective of sovietized Mennonites whose realistic expectation is to raise their children in that society, may point to the inadequacy of the common North American framework of the story. To tell it as a story of immigration to Russia after 1789 for reasons of conscience followed by emigration from Russia after 1874 or 1923 for similar reasons leaves out the Soviet Mennonites. To tell the story as one of persecution of an innocent religious community where God stepped in to save by opening the door of emigration, does not fit, neither is it accurate. Rather it reminds them of the reputation Mennonites have developed of not taking Soviet citizenship seriously.

Telling the story of suffering, of death, of recovery and of resurrection as a people of God is the Soviet Mennonites' story, as it is also the story of many, many other Soviet citizens. Perhaps that is why carefully listening to each other's stories, as they become increasingly coloured by each other's national context and loyalties, may be the way to distinguish the hand of God in history, from the hand of the evil one, and thus to see the way ahead — a way that might, or might not, use Mennonite terminology. Nevertheless it will be a story told in the common language of the people of God.

October 1988

Postscript *

Quite suddenly in February 1987, emigration once again became a possibility for Soviet Germans. This was in sharp contrast to the situation only two years before when the prospect for reunification with family members in West Germany had become quite unrealistic for most — it seemed they would have to stay in the Soviet Union, become culturally more adjusted, and gradually also increase their religious freedoms. So rapid was the emigration that by October 1989, *Mennonitische Umsiedlerbetreuung* had listed 17,500 additional names of Mennonites and Baptists of Mennonite lineage who had left. The *Umsiedler* II movement (1987 and following) is turning out to be the largest and perhaps the last major Mennonite migration. To emigrate or to stay was the primary issue which visitors to Soviet Mennonite communities have reported since then. Others called it quite simply emigration fever.

Yet in August 1989 Soviet Mennonites met in Zaporozh'e (formerly Chortitza) to celebrate the bicentennial of their settlement in Russia. It was the first such national gathering permitted by the authorities since that fateful "Martyr's Conference" of 1925. The bicentennial celebration was initiated and organized by Soviet Mennonites, Viktor Fast of Karaganda being the primary organizer. Hundreds of Mennonites came to the old oak tree on Khortitsa Island to remember the pain and the blessing, to reflect on the "graciousness and the strictness of God," as one invitation bulletin put it. With placards, lapel buttons and even a mass meeting of 10,000 people in a nearby stadium they reminded each other of the oft-repeated biblical affirmation, "Bis hieher hat uns der Herr geholfen," only this time they proclaimed it in Russian.

Indeed, reflections about the past seemed muted compared to the new need of the moment. The main sermon text in the stadium was John 3:16 and hundreds responded to the altar call. Thousands

Mennonite bicentennial celebrations at the great oak in Chortitza in August 1989.   Photo: Walter Sawatsky

stretched out their hands for a copy of a New Testament or Bible. Eight tons of Christian literature had arrived by truck the day before, a major legal importation of such materials. Mennonites from Orenburg, Karaganda and elsewhere in Central Asia returned home by train, a trip of many hours. Whenever the train stopped at a larger station the young people started distributing Christian literature, singing Christian songs or engaging interested bystanders in deep conversations about faith.

Some Soviet Mennonites questioned the validity of these celebrations when the Mennonites are leaving the Soviet Union. Others responded that this was a perfect time to praise God for leading them throughout the 200 years and to do so by giving a verbal witness to unbelievers around them. Emigration and/or mission are indeed the two dominant themes of 1989.

Most of the visitors at the bicentennial celebration in Zaporozh'e were local Ukrainian evangelicals. One of their leaders concluded his historical account of the Mennonite contribution with the appeal: "Please don't all go away from the Soviet Union. Please don't leave us alone." But, as one Mennonite who had been a pastor in a Russian congregation for nearly forty years saw it, to stay meant to become totally russified. "Russians are a very nationalistic people. It is impossible to merge the two cultures: German/Dutch and Russian. They will not mix. . . . Now if Mennonites could become like the Russians, totally adjusted to their way of thinking, feeling, speaking and acting . . . and at the same time retain their Anabaptist-Mennonite faith, then they would have a future, but that is utterly impossible. The Mennonites in Russia are tired," he said. "The leadership has no energy to move into new frontiers such as evangelization or attempting to find new contacts and build bridges to the Russian people."

Most Mennonites who leave try to justify it by claiming both possibilities: emigration and mission. Even though some people are leaving every week for Germany, other persons are becoming converted and joining the church. In the town of Bergthal, Kirgizia, for example, the congregation of nearly 900 members in 1987 had declined in membership to 350 by June 1989, with only 80 of the membership non-German. Yet they took the opportunity (possible under *glasnost* and *perestroika*) to build a new church building to more adequately accommodate the members and to make it more attractive to outsiders.

Why are they leaving? As earlier in Mennonite history, the motives are complex. In this case they are a traumatized people. They applaud the new freedoms, they affirm *perestroika*, but they worry that the changes will not last. As one observer put it, "They praise Gorbachev but they aren't with him." Invariably *Umsiedler* will explain that they seek religious freedom for their children, even if they themselves have learned to cope.

Additional explanations for this latest emigration are explicit warnings from surrounding Muslim peoples, specifically in Uzbekistan, to get out before those national groups vent their accumulated animosity on the Russians and other foreigners such as the Germans. Invariably too, recent visitors are asked about the return of the Lord. There is a heightened sense that when the time of tribulation comes — premillenial teachings seem widespread — they would like to be away from the epicentre. *Umsiedler* insist that material attractions of the West are not the real motive but they are obviously powerful magnets, particularly since predictions for Soviet economic recovery remain pessimistic. Even here there is a moral element. Since so much of the Soviet economy survives on corruption, it becomes a daily challenge for an individual to participate in the producing, buying and selling process with openness and honesty.

Recent visitors to the Soviet Union have become participants in farewell services. Elfrieda Dyck attended such a service in Donskoe, Orenburg, at the time that the leader, Daniel Janzen, and five other families left. "It was very moving. There were tears; men and women got up and told them that they believe that it is the Lord's will that they should leave. All of them ended by saying that if they had wronged anyone they asked forgiveness. When the person had finished speaking the pastor always rose and said, 'You have heard their request for peace. They ask for forgiveness.' Then the entire congregation rose and with one voice said, 'We forgive; we wish them peace.' "

They do forgive, of course, but it is still painful. Several ministers remarked to this writer that people often leave with a bad conscience because they have not told anyone about their plans. In such cases the actual moment of requesting permission to leave in peace becomes an offence because the congregation was not included in the decision-making. Once when an ordained minister announced he was leaving, the elder asked him why he had not asked the congregation for permission to leave. "What if the congregation says no?" was the reply. That elder, who is still firmly committed to staying, felt that a minister's ordination to the local church was his first line of responsibility; therefore the congregation must be asked for help in the decision, and its response should be taken seriously.

The issue of leaderless flocks is an urgent one. In June 1989 Jake

Tilitzky of Canada was sent as visiting minister for a six-week period in response to a written request for help from *Kirchliche* Mennonites. In numerous places he and other Mennonite representatives from the West were asked what should be done for those persons who remained. Should they be encouraged to go to the Baptist church? Would they be denied communion there unless they allowed themselves to be rebaptized by immersion? In Politotdel near Alma Ata, Kazakhstan, the local Baptists promised to accept into full fellowship the remaining eight older women when that Mennonite fellowship was dissolved in June 1989. Elsewhere that response seems unlikely.

The bicentennial year for Mennonites in the Soviet Union is indeed a momentous time. Never before have so many Bibles been sent to the Soviet Union and distributed also to Mennonites. It finally seems possible to organize a Mennonite conference or union, as far as government permission is concerned, but by now the will to organize seems to have disappeared. It has become possible to launch an evangelical seminary or to send students abroad for theological study, but instead young *Umsiedler* have organized themselves for teaching ministries which extend from West Germany to the Soviet Union. It has become possible for believers to get involved in social services and in charity *(miloserdie)* societies, to cooperate with Mennonite Central Committee in such new projects in the Soviet Union, but the majority of active Mennonite Christians (*Kirchliche,* Mennonite Brethren and Baptist Mennonites) appear to be leaving. Their involvement in service and mission in Germany has scarcely developed beyond their own rituals of worship, even for those *Umsiedler* who came a decade ago.

Soviet believers have been referring to 1989 as a year for the evangelization process. They are anxious that no existing church building revert back to a club or warehouse simply because people move away. The new AUCECB Information Bulletin carried an invitation from some Orenburg Mennonite villages for Christians to purchase the empty houses (25 were standing empty in Village No. 3) to join the fellowship and to get involved in new cooperative farming enterprises. There are many active Mennonites, Viktor Fast of Karaganda MB church being the most prominent organizer of evangelistic projects this summer. So many of them, however, are emotionally and physically tired, still traumatized by the persecutions of the past. That Mennonites from the West might consider moving into those empty houses and apply their agricultural and management skills is no longer mentioned only in jest; a number of Soviet officials are serious when they suggest such a possibility.

The Russian/Soviet Mennonites are contemplating religious freedom, emigration and the prospect of the evangelization and moral
renewal of the Soviet people. As they do so, their issues once again
become the issues for all those of Russian Mennonite origin.

September 26, 1989

* Data is based on a composite of 1989 travel accounts, including those provided by persons who attended bicentennial events in Zaporozh'e and Karaganda. Peter and Elfrieda Dyck represented North American Mennonites; Hans
and Leni von Niessen, Daniel Janzen and Gerhard Woelk represented European
Mennonites.

Notes

1. See for example, Stephen F. Cohen, *Rethinking the Soviet Experience:
Politics and History since 1917* (New York: Oxford University Press, 1985) which
discusses the degree to which scholarly assessments of Soviet developments
were motivated by right wing and conservative ideologies. Cohen argues for a
sober, non-ideological examination of the uneven developments in various
spheres of life, which is the revisionist approach that I identify with. In what
follows I am also more interested in recent studies of the Soviet nationality
problem such as Rasma Karklins, *Ethnic Relations in the USSR* (Boston: Allen &
Unwin, 1986) and Edward Allworth, ed., *Ethnic Russia in the USSR: The
Dilemma of Dominance* (New York: Pergamon Press, 1983), than in the views
and practices of Joseph Stalin as described by Richard Pipes in *The Formation of
the Soviet Union: Communism and Nationalism, 1917-1923* (Cambridge: Harvard University Press, 1954).

2. For a more developed argument, see my *Soviet Evangelicals since World
War II* (Scottdale, Pennsylvania: Herald Press, 1981), 16-17; 337ff; 448.

3. A.N. Ipatov, *Kto takie mennonity?* (Alma Ata: Izdatelstvo Kazakhstan, 1977);
in German, *Wer sind die Mennoniten?* (Alma Ata: Verlag Kazachstan, 1977). See
also A.F. Belimov, *Kto takie mennonity?* (Frunze: Kyrgystan, 1967).

4. Ingeborg Fleischhauer, "'Operation Barbarossa' and the Deportation" in
Ingeborg Fleischhauer & Benjamin Pinkus, *The Soviet Germans Past and
Present* (London: C. Hurst & Co., 1986), 81.

5. This is now well documented in Nicholas Bethell, *The Last Secret* (London:
Andre Deutsch, 1974); Nikolai Tolstoy, *Victims of Yalta* (London: Hodder &
Stoughton, 1977), published in the United States as *The Secret Betrayal: 1944-47*
(New York, 1978); and Mark R. Elliott, *Pawns of Yalta: Soviet Refugees and
America's Role in their Repatriation* (Urbana: University of Illinois Press, 1982).

6. Fleischhauer, "'Operation Barbarossa,'" 69. See also her longer book, *Das
Dritte Reich und die Deutschen in der Sowjetunion* (Stuttgart: Deutsche Verlags-
Anstalt, 1983).

7. A. Nekrich, *The Punished Peoples: The Deportation and Fate of Soviet Minorities at the End of the Second World War* (New York: W.W. Norton, 1978). This is a careful study, relying on some generally inaccessible Soviet doctoral dissertations, on *samizdat*, as well as on the author's own extensive interviewing before being ousted from the Soviet Union in 1965. Nekrich's focus is on the Crimean Tatars.

8. Benjamin Pinkus, "The Germans in the Soviet Union since 1945," in Fleischhauer & Pinkus, *The Soviet Germans*, 106.

9. Ibid., 104; Nekrich, *The Punished Peoples*, 118.

10. Pinkus, "The Germans in the Soviet Union," 104-5.

11. Ibid., 107. Nekrich indicates that overall direction was in the hands of Lavrenti P. Beria, assisted by his deputies, B. Kobulov and I. Serov, the latter surviving the 1953 fall of Beria under Khrushchev's patronage, 108.

12. Pinkus, "The Germans in the Soviet Union," 107.

13. Nekrich, *The Punished Peoples*, 130f., reports that children under 10 no longer needed to report after Stalin's death.

14. Collectivization and dekulakization were closely linked. A recent scholar argues that the worst excesses appeared where local leaders stressed removal of the kulak class before redistributing the land. Lynne Viola, "The Campaign to Eliminate the Kulak as a Class, Winter 1929-30: A Reevaluation of the Legislation," *Slavic Review* (Fall 1986): 503-524. For general treatments see the recent works by R.W. Davies, *The Socialist Offensive: The Collectivization of Soviet Agriculture, 1929-1930* (Cambridge: Harvard University Press, 1980) and Dorothy Atkinson, *The End of the Russian Land Commune 1905-1930* (Stanford, California: Stanford University Press, 1983).

15. The most recent detailed description is in Robert Conquest, *The Harvest of Sorrow: Soviet Collectivization and the Terror-Famine* (New York: Oxford University Press, 1986), especially 117-143.

16. Walter Sawatsky, "Mennonite Congregations in the Soviet Union Today," *Mennonite Life* 33 (March 1978): 12-26. Recently more memoir literature has appeared, some of it in the form of short articles in *Der Bote* or in private publications such as Johann Epp, *Freuden und Leiden der Familie Olga Wiebe und Johann Epp* (Espelkamp: Selbstverlag, 1984); Franz Thiessen, ed., *Neuendorf in Bild und Wort: Chortitzaer Bezirk, Ukraine 1789-1943* (Espelkamp: Selbstverlag, 1984) which devotes nearly half of its 400 pages of photos and story to the period after 1943. An excellent survey and critique in English is Lawrence Klippenstein, "An Unforgotten Past: Recent Writings by Soviet Emigre Baptists in West Germany," *Religion in Communist Lands* 14 (Spring 1986): 17-32. This covers the semi-fictional novels of Herman Hartfeld, although not his latest *Heimkehr in ein fremdes Land* (Wuppertal: Brockhaus, 1986); Johann Epp, *Von Gottes Gnade getragen* (Gummersbach: Verlag Friedensstimme, 1984); Abram and Maria Hamm, *Die Wege des Herrn sind lauter Güte* (Gummersbach: Verlag Friedensstimme, 1985); Jacob Esau, et al., *Unter dem Schirm des Höchsten: Drei kurze Biographien von Christen im Untergrund* (Wuppertal: Brockhaus, 1979). See in addition Gerhard Hamm, *Gottes Wort ist nicht gebunden: Geschichten und Gleichnisse aus Rußland* (Wuppertal: Oncken, 1980) which is more episodic.

17. See Pinkus, "The Germans in the Soviet Union," 117f., for numerous

statistical illustrations. Nekrich, *The Punished Peoples*, cites data in 1949 that 118,259 special settlers in the Kazakh Republic regions of Akmolinsk, Kokchetav, Kustanai, North Kazakhstan and Semipalatinsk were "in extreme need in regard to food." As he summarizes at one point, "the special settlers were ill-clad, ill-fed and ill-housed," 123, 125.

18. Walter Wedel, *Nur Zwanzig Kilometer* (Wuppertal: Brockhaus, 1979), passim.

19. Franz Thiessen, *Neuendorf*, 381-2.

20. Thiessen, *Neuendorf*, 74, and interview with author, October 1986.

21. Fleischhauer & Pinkus, *The Soviet Germans*, 78, 82, 117-9.

22. Sawatsky, *Soviet Evangelicals*, 55-64. The widespread myth that Roosevelt forced Stalin to reopen Baptist churches has no basis in fact.

23. Based on *Umsiedler* interviews and selected court documents, cf., Franz Thiessen, *Neuendorf* 34.

24. I have been unable to obtain more information on the location of the Buettner camp or to identify the American (Old) Mennonites involved.

25. Pinkus, "The Germans in the Soviet Union," 109.

26. The major era of work was 1957-67, with Peter J. Dyck and Doreen Harms the primary administrators, yet even into the late seventies this resource still helped persons locate each other. Another common resource was the newsletter of the Landsmannschaft der Russland Deutschen. See also Karl Boehme, *Gesucht wird: Die dramatische Geschichte des Suchdienstes* (Munich, 1965).

27. Russian language sources speak of Brethren Mennonites and Church *(Kirchliche)* Mennonites, and also refer to the Mennonite Brethren as New Mennonites. There is in general no awareness of any other Mennonite groupings. I am using Mennonite Brethren and Mennonite as more common English distinctions. Mennonite can refer to all Mennonites or to the Church Mennonites. Where the context leaves the intended meaning in doubt, I will use the more awkward "Church Mennonites."

28. MCC files (Trip Reports, 1956ff.).

29. A problem was the fact that Ivan V. Polianskii had just died and his successor, A.N. Puzin, had not yet been appointed.

30. Alexei Bychkov, in his reflections on the 20-year period 1961-81 quoted the following excerpt from his predecessor Alexander Karev's report to the Congress of 1966: "With reference to the Church Mennonites, the expanded Plenum of the AUCECB of 2 September 1964 took the following decision: to permit them, on the basis of their conversion and Christian life, to preach in our congregations, and also to sing in the choir. Moreover, in the case of a negative response on the part of a member of our congregation to their participation in our communion services, that we permit them to conduct separate communion services in our prayer houses." *Bratskii Vestnik (BV)* 5 (1982): 67; quoted from *BV* 6 (1966): 31. See *BV*, 4 (1958): 75; *BV* 4 (1967): 42.

31. MCC Files. Members of the delegation were Gerhard Lohrenz, Frank C. Peters, David P. Neufeld and Peter J. Dyck.

32. V.F. Krest'ianinov, *Mennonity* (Moscow: Politizdat, 1967). Krest'ianinov claims they met to discuss "the question of legalizing congregations by means of uniting with the Baptists. Here a program for creating a single leading Mennonite centre in the USSR was considered," 78.

33. See Sawatsky, *Soviet Evangelicals,* chapter 5 for a survey of the overall Khrushchev campaign.

34. Walter Sawatsky, "What Makes Russian Mennonites Mennonite?" *Mennonite Quarterly Review* 53 (January 1979): 5-20; Sawatsky, "A Call for Union of Baptists and Mennonites Issued by a Russian Baptist Leader," *Mennonite Quarterly Review* 50 (July 1976): 230-239.

35. Pinkus, "The Germans in the Soviet Union," 110.

36. Ibid.

37. Ibid, 119-153 for numerous statistical indicators. Alexander Solzhenitsyn in *The Gulag Archipelago* (New York: Harper & Row, 1973-78), Vol. V-VII stated that "By the 1950s the Germans — in comparison with other exiles and even with the locals — had the stoutest, roomiest, and neatest houses, the biggest pigs, the best milk cows. Their daughters grew up to be the most-sought-after brides, not only because their parents were well-off, but — in the depraved world around the camps — because of their purity and strict morals," 401.

38. Ibid.; cf., Rasma Karklins, *Ethnic Relations in the USSR* for more data on the status of non-Russian nationalities, which also relies on 200 interviews with German *Umsiedler.*

39. See the background on Peter Vins in Georgi P. Vins, *Prisoner of Conscience* (Elgin, Illinois: David C. Cook Publishers, 1975, 1979), also with the title *Testament From Prison and Three Generations of Suffering,* 35-62; Albert W. Wardin, Jr., "Jacob J. Wiens: Mission Champion in Freedom and Repression," *Journal of Church and State* 28 (Autumn 1986): 495-514.

40. There was seldom a full contingent of members. Kreker was a leader in the Western Siberia region until about 1985 when disagreements with President Kriuchkov developed. Kreker was released from prison as part of the new amnesty in 1987.

41. A youth evangelist born in 1944 who had never married, Peters was released in early 1987 from his fifth full imprisonment. At his homecoming the authorities issued a fine and imposed a curfew that was equivalent to house arrest, so Peters went underground again. His brother, Heinrich, and uncle, Dimitri, were also in prison at the same time.

42. For example, Ivan Plett, Ivan I. Leven, David I. Koop.

43. The movement is discussed at length in my *Soviet Evangelicals,* somewhat more updated in my "The Reform Baptists Today," *Religion in Communist Lands* 8 (Spring 1980): 28-38. A retelling of the story from their own *samizdat* documents appeared serially during 1987 in *Nachrichten von den Feldern der Verfolgung,* a monthly publication of *Missionswerk Friedensstimme* in Gummersbach, West Germany.

44. The fragmenting of the CCECB and the establishment of up to 115 congregations as autonomous ECB churches with their own "Fraternal Agreement" (1983) awaits separate treatment.

45. Ipatov, *Kto takie mennonity,* 3.

46. The impression given in Heinrich & Gerhard Woelk, *A Wilderness Journey: Glimpses of the Mennonite Brethren Church in Russia 1925-1980,* trans. Victor G. Doerksen (Fresno, California: Center for Mennonite Brethren Studies, 1982) is somewhat misleading.

47. Woelk, *A Wilderness Journey,* provides the most detailed history of the

Karaganda Mennonite Brethren church. I have used additional information from *Umsiedler* to obtain a more complete picture since there is a strong bias in how Woelk's sources interpret events. For example, the fact that Church Mennonites also contributed their services to constructing the building is not even mentioned in Woelk.

48. Pinkus, "The Germans in the Soviet Union," 111. Nekrich devotes a major section of *The Punished Peoples* to the Crimean Tatars who were considered such an "enemy nationality" whose rehabilitation has consistently lagged behind that of other groups.

49. Pinkus, "The Germans in the Soviet Union," 153 and other official sources for 1981-86.

50. Walter Sawatsky, "The New Soviet Law on Religion," *Religion in Communist Lands* 4 (Summer 1976): 4-10. The new Brezhnev Constitution of 1977 may also have been influential.

51. The 10 congregations in the Orenburg region with membership and leading minister were: Chortitza 100 (A.A. Giesbrecht), Petrovka 104 (Johann H. Walmann), Kantserovka 35 (Jacob J. Dyck), Zhdanovka 110 (Peter P. Bartel), Nikolaevka 60 (Heinrich J. Klippenstein & B.B. Rempel), Feodorovka 50 (Heinrich Wiebe), Kitchkas 96 (Dietrich Johann Thiessen), Pretoriia 35 (?), Stepanovka 100 (Johann Johann Martens), Sol-Iletsk 60 (Johann Abram Friesen). Recorded Church Mennonite congregations elsewhere are: Karaganda 402 (Julius Siebert), Alma Ata 145 (Jacob Sudermann), Novosibirsk 180 (Bernhard [or Boris] Sawadsky d. 1988), Krasnaia Rechka 167 (Peter Braun), Tokmak 214 (Johann Schellenberg), Romanovka 140 (Abram Abrams), Dzhambul 135 (Viktor Schmidt), Politotdel, a group near Alma Ata (Peter Klassen), Martuk 143 (Peter Peters), Dzhetisai 60 (Dietrich Neufeld), Dushanbe 30 (Jacob Unger).

52. Short history by Johann Neufeld in Woelk, *The Wilderness Journey*, 123-25. It fails to discuss the nature of the relationship to the much larger Mennonite contingent in the Frunze ECB church nearby.

53. Supplementing Woelk, 128-32.

54. Some of this is now documented in print in Abram and Maria Hamm, *Die Wege des Herrn*, 69-72, 93-95 and summarized in English in Klippenstein, "An Unforgotten Past," 23-24. Krest'ianinov, *Mennonitey*, also cites numerous cases of illegal religious activity.

55. A very abbreviated and incomplete record in Woelk, *The Wilderness Journey*, 27-28.

56. In 1985 the local plenipotentiary for religious affairs, G.M. Iudin, sent an article to the Soviet press which stated that there were 4,000 Germans in the four raiony under his jurisdiction (Aleksandrovsk, Krasnogvardeisk, Novosergievsk and Perevolotsk) and including the cities of Orenburg, Sol-Iletsk and Orsk. Of these, 4,000 were believers, divided into six AUCECB, 14 MB and 11 Mennonite societies, all with their own prayer houses. The article proceeded to laud the good citizenship qualities of these believers.

57. They were: Chortitza 23 (Johann Isbrand Risen), Petrovka 43 (Jakob Jacob Tews), Kantserovka 154 (Peter Heinrich Tissen), Kamenka 192 (Peter David Siemens), Zhdanovka 165 (David Petrovich Blok), Nikolaevka 17 (Viktor Tissen), Feodorovka 69 (Johann Kornelius Dyck), Rodnichnoe 57 (Johann Abram Klassen), Suvorovka 30 (Heinrich David [or Andrei Ivanovich] Wiebe),

Pretoriia 181 (Johann Petrovich Epp), Kubanka 163 (Erwin Abram Petkau), Stepanovka 100 (Johann Heinrich Dyck), Alisovo 42 (Heinrich Isaak Schmidt), Susanovo 360 (Abram Heinrich Neufeld).

58. They were: Donskoe 430 (Daniel Johan Janzen), Podolsk 150 (Abram Jacob Tissen), Ishchalka 60 (Wilhelm Heinrich Wurms), Klinok 34 (Johann Jacob Hamm), Totskoe (Vodomasovoe) 50 (Johann Langemann), Lugovskoe 120 (Ivan Henrikovich Spenst), Krasikovo 150 (Heinrich Heinrikovich Gerzen), Kuterlia 106 (Ivan Henrikovich Thiessen), Koltan 40 (Ivan Leven).

59. David Redekop (Winnipeg), John B. Toews (Fresno) and Johann Koehn (Waldbröl) visited the Orenburg area in September 1985. The following year Redekop and Henry Brucks attended the dedication of the remodelled ECB church in Orenburg and visited the colonies. A Mennonite World Conference delegation also visited in late 1986, followed by an MCC delegation in February 1988.

60. Based on a composite of private sources available to the writer, since foreigners did not normally attend the elections nor were actual votes made public.

61. This decision could never be implemented because of residence restrictions in Moscow. Logvinenko traded apartments with a family that moved to Kiev; Kolesnikov commuted from Alma Ata for many years, as did Fast who came for the monthly Presidium meetings and who also travelled extensively throughout the USSR and abroad.

62. For example, *Bratskii Vestnik (BV)* 2 (1983): 57; 1 (1985): 59.

63. *BV* 1 (1985): 53-59; 2 (1985): 45-49.

64. Paul N. Kraybill, "Can Culture Cradle the Faith?" *Festival Quarterly* 12 (Fall 1985): 7-10.

65. *MWC Courier* (First Quarter 1987): 1-3; and Jake Pauls, "Mennonites: East and West (Who Are We?)," News release, Mennonite World Conference, December 9, 1986.

66. Fleischhauer & Pinkus, *The Soviet Germans,* 157. A new wave of emigration (family reunification) began in February 1987, resulting in over 37,000 Germans leaving by September 1988, of which 34 percent were identified as Mennonite or Baptist. This time it has resulted in a rapid depletion of the ranks of church activists and leaders, causing growing concern about the ongoing viability of some of these congregations.

Under Tsarist Crown and Soviet Star:
An Historiographical Survey

Peter J. Klassen

Since the Second World War, there has been a remarkable resurgence of interest in Russian Mennonite historiography. The wide variety of literature that has appeared about Russian Mennonites has been stimulated by a number of factors, including the dramatic and tragic events associated with the collapse of traditional life in Russia, the current interest in *Heimat und Herkunft,* the increased awareness and sophistication of writers of Russian Mennonite background and the recognition that the Russian Mennonite experience is an interesting historical, religious and sociological phenomenon.

In what has been described, perhaps imprecisely, as the "Golden Age" of Russian Mennonitism, i.e., the decades prior to World War I, there was a considerable body of literature, much of it by Mennonites in Russia, that portrayed the challenges and accomplishments of that body. The massive volume by P.M. Friesen, *Die alt-evangelische mennonitische Brüderschaft in Rußland 1789-1910,* published in 1911 in Halbstadt, Molotschna, may be viewed as the culmination of such literary activity.

The calamities of war, revolution, civil strife and famine silenced the voice of Russian Mennonites, except for the anguished cries for help that sometimes managed to reach the outside world. With the ensuing sovietization of Mennonite communities, former Mennonite institutions that had served to foster and develop historical expression were destroyed. At least for a time, it was evident that Mennonites living elsewhere, or those who had recently emigrated from Russia, would have to become the voice of Mennonites in Russia.

Not surprisingly, writing that arose out of this context focused on the tragedies known to be unfolding behind closed doors. The 1930 Mennonite World Conference, meeting in Danzig, attempted to address these problems and reflected the intense interest generated by the tragedies in Russia. At the same time, emigrants from Russia graphically illustrated the fact that an age had ended. Accounts of suffering, flight, hunger, pillage, expropriation, banishment and death now became the stuff of which the new body of literature was made. Nostalgia for the old and abhorrence for the new were everywhere in evidence as the dispossessed recounted their tales.

In the aftermath of World War II and with the emigration of another wave of Russian Mennonites, new drama was added. At the same time, an increasing number of scholars began a more careful and historical analysis of the entire Russian Mennonite experience. Gradually, attention shifted from gripping personal tragedy to a more detached, scholarly examination of factors that had shaped the Mennonite world in Russia. Today, Russian Mennonite historiography is experiencing an intensity of interest and a depth of understanding probably never before equalled.

Since the beginning of their settlement in Russia, Mennonites have formed part of the larger German-speaking minority in Russia. It is thus not surprising that studies of Germans in tsarist Russia or the Soviet Union often include significant sections on Mennonites. At the same time it should be noted that, at least until the early 1870s when many aspects of the privileged status of the settlers were abolished, Russian officials as well as the settlers themselves usually distinguished between the "Mennonites" *(mennonity)* and "colonists" *(kolonisty)*. The latter term was almost exclusively applied to Lutherans and Catholics. During the Soviet era, these distinctions have largely disappeared in official documents.

Over the decades, historians have created a substantial body of literature depicting the life of a group that, according to the 1979 Soviet census, numbers almost two million.[1] In addition, of course, thousands of Germans (including Mennonites) have emigrated from Russia in the last century.

Especially in Germany, Canada and the United States, the 20th century has witnessed the steady growth of interest in this theme. Since World War II this interest has mushroomed, as is reflected in the formation of a number of historical societies which facilitate systematic study of Germans in and from Russia. Organizations such as the Landsmannschaft der Deutschen aus Rußland, the American Historical Society of Germans from Russia, the North Dakota Historical Society of Germans from Russia, and several Mennonite historical societies in Canada, the United States and West Germany, through journals, lectures and special events, have stimulated a broad-based interest in this subject. Today a substantial body of literature and extensive bibliographies invite the interested scholar to further analysis and interpretation.

Although this paper does not attempt to survey the rich sources available in Soviet archives and libraries, it should be noted, as David Rempel has often stated, that these materials remain largely untouched. I am grateful to him for numerous suggestions and also for the following list of 19th-century journals that contain pertinent studies: *Izvestiia Petrovskoi sel'skokhoziaistvennoi Akademii* (Notes of the Petrovskii Rural Economy Society); *Obshchestvo sel'skago khoziaistva iushnoi Rossii* (The Society or Association of Rural Economy of the South of Russia); *Sbornik statei Ekaterinoslavskago nauchnago obshchestvo po izsledovanii kraia* (Collection of articles of the Scientific Society of Ekaterinoslav for the Study of the Region); *Trudy Imperatorskago Vol'nago Ekonomicheskago Obshchestva* (Transactions of the Imperial Free Economic Society); *Tsentral'nyi Statisticheskii Komitet* (Central Statistical Committee); *Zapiski Odesskago Obshchestvo Istorii i Drevnostei* (Notes of the Odessa Society of History and Antiquity); and *Zhurnal Ministerstva Gosudarstvennykh Immushchestvo* (The Journal of the Ministry of State Domains). In addition, valuable bibliographic information on the larger Russian context is provided by Patricia K. Grimsted in several of her publications such as *Archives and Manuscript Repositories in the USSR: Moscow and Leningrad* (Princeton, 1972); *Recent Soviet Archival Literature: A Review and Preliminary Bibliography of Selected Reference Aids* and *The Archival Legacy of the Soviet Ukraine: Problems of Tracing the Documentary Records of a Divided Nation* (The Kennan Institute for Advanced Studies, 1985 and 1986).

Bibliographic Guides

The German-speaking element in Russia has been the subject of a number of bibliographies. The following are especially useful: Karl Stumpp, *Das Schrifttum über das Deutschtum in Rußland: Eine Bibliographie.* 5. erweiterte Ausgabe (Stuttgart, 1980), the most extensive bibliography of German-language materials on the subject; and James Long, *The German Russians: A Bibliography of Russian Materials . . . in Major Soviet and American Libraries* (Santa Barbara, 1978).

Several other bibliographies provide important references: *Bibliography of the American Historical Society of Germans from Russia* (Lincoln, 1978), with several later supplements; Marie Miller Olson, comp., *A Bibliography on the Germans from Russia: Materials Found in the New York Public Library* (Lincoln, 1976); and F.P. Schiller, *Literatur zur Geschichte und Volkskunde der deutschen*

Kolonien in der Sowjet-Union für die Jahre 1764-1926 (Pokrovsk, 1927). Also worth noting are the bibliographies published by the Bücherei des deutschen Ostens in Herne, West Germany. A five-volume bibliography lists hundreds of studies devoted to Germans in and from Russia and former German territories in East Europe. Also worth noting is *Das Deutschtum im Ausland* (Berlin, 1925), especially the section devoted to the changing legal status of Germans in Russia after 1914. Similarly, Richard Mai, in his *Auslanddeutsche Quellenkunde, 1924-1933* (Berlin, 1936), lists numerous publications reflecting the impact of the social upheaval of the 1920s.

For the student of the Russian Mennonites, several very helpful bibliographic guides are available. The annual "Radical Reformation and Mennonite Bibliography" in *Mennonite Life* (North Newton, Kansas) has established itself as the most current and comprehensive bibliography that lists Russian Mennonite sources and appears regularly. Numerous references to Russian Mennonite literature will also be found in Nelson Springer and A.J. Klassen, eds., *Mennonite Bibliography, 1631-1961*, 2 vols. (Scottdale, 1977). Another useful source is Nadezhda Simon's unpublished "Bibliography of Russian Mennonites" which lists materials available at the Lenin Library in Moscow, U.S.S.R.

As scholarly studies on Russian Mennonites continue to appear, it is of course not surprising that many are accompanied by very extensive bibliographies. Doctoral dissertations such as those by David Rempel, "The Mennonite Colonies in New Russia" (Stanford University, 1933) and by James Urry, "The Closed and the Open: Social and Religious Change amongst the Mennonites in Russia, 1789-1889" (Oxford University, 1978), provide especially detailed guides to the relevant literature. Numerous articles in the *Mennonite Encyclopedia* and the *Mennonitisches Lexikon* also list important sources.

Early Settlement

The beginning of Mennonite settlement in South Russia needs to be seen as part of a large colonization program vigorously implemented by the Russian government. In particular, Catherine's Manifesto of 1763 stressed the need to find settlers for the "great many places" that remained "yet uncultivated." Her invitations were sent to many courts and countries, both in Europe and Asia. Conditions in Europe at this time led Germans in particular to take advantage of the opportunity. Ironically, at the very moment when Mennonites began to leave Poland and Prussia for the Ukraine, King Frederick William II was also attempting to draw new settlers to Prussia.

In his book, *Human Capital: The Settlement of Foreigners in Russia 1762-1804* (Cambridge, 1979), Roger Bartlett has provided an overview of colonization in Russia that portrays Mennonite immigration as part of a vast social phenomenon. At the same time, he raises provocative questions about reaction to the settlement, underlying reasons for the open door policy and implications of granting sweeping liberties to foreign settlers when native peasants were still serfs. An important overview of laws governing land use in the new colonies is to be found in Johann von Keussler, "Das Grundbesitzrecht in den deutschen Kolonien Südrußlands."[2] The same volume has another informative article by Friedrich Matthai, "Über die Kolonisation von Ausländern in Rußland und die Bauernfrage."[3] Phillip Wiebe deals with Mennonite agricultural pursuits in his article, "Ackerbauwirtschaft bei den Mennoniten im südlichen Rußland."[4]

Numerous visitors to tsarist Russia have left accounts of their impression and experiences. Among those who travelled in New Russia and described, in varying detail, life in the Mennonite colonies, the following may be mentioned: August von Haxthausen, *Studien über die inneren Zustände, des Volkslebens und insbesondere die ländlichen Einrichtungen Rußlands* (Hannover, 1847; Berlin, 1852); Xavier Hommaire de Hell, *Travels in the Steppes of the Caspian Sea, the Caucasus, etc.* (London, Berlin, 1847); Johann G. Kohl, *Reisen in Südrußland* (Dresden, 1841); Alexander Petzhold, *Reise im westlichen und südlichen europäischen Rußland im Jahre 1855* (Leipzig, 1864). In 1963 Gerhard Wiens published an abridged version of Petzhold's book under the title, *Besuch bei unseren Vätern: Auszüge aus Alexander Petzholds "Reise im europäischen Rußland im Jahre 1855"* (Norman, 1963).

Other significant studies that depict the larger scene are the following: Otto Auhagen, *Die deutschen Kolonien an der Wolga* (Stuttgart, 1919); Ingeborg Fleischhauer, *The Soviet Germans: Past and Present* (New York, 1986); Adam Giesinger, *From Catherine to Khrushchev* (Winnipeg, 1974); B. Ischchanian, *Die ausländischen Elemente in der russischen Volkswirtschaft* (Berlin, 1913); Konrad Keller, *The German Colonies in South Russia*, 2 vols., trans. A. Becker (Saskatoon, 1968, 1973); Lothar Koenig, *Die Deutschtumsinsel an der Wolga* (Dulmen/Westphalen, 1938); Manfred Langhans-Ratzeburg, *Die Wolgadeutschen: ihr Staats- und Verwaltungsrecht* (Berlin, 1929) (This volume has special value for the researcher since it provides summaries of government decrees regulating life in the Volga German colonies); Fred Koch, *The Volga Germans in Russia and the Americas from 1763 to the Present* (University Park, 1977); Georg Leibbrandt, *Die deutschen Siedlungen in der Sowjetunion* (Berlin, 1941); Karl Lindemann, *Von den deutschen Kolonisten in Rußland* (Stuttgart, 1924); Josef Malinowsky, *Die Planerkolonien am Asowschen Meere* (Stuttgart, 1928); Friedrich Matthai, *Die deutschen Ansiedlungen in Rußland* (Leipzig, 1866); C.B. Peterson, "Geographical Aspects of Foreign Colonization in Pre-Revolutionary New Russia;"[5] Johannes Schleuning, *Die deutschen Siedlungsgebiete in Rußland* (Wuerzburg, 1955); Viktor Schirmunski, *Die deutschen Kolonien in der Ukraine* (Charkov, 1928); David Schmidt, *Studien über die Geschichte der Wolgadeutschen* (Pokrovsk, 1930); Joseph Schnurr, ed., *Die Kirchen und das religiöse Leben der Rußlanddeutschen* (Stuttgart, 1972); Gerhard Schroeder, *Miracles of Grace and Judgment* (Kingsport, 1974); Heinrich Schroeder, *Die systematische Vernichtung der Rußland-deutschen* (Langensalza, 1934); Jakob Stach, *Die deutschen Kolonien in Südrußland* (Prischib, 1904) and *Das Deutschtum in Sibirien, Mittelasien und dem Fernen Osten* (Stuttgart, 1938); S.F. Starr, ed., *Studies on the Interior of Russia: August von Haxthausen*, trans. E.L. Schmidt (Chicago, 1972) in which the author describes his meeting with Johann Cornies; Karl Stumpp, *The German-Russians: Two Centuries of Pioneering*, trans. Joseph Height (Bonn, 1967); and Stumpp, *The Emigration from Germany to Russia in the Years 1763-1862* (Lincoln, 1978); Margarethe Woltner, *Gemeindeberichte der Schwarzmeerdeutschen* (Leipzig, 1941); Hattie Plum Williams, *The Czar's Germans,* ed. Emma Haynes, et al. (Lincoln, 1975) and "A Social Study of the Russian German."[6]

Self-Perception in Tsarist Times

Late in the nineteenth century when the Mennonite Brethren Church in Russia asked Peter M. Friesen, a teacher and minister, to write its history, the result was a massive volume on Mennonites with special emphasis on their development in imperial Russia. Published in 1911, it contained extensive documentary quotations and focused primarily on religious issues.[7] Its irenic tone indicated that at least some writers were prepared to move beyond the strife that had characterized inter-Mennonite relations in Russia since 1860.

Although a number of other writers from within the Russian Mennonite community presented historical studies prior to World War I, these efforts tended to be characterized by a narrow perspective and a pronounced didacticism. In his "Introduction to Russian

Mennonite Historiography,"[8] David G. Rempel has examined some of these early studies and has concluded that, despite their limitations, they provide significant glimpses into the Mennonite world. The prominent Mennonite leader, David H. Epp, became a pioneer in developing a body of literature that provided a respectable beginning for Russian Mennonite historiography. His works included *Die Chortitzer Mennoniten* (Rosenthal, 1889); *Johann Cornies: Züge aus seinem Leben und Wirken* (Ekaterinoslav, 1909); *Die Memriker Ansiedlung* (Kalinovo, 1910); *Heinrich Heese und seine Zeit* (serialized in *Der Botschafter*, 1910). Rempel also examines a significant document by Peter Hildebrandt, *Erste Auswanderung der Mennoniten aus dem danziger Gebiet nach Südrußland* (Halbstadt, 1888) and concludes that the author was unfortunately "evasive" when narrating unpleasant events.

Other insights into the life of Mennonites in imperial Russia are provided by Franz Isaac in *Die Molotschnaer Mennoniten* (Halbstadt, 1908), of special note because of its analysis of the bitter struggle between the landed and the landless colonists; by Alexander Klaus, a Volga German in government service who provided an overview of German settlements in *Nashi kolonii* (St. Petersburg, 1869)[9] and in Adolf Ehrt's history of Mennonites in Russia, *Das Mennonitentum in Rußland von seiner Einwanderung bis zur Gegenwart* (Langensalza-Berlin-Leipzig, 1932).

Early in the twentieth century Mennonites in Russia began publishing two periodicals, *Der Botschafter*[10] and *Die Friedensstimme*.[11] The former was published by David Epp and served as the organ of the *Kirchliche* Mennonites while *Die Friedensstimme*, published by the brothers Jakob and Abraham Kroeker, established itself as the semi-official voice of the Mennonite Brethren. Other periodicals, such as *Mennonitisches Jahrbuch*, published by Heinrich Dirks, and *Christlicher Familienkalender*, also contained a great deal of information about the Mennonite community. After the Revolution, some Mennonites attempted to launch new periodicals that emphasized economic rather than religious ties. *Der praktische Landwirt* (Moscow, 1925-1926) and *Unser Blatt* (Moscow, 1925-1928) briefly provided a literary bond among Mennonite colonies.

Some earlier, non-Mennonite publications such as *Die Odessaer Zeitung* (Odessa, 1863-1914); *Das Unterhaltungsblatt für deutsche Ansiedler im südlichen Rußland* (Odessa, 1846-1862); *Der Molotschnaer Volkskalendar* (Prischib, 1881-1914) often contained information about Mennonite colonies. The *Unterhaltungsblatt* in particular carried articles by prominent Mennonite leaders such as

Johann Cornies, often regarded as the spokesman of the Mennonites by Russian authorities, and Philipp Wiebe, chairman of the Agricultural Union of the Moloschna settlement.

Disintegration of the Russian Mennonite World

World War I and the following decades brought tragedy and destruction to Mennonite communities in Russia. Shadows of change were already appearing during the war, for tsarist decrees of expropriation of lands held by "German" colonists indicated that the tide of Russian nationalism would overwhelm Mennonite communities. The defeat of the tsar's armies brought temporary reprieve; then came revolution, civil war and famine, soon to be followed by the collectivization of agriculture and the loss of landed private property. This, coupled with the forced exile or imprisonment of many kulaks, clergymen, businessmen and various professional persons, jeopardized the continued existence of all things Mennonite.

For a time following the Peace of Brest-Litovsk, the collapse of internal political, social and economic structures threatened to plunge Russia into anarchy. Indeed, in Ukraine the anarchist Nestor Makhno and his bands spread terror and destruction. Part of that story is told in Victor Peters, *Nestor Makhno: The Life of an Anarchist* (Winnipeg, 1970) and in Michael Palij, *The Anarchism of Nestor Makhno* (Seattle, 1976). Famine added to the distress, and the vigorous response of Mennonites in North America and Europe saved the lives of many, as depicted in P.C. Hiebert, ed., *Feeding the Hungry* (Scottdale, 1929) and in Benjamin H. Unruh, *Fügung und Führung im mennonitischen Welt-Hilfswerk 1920-1933* (Karlsruhe, 1966). Other accounts such as *Brüder in Not! Dokumente der Hungersnot unter den deutschen Volksgenossen in Rußland* (Berlin, 1933) described the even more deadly famine a decade later.

The changing world of German-speaking communities during the interwar years is depicted in numerous studies. A good introduction is provided by the following: O. Auhagen, *Die Schicksalswende des rußlanddeutschen Bauerntums in den Jahren 1927-1930* (Leipzig, 1942); and Meir Buchsweiler, *Volksdeutsche in der Ukraine am Vorabend und Beginn des zweiten Weltkriegs* (Gerlingen, 1984).

In a brief interval during the Russo-German pact (1939-1941) the pressure on Mennonites was somewhat relaxed and some prisoners were permitted to return to their homes. Then, with the coming of the war in 1941, the full fury of Soviet power was unleashed on the numb Mennonite villages. Charged with collaboration with Germany, most citizens of German background, including Mennonites, were ordered deported to Asiatic Russia. The ensuing dislocation, suffering and death have often been chronicled by participants and observers.

In *Lost Fatherland* (Scottdale, 1967), John B. Toews has depicted the drama of the collapse of the Mennonite commonwealth and the ensuing desperate attempts to come to terms with the new regime. When these efforts failed, mass emigration was the response of a people deprived of traditional rights and privileges. Toews also demonstrated how the successive waves of calamity taught Mennonites the need for cooperation, mutual trust and support. The dramatic developments of these days are reflected in a collection of documents published in 1975.[12]

In a related study, Frank Epp in *Mennonite Exodus* (Altona, 1962) has examined the emigration of 20,000 Mennonites from Russia and their settlement in Canada. Epp has captured the drama of peril and heroism, of suffering and hope.

Not surprisingly, many of those who emigrated from the Soviet Union in the 1920s or later have come to view their experiences from the standpoint of those driven from the Garden of Eden. The recording of their recollections sometimes exaggerates the beauty of a lost paradise; usually, there is no reference to the injustices that characterized social structures in tsarist days. The cries of anguish over injustices done are understandable; however, they need to be seen in the context of a nation in convulsive change. At the same time, the accounts provide important vistas of a people confronted by forced labour camps, prison, starvation, expropriation and death.

These recollections are too numerous to list *in extenso*. The following portraits are illustrative: Helene Harder, *Feuerproben: Lebensschicksale eines deutschen Siedlers in Rußland* (Wernigerode, 1934); Dietrich Neufeld, *Ein Tagebuch aus dem Reiche des Totentanzes* (Emden, 1921), trans. and ed. Al Reimer as part of *A Russian Dance of Death* (Winnipeg, 1977); Jacob A. Neufeld, *Tiefenwege, Erfahrungen und Erlebnisse von Rußland-Mennoniten in zwei Jahrzehnten bis 1949* (Virgil, n.d.); A.A. Toews, *Mennonitische Märtyrer*, 2 vols. (Winnipeg, 1949, 1954); Heinrich Toews, *Eichenfeld-Dubowka: Ein Tatsachen Bericht aus der Tragödie des Deutschtums in der Ukraine* (Karlsruhe, n.d.).

Colony Narratives

Another historical record that constitutes an important source for the study of Russian Mennonites is the colony account. Often, this is the summary of recollections of emigrés who left the Soviet Union in the 1920s or after World War II; at other times, carefully researched narratives present a scholarly overview of the development of a particular settlement. These sources thus reflect a wide range in their quality and reliability; frequently, memories of events that occurred twenty or more years ago have become all too fuzzy. Fortunately, volumes reflecting little more than anecdotal collections of personal perceptions are offset by studies that demonstrate careful research. In any event, the accounts are useful in permitting the reader to see how participants in the drama viewed the life of the community. It is not surprising that frequently heavy emphasis is placed on tragedies that followed the two world wars.

Many of those Mennonites who emigrated from Russia after the Revolution and Civil War, or who were part of the exodus during and after World War II, attempted to preserve accounts of their colonies and so wrote a large number of rather cursory accounts. The following are typical: Peter Dyck, *Orenburg am Ural* (Yarrow, 1951); Gerhard Fast, *Das Ende von Chortitza* (Winnipeg, 1973); H. Goerz, *Die Molotschnaer Ansiedlung: Entstehung, Entwicklung und Niedergang* (Steinbach, 1951) and *Die mennonitischen Siedlungen der Krim* (Steinbach, 1957); Bernhard J. Harder, *Alexandertal: Die Geschichte der letzten deutschen Stammsiedlung in Rußland* (Berlin, n.d.); Gerhard Hein, ed., *Ufa: The Mennonite Settlements (Colonies) in Ufa, 1894-1938* (Winnipeg, 1977); I.P. Klassen, *Die Insel Chortitza* (Steinbach, 1979); N.J. Kroeker, *First Mennonite Villages in Russia: Khortitsa-Rosental, 1789-1943* (Vancouver, 1981); C.P. Toews and Heinrich Friesen, *Die Kubaner Ansiedlung* (Steinbach, 1953); Gerhard Lohrenz, *Sagradowka: Die Geschichte einer mennonitischen Ansiedlung im Süden Rußlands* (Rosthern, 1947); Johann J. Neudorf, et al., *Osterwick, 1812-1943* (Clearbrook, n.d.); Franz Thiessen, ed., *Neuendorf in Bild und Wort: Chortitzaer-Bezirk, Ukraine, 1789-1943* (Espelkamp, 1984); Peter Rahn, *Mennoniten in der Umgebung von Omsk* (Winnipeg, 1975); C.P. Toews, *Die Tereker Ansiedlung* (Steinbach, 1945); Gerhard Toews, *Schoenfeld, Werde- und Opfergang einer deutschen Siedlung in der Ukraine* (Winnipeg, 1939).

There is also a considerable body of biographical and autobiographical literature that depicts the life of those who grew up in tsarist Russia, then emigrated or fled to Germany or the Americas. Often these sketches portray a rather idyllic Russia up to World War I, then recount the tragedy of war, revolution, expropriation, civil war, famine, emigration and gradual acculturation in a new homeland. Accounts are often similar, but they nonetheless provide glimpses of how various persons responded to challenges that totally disrupted a way of life.

The following volumes are illustrative of this genre: Cornelius DeFehr, *Erinnerungen aus meinem Leben* (Winnipeg, 1976); Anna Reimer Dyck, *Anna: From the Caucasus to Canada,* ed. Peter J. Klassen (Hillsboro, 1979); Gerhard Fast, *Im Schatten des Todes* (Wernigerode, 1935); Cornelius Funk, *Escape to Freedom,* trans. and ed. Peter J. Klassen (Hillsboro, 1982); Gerhard Hamm, *Du hast uns nie verlassen* (Wuppertal, 1978); Martin Hamm, *Aus der alten in die neue Heimat: Lebensgeschichte eines schlichten Mennoniten* (Winnipeg, 1971); Gerhard Lohrenz, *Storm Tossed: The Personal Story of a Canadian Mennonite from Russia* (Winnipeg, 1983); Gerhard Lohrenz, *Mia, oder über den Amur in die Freiheit* (Winnipeg, 1981); Herman A. Neufeld, *Herman and Katharina: Their Story,* trans., ed., Abram H. Neufeld (Winnipeg, 1984); Anita Priess, *Exiled to Siberia* (Steinbach, 1972); John B. Toews, *With Courage to Spare: The Life of B.B. Janz* (Winnipeg, 1978).

Changing Historical Perspectives

During the past several decades, Mennonite historians have continued to reflect a strong, indeed, growing fascination with the experiences of Russian Mennonites. At the same time, different approaches and perspectives have become readily apparent as the literature has become more realistic, less didactic, less defensive and more critical.

Probably no analyst of the Russian Mennonite scene has done more to introduce sober correctives than David G. Rempel. He has long contended that Mennonites must be seen in the context of their Russian cultural, economic, religious, political and social setting. While Mennonites may indeed have constituted an "island," they were certainly profoundly shaped by the vast Russian sea that surrounded them. Several studies by Rempel have helped to clarify the scene: "Mennonite Commonwealth in Russia: A Sketch of its Founding and Endurance, 1789-1919,"[13] as well as his doctoral dissertation, "The Mennonite Colonies in New Russia: A Study of the Settlement and Economic Development from 1789 to 1914."[14]

A number of recent studies have raised questions about the presuppositions of idyllic conditions in tsarist times. Some writers, such as Harvey Dyck and James Urry, have contended that the imagined paradise never existed. In a provocative study of Mennonites in confrontation with powerful forces of change in their Russian homeland,[15] Dyck has shown that the decades prior to World War I, far from being a time when all was well, were times of growing strain and apprehension. In these years Mennonites increasingly encountered the larger Russian community. A vigorous Russian nationalism that, at least in part, was responding to a militaristic and often chauvinistic German nationalism in imperial Germany, showed little sympathy for ethnic cultural islands that were regarded as outposts of a rival and potential enemy on the western borders. The drive for Russification late in the 19th century was a powerful factor in stimulating emigration in the 1870s. Mennonites who stayed had to come to terms with currents of change that, already in tsarist times, threatened Mennonite culture and belief.

Another perspective on Mennonite history has been developed by James Urry. In his doctoral dissertation[16] and in other studies, such as "Through the Eye of a Needle: Wealth and Mennonite Experience in Imperial Russia,"[17] Urry has argued that factors such as the inequitable distribution of wealth, acculturation and increasingly strong inroads of secularization all too often seemed to demonstrate that Mennonite ideals of love, compassion, mutual assistance and social justice were little more than hollow memories. Like many of their Russian counterparts, Mennonites were fully prepared to participate in the opportunities presented by new forces of capitalist change and industrial expansion. Urry suggests that apparent religious renewal, such as the rise of the Mennonite Brethren, was less a religious phenomenon than an expression of entrepreneurial and academic challenge to traditional structures.

A long-neglected dimension of Russian Mennonite historiography is the view which Russians developed about their Mennonite neighbours. Just a century after the beginning of Mennonite settlement in New Russia, a staunch Russian nationalist, A.A. Paltov, published a series of articles in which he contended that German colonies, including the Mennonites, should be regarded as posing a threat to Russian security. One of his articles appeared under the title, "The German Conquest of Southern Russia,"[18] and depicted Mennonites (and other Germans) as disloyal to the Russian state and subversive of Russian culture. Some Russian scholars, as well as German periodicals and writers, challenged Paltov's controversial charges; nonetheless, the diatribe continued to be an unsettling warning of things to come. Anti-German sentiment came to violent expression in World War I, when various anti-German decrees of the tsar's government deprived Mennonites of many traditional privileges, although military reverses prevented the government from carrying out its intentions. Despite belated efforts at acculturation, despite an almost fawning attitude toward the tsar and despite repeated identification with the Russian nation and its aspirations, Mennonites found themselves outside the pale.

It is not surprising that some of these charges were revived in the xenophobia of World War II. This time, charges of disloyalty provided the basis for massive deportation efforts. Part of this story is told in Ingeborg Fleischhauer, *Das Dritte Reich und die Deutschen in der Sowjetunion* (Stuttgart, 1983).

Surveys of Russian Mennonite History

There are, of course, many surveys of Mennonite history that also include significant sections on the Russian setting. C. Henry Smith's *Story of the Mennonites,* ed. Cornelius Krahn (Newton, 1981) and C.J. Dyck's *An Introduction to Mennonite History* (Scottdale, 1967) provide such integrated overviews. For the Russian scene, however, no adequate portrait existed until John B. Toews published his *Czars, Soviets and Mennonites* (Newton, 1982). This study is based on an examination of diaries, documents of various agencies, newspapers, letters and various other sources. Although major emphasis is placed on events since World War I, the earlier setting is sufficiently sketched to provide a setting that makes the twentieth century comprehensible.

As Toews himself noted, he chose to tell the "Mennonite story" without extensive analysis of the larger Russian scene. Critics may fault him for avoiding the larger perspective. However, it may be more profitable to suggest that the time is now ripe for a systematic analysis of Russian (and other) primary sources which will further illuminate the drama of Mennonite life in a setting where an overall view will reveal that the Mennonite community constituted a miniscule element in the vastness of Russia. In any event, Toews has presented a gripping and often heroic account of how a people responded when they saw their world collapsing all around them.

A number of works have also presented a pictorial overview of the Mennonite setting. Obviously not designed to be scholarly analyses, they nonetheless are important means whereby popular interest in the theme is stimulated. In addition, they are significant in their own right, recreating a world through photographs. The following such pictorial reviews are especially noteworthy: Gerhard Lohrenz, *Heritage Remembered: A Pictorial History of Mennonites in Prussia and Russia* (Winnipeg, 1974; rev. ed., 1977); Walter Quiring and Helen Bartel, *In the Fullness of Time* trans. Katherine Janzen (Kitchener, 1974); Horst Gerlach, *Bildband zur Geschichte der Mennoniten*

(Uelzen-Oldenstadt, 1980).

During their one and one-half centuries' development in Russia, several religious renewal movements generated separate entities. The first major "reform" movement has been examined by Delbert Plett in *The Golden Years: The Mennonite Kleine Gemeinde in Russia, 1812-1849* (Steinbach, 1985) and in *Storm and Triumph: The Mennonite Kleine Gemeinde (1850-1875)* (Steinbach, 1986), while A.H. Unruh in *Geschichte der Mennoniten-Brüdergemeinde* (Winnipeg, 1955) and John A. Toews in *A History of the Mennonite Brethren Church* (Fresno, 1975) have examined events associated with the upheaval of the 1860s. The memoirs of one of the participants in that division have been printed as Jacob P. Bekker, *Origin of the Mennonite Brethren Church* (Hillsboro, 1973). The account is unfortunately coloured by excessive polemic and bias. Another "founding father" has been accorded recognition in a somewhat fictionalized biography: Elizabeth S. Klassen, *Trailblazer for the Brethren: The Story of Johann Claassen, a Leader in the Early Mennonite Brethren Church* (Scottdale, 1978).

Specialized Studies of Aspects of Mennonite Life

One of the most cherished privileges granted Mennonites when they came to Russia was exemption from military service. In the 1870s, when the government changed that policy, many Mennonites chose to emigrate; others chose to accept forms of alternative service. A careful study of the loss of that exemption and the imposition of military service in Soviet times is presented in Lawrence Klippenstein, "Mennonite Pacifism and State Service in Russia: A Case Study of Church-State Relations, 1789-1936."[19] Klippenstein has also presented other aspects of this theme in studies such as "Exercising a Free Conscience: The Conscientious Objectors of the Soviet Union and the German Democratic Republic."[20] This issue is further illuminated in Hans Rempel, comp. and ed., *Waffen der Wehrlosen: Ersatzdienst der Mennoniten in der UdSSR* (Winnipeg, 1980). An earlier survey by Abraham Goerz, *Ein Beitrag zur Geschichte des Forstdienstes der Mennoniten in Rußland* (Gross-Tokmak, 1907), also provides documentary readings on the subject.

Few themes recur so frequently in Mennonite history as does emigration. The quest for new homes has often provided an escape from a difficult situation. The motif has not yet been fully explored; nonetheless, a number of important portraits have been drawn. Several studies have examined Mennonite migration to Russia: Paul

Karge, "Die Auswanderung west- und ostpreußischer Mennoniten nach Südrußland 1787-1820;"[21] and David Rempel, "The Mennonite Emigration to New Russia, 1787-1870."[22] Other authors have examined the emigration to North America. Among these may be mentioned the accounts by Gustav E. Reimer and G.R. Gaeddert, *Exiled by the Czar: Cornelius Jansen and the Great Mennonite Migration* (Newton, 1956); and Gerhard Wiebe, *Causes and History of the Emigration of the Mennonites from Russia to America*, trans. Helen Janzen (Winnipeg, 1980). A glimpse into the uncertainty and hope caused by the expectation of emigration is provided in Leonhard Sudermann, *Eine Deputationsreise von Rußland nach Amerika* (reprint, Steinbach, 1975). The studies by Fred Richard Belk, *The Great Trek of the Russian Mennonites to Central Asia, 1880-1884* (Scottdale, 1976) and Franz Bartsch, *Unser Auszug nach Mittelasien* (Steinbach, 1948) examine migration as a response to apocalyptic teachings and expectations, while Abram J. Loewen in *Immer Weiter nach Osten: Südrußland-China-Kanada* (Winnipeg, 1981) allows the reader to sense some of the drama of the hazardous escape across the Amur River.

Mennonites within the Soviet Union

As Part of the Larger German-Speaking Community

During the past several decades a considerable body of literature on Germans in the Soviet Union has appeared. Attempts to emigrate coupled with an often strident anti-Soviet tone in parts of the West German press, especially by advocates of a more liberal emigration policy, have brought considerable attention to this minority. Mennonites have been very much involved in emigration efforts, and the *Umsiedler* have been given considerable attention in the Mennonite and the West German press. At the same time, the 1.9 million ethnic Germans still in the Soviet Union continue to generate interest both in the Soviet Union and abroad.

In a recent study, *The Soviet Germans in the USSR Today* (Koeln, 1980), Sidney Heitman has given a careful analysis of the status of Germans in that country today. Using information from a variety of sources, such as official periodicals, historical studies, underground reports, *Umsiedler* accounts and archival documents, Heitman examines issues such as the current locations and occupations of the Germans, their restrictions and the extent of their cultural assimilation. He concludes that the "German religion" is destined to disappear.

As Part of the Larger Protestant Community

With the coming of the Second World War, a new era began for churches in the Soviet Union. The Soviet government, confronted with massive invasion on its western front, tried to gain support from all segments of the population in its "Great Patriotic War." The churches were now viewed as potentially significant sources of support. Consequently, the policy of repression was swiftly changed.

For the Protestant churches the new climate also permitted a greater measure of expression. Efforts were made to develop a united Protestant position and, by 1944, the All-Union Council of Evangelical Christians-Baptists (AUCECB) expressed this ecumenical drive. For the Mennonites, this new administrative unit provided an umbrella under which they could gain legal standing. A number of them joined. Others, however, were not prepared to surrender their hope for recognition as an independent, autonomous entity. Thus the Mennonite community faced an uncertain future.

In the following decades, the AUCECB has continued to attract Mennonites, and in many contexts the identity of Mennonites as a distinct religious denomination has become blurred. At the same time, it should be noted that some Mennonite leaders have insisted that joining the larger, predominantly Baptist body did not mean that they ceased to be Mennonites. Thus, there are presently a number of Mennonite congregations functioning as independent bodies while others are an integral part of AUCECB. The separate Mennonite bodies may enjoy legal standing, although this is not necessarily the case.

In *The Russian Protestants: Evangelicals in the Soviet Union, 1944-1964* (Rutherford, 1969), Steve Durasoff has analyzed various factors shaping Protestant movements, and has devoted special attention to the formation of AUCECB. He has also noted the position taken by Mennonites, although the role played by those who declined to join the merger is not examined. Durasoff suggests that the vigorous earlier attempts to assert traditional Mennonite rights may have in part sparked an especially hostile antireligious drive by the communist government, culminating in the repressive Law of 1929.

Several other general surveys of religion in the Soviet Union help to provide a broader view of the setting in which Mennonite congregations functioned. Among these may be mentioned Erik Amburger, *Geschichte des Protestantismus in Rußland* (Stuttgart, 1961); Trevor Beeson, *Discretion and Valour: Religious Conditions in Russia and Eastern Europe*, rev. ed. (Philadelphia, 1982); Michael Bourdeaux,

Religious Ferment in Russia (London, 1958); Leopold Braun, *Religion in Russia from Lenin to Khrushchev* (Patterson, 1959); William Fletcher, *Soviet Believers: The Religious Sector of the Population* (Lawrence, 1981); William Fletcher and Anthony Strover, eds., *Religion and the Search for New Ideals in the USSR* (Munich, 1960); Boris Iwanow, ed., *Religion in the USSR* (Munich, 1960); Wilhelm Kahle, *Evangelische Christen in Rußland und der Sowjetunion* (Wuppertal, 1978); A.V. Karev, "The Russian Evangelical Baptist Movement, or Under His Cross in Soviet Russia," trans. Frederick Loman (Evansville, n.d., unpub.); Walter Kolarz, *Religion in the Soviet Union* (New York, 1961); Christel Lane, *Christian Religion in the Soviet Union* (London, 1978); William H. Melish, *Religion Today in the USSR* (New York, 1945); Johannes Reimer, *Ostslawischer Protestantismus: Quellen, Wege, Prägungen* (dissertation, Theologisches Seminar Hamburg-Horn, 1983); J.H. Rushbrooke, *Baptists in the U.S.S.R.* (Nashville, 1943); Joseph Schnurr, *Die Kirchen und das religiöse Leben der Rußlanddeutschen* (Stuttgart, 1978); Matthew Spinka, *The Church in Soviet Russia* (New York, 1956); Boleslaw Szczesniak, ed., *The Russian Revolution and Religion: A Collection of Documents Concerning the Suppression of Religion by the Communists, 1917-1925* (Notre Dame, 1959); N.S. Timasheff, *Religion in Soviet Russia, 1917-1942* (New York, 1942); Charles West, *Communism and the Theologians* (New York, 1958).

Certainly one of the most informed surveys of Protestants in the Soviet Union today is the recent overview presented by Walter Sawatsky in *Soviet Evangelicals Since World War II* (Scottdale, 1981). He has drawn on a wealth of documents, personal interviews and observations and extensive travel to present the most informative volume on the subject available today. Included is a review of Mennonites, their geographical location, their relations with other churches and with the Soviet authorities and the nature of their present church life.

Another glimpse into some present-day Mennonites churches in the Soviet Union is presented by Heinrich and Gerhard Woelk, *Die Mennoniten Brüdergemeinde in Rußland, 1925-1980* (Fresno, 1981). An English translation by Victor G. Doerksen appeared under the title, *A Wilderness Journey: Glimpses of the Mennonite Brethren Church in Russia, 1925-1980* (Fresno, 1982). The brief volume expresses personal views and experiences of the authors, and thus is a firsthand account of a heroic and difficult chapter in the life of Mennonites in Russia. At the same time, perspectives are very limited, cultural distinctives are sometimes confused with faith and judgments tend to be harsh and one-sided. A more comprehensive treatment is badly needed.

Some of the theological and sociological problems reflected in *A Wilderness Journey* are now beginning to be discussed as recent emigrés from the Soviet Union publish accounts of their expectations and experiences. Some implications of a clash of cultures can be discerned in books such as Hermann Hartfeld, *Heimkehr in ein fremdes Land* (Wuppertal, 1986). Clearly, the coming of the *Umsiedler* has raised complex questions about faith and practice.

Mennonites from a Soviet Perspective

One of the more fascinating areas of Mennonite historiography is the interpretation of Mennonites by Soviet writers. Although the *Great Soviet Encyclopedia* dismisses Mennonites as insignificant in number,[23] a substantial body of literature has been created by Soviet scholars as they have examined this ethnic and religious phenomenon.

Early Soviet German Periodicals

In the aftermath of the Bolshevik victory, a number of new publications reflecting communist perspectives appeared in the German colonies. Not surprisingly, the tone tended to be virulently antireligious. Since churches were largely silenced, the new periodicals were left without published rebuttals. The Mennonite community faced a situation where its publications were suspended and where the new regime insisted on complete control of the press.

Several new publications appeared in the heartland of Russian Mennonitism and freely denounced traditional beliefs and values. A few titles may be listed to illustrate this approach. In Kharkov in 1930, the journal *Neuland, antireligiöse Zweiwochenschrift der Sowjetdeutschen* appeared to provide antireligious guidance for schools. Evidently many Mennonites resisted its blandishments, for an issue in 1932 complained that relatively few Mennonites had joined the Verband der kämpfenden Gottlosen (League of the Militant Godless), while another writer blamed kulaks and preachers for the passion to emigrate.[24] Another publication, *Der deutsche Kollektivist*,[25] was issued in the village that had so long served as a nerve centre for many Russian Mennonites, Halbstadt, while in Chortitza *Der Stürmer*[26] made its appearance. Both papers combined comments about new agricultural and political developments with denunciations of old social and religious systems. By this time, most Mennonite churches had been confiscated by the state and the ministers exiled. The long night had descended upon Russian Mennonitism.

With the coming of World War II, publication of these and other German-language periodicals in Russia ceased. Only gradually after the war did such periodicals reappear.

In the Soviet Scholarly Press

In 1931, A.I. Klibanov published *Mennonity* (The Mennonites) (Moskva-Leningrad, 1931), which was followed by an impressive number of other publications in which he continued his analysis of religious movements including Mennonitism. In the process he attempted to show that Marxism-Leninism could explain the growth of this "sect," and that, as Lenin had noted, "any...justification of the idea of God is a justification of reaction." Mennonite belief and practice had flourished on ignorance of the populace and exploitation of the poor, especially the very poor in villages near Mennonite communities. In *Istoriia religioznogo Sektantstva v Rossii* (Moskva, 1965)[27], Klibanov examined the Mennonites as part of the larger spectrum of Russian sectarianism. He concluded that the rise of the "Neo-Mennonites" (Mennonite Brethren) demonstrated the strength of the spirit of capitalism and the impact of bourgeois stratification.[28] At the same time, the Oncken confession of faith, circulated widely among the early members of the movement, stressed human sinfulness and "devalued man."[29] Klibanov further argues that in the revolutionary upheaval of 1905-06, the "Mennonite-Baptist party"[30] aligned itself with the Kadets and held a generally reactionary position, all the while deluding the masses with its "Christian-social demagogy."[31]

Another attack on the Mennonites had appeared in 1930. Entitled *Mennonity,* and authored by two former Mennonites, it was published in Moscow by the National Soviet League of Atheists. The authors were listed as A. Reinmarus (Penner) and G. Frizen (Friesen). They subsequently wrote other attacks on Mennonites, such as *Under the Yoke of Religion* (Moscow, 1931), published in Russian as *Pod gnietom religii.*

Among other Soviet interpreters of the Russian Mennonite experience, the following are worth noting: V.F. Krest'ianinov, *Mennonity* (Moscow, 1967); and A.N. Ipatov, *Mennonity* (Moscow, 1978). Their interpretation of Mennonites is similar to that of Klibanov.

Occasionally Mennonites are examined in Soviet scholarly journals. Sometimes these articles express surprise at the continuing attraction of religion for young people and suggest ways in which religion may be combated. A typical illustration may be found in N.I. Il'inykh, whose article on Mennonites in *Soviet Sociology* 10 (Fall, 1972) was printed in translation as "The Orenburg Mennonites, 1972: A Soviet Description."[32] Other illustrations of vitriolic attacks may be found in periodicals such as the journal, *Nauka i religiia* (Science and Religion). Begun in 1959, it has carried numerous articles attacking religion and has sometimes singled out Mennonites for specific denunciation.[33] On the other hand, some studies, such as A. B. Kalyshev, "Interethnic Marriages in Rural Areas of Kazakhstan (Based on material from Pavlodar Oblast, 1926-1979)"[34] present insights into ethnic assimilation.

German Publications in the Soviet Union since World War II

One of the still largely unexplored areas in Soviet literature today is that of German-language publications, some of them by Mennonites, former Mennonites or descendants of Mennonites. Various political and religious practices and developments have made differentiation difficult. Since all government-approved publication in the Soviet Union is subject to official censorship, writing reflects the antireligious position of the government. Nonetheless, several periodicals and other publications provide considerable information about the life of those who still maintain their religious Mennonite identity and those who, although they may have abandoned the faith of their forebears, still retain a measure of identification with the culture that nourished them.

Since World War II, at least three German-language newspapers have been published in the Soviet Union. The earliest, *Arbeit*, appeared briefly in 1955 and 1956. It was issued in Barnaul, one of the most important centres of Mennonite settlement in Siberian Russia. *Neues Leben*, published in Moscow since 1957, sometimes carries articles deploring the religious activities of some German-speaking believers. The context suggests that reference is being made to Mennonites. At the present time, the largest concentration of German-speaking Soviet citizens is to be found in Kazakhstan and the neighbouring republics of Kirgizia and Tadzhikistan. Since 1967, *Freundschaft* has been published in this area, first in the important administrative and economic centre, Tselinograd, now in Alma Ata. Frequent reports about agricultural developments in the collective farms allow the careful reader to glean considerable information about life among the Mennonites and other German-speaking persons.

358

Some recent Soviet belletristic literature also permits limited glimpses into Mennonite or former Mennonite community life: *Anthologie der sowjetdeutschen Literatur,* 3 vols. (Alma Ata, 1981, 1982); Berta Bachmann, *Erinnerungen aus Kasachstan* (Wuppertal, 1980-81); David Loewen, *Es eilen die Jahre* (Alma Ata, 1974); Viktor Klein and J. Warkentin, eds., *Poesie und Prosa der deutschsprachigen Schriftsteller in der UdSSR* (Moskau, 1977); Alexander Ritter, ed., *Nachrichten aus Kasachstan* (New York, 1974).

Selected Periodical Literature

A substantial body of periodical literature also depicts life in religious circles in Russia. Mennonites often form part of the larger picture of religion in the USSR that is presented in publications such as the following: *Bratskii Vestnik* (Fraternal Messenger), published in Moscow by the Baptists; *Glaube in der 2. Welt: Zeitschrift für Religionsfreiheit und Menschenrechte* (Zollikon, Switzerland); *Occasional Papers on Religion in Eastern Europe* (Rosemont, Pennsylvania); *Religion in Communist Dominated Areas* (New York); *Religion in Communist Lands* (Keston College, Keston, U.K.).

Another important source of information about various religious groups, including Mennonites, in the Soviet Union is the underground press. Its publications, often referred to as *samizdat,* appear in various forms and on numerous subjects. Keston College (England) has a substantial collection on religious themes, as does the *samizdat* archive maintained by Radio Free Europe (Munich).

Russian Mennonite themes also appear frequently, of course, in the larger Mennonite press. The following periodicals are illustrative: *Der Mennonit, The Mennonite, Der Bote, Canadian Mennonite, Mennonite Reporter, Mennonite Weekly Review, Mennonite Mirror, Mennonitische Blätter, Mennonitische Rundschau, Mennonite Brethren Herald, Die Steinbach Post* and *Mennonite Historian.*

More scholarly articles and analyses are to be found in journals such as *Conrad Grebel Review, Journal of Mennonite Studies, Mennonitische Geschichtsblätter, Mennonite Life* and *Mennonite Quarterly Review.* Significant articles have also appeared in *Journal of the American Historical Society of Germans from Russia* (Lincoln, Nebraska) and *Heritage Review* (Bismark, North Dakota), published by the Germans from Russia Historical Society. Similarly, *Heimatbuch der Deutschen aus Rußland* and *Volk auf dem Weg,* both published by the Landsmannschaft der Deutschen aus Rußland in Stuttgart, sometimes carry pertinent reports.

Topics for Further Analysis

For some time, David G. Rempel has been stressing the need for a far greater emphasis upon the Russian context in any examination of Russian Mennonites. Too often, he has written, historical studies have been based largely upon Mennonites sources, especially those recorded by ministers and other leaders in the communities. Russian sources, available in various government documents, scholarly publications, village and area records, have too often been neglected. Themes that need further examination include, for example, such topics as the following: causes of migration to Russia; conditions set by Russian authorities relative to colony development and practice; interaction with the larger communities in Russia; attitudes toward other cultural, ethnic and religious groups. It might also be noted that too much writing reflects a patronizing and condescending attitude toward Slavic culture and accomplishments. In this arena, historians might well have reflected more of the sentiment so movingly expressed in that traditional Orthodox prayer, *Gospodi pomilui* ("Lord, have mercy").

Other opportunities for further analysis are provided by various documentary collections such as those in Russian archives and libraries. The extent of collections still available in centres such as Dnepropetrovsk remains unclear. During the German occupation of this area in 1941-1943, the historian Dr. Karl Stumpp prepared extensive lists of materials held in the archives in that city.[35] At that time substantial and significant holdings were available on the economic, political and social conditions in the colonies in that area from earliest times to the 20th century. A brief survey of pertinent holdings in archival collections in Odessa and Nikolaiev is contained in "Quellen zur Erforschung der deutschen Kolonistensiedlungen am Schwarzen Meer."[36]

Numerous documents prepared by Dr. Stumpp and his associates record various aspects of life in German-speaking communities in South Russia. These can be found in the Bundesarchiv in Koblenz. Documents collected by Stumpp and his associates include numerous accounts of imprisonment and exile in the 1930s.[37] Microfilm copies of many of those documents are available from the National Archives in Washington.[38] The Koblenz archives also have lists of emigrants from Prussia to Russia at various times in the 18th and 19th centuries. Included among these records is a statement by King Frederick Wilhelm in 1809. Commenting on Mennonite emigration, he noted laconically, "für einige Mennonisten dürften allerdings Gewissensskrupel mitwirken. . . ."[39] Letters between Mennonites in

Russia and Prussia are also to be found.[40]

Similarly, government documents, personal letters, reports from settlements in Russia and related sources are to be found in several Polish collections, such as the state archives and the city library in Gdansk. Letters preserved here demonstrate that Mennonites in Prussia long continued to play a direct role in the life of the new colonies in Russia. This relationship, as depicted in Polish archives, remains largely unexplored. Other important documents are available in the archives in Torun and Warsaw. Also, substantial collections of pertinent documents are available in Mennonite historical libraries in Germany, The Netherlands, Canada and the United States. Professor David Rempel's private collection, to be located at Conrad Grebel College, Waterloo, Ontario offers especially rich sources.

Notes

1. The *Ständiges Sekretariat für die Koordinierung der Bundesgeförderten Osteuropaforschung* maintains extensive statistical information. See its publication, *Deutsche in der Sowjetunion* (Koeln, 1982).

2. *Russische Revue* 23 (St. Petersburg, 1883): 385-436.

3. Ibid., 359-378.

4. *Archiv für Wissenschaftliche Kunde von Rußland* (Berlin, 1853) 12: 429-436.

5. Ph.D. dissertation, University of Washington, 1969.

6. *University Studies* (University of Nebraska, 1916) 16: 127-227.

7. Peter M. Friesen, *Die alt-evangelische mennonitische Brüderschaft in Rußland, 1789-1910* (Halbstadt: Raduga, 1911). For a discussion of some of the issues associated with this monumental publication see Abraham Friesen, ed., *P.M. Friesen and His History: Understanding Mennonite Brethren Beginnings* (Fresno, California: Center for Mennonite Brethren Studies, 1979).

8. *Mennonite Quarterly Review* 48 (October 1974): 409-446.

9. Trans. J. Toews, *Unsere Kolonien* (Odessa: Verlag der Odessaer Zeitung, 1887).

10. It was published in Ekaterinoslav, then Berdiansk, from 1905 to 1914. A virtually complete file is available in the Lenin State Library, Moscow. Copies have been acquired by various libraries.

11. Except for a few issues, it was published in Halbstadt from 1903-1914. The periodical reappeared in 1917 as *Nachrichten des "Volksfreund,"* then simply as *Volksfreund.* It briefly reappeared under its original title, then ceased publication in 1920. See John B. Toews, "A Voice of Peace in Troubled Times," *Mennonite Life* 27 (September 1972): 93-94.

12. John B. Toews, ed. *Selected Documents: The Mennonites in Russia from 1917 to 1930* (Winnipeg, Manitoba: Christian Press, 1975).

13. *Mennonite Quarterly Review* 47 (October 1973): 259-308; 48 (January 1974): 5-54.

14. Ph.D. dissertation, Stanford University, 1933.

15. See Harvey Dyck, "Russian Mennonitism and the Challenge of Russian Nationalism, 1889," *Mennonite Quarterly Review* 56 (October 1982): 307-341.

16. James Urry, "The Closed and the Open: Social and Religious Change amongst the Mennonites in Russia, 1789-1889" (D. Phil. dissertation, Oxford University, 1978).

17. *Journal of Mennonite Studies* 3 (1985): 7-35.

18. Paltov wrote under the pseudonym of A.A. Velitsyn. For a translation of the article, together with an informative analysis of the historical context of Paltov's document, see Dyck, "Russian Mennonitism."

19. Ph.D. dissertation, University of Minnesota, 1984.

20. *Mennonite Life* 40 (September 1985): 21-26.

21. *Elbinger Jahrbuch* 3 (1923): 65-98.

22. *Mennonite Quarterly Review* 9 (April, July 1935): 71-91; 109-128.

23. *Great Soviet Encyclopedia*, vol. 16, 123-124.

24. *Neuland* IV (1930): 13ff.

25. Published in Molochansk, 1929.

26. Published in Chortitza, 1933-.

27. In translation, A.I. Klibanov, *History of Religious Sectarianism in Russia* (1860s-1917), trans. Ethel Dunn, ed. Stephen Dunn (New York: Pergamon Press, 1982).

28. Ibid., 238.

29. Ibid., 250.

30. Ibid., 320.

31. Ibid., 321.

32. *Mennonite Life* 36 (March, 1981): 19-23.

33. For example, see P. Ervin, "Mennonity," in *Nauka i religiia* 5 (1963): 25-28. Also, for a brief examination of tactics used by editors of this journal, see Walter Sawatsky, *Soviet Evangelicals Since World War II* (Scottdale, Pennsylvania: Herald Press, 1981), 135-145. Religious persons have been routinely depicted as enemies of the state and "mental cripples."

34. *Soviet Sociology* 22 (Fall 1984): 28-42.

35. In his "Abschlußbericht über die Tätigkeit des Arbeitsstabs," dated October 15, 1943, Stumpp wrote, "In folgenden Archiven ist Deutschtumsmaterial vorgefunden worden: Dnjepropetrowsk, Saporoshje (jetzt Chortitza), Nikoleajew, Cherson, Melitopol und Kriwoj-Rog. Der weitaus größte Teil befindet sich in Dnjepropetrowsk"(Captured German Documents, Deutsches Ausland-Institut, National Archives, Washington, roll 636, frame 5437409). Many of the important documents are listed in "Verzeichnis der wichtigsten Urkunden im Historischen Gebietsarchiv der Stadt Dnjepropetrowsk über die deutschen Kolonisten in Süd-Rußland" (unpublished manuscript) in the author's possession.

36. Bundesarchiv, R6/109.

37. See, for example, "Deutsches Kolonistenschicksal" (Bundesarchiv,

R69/119).

38. See Adam Giesinger "Captured German Documents," *AHSGR Work Paper* 13 (December 1973).

39. Captured German War Documents, Deutsches Ausland-Institut, National Archives, Washington (roll 626, frame 5422905-8).

40. For an overview of some sources available in the Federal Republic of Germany, see Peter J. Klassen, "Sources for Russian Mennonite Research in German Archives and Libraries," *Mennonite Quarterly Review* 52 (January 1978): 21-34.

A Select Bibliography

With a Note on Archival Sources

Introduction

An exhaustive published bibliography of literature dealing with Mennonites in Russia and the Soviet Union still does not exist. The volumes listed here include essentially all the titles which have been used for the essays in this publication. Added to these are reference works, periodicals and other items which represent more recent research in the field of Russian Mennonite history.

A list of books written by Gerhard Lohrenz on Mennonites in Russia and the Soviet Union appears separately in this volume. Articles by Lohrenz found in *Der Bote, Mennonite Life, The Mennonite Encyclopedia* and elsewhere have not been listed, but can be located by means of indexes available for these publications.

Journal and newspaper articles used in the essays, or others related to the theme of the book, are not included in this selection. The most important sources for these materials can be found in the section on periodicals and newspapers or in the reference books noted below.

I. Reference Works

Bender, H.S., C. Henry Smith, Cornelius Krahn, and Melvin Gingerich, eds. *The Mennonite Encyclopedia.* Vols. I-IV. Hillsboro, Kansas: Mennonite Publication Office, and Scottdale, Pennsylvania: Mennonite Publishing House, 1955-1959.

Hege, Christian, and Christian Neff, et al., eds. *Mennonitisches Lexikon.* Vols. I-II. Frankfurt am Main and Weierhof (Pfalz): Selbstverlag, 1913, 1937. Vols. III-IV. Karlsruhe: Heinrich Schneider, 1958, 1967.

Hildebrand, J.J. *Chronologische Zeittafel: 1500 Daten historischer Ereignisse und Geschehnisse aus der Zeit der Geschichte der Mennoniten Westeuropas, Rußlands und Amerikas.* Winnipeg, Manitoba. By the author, 1945.

Long, James, ed. *The German Russians: A Bibliography of Russian Materials with Introductory Essay, Annotations and Locations of Materials in Major American and Soviet Libraries.* Oxford: Woodside House, and Santa Barbara, California: Clio Press, 1978.

Rempel, Peter H., and Adolf Ens, eds. *Der Bote Index, 1924-1947.* Vol. I. Winnipeg, Manitoba: CMBC Publications, 1976.

Springer, Nelson P., and A.J. Klassen, comps. *Mennonite Bibliography, 1631-1961.* Vols. I-II. Scottdale, Pennsylvania, and Kitchener, Ontario: Herald Press, 1977.

Stumpp, Karl, ed. *Das Schrifttum über das Deutschtum in Rußland: Eine Bibliographie.* 5th enlarged edition. Stuttgart: Landmannschaft der Deutschen aus Rußland e.V., 1980.

II. Books

Anthologie der sowjet-deutschen Literatur. Vols. I-III. Alma-Ata: Kasachstan, 1981, 1982.

Baerg, Anna. *Diary of Anna Baerg, 1916-1924.* Trans. and ed. Gerald Peters. Winnipeg, Manitoba: CMBC Publications, 1985.

Bartlett, Roger P. *Human Capital: The Settlement of Foreigners in Russia, 1762-1804.* Cambridge: Cambridge University Press, 1979.

Bartsch, Franz. *Unser Auszug nach Mittelasien.* Halbstadt, Taurien: H.J. Braun, 1907.

Bekker, Jacob P. *Origin of the Mennonite Brethren Church.* Trans. D.E. Pauls and A.E. Janzen. Hillsboro, Kansas: Mennonite Brethren Historical Society of the Midwest, 1973.

Belimov, A.F. *Kto takie mennonity?* Frunze: Kyrgyzstan, 1967.

Belk, Fred Richard. *The Great Trek of the Russian Mennonites to Central Asia 1880-1884.* Scottdale, Pennsylvania: Herald Press, 1976.

Berg, Wesley. *From Russia with Music: A Study of the Mennonite Singing Tradition in Canada.* Winnipeg, Manitoba: Hyperion Press, 1985.

Bethell, Nicholas. *The Last Secret.* London: André Deutsch Ltd., 1974.

Bondar, S.D. *Sekta Mennonitov v Rossii v sviazi s istorii niemietzkoi kolonizatzii na iuge rossii.* Petrograd: Tipo V.D. Smirnova, 1916.

Brock, Peter. *Pacifism in Europe to 1914.* Princeton, New Jersey: Princeton University Press, 1972.

Brons, A. *Ursprung, Entwickelung und Schicksale der altevangelischen Taufgesinnten oder Mennoniten.* Norden: Diedr. Soltan, 1891.

Buchsweiler, Meir. *Volksdeutsche in der Ukraine am Vorabend und Beginn des Zweiten Weltkriegs – ein Fall doppelter Loyalität?* Gerlingen, W. Germany: Bleicher Verlag, 1984.

Chamberlin, William H. *The Russian Revolution 1917-1921.* Vols. I-II. New York, New York: Macmillan, 1952.

Conquest, Robert. *The Great Terror: Stalin's Purge of the Thirties.* New York, New York: Macmillan, 1968; revised edition, 1973.

Der Mariupoler Kolonisten- und Mennoniten-Bezirk: Jahrbuch des Landwirts: Eugenfeld, 1914.

Derksen, Peter (Isaak). *Es wurde wieder ruhig: Die Lebensgeschichte eines mennonitischen Predigers aus der Sowjetunion.* Ed. Lawrence

Klippenstein. Winnipeg, Manitoba: Mennonite Heritage Centre, 1989.

Doerksen, Victor G., et al. *Collected Works – Arnold Dyck – Werke.* Vol I. Winnipeg, Manitoba: Manitoba Mennonite Historical Society, 1985.

Durksen, Martin. *Die Krim war unsere Heimat.* Winnipeg, Manitoba: By the author, 1980.

Dyck, Anna Reimer. *Anna: From the Caucasus to Canada.* Trans. and ed. Peter J. Klassen. Hillsboro, Kansas: Mennonite Brethren Publishing House, 1979.

Dyck, John P., ed. *Troubles and Triumphs, 1914-1924: Excerpts from the Diary of Peter J. Dyck, Ladekopp, Molotschna Colony, Ukraine.* Springstein, Manitoba: By the author, 1981.

Dyck, Peter P. *Orenburg am Ural: Die Geschichte einer mennonitischen Ansiedlung.* Yarrow, British Columbia: Orenburg Reunion Committee, 1951.

Ediger, Heinrich, ed. *Beschlüsse der von den geistlichen und anderen Vertretern der Mennonitengemeinden Rußlands abgehaltenen Konferenzen für die Jahre 1879 bis 1913.* Berdjansk: Verlag von Heinrich Ediger u.K., 1914.

Ehrt, Adolf. *Das Mennonitentum in Rußland von seiner Einwanderung bis zur Gegenwart.* Langensalza-Berlin-Leipzig: Verlag von Julius Beltz, 1932.

Epp, David H. *Die Chortitzer Mennoniten: Versuch einer Darstellung des Entwickelungsganges desselben.* Rosenthal bei Chortitz, 1888.

Epp, David H., and Nikolai Regehr. *Heinrich Heese/Johann Philipp Wiebe: Zwei Vordermänner des südrussischen Mennonitentums.* Steinbach, Manitoba: Echo-Verlag, 1952.

Epp, David H. *Johann Cornies: Züge aus seinem Leben und Wirken.* Rosthern, Saskatchewan, and Steinbach, Manitoba: Echo-Verlag, 1946.

Epp, David H. *Sketches from the Pioneer Years of the Industry in the Mennonite Settlements of South Russia.* Trans. Jacob P. Penner. Leamington, Ontario: Jacob Penner, 1972.

Epp, Frank H. *Mennonite Exodus: The Rescue and Resettlement of the Russian Mennonites since the Communist Revolution.* Altona, Manitoba: Canadian Mennonite Relief and Immigration Council and D.W. Friesen and Sons Ltd., 1962.

Epp, Heinrich, ed. *Heinrich Epp, Kirchenältester der Mennonitengemeinde zu Chortitza (Südrußland).* Leipzig, 1897.

Epp, Johann. *Freuden und Leiden der Familie Olga Wiebe und Johann Epp.* Espelkamp: Selbstverlag, 1984.

Epp, Johann. *Von Gottes Gnade getragen.* Gummersbach: Verlag Friedensstimme, 1984.

367

Epp, Peter. *Ob tausend fallen . . .: Mein Leben im Archipel Gulag.* Weichs, W. Germany: Memra-Verlag, 1988.

Esau, Jacob, et al. *Unter dem Schirm des Höchsten: Drei kurze Biographien von Christen im Untergrund.* Wuppertal: Brockhaus, 1979.

Fast, Gerhard. *Das Ende von Chortitza.* Winnipeg, Manitoba: Selbstverlag, 1973.

Fast, Isaac P. *Züge aus meinem Leben.* Winnipeg, Manitoba: A.J. Fast, 1932.

Fast, Karl. *Gebt der Wahrheit die Ehre!: Ein Schicksalsbericht.* Second edition. Winnipeg, Manitoba: Canzona Publishing, 1989.

Fast, Martin B. *Geschichtlicher Bericht wie die Mennoniten Nordamerikas. . . /Meine Reise nach Sibirien und zurück.* Reedley, California: By the author, 1919.

Fast, Martin B. *Meine Reise nach Rußland und zurück.* Scottdale, Pennsylvania: By the author, 1910.

Fleischhauer, Ingeborg. *Das Dritte Reich und die Deutschen in der Sowjetunion.* Stuttgart: Deutsche Verlags-Anstalt, 1983.

Fleischhauer, Ingeborg. *Die Deutschen im Zarenreich: Zwei Jahrhunderte deutsch-russische Kulturgemeinschaft.* Stuttgart: Deutsche Verlags-Anstalt, 1986.

Friedmann, Robert. *Mennonite Piety through the Centuries: Its Genius and Its Literature.* Goshen, Indiana: The Mennonite Historical Society, 1949.

Friesen, Abram., ed. *P.M. Friesen and His History: Understanding Mennonite Brethren Beginnings.* Fresno, California: Center for Mennonite Brethren Studies, 1979.

Friesen, P(eter) M. *Die Alt-Evangelische Mennonitische Brüderschaft in Rußland (1789-1910) im Rahmen der mennonitischen Gesamtgeschichte.* Halbstadt, Taurien: Verlagsgesellschaft "Raduga", 1911. Trans. Abraham Friesen, et al, *The Mennonite Brotherhood in Russia (1789-1910).* Fresno, California: Board of Christian Literature, General Conference of Mennonite Brethren Churches, 1978.

Froese, Leonhard. "Das pädagogische Kultursystem der mennonitischen Siedlungsgruppe in Rußland." D.Phil. dissertation, Universität zu Goettingen, 1949.

Giesinger, Adam. *From Catherine to Khrushchev: The Story of Russia's Germans.* Winnipeg, Manitoba: By the author, 1974.

Goerz, A. *Ein Beitrag zur Geschichte des Forstdienstes der Mennoniten in Rußland.* Gross Tokmak: H. Lenzmann, 1907.

Goerz, H. *Memrik: Eine mennonitische Kolonie in Rußland.* Rosthern, Saskatchewan: Echo-Verlag, 1954.

Goerz, H. *Die mennonitischen Siedlungen der Krim.* Winnipeg, Manitoba: Echo-Verlag, 1957.

Goerz, H. *Die Molotschnaer Ansiedlung: Entstehung, Entwicklung und*

Untergang. Steinbach, Manitoba: Echo-Verlag, 1951.

Guenther, Waldemar, David P. Heidebrecht and Gerhard I. Peters, eds. *"Onsi Tjedils": Ersatzdienst der Mennoniten in Rußland unter den Romanovs.* Clearbrook, British Columbia: By the authors, 1966.

Gutsche, Waldemar. *Westliche Quellen des russischen Stundismus: Anfänge der evangelischen Bewegung in Rußland.* Kassel: J.G. Oncken Verlag, 1956.

Hamm, Abram and Maria. *Die Wege des Herrn sind lauter Güte.* Gummersbach: Verlag Friedensstimme, 1985.

Hamm, Gerhard. *Gottes Wort ist nicht gebunden: Geschichten und Gleichnisse aus Rußland.* Wuppertal: Oncken Verlag, 1980.

Hamm, Oscar H., ed. *Memoirs of Ignatievo in the Light of Historical Change.* Trans. Margaret Neufeld. Saskatoon, Saskatchewan: Ruth F. Hamm, 1984.

Harder, Hans. *No Strangers in Exile.* Trans., ed. and expanded by Al Reimer. Winnipeg, Manitoba: Hyperion Press, 1979.

Hartfeld, Herman. *Heimkehr in ein fremdes Land.* Wuppertal: Brockhaus, 1986.

Hein, Gerhard, ed. *Ufa: The Mennonite Settlements in Ufa, 1894-1938.* Winnipeg, Manitoba: N.J. Neufeld, et al., 1977.

Hiebert, P.C. and Miller, Orie, eds. *Feeding the Hungry: Russia Famine 1919-1925.* Scottdale, Pennsylvania: Mennonite Central Committee, 1929.

Hildebrand, Peter. *Erste Auswanderung der Mennoniten aus dem Danziger Gebiet nach Südrußland.* Halbstadt: Typographie von P. Neufeld, 1888.

Holborn, Hajo. *A History of Modern Germany, 1648-1840.* New York, New York: Alfred A. Knopf, 1968.

Hostetler, John A. *Hutterite Society.* Baltimore, Maryland, and London: The Johns Hopkins University Press, 1974.

Huebert, Helmut T. *Hierschau: An Example of Russian Mennonite Life.* Winnipeg, Manitoba: Springfield Publishers, 1986.

Ipatov, A.N. *Kto takie mennonity.* Alma Ata, U.S.S.R.: Izdatelstvo "Kazakhstan," 1977.

Ipatov, A.N. *Wer sind die Mennoniten?* Alma Ata: Verlag Kazachstan, 1977.

Ipatov, A.N. *Mennonity (Voprosy formirovaniia i evolutsii etnoconfessional'noi obshchnosti').* Moskva: "Mysl," 1978.

Isaak, Franz. *Die Molotschnaer Mennoniten: Ein Beitrag zur Geschichte derselben.* Halbstadt, Taurien: H.J. Braun, 1908.

Janzen, Johannes Heinrich. *Das Märchen vom Weihnachtsmann.* Herausgegeben und mit einem Nachwort versehen von Waldemar Janzen. Winnipeg, Manitoba: CMBC Publications, 1975.

Kamenskii, P.V. *Vopros ili nedorazumienie? (K voprosy ob innostranny poseleniia na iuge rossii).* Moskva: T-vo A.A. Levenson, 1895.

Klaassen, Martin. *Geschichte der wehrlosen taufgesinnten Gemeinden von den Zeiten der Apostel bis auf die Gegenwart.* Koeppenthal, Am Trakt: Der Vorstand der Mennonitengemeinde, 1873.

Klassen, Abram J. "The Roots and Development of Mennonite Brethren Theology to 1914." M.A. thesis, Wheaton College, 1966.

Klassen, Doreen. *Singing Mennonite: Low German Songs of the Mennonites.* Winnipeg, Manitoba: University of Manitoba Press, 1989.

Klassen, Elizabeth Suderman. *Trailblazer for the Brethren: The Story of Johann Claassen, a Leader in the Early Mennonite Brethren Church.* Scottdale, Pennsylvania: Herald Press, 1978.

Klassen, Isaac P. *Die Insel Chortitza: Stimmungsbilder, Gedanken, Erinnerungen.* Winnipeg, Manitoba: By the author, 1979.

Klaus, Alexander. *Nashi Kolonii: Opyty i materialy po istorii i statistike inostrannoi kolonizatsii v Rossii.* Sankt Petersburg: Tipografiia V.V. Nusvalta, Liteinaia, 1869.

Klaus, Alexander. *Unsere Kolonien: Studien und Materialien zur Geschichte und Statistik der ausländischen Kolonisation in Rußland.* Trans. and ed. J. Toews. Odessa, Ukraine: Verlag der "Odessaer Zeitung," 1887.

Klibanov, A.I. *Mennonity.* Moskva: Ogiz-Moskovskii Rabochii, 1931.

Klippenstein, Lawrence. "Mennonite Pacifism and State Service in Russia: A Case Study in Church-State Relations, 1789-1936." Ph.D. dissertation, University of Minnesota, 1984.

Koch, Fred C. *The Volga Germans in Russia and the Americas from 1763 to the Present.* University Park, Pennsylvania, and London: Pennsylvania University Press, 1977.

Krest'ianinov, Viktor F. *Mennonity.* Moskva: Politizdat, 1967.

Kroeker, Abraham Jacob. *Pfarrer Eduard Wuest: Der große Erweckungsprediger in den deutschen Kolonien Südrußlands.* Leipzig: Selbstverlag, 1903.

Kroeker, Nick J. *First Mennonite Villages in Russia, 1789-1943: Khortitsa-Rosental.* Vancouver, British Columbia: By the author, 1981.

Kuppeler, Andreas, Boris Meissner and Gerhard Simm, eds. *Die Deutschen in Russischen Reich und im Sowjetstaat.* Koeln: Markus Verlag, 1987.

Kurze älteste Geschichte der Taufgesinnten (Mennoniten genannt). Odessa: Franzow und Nitzsche, 1852.

Letkemann, Peter. "The Hymnody and Choral Music of Mennonites in Russia, 1789-1915." Ph. D. dissertation, University of Toronto, 1985.

Lindemann, Karl Eduardovich. *Von den deutschen Kolonisten in Rußland: Erlebnisse einer Studienreise 1919-1921.* Stuttgart: Ausland und Heimat Verlags-Aktiengesellschaft, 1924.

Loewen, A., and A. Friesen. *Die Flucht über den Amur: Ein mennonitisches Dorf flüchtet (1930) aus dem sowjetrussischen Sibirien in die chinesische Mandschurei.* Rosthern, Saskatchewan, and Steinbach, Manitoba: Echo-Verlag, 1946.

Loewen, Heinrich. *In Vergessenheit geratene Beziehungen: Frühe Begegnungen der Mennoniten-Brüdergemeinde mit dem Baptismus in Rußland – ein Überblick.* Bielefeld, West Germany: Logos-Verlag, 1989.

Malinowsky, J. Aloys. *Die Planerkolonien am Asowschen Meer.* Stuttgart: Ausland und Heimat Verlags-Aktiengesellschaft, 1928.

Mannhardt, H.G. *Die Danziger Mennonitengemeinde: Ihre Entstehung und ihre Geschichte von 1569-1919.* Danzig: Selbstverlag der Danziger Mennonitengemeinde, 1919.

Mannhardt, H.G. *Jahrbuch der Altevangelischen oder Mennoniten Gemeinde.* Danzig: Selbstverlag, 1888.

Mannhardt, Wilhelm. *Die Wehrfreiheit der alt-preußischen Mennoniten.* Marienburg: Altpreußischen Mennonitengemeinden, 1863.

Martens, Wilfred. *River of Glass.* Scottdale, Pennsylvania, and Kitchener, Ontario: Herald Press, 1980.

Neufeld, Abram H., trans. and ed. *Herman and Katharina: Their Story: The Autobiography of Elder Herman A. and Katharina Neufeld.* Winnipeg, Manitoba: Centre for Mennonite Brethren Studies, 1984.

Neufeld, Diedrich. *The Russian Dance of Death: Revolution and Civil War in the Ukraine.* Trans. and ed. Al Reimer. Winnipeg, Manitoba: Hyperion Press, 1977.

Neufeld, Jacob A. *Tiefenwege: Erfahrungen und Erlebnisse von Rußlandmennoniten in zwei Jahrzehnten bis 1949.* Virgil, Ontario: By the author, 1954.

Nickel, John P., ed. and trans. *Hope Springs Eternal: A Legacy of Service and Love in Russia During Difficult Times: Sermons and Papers of Johann J. Nickel (1859-1920).* Nanaimo, British Columbia: Nickel Publishers, 1988.

Nickel, Katherine. *Seed from the Ukraine.* New York, New York: Pageant Press, 1952.

Nottarp, Hermann. *Die Mennoniten in den Marienburger Werdern: Eine kirchenrechtliche Untersuchung.* Halle: Max Niemeyer Verlag, 1929.

Palij, Michael. *The Anarchism of Nestor Makhno 1918-1921: An Aspect of the Ukrainian Revolution.* Seattle and London: University of Washington Press, 1976.

Penner, George. *Mennoniten dienen in der Roten Armee.* Winnipeg, Manitoba: By the author, 1975.

Penner, Horst. *Die ost- und westpreußischen Mennoniten in ihrem religiösen und sozialen Leben in ihren kulturellen und wirtschaftlichen Leistungen.* Band I-II. Weierhof: Mennonitischer Geschichtsverein,

371

1978, 1987.

Peters, Klaas. *Die Bergthaler Mennoniten und deren Auswanderung aus Rußland und Einwanderung in Manitoba.* Hillsboro, Kansas: Mennonite Brethren Publishing House, n.d.

Peters, Victor. *Nestor Makhno: The Life of an Anarchist.* Winnipeg, Manitoba: Echo Books, 1970.

Peters, Victor. *Zwei Dokumente: Quellen zum Geschichtsstudium der Mennoniten in Rußland.* Winnipeg, Manitoba: Echo-Verlag, 1965.

Pisarevskii, Grigorii. *Iz istorii inostrannoi kolonizatzii v rossii v XVIII v.* Moskva: Suegerev, 1909.

Pisarevskii, Grigorii. *Pereselenie prusskikh mennonitov v Rossiu pri Alexandre I.* Rostov-on-Don: Tipogragiia S. S. Sivozhelezov, 1917.

Plett, Delbert, ed. *Storm and Triumph: The Mennonite Kleine Gemeinde (1850-1875).* Steinbach, Manitoba: D.F.P. Publications, 1986.

Plett, Delbert. *History and Events: Writings and Maps pertaining to the history of the Mennonite Kleine Gemeinde from 1866 to 1876.* Steinbach, Manitoba: D.F. Plett Farms Ltd., 1982.

Plett, Delbert. *The Golden Years: The Mennonite Kleine Gemeinde (1812-1849).* Steinbach, Manitoba: D.F.P. Publications, 1985.

Polnoe Sobranie Zakonov Rossiiskoi Imperii s 1649 goda. (PSZ) Vols. I-III. Sankt Petersburg: Otdieleniia Sobstvennoi Ego Imperatorskogo Velichestva Kantseliarii, 1830-1916.

Priess, Anita. *Exiled to Siberia.* Steinbach, Manitoba: Derksen Printers, 1972.

Quiring, Jacob (Walter). *Die Mundart von Chortitza in Süd-Rußland.* Muenchen: Druckerei Studentenhaus Muenchen Universitaet, 1928.

Quiring, Walter and Helen Bartel, eds. *In the Fullness of Time: 150 Years of Mennonite Sojourn in Russia.* Third edition. Waterloo, Ontario: Aaron Klassen, 1974.

Rahn, Peter. *Mennoniten in der Umgebung von Omsk.* Vancouver, British Columbia: By the author, 1975.

Randt, Erich. *Die Mennoniten in Ostpreußen und Litauen bis zum Jahre 1772.* Koenigsberg: Otto Kümmel, 1912.

Redekopp, Jakob. *Es war die Heimat . . .: Baratow-Schlachtjin.* Filadelfia, Paraguay: By the author, 1966.

Regehr, Ted D., and Jacob Regehr, *For Everything a Season: A History of the Alexanderkrone Zentralschule.* Winnipeg, Manitoba: CMBC Publications, 1988.

Reimer, Al. *My Harp is Turned to Mourning.* Winnipeg, Manitoba: Hyperion Press, 1985.

Reimer, Gustav E., and G.R. Gaeddert. *Exiled by the Czar: Cornelius Jansen and the Great Mennonite Migration, 1874.* Newton, Kansas: Mennonite Publications Office, 1956.

Reinmarus, A. (Penner). *Anti-Menno: Beiträge zur Geschichte der Men-*

noniten in Rußland. Moskau: Zentral Voelker Verlag, 1930.

Reinmarus, A. and G. Frizen, *Mennonity.* Moskva: AKtz. Izd. O-Bo, "Biesbozhnik," 1930.

Rempel, David G. "The Mennonite Colonies in New Russia: A Study of their Settlement and Economic Development from 1789-1914." Ph.D. dissertation, Stanford University, 1933.

Rempel, Hans and George Epp, eds. *Waffen der Wehrlosen: Ersatzdienst der Mennoniten in der UdSSR.* Winnipeg, Manitoba: CMBC Publications, 1980.

Rempel, Olga. *Einer von Vielen: Die Lebensgeschichte von Prediger Aron P. Toews.* Winnipeg, Manitoba: CMBC Publications, 1979.

Rempel, Olga. *Siberian Diary of Aron P. Toews with a Biography by Olga Rempel.* Trans. Esther Klaassen Bergen and ed. Lawrence Klippenstein. Winnipeg, Manitoba: CMBC Publications, 1984.

Rimland, Ingrid. *The Wanderers: The Saga of Three Women Who Survived.* St. Louis, Missouri: Concordia, 1977.

Ritter, Alexander, ed. *Nachrichten aus Kasachstan: Deutsche Dichtung in der Sowjetunion.* Hildesheim, New York: Olms Presse, 1974.

Sawatsky, Walter. *Soviet Evangelicals Since World War II.* Kitchener, Ontario: Herald Press, 1981.

Sawatzky, Heinrich. *Templer mennonitischer Herkunft.* Winnipeg, Manitoba: Echo-Verlag, 1955.

Schaefer, Paul J. *Woher? Wohin? Mennoniten! Teil II.* Altona, Manitoba: Mennonite Agricultural Advisory Committee, 1942.

Schilder, N.K. *Graf Eduard Ivanovich Totleben: Ego Zhizn'i diatelnost'.* Vols. I-II. Sankt Petersburg, 1885-1886.

Schreiber, William. *The Fate of the Prussian Mennonites.* Goettingen: Goettingen Research Committee, 1955.

Schroeder, George P. *Miracles of Grace and Judgment: A Family Strives for Survival during the Russian Revolution.* Lodi, California: By the author, 1974.

Schroeder, William. *The Bergthal Colony.* Revised edition. Winnipeg, Manitoba: CMBC Publications, 1986.

Schultz, Henry H. *Snowborne: The Siberian Chronicles of Henry Schultz.* Revised edition. Campbell River, British Columbia: By the author, 1982.

Senn, Fritz [Gerhard Johann Friesen]. *Gesammelte Gedichte und Prosa.* Ed. Victor G. Doerksen. Winnipeg, Manitoba: CMBC Publications, 1987.

Simon, Gerhard. *Church, State and Opposition in the U.S.S.R.* Trans. Kathleen Matchett. London: C. Hurst & Company, 1974.

Smith, C. Henry. *Smith's Story of the Mennonites.* 5th edition. Revised by Cornelius Krahn. Newton, Kansas: Faith and Life Press, 1981.

Stach, Jakob. *Der Kreis Mariupol im Gouvernement Jekaterinoslaw:*

Jahrbuch des Landwirts. Eugenfeld, 1914.

Stach, Jakob. *Ocherki iz istorii i sovremennoi zhizni iuzhnorusskikh kolonistov.* Moskva: Tovarishchestvo tipografii A.I. Mamontova, 1916.

Stumpp, Karl. *The Emigration from Germany to Russia in the Years 1763 to 1862.* Trans. Joseph S. Height. Lincoln, Nebraska: AHSGR, 1982.

Sudermann, Leonhard. *Eine Deputationsreise von Rußland nach Amerika.* Elkhart, Indiana: Mennonitische Verlagshandlung, 1897.

Surukin, V. *Am Trakt: Eine mennonitische Kolonie im mittleren Wolgagebiet.* Trans. and ed. Johann J. Dyck. Winnipeg, Manitoba: Echo-Verlag, 1948.

Szdzucki, Lech. *Socinianism and Its Role in the Culture of the XVIIth and XVIIIth Centuries.* Warsaw-Lodz: Polish Academy of the Sciences, 1983.

Thiessen, Franz C. *P.M. Friesen 1849-1914: Personal Recollections.* Winnipeg, Manitoba: Board of Christian Literature, General Conference of the Mennonite Brethren, 1974.

Thiessen, Franz, ed. *Neuendorf in Bild und Wort: Chortitzaer Bezirk, Ukraine 1789-1943.* Espelkamp, West Germany: Selbstverlag, 1984.

Tiessen, Henry B. *The Molotschna Colony: A Heritage Remembered.* Kitchener, Ontario: By the author, 1979.

Toews, A.A., ed. *Mennonitische Märtyrer der jüngsten Vergangenheit und der Gegenwart.* Band I-II. Clearbrook, British Columbia: By the author, 1949, 1954.

Toews, C.P. *Die Tereker Ansiedlung: Mennonitische Kolonie im Vorderkaukasus: Entstehung, Entwicklung und Untergang, 1901-1918/1925.* Rosthern, Saskatchewan, and Steinbach, Manitoba: Echo-Verlag, 1945.

Toews, John B. *Czars, Soviets & Mennonites.* Newton, Kansas: Faith and Life Press, 1982.

Toews, John B. *Lost Fatherland: The Story of the Mennonite Emigration from Soviet Russia, 1921-1927.* Scottdale, Pennsylvania: Herald Press, 1967.

Toews, John B., ed. *The Mennonites in Russia from 1917 to 1930: Selected Documents.* Winnipeg, Manitoba: Christian Press, 1975.

Toews, John B. *Perilous Journey: The Mennonite Brethren in Russia, 1860-1910.* Winnipeg, Manitoba, and Hillsboro, Kansas: Kindred Press, 1988.

Tolstoy, Nikolai. *Victims of Yalta.* London: Hodder & Stoughton, 1977.

Unruh, Abraham H. *Die Geschichte der Mennoniten-Brüdergemeinde 1860-1954.* Hillsboro, Kansas: The General Conference of the Mennonite Brethren Church of North America, 1955.

Unruh, Abe J. *The Helpless Poles.* Montezuma, Kansas: By the author,

1973.

Unruh, Benjamin H. *Die niederländisch-niederdeutschen Hintergründe der mennonitischen Ostwanderung im 16. 18. und 19. Jahrhundert.* Karlsruhe: Heinrich Schneider, 1955.

[Unruh, Benjamin H., and T. Hylkema]. *Die Mennoniten-Gemeinden in Rußland während der Kriegs- und Revolutionsjahre 1914-1920.* C.B. Heilbronn a. Neckar: Kommissions Verlag der mennonitischen Flüchtlingsfürsorge, 1921.

Urry, James. "The Closed and the Open: Social and Religious Change amongst the Mennonites in Russia (1789-1889)." D.Phil. dissertation, Oxford University, 1978.

Urry, James. *None but Saints: The Transformation of Mennonite Life in Russia.* Winnipeg, Manitoba: Hyperion Press, 1989.

Velitzyn, A.A. *Niemtsy v Rossii; ocherki istoricheskago razvitiia i nastoiaschago polozheniia niemietskikh kolonii na iuge i vostoke rossii.* Sankt Petersburg: Izdanie russkago vestnika, 1893.

Vins, Georgi P. *Prisoner of Conscience.* Elgin, Illinois: David C. Cook Publishers, 1975.

Wedel, Walter. *Nur Zwanzig Kilometer.* Wuppertal: Brockhaus, 1979.

Wiebe, George. "The Hymnody of the Conference of Mennonites in Canada." M.A. thesis, University of Southern California, 1962.

Wiebe, Gerhard. *Causes and History of the Emigration of the Mennonites from Russia to America.* Trans. Helen Janzen. Winnipeg, Manitoba: Manitoba Mennonite Historical Society, 1981.

Wiebe, Herbert. *Das Siedlungswerk niederländischer Mennoniten im Weichseltal zwischen Forden und Weisenberg bis zum Ausgang des 18. Jahrhunderts.* Marburg a.d. Lahn: Johann Gottfried Herder Institut, 1952.

Wiebe, Johann. *Die Auswanderung von Rußland nach Kanada – 1875 – in Form einer Predigt.* Cuauhtémoc, Mexico: 1972.

Wiebe, Rudy. *The Blue Mountains of China.* Toronto, Ontario: McClelland and Stewart, 1970.

Willms, H.J., ed. *At the Gates of Moscow: God's Gracious Aid Through a Most Difficult and Trying Period.* Trans. George Thielman. Yarrow, British Columbia: By the author, 1964.

Winter, Henry H. *Ein Hirte der Bedrängten: Heinrich Winter, letzter Ältester von Chortitza.* Wheatley, Ontario: By the author, 1988.

Woelk, Heinrich, and Gerhard Woelk. *A Wilderness Journey: Glimpses of the Mennonite Brethren Church in Russia 1925-1980.* Trans. Victor G. Doerksen. Fresno, California: Center for Mennonite Brethren Studies, 1982.

Woltner, Marguerite. ed. *Die Gemeindeberichte von 1848 der deutschen Siedlungen am Schwarzen Meer.* Leipzig: Verlag S. Hirzel, 1941.

Zieglschmid, A.J.F. *Das Klein Geschichtsbuch der Hutterischen Brueder.*

Philadelphia, Pennsylvania: The Carl Schurz Memorial Foundation, 1947.

III. Periodicals and Newspapers

Aufwärts. Davlekanovo, Ufa, Russia, 1909-1910.

Bote, Der. Rosthern and Saskatoon, Saskatchewan, Canada, 1924-1977; Winnipeg, Manitoba, 1977-.

Botschafter, Der. Ekaterinoslav and Berdiansk, Ukraine, 1905-1914.

Christlicher Bundesbote. Berne, Indiana, and Newton, Kansas, U.S.A., 1882-1947.

Christliches Jahrbuch zur Belehrung und Unterhaltung. Spat, Crimea, Russia, 1902-1904; Halbstadt, Ukraine, 1905. Name changed to *Fürs christliche Haus: Belehrendes und Unterhaltendes für Jung und Alt* in 1905.

Freundschaft. Tselinograd and Alma Ata, U.S.S.R., 1966-.

Friedensstimme, Die. Berlin, Germany, 1903-1905; Halbstadt, Ukraine, 1906-1914, 1918-1920.

Gemeindeblatt der Mennoniten, Das. Sinsheim a. Elsenz, Germany, 1870-1926; Karlsruhe, 1926-1941.

Heimatbuch der Deutschen aus Rußland. Stuttgart, Germany, 1954. Ran as *Heimatbuch der Ostumsiedler,* 1954-1955.

Heritage Review. Germans from Russia Heritage Society, Bismarck, North Dakota, U.S.A., 1971. Organization name was North Dakota Historical Society of Germans from Russia, 1971-1979.

Journal. American Historical Society of Germans from Russia, Greeley, Colorado, U.S.A., 1969-1973; Lincoln, Nebraska, 1973-. Periodical called *Workpaper,* 1969-1977.

Journal of Mennonite Studies. Winnipeg, Manitoba, Canada, 1983-.

Mennonite Historian. Winnipeg, Manitoba, Canada, 1975-.

Mennonite Life. North Newton, Kansas, U.S.A., 1946-.

Mennonite Mirror. Winnipeg, Manitoba, Canada, 1971-.

Mennonite Quarterly Review. Goshen, Indiana, U.S.A., 1927-.

Mennonitische Blätter. Danzig, West Prussia, 1854-1941.

Mennonitische Jugendwarte. Ibersheim (Worms), Germany, 1920-1923; Friedelsheim (Pfalz), 1923-1927; Monsheim (Rheinhessen), 1927-1939.

Mennonitische Rundschau, Die. Elkhart, Indiana, 1880-1908; Scottdale, Pennsylvania, 1908-1923; Winnipeg, Manitoba, Canada, 1923-.

Mennonitische Volkswarte. Steinbach, Manitoba, Canada, 1935-1938.

Mennonitisches Jahrbuch. North Newton, Kansas, U.S.A., 1948-1957.

Molotschnaer Volkskalender für die deutschen Ansiedler in Südrußland, Der. Prischib, Ukraine, 1861-1914.

Neuer Haus- und Landwirtschafts Kalender für deutsche Ansiedler im südlichen Rußland. Odessa, Ukraine, 1865-1914.

Neues Leben. Moskva, U.S.S.R., 1957-.

Odessaer Zeitung, Die. Odessa, Ukraine, 1863-1914.

Praktische Landwirt, Der. Moskau, U.S.S.R., 1925-26.

Unser Blatt. Gross Tokmak, U.S.S.R., 1925-1928.

Unterhaltungsblatt für deutsche Ansiedler im südlichen Rußland. Odessa, Ukraine, 1846-62.

Zur Heimath. Summerfield, Illinois, U.S.A., 1875; Halstead, Kansas, 1875-1881.

IV. Archival Sources

A comprehensive inventory of related archival material is not yet available. Such holdings are located mainly in various Mennonite institutions which have consciously gathered unpublished materials. The Mennonite Library and Archives (MLA) at Bethel College, North Newton, Kansas, can claim to be a pioneer in this regard. Dr. Cornelius Krahn, retired professor of history at the College and long-time director of the archives, led the search for archival items related to Russian Mennonite history during his years of active service there. The personal papers of Cornelius Janzen, of Berdiansk, south Russia, and later a resident of the U.S.A., as well as those of A.A. Friesen, an emigrant from Ukraine, who eventually retired in Rabbit Lake, Saskatchewan, are some of the more prominent collections of the MLA holdings. Complete sets of all the important Russian Mennonite periodicals such as *Mennonitisches Jahrbuch, Christlicher Familienkalender, Praktischer Landwirt* and *Unser Blatt* are an important supplement to individual collections.

The records of the Canadian Mennonite Board of Colonization, the personal papers of individuals such as Gerhard Lohrenz, J.J. Hildebrand, Kaethe Hooge, Olga Rempel, John P. Dyck, Alexander Rempel, D.H. Epp, as well as a large collection of maps and photos related to the Russian Mennonite story, are central to the holdings of the Mennonite Heritage Centre Archives (MHCA) in Winnipeg, Manitoba. Relevant journals, periodicals, newspapers, such as *Der Bote,* and a number of Soviet publications on Mennonites are also part of the MHCA holdings.

The Mennonite Brethren centres of research at Fresno, California, Hillsboro, Kansas, and Winnipeg, Manitoba, hold substantial collections of items related to MB history in Russia and elsewhere. The B.B. Janz and C.F. Klassen papers at the Centre for MB Studies (CMBS) in Winnipeg are examples of such materials. Substantial collections of personal correspondence originating in the Soviet Union after 1917, and received by relatives in Canada, can be found there as well. The newspapers *Mennonitische Rundschau, Unterhaltungsblatt der deutschen Ansiedler in Rußland* (1846-1862) and *Die Odessaer Zeitung* (1863-1914) are other important sources of the CMBS holdings.

Some historical documents brought to West Germany by *Umsiedler* (recent immigrants from the Soviet Union) have found their way to the Fresno centre, where Dr. J.B. Toews, retired president and professor of the Mennonite Brethren Seminary, has been a vigorous collector of Russian Mennonite materials.

At Conrad Grebel College, Waterloo, Ontario, a major portion of the David G. Rempel papers form the core of a growing archival collection related to Russian Mennonite themes. An oral history project dealing with conscientious objectors has brought together autobiographical data related to the Russian experience.

The Ernst Crous personal collection, as the founding materials for the archival holdings of the Mennonitische Forschungsstelle of the Weierhof in West Germany, includes a portion of the Benjamin Unruh papers, especially as they concern relief work in the Soviet Union and Germany after World War I. West Germany is also home to important related materials at the Bundesarchiv in Koblenz, and the "Captured German War Documents," of which duplicates are at the Library of Congress and National Archives in Washington, D.C.

Index

Memel River 14
Memrik 164, 228
Mennonite Brethren 150-160, 164-172, 205-10, 215, 226, 230, 247-48, 284-85, 290, 296, 309-11, 314-16, 320, 322, 325
Mennonitische Blätter 223, 259
Mennonitische Rundschau 223
Mennonitisches Jahrbuch 170, 229
military exemption 19, 46, 120, 127ff, 157-58, 165, 278, 281-82, 352
military service 14, 45, 62, 120, 127-28, 139, 161, 266, 308, 323
Miller, Orie 310
Millerovo 243, 248
mills, milling 20, 22-23, 113, 240, 242-43, 246-48, 250-51, 253-55
ministers 44, 46-49, 60-61, 116, 168-69, 275, 336-37 n.51, 57, 58
missions 19, 60-62, 64, 66, 168, 329
Mogilev 25, 47
Moldavia 317, 320
Molochnaia River 18, 34, 55-56
Molokans 154
Molotschna 34, 52, 55-71, 103, 110-111, 115, 154, 158, 161, 163, 169, 172, 184-85, 196, 204-05, 208-09, 211, 214, 215, 228, 232, 240, 243, 245-48, 250-53, 256, 269-70, 272-75, 280
Moody 211
Moravian Brethren 63, 65, 204
Moritz 62
Moskovka River 241, 253
Moskow 251, 257, 277, 280
Muenster 162
Muensterberg 34
Muntau 34, 278
music & singing 66, 203-17
Muslims 296-97

Nachtigal, Abraham 173
Naegeli, Hans 212
Nartan 320
Narym 303
nationalism 130-31, 135, 139, 350
nationalization 84, 120
Natorp, B.C.L. 204
Naumenko 247
Nepluiev 196
Neu Chortitza 163
Neu Halbstadt 83, 223, 228, 278
Neu Samara 320
Neu Schoensee 2
Neuenburg 28, 48, 277

Neuendorf 17, 28, 48, 276
Neufeld, A.A. 81, 83, 224
Neufeld, Gerhard 25, 47
Neufeld, Heinrich 153
Neufeld, Kornelius G. 213-14, 230
Neufeld, Peter J. 223, 228
Neufeld, Wilhelm 211-12, 224
Neugarten 18, 22
Neuhoffnung 151
New Russia 43, 55, 101ff, 343
New York 117, 163
Nicholas I 130-31, 187, 197
Nickel, J. 248
Niebuhr, Hermann 253
Nieder Chortitza 276
Nikolaiev 3
Nikolaifeld 163-64
Nikopol 190, 242, 250-51
Nitvia 309
Nogai 33, 62
Nogat River 28, 45
nonresistance 59-60, 62, 130, 133, 135, 139, 157, 266, 281-82, 314, 326
Norilsk 290
Novaia Lialia 309
Novo Pavlovka 320
Novokovno 188
Novomoskov 26
Novopodolsk 188, 194
Novosibirsk 300, 306, 313, 315, 318, 323-24
Novovitebsk 188, 190, 194
Novozhitomir 188

Oberschulz 34, 50, 58, 64, 66
October Revolution 268, 274, 283, 292
Odessa 65-66, 243, 251-52
Odessaer Zeitung 223, 227-28
Ohrloff 34, 54, 58, 61-63, 65, 69-70, 78, 154, 159, 165, 170, 224, 248, 267-68
Old Believers 115
Olgopol 26
Omsk 161, 250, 290, 300
Oncken, Johann G. 157
Orekhov 33, 242, 246-48, 258
Orenburg 109, 163, 290, 304, 320, 322-26, 329-31, 358
Orsk 322
Orthodox Church 19, 173, 244
Ostrog 70

Paul I 21, 30, 32, 51, 127
Pauls, Franz 27
Pavlodar 250-51, 309
Penner, Behrend (Bernhard) 25, 47-49, 55

383

Glossary

Ältester — a Mennonite leader of a congregation or group of congregations.

Anwohner — literally "people who live beside." The term was used for landless Mennonites in Russia who lived beside or at the end of the village.

AUCECB — All-Union Council of Evangelical Christians-Baptists, the Soviet government's umbrella organization for all Protestant and Evangelical churches.

dessiatina — a measure of land, approximately 2.7 acres.

Einwohner — people who leased property, usually residences.

Forsteidienst — forestry service, the form of alternative service required of Mennonite men after 1880.

Fürsorgekomitee — an organization established by the Russian government to supervise foreign, including Mennonite, settlements.

Gebietsamt — a Mennonite settlement's civic administrative office.

Handelsschule — literally, a "school of commerce" but, in fact, more like a senior high school.

Kirchenkonvent — a Mennonite church association consisting of all the religious leaders, namely the *Ältesten* and *Lehrer* (ministers), for all the settlements.

khutor — a Russian term for a large estate or land holding.

Lehrer — the traditional term used for a Mennonite minister.

Lehrdienst — the church leadership group in each church, consisting of *Ältester*, *Lehrer* and deacons.

Mädchenschule — a girls' school approximately on the junior high school level.

Oberschulz — the elected head of civic government in Mennonite settlements.

Pietism — a collective term describing numerous renewal movements, most of which originated in Germany.

Plattdeutsch or Plautdietsch — the Low German language which Mennonites learned from their neighbours in Poland/Prussia and continued to use as the main language of everyday communication in Russia.

Privilegium — an agreement which spelled out rights and obligations between Mennonites and various governments, e.g. Polish, Prussian and Russian.

Schulz — the elected head (mayor) of a Mennonite village.

Vereinsschule — a school owned and operated by an association of people, in contrast to a school run by a whole community.

verst — a Russian measure of distance, approximately one kilometre or five-eighth of a mile.

Vorsänger — the song leader in Russian Mennonite congregations. His duties were to select hymns and lead out in, but not direct, congregational singing.

Waisenamt — a Mennonite institution which handled the estates of widows and orphans. Eventually it also became a lending and depositing institution.

Zentralschule — a school following grade school on approximately the junior high school level.